THE ADOLESCENT
IN THE
AMERICAN NOVEL
1920-1960

W. TASKER WITHAM

Associate Professor of English,
Indiana State College, Terre Haute

FREDERICK UNGAR PUBLISHING CO.
NEW YORK

To
JOHN T. FLANAGAN
for inspiration and guidance

Some material in this book was included in the author's
The Forge of Life: Problems of Adolescents
in American Literature, 1920-1958

Third Printing, 1978

ISBN 0-8044-3320-8
Copyright © 1964 by
Frederick Ungar Publishing Co., Inc.
Printed in the United States of America
Library of Congress Catalog Card Number 63-8849

TABLE OF CONTENTS

Contents

Contents

Contents

PREFACE

In America between the two world wars, and especially after the close of the second, the general public interest in the problems of adolescents grew from an attitude of amused condescension to one of overwhelming concern mingled with helpless bewilderment. Novels published during these years indicate changes in public interest; but more than that, they often supply an unusually sensitive insight into the nature and causes of human problems. Sigmund Freud himself early acknowledged the aid which psychologists may receive from novelists, as he analyzed Wilhelm Jensen's novel *Gradiva:*

> Story-tellers are valuable allies, and their testimony is to be rated high, for they actually know many things between heaven and earth that our academic wisdom does not even dream of. In psychic knowledge, indeed, they are far ahead of us ordinary people, because they draw from sources that we have not yet made accessible for science.[1]

The psychologist, then, might profit as well as the student of literature —to say nothing of the sociologist, the social worker, the clergyman, the teacher, the parent, and that indispensable friend to all purposeful readers, the librarian—all these people might profit from a survey of the American novels, published between 1920 and 1960, which feature the problems faced by adolescents.

The present survey begins with a rather short chapter sketching the literary and cultural background of the American novel of adolescence in the period discussed. The five following chapters present, in order of importance, the five areas in which adolescents face their most difficult problems of adjustment: sex and love, the family, school and college, the community environment, and the finding of a career and a world outlook which will suit each individual in his adult life. The seventh chapter discusses smaller groups of problems encountered by many adolescents but not by all of them. The final chapter sums up the observations made in earlier chapters and, on the basis of these, ventures a prophecy as to future trends in novels of adolescence.

In order to trace the changing attitudes of novelists both chronologi-

1

cally and regionally, I have included not only the works of important writers like Wolfe, Farrell, and Salinger, but every novel of adolescence (within certain arbitrary limits) which received a reasonable amount of critical or popular acclaim. Since these novels total well over five hundred, they could not all be discussed in any detail; but they are all listed in the appendix, which I hope will prove very useful in a number of ways. The main body of this survey gives special emphasis to the novels of greatest literary value, but it includes specific comments on less important novels when these present striking examples of characteristic or otherwise notable attitudes toward the problems of adolescents.

The year 1920 was chosen for the beginning of this survey because it is a convenient date that marks as well as any the turning point between the genteel tradition that had dominated American literature for half a century, and the new tradition of frankness and iconoclasm that characterized the novelists appearing after World War I. It was also a year when two important and influential novels of adolescence were published: Floyd Dell's *Moon-Calf* and F. Scott Fitzgerald's *This Side of Paradise*. The year 1960 was chosen for the end of the survey simply because it is the most recent year which marks the close of a decade. Within this forty-year period, many of the novels belong clearly in a survey such as this; but a number of works might or might not be considered American novels of adolescence. It was particularly important for me to define, for my own guidance, the terms *American, novel,* and *adolescent.*

The term *American* in this survey refers to novels written by American authors, with settings within the United States. Since few novelists writing after 1920 could personally recall events and settings prior to 1870, novels with settings before 1870 have also been excluded. The survey does include a few novels whose authors changed their citizenship either to or from American, or whose protagonists had some adolescent experiences abroad or before 1870; but in each case the chief emphasis is on adolescent experiences in this country after 1870.

The term *novel* is used here in its broadest sense, meaning an extended fictional prose narrative. Still there are borderline works: for example, should Sherwood Anderson's *Tar* be classed as autobiographical fiction or as fictionalized autobiography? should Hemingway's *In Our Time* and Jessamyn West's *Cress Delahanty* be classed as episodic novels or as collections of short stories? and should Faulkner's "The Bear" and Steinbeck's "The Red Pony" be classed as short novels or as long short stories? Since each of the works here mentioned is important and influential in the development of recent novels about adolescents, all of them are included in the survey. Some less important borderline works are included on the following basis: autobiographies written in an obviously fictionalized style, with emphasis on story and character development rather than precise recording of facts; collections of stories when they are arranged to show continuous development of one or more adolescent characters; and narratives long enough to have been published in separate volumes of about a hundred pages, even when they have not been so published. All of these borderline works are clearly indicated in the appendix.

The term *adolescent* was the most difficult to define. It seemed inadvisable to set specific chronological ages for the beginning and end of adolescence, because fictional characters, like those in real life, vary considerably in respect to the exact ages at which this stage of development commences and finishes. Physical adolescence, which is the easiest to observe, may begin at any age from ten to fourteen and may finish at any age from fifteen to twenty-two; the ages for intellectual, social, moral, and emotional adolescence may vary much more. Indeed, it is often said that, in a nonphysical sense, some people never progress beyond adolescence. But if this study were to include characters of any age who behaved like adolescents, almost any character in literature might be included! Finally I decided to include as adolescents only those who have begun to show physical and social signs of maturing but have not yet assumed full adult responsibility. The great majority of the adolescents here studied are between the ages of twelve and twenty-one. In no cases, I think, are they younger than ten or older than twenty-four. In each of the novels here presented, the problems of one or more adolescents are a major concern of the novelist, although they may not be his main concern.

For the most part, this study omits novels which seem to have been written primarily for sensational appeal or for interest to juvenile readers; but it does include a few books by the more mature writers of juveniles, such as John R. Tunis and Mary Stolz, and by sensational novelists who show insight and sincerity, such as Hal Ellson and Irving Shulman.

To avoid an excessive use of footnotes, I have given most page references in parentheses immediately following a quotation or other citation. Unless otherwise noted, the reference is always to the first American

3

edition, as listed in my bibliography. I have used notes, however, when a mere page reference would not be sufficiently clear. Notes for the preface and all chapters are located at the end of the final chapter. Cross references to other pages in this work are always accompanied by the word "above" or "below."

Most of the material appearing in this volume was incorporated in my doctoral thesis, *The Forge of Life: Problems of Adolescents in American Novels, 1920–1958*, which was accepted by the Graduate College of the University of Illinois in September, 1961. I am therefore indebted to the Department of English of the University of Illinois for permission to use this material as the basis of the present book. Especially am I indebted to my thesis director, Professor John T. Flanagan, for inspiration and patient guidance. I am grateful also for suggestions made by members of my examining committee, especially Professors Bruce Harkness and Cornelia Kelley, who took the trouble to write out some detailed critical comments. I owe a great deal to many faculty members and students at both the University of Illinois and Indiana State College for questions and suggestions that have helped me to a deeper understanding of my subject. Particularly helpful comments have come from Professors James F. Light and James H. Mason of Indiana State, and from my publisher, Mr. Frederick Ungar, and his editor, Miss Ruth Selden. In extending my survey from 1958 to 1960, I have had the competent assistance of George Dean, a student at Indiana State.

For nontechnical assistance I am indebted to the Danforth Foundation for a generous summer study grant for the summer of 1961; to President Raleigh W. Holmstedt of Indiana State for making this grant available to me; to the late Richard E. Thursfield, Dean of Studies at Indiana State, for a further grant for additional research; and to my wife Drusilla and my children, who have patiently tolerated my neglect of family obligations while I devoted evenings and week ends to this study.

W. T. W.

THE ADOLESCENT
IN THE AMERICAN NOVEL
1920-1960

Chapter I

LITERARY AND CULTURAL BACKGROUND

THE GENTEEL TRADITION—DEFINITIONS AND EXAMPLES

In order to appreciate the trends in the treatment of specific problems in the novels of adolescence published since 1920, one should know something about the novels of this sort published before 1920, both in this country and abroad, and should know something of the trends in literature and culture which affected novels published before 1920 as well as the trends affecting later novels.

The dominant trend in American letters from about 1870 to 1920 is generally known as "the genteel tradition"—a term first used in a lecture by George Santayana in 1911.

> America is not simply . . . a young country with an old mentality: it is a country of two mentalities, one a survival of the beliefs and standards of the fathers, the other an expression of the instincts, practice and discoveries of the younger generations. In all higher things of the mind—in religion, in literature, in the moral emotions—it is the hereditary spirit that still prevails, so much so that Mr. Bernard Shaw finds that America is a hundred years behind the times. The truth is that one half of the American mind, that not occupied intensely in practical affairs, has remained, I will not say high-and-dry, but slightly becalmed; it has floated gently on the backwater, while, alongside, in invention and industry and social organization, the other half of the mind was leaping down a sort of Niagara Rapids. This division may be found symbolized in American architecture: a neat reproduction of the Colonial mansion—with some modern comforts introduced surreptitiously—stands beside the skyscraper. The American will inhabits the skyscraper: the American intellect inhabits the Colonial mansion. The one is the sphere of the American man; the other, at least predominantly, of the American woman. The one is all aggressive enterprise; the other is all genteel tradition.[1]

Although some American writers did show aggressive enterprise—notably Mark Twain in his great novel of adolescence, *Huckleberry Finn* (1884) —it was not until the "Little Renaissance" of 1912 to 1925 that a considerable number of them made a concerted and successful effort to

7

move from the "backwater" of the genteel tradition to the strong current that has carried modern American literature to a position of world leadership.

It is as difficult to find an exact definition for the term "genteel tradition" as it is for the term "romanticism." Santayana traced the tradition back to Calvinism—not to the specific teachings of John Calvin, but rather to "an expression of the agonized conscience" which beset the New England Calvinists of the Colonial period. These New England Calvinists, convinced "that sin exists, that sin is punished, and that it is beautiful that sin should exist to be punished," were torn between tragic concern about their own sinful natures and tragic exultation at the status and punishment of sin in the universe.[2] The genteel tradition, with its excessive emphasis on morality, grew out of this early New England agony.

But American critics writing after 1920, using Santayana's term to belittle the tendencies that had long prevailed in American literature, expanded its meaning. Malcolm Cowley, in his introduction to *After the Genteel Tradition* (pp. 17–19), described the genteel tradition as a combination of New England sin-consciousness with Victorian prudery, plus an optimism growing out of the material success that had accompanied hard work in this land of opportunity, and an admiration for the wealth and polish to be found on the Atlantic seaboard with its minor "shrines of culture" such as Boston and New York, Harvard and Princeton, and particularly in Europe with its major shrines such as London and Oxford.

William Van O'Connor, in *An Age of Criticism: 1900–1950*, listed seven different works in which discussions of the genteel tradition might be found,[3] but he cautioned his readers:

> One begins to suspect that there are two genteel traditions: the one that might exist for the disinterested historian and the one that was mythologized by Sinclair Lewis and his contemporaries. . . . They did create a rather grotesque effigy of the genteel writer and critic, but it was true that the group they opposed, so far as it was homogeneous, did not encourage the expression in literature of the bristling vigor, the commercialization, the scheming and plodding in American life. (Pp. 3–4.)

More recently Henry F. May, in *The End of American Innocence*, equated the genteel tradition with a sort of innocence, "the absence of guilt and doubt and the complexity that goes with them," which had

8

been characteristic of American culture before World War I, but was rapidly disappearing during the war decade and was almost completely gone in the 1920's:

> This innocence had often been rather precariously maintained. Many had glimpsed a world whose central meaning was neither clear nor cheerful, but very few had come to live in such a world as a matter of course. Exceptions to innocence had existed in all camps—they had included unhappy elder thinkers like Henry Adams, rueful naturalists like Dreiser, and vigorous skeptics like Mencken. None of these had yet deeply affected the country's image of itself; all, including Henry Adams, who died in 1918, were to become influential in the twenties.
>
> This change, on the way for a long time and precipitated by the war, is worth looking at very briefly as it affected several segments of the increasingly divided nation. The most obvious aspect of change was the complete disintegration of the old order, the set of ideas which had dominated the American mind so effectively from the mid-nineteenth century until 1912. The heresies of the nineties had undermined this set of beliefs; the Rebellion had successfully defied it; the twenties hardly had to fight it. After the war it was hard to find a convincing or intellectually respectable spokesman for the prewar faith. (Pp. 393–94.)

BASIC NOVELS OF ADOLESCENCE BEFORE 1920

The various characteristics of the genteel tradition can be seen in the majority of the novels of adolescence published in the first two decades of this century. The most popular authors of such novels were Harold Bell Wright, Gene Stratton-Porter, Booth Tarkington, and Burt L. Standish, with Owen Johnson almost as celebrated. Wright's most popular novel was *The Winning of Barbara Worth* (1911), a sentimental tale of a foundling girl raised by noble Westerners, bringing happiness to her foster parents and proving a worthy prize for a young mining engineer of distinguished Eastern family background. Wright shows his gentility not by praising the culture of the East, but by appealing to well-established prejudices of his readers: that the frank sincerity of the Westerner is worth more than the ancestry of the Easterner; that a young girl, especially an orphan, must be virtuous; that hard work and contact with nature almost invariably make a person spiritually better. Mrs. Porter's novels have a similar appeal. *Freckles* (1904) concerns a miserable, homeless boy who believes himself to be an orphan. After ennobling

9

contacts with nature in the swamps and forests of Indiana, he is claimed by a long-lost wealthy father. (In later novels, the finding of such a father is likely to be a theme of adolescent daydreams, but not an actual occurrence. See, for example, the comments on Sherwood Anderson's *Tar,* p. 79 below.) *A Girl of the Limberlost* (1909) tells of Freckles' companion Eleanora, who wanders about the swamps and woods collecting moths, which she sells to earn herself an education. William Gilbert Patten, better known by his pseudonym "Burt L. Standish," began in 1896 to turn out quantities of cheap novels about the fabulous Frank Merriwell, a college athlete who was as remarkable for his constant adherence to the rules of fair play as for his ability to save the game in the last few seconds. According to James D. Hart's *Oxford Companion to American Literature,* Standish wrote more than two hundred Frank Merriwell novels, which sold a total of more than twenty-five million copies. Owen Johnson presented somewhat more realistic pictures of school and college life, but he too depended on the well-established appeal of the good-hearted though mischievous schoolboy, who is guilty of occasional pranks but never of dishonesty, bullying, or sexual indulgences: *The Varmint* (1910) and *The Tennessee Shad* (1911) present an assortment of likable and memorable boys at Lawrenceville Prep School in New Jersey, while *Stover at Yale* (1911) follows the hero of *The Varmint* into college life.

Booth Tarkington deserves more serious consideration. In *Penrod* (1914) he created one of the enduring adolescents of American fiction, whose further troubles and escapades appear in inferior sequels, *Penrod and Sam* (1916) and *Penrod Jashber* (1929). Twelve-year-old Penrod suffers acutely in adjusting to some of the problems of early adolescence: his expected public appearance in a school play in what he considers a most unvirile costume, the temptation to bring discomfort and disgrace upon the model boy of the neighborhood, the pangs of first love for a pretty coquette of his own age but of considerably more experience in heterosexual relations. Tarkington showed inventiveness and acute observation in relating these sufferings, but his condescending attitude is clearly apparent in this comment in *Penrod:*

> Perhaps middle-aged people might discern Nature's real intentions in the matter of pain if they would examine a boy's punishments and sorrows, for he prolongs neither beyond their actual duration. With a boy, troubles must be of Homeric dimensions to last overnight. To him, every next day is really a new day. (P. 283.)

10

In *Seventeen* (1916) he presented an older adolescent, Willie Baxter, but again his attitude was that a boy's problems will disappear in time and should not be taken seriously. However, Tarkington's realization of the possible lasting effects of an adolescent's difficulties appears in *The Magnificent Ambersons* (1918), in which George Amberson Minafer grows up with an exalted idea of his own importance because he is related to one of the most prominent families in his home town. In later years, partly because of his arrogance and partly because of fortuitous accidents, George experiences poverty and misery and the Amberson name falls into oblivion. Following the tested formula for a sentimental novel, Tarkington demonstrated that pride would fall and patient merit would be rewarded: he allowed George to become dependent on the "queer-looking duck" he had long despised as his mother's devoted but unworthy admirer. Especially sentimental is the final reconciliation scene in the hospital, presided over by the "duck's" lovely daughter and the spirit of George's dead mother.

Both the condescending humor and the sentimental drama exemplified in these novels are characteristic of the genteel tradition in literature, and go back to well-established antecedents. The pranks and problems of schoolboys are treated in a light-hearted manner in George Wilbur Peck's sketches collected in *Peck's Bad Boy* (1883), and almost as casually in Thomas Bailey Aldrich's *Story of a Bad Boy* (1870) and Mark Twain's *Tom Sawyer* (1876) and *Huckleberry Finn* (1884); this tradition goes back through English fiction even to Fielding's *Tom Jones* (1749). Similarly, the conditioned emotional response to the mistreated innocence of adolescents has been the stock in trade of many of the most popular American and English novelists, as evidenced by the seemingly endless Elsie Dinsmore series (1867–1905) of Martha Farquharson, the rags-to-riches romances (1866–1899) of Horatio Alger, Louisa May Alcott's *Little Women* (1868–69) and *Little Men* (1871), Charles Dickens' *Oliver Twist* (1837–38) and *Old Curiosity Shop* (1840–41), and even the eighteenth-century novels of Samuel Richardson.

The genteel tradition did not, of course, end abruptly in 1920, nor was it the only influence on the fictional treatment of adolescence before that date. The most powerful literary force against it was naturalism, originating in France with the novels of Zola, Flaubert, and the brothers Goncourt and with the criticism of Hippolyte Taine, and making its first American appearance in Stephen Crane's *Maggie: A Girl of the Streets* (1893). This short novel—telling of an adolescent girl in the New York

11

slums driven into prostitution and eventually to suicide by the sordidness of her environment and the callous indifference of her mother, her brother, and her lover—presents such a one-sided picture in language so loaded with pathos that it seems today almost as sentimental as *Elsie Dinsmore*. Crane showed much more restraint and psychological subtlety in *The Red Badge of Courage* (1895), which presents the adolescent Henry Fleming initiated into adulthood by the searing experience of war. Theodore Dreiser's first novel, *Sister Carrie* (1900), presents a naturalistic picture of an eighteen-year-old girl trying to support herself in Chicago; but the bulk of the novel is concerned with Carrie's problems as an adult. Similarly, the first few chapters of Dreiser's novel *The Financier* (1912) show the adolescence of Frank Cowperwood; but the novel, like its sequel, is more concerned with Cowperwood's adult life. Actually, few of the early American naturalistic novels are concerned primarily with adolescents, but the trend toward naturalism may have influenced some serious novelists to treat adolescents more realistically than the genteel tradition would have treated them.

Ernest Poole's *The Harbor* (1915) shows realistically the effect that the Brooklyn docks may have on a boy who grows up beside them, even when he goes away to college and then travels across the sea to Paris. Although only about one-eighth of the novel—something less than fifty pages—is devoted directly to Billy's adolescence, Poole vividly presents the problems of a youth growing into adulthood while torn between the genteel influence of his ex-school-teacher mother and the harsh realities learned during furtive visits to the docks in childhood—realities later emphasized by the muck-raking harangues of his college friend Joe Kramer. Sherwood Anderson showed Ohio village life to be anything but idyllic in *Windy McPherson's Son* (1916) and in some of the sketches in *Winesburg, Ohio* (1919); he described an unhappy adolescence even more specifically in *Poor White* (1920). Willa Cather in two of her early novels presented realistically the problems of adolescent girls of immigrant families in Nebraska—the Swedish Thea Kronborg in *The Song of the Lark* (1915) and the Bohemian Antonia Shimerda in *My Ántonia* (1918). In both novels the harshness of prairie farm life is fully realized, but both girls—unlike the protagonists of naturalistic novels—have nobility of character to triumph over their stultifying environment. Adolescent males, who have less success with their problems than do her females, appear in Miss Cather's early short story "Paul's Case" (1905) and in her later novel *A Lost Lady* (1923), which is discussed below on pages 39–40. Dorothy Canfield Fisher won both critical and popular acclaim with her realistic treatment of adolescence in *The Bent Twig* (1915); but a survey of the best-seller lists of the first third of the twentieth century shows that it was 1920 before the sentimental novelists like Harold Bell Wright, Gene Stratton-Porter, and Eleanor H. Porter were replaced in popular favor by moderate realists like Mrs. Fisher, Sinclair Lewis, and F. Scott Fitzgerald.

Besides the growth of naturalism in this country, one of the chief influences toward a franker treatment of adolescence in American fiction was a similar trend in English fiction. As early as 1859 George Meredith had presented, in *The Ordeal of Richard Feverel*, the tragic effects of a parent's well-intentioned but misguided "system" for educating an adolescent son. In 1903, Samuel Butler's posthumous autobiographical novel *The Way of All Flesh* showed how the frustrations of parents may lead to destructive relations with an adolescent child. Somerset Maugham's Philip Carey in *Of Human Bondage* (1915) has about the same relations with his straitly religious aunt and uncle that Butler's Ernest Pontifex has with his sanctimonious parents. Modern psychological problems appear in the mother fixation of Paul Morel in D. H. Lawrence's *Sons and Lovers* (1913) and in Stephen Dedalus' rebellion against home, religion, and country in James Joyce's *Portrait of the Artist as a Young Man* (1916). All of these novels present adolescence as a solemn and influential time of life, and all of them served as models for some of the serious American novelists.

A third important influence was the development of psychology as a science. Increased understanding of psychology brought not only better understanding and franker expression of the more obvious workings of the mind, but also a new appreciation of the obscure motives of the subconscious mind, indicating their presence and direction symbolically. This latter aspect of psychology became increasingly influential toward the middle of the century, when the frank portrayal of the physical facts of life became so complete that it was necessary to look beneath the surface to find fresh literary material. There is no doubt that Freud and his followers—particularly Carl Jung—have been of greatest importance in bringing this psychological influence into literature, but Frederick J. Hoffman, in *Freudianism and the Literary Mind* (pp. 313–21), points out that Schopenhauer and Nietzsche in Germany and Dostoevski in Russia

13

have also helped to bring new psychological understanding into the literature of Europe and America. And one should not overlook the influence of Henry James, whose works are as concerned with mental processes as are those of his psychologist brother.

TRENDS IN AMERICAN FICTION, 1920–1960

If one were to seek labels for the literary trends of each decade of American literature between 1920 and 1960, he could probably find no better label for the trends of the twenties than that of frank rebellion against the gentility and false optimism of the immediately preceding period. Such terms as "The Roaring Twenties" and "The Jazz Age," traditionally applied to the period, seem inappropriate when the fiction of the twenties is compared to that of later decades, particularly the fifties— even though it was roaring and jazzy when compared with earlier fiction. In the *Atlantic Monthly* for September, 1920, a young man answered charges by members of the older generation that youth had lost chivalry, modesty, and religion:

> A keen interest in political and social problems, and a determination to face the facts of life, ugly or beautiful, characterizes us, as it certainly did not characterize our fathers. We won't shut our eyes to the truths we have learned. . . . Now I think this is the aspect of our generation that annoys the uncritical and deceives the unsuspecting oldsters who are now met in judgment upon us: our devastating and brutal frankness. And this is the quality in which we really differ from our predecessors. We are frank with each other, frank, or pretty nearly so, with our elders, frank in the way we feel toward life and this badly damaged world. It may be a disquieting and misleading habit, but is it a bad one? [4]

Undoubtedly, frankness and rebellion characterize the entire period of this study, and become increasingly prominent in American fiction at least until the late 1940's; but after 1930, as I shall point out, other characteristics take precedence in the most important novels, and in some cases even obscure the author's intention, thus counteracting his frankness to some extent. In the 1920's, frankness itself was a novel and striking feature, and Dreiser, Anderson, Fitzgerald, and Dell shocked and startled the public merely by relating what everyone knew but had previously considered unsuitable for literature.

In the thirties, the Great Depression was an ever present threat, and in many cases an actual torment, which inevitably affected the literature of the time. Writers who had not been disillusioned with gentility by World War I and its aftermath were pushed into left-wing positions by the stock-market crash and the insecurity that followed it. Most important writers stressed social criticism, and a considerable number of them became either Communists or fellow travelers. Frederick Hoffman in *The Modern Novel in America, 1900–1950* outlined a "formula of proletarian fiction" as he observed it in many novels of the decade:

> First, it ought to be a novel of action—which meant that it usually contained much action and that the pace was relatively fast; as for the reader, he was supposed to be stimulated, if not to action, at least to a very active sympathy with the patently "right cause" about which the fiction left no doubt. Second, in this kind of novel thought was subordinated to the action as it was seen preparing and occurring. The intellectual development of the characters was both logically simple and ideologically determined. . . . Third, there was a measure of documentation in every one of these novels, and some of them were nothing but documentation. Never in the history of American fiction were facts of the American scene so abundantly supplied or so frequently reiterated. (Pp. 133–34.)

The hero of the proletarian novel, said Hoffman, "must carry the burden of ideological conviction"; and therefore, whether he began as an uneducated worker or as a reactionary, he must learn in the course of the novel, both through events and through doctrinal persuasion by others, that the rights of the worker are of paramount importance. Thus the dialogue in such a work of fiction was likely to take the form of "a dialectic catechism."

Several of the proletarian novelists of the thirties, such as Albert Halper, Meyer Levin, and Erskine Caldwell, rose above this crude formula and produced novels of better-than-average quality, some of them dealing with adolescents. Nelson Algren followed the formula fairly closely in his first novel, *Somebody in Boots* (1935), but showed an originality that was to make some of his later novels outstanding. A few left-wing writers of the thirties—John Dos Passos, John Steinbeck, and James T. Farrell—completely avoided the formula and produced novels which, though obviously intended to preach social reform, became really important contributions to American literature.

Although social criticism is the outstanding characteristic of fiction in the thirties, two of the greatest novelists of the period—Thomas Wolfe and William Faulkner—showed very little if any proletarian fervor. All through the decade, their work showed characteristics that were to be more typical of novels in the forties, particularly after World War II: the complex interplay of original, almost freakish characters; the probing of the depths of the human mind below the level of consciousness; and the presentation of characters, thoughts, and actions through symbols and indirect suggestions of a kind that had previously been considered more appropriate for poetry than for prose fiction.

There is far less unity of technique and of emphasis in the novels of the forties than in those of the thirties. As the insistent demands of World War II divided the decade for all Americans into prewar, wartime, and postwar periods, so the aims and interests of novelists were divided until a few years of peacetime productivity had a chance to establish a dominant position. James T. Farrell, Erskine Caldwell, and Richard Wright continued to write left-wing propaganda novels in the naturalistic tradition. Faulkner continued his experimental probing of the depths of unusual minds. Two important women writers emerged in the early forties—Carson McCullers and Jean Stafford—both of whom followed Faulkner into unexplored depths of the mind, using symbols not only to communicate what they found but also to snare elusive thoughts and impulses and tie them into narratives. Perhaps as a reaction to the long, exhausting tension of a depression followed by a war, there was a rather striking tendency to revive the Tarkington tradition of the lovable, laughable adolescent. There was even a revival of the sentimental treatment of adolescence in the novels of William Saroyan, Betty Smith, Mary O'Hara, and Robert Nathan. Of course there was an outpouring of war novels. And when the return of peace allowed parents the opportunity to observe what had happened to their children during the years of absentee parenthood, there began an almost equal outpouring of novels of juvenile delinquency. Probably the most important trend all through the decade, and one which was well established by the closing years, was the use of depth psychology and symbolism in novels of careful and conscious artistry.

Meanwhile, the struggle against prudery, which had begun in the 1890's but had shown little progress until the 1920's, had advanced so far that by the end of the 1940's there was practically no phase of human thought, language, or action that could not be stated frankly and forthrightly in print. But whatever was stated frankly and forthrightly was likely to be of less importance to the real significance of a novel than what was implied and suggested by symbols.

In the fifties both symbolism and depth psychology became more firmly established as methods of fiction, while naturalism was on the decline, though by no means extinct. The numerous novels on juvenile delinquency were especially documentary. Meanwhile, a new attitude became apparent in American literature—the flippant, intellectual despair and rebellion of the "beat generation." Born of an awareness of the tenuous uncertainty of humanity's future in an atomic age, this attitude found expression in novels glorifying the pointlessness of life, and the pleasures to be found in rejecting all inhibitions and in finding release through jazz, drugs, speed, and sexual promiscuity. It is an attitude typical of a desperate and lost adolescent, and the chief novelist of the beat generation, Jack Kerouac, peopled his novels with young men who, though chronologically mature, remained emotionally adolescent. A few outstanding novelists, notably James Agee and James Baldwin, sought meaning in life through religion; but for most intellectual writers, the only approach to purposiveness in life that had much appeal was existentialism. For many, the metaphysics of two thousand years ago seemed anachronistic in an age of rapidly increasing scientific knowledge; yet science left many areas of human nature unexplained. Existentialism offered an escape from naturalism without involving a retreat to discarded traditions of Judeo-Christian religion.

Generalizations About American Novels of Adolescence, 1920–1960

Even a cursory glance at the fiction about adolescence published in the forty years of this survey reveals two very obvious facts and two somewhat less obvious ones, all of which should be taken into account in any study of this literature. First, the majority of novels emphasizing the adolescence of the protagonist are first novels, and secondly, most of them are largely autobiographical. These facts are not surprising. A beginning novelist naturally writes about the people, places, and situations he knows best. Probably he has not lived long enough to have experienced many dramatic situations, but certainly he has experienced the promising yet terrifying adventure of growing into adulthood. He fictionalizes his experiences, and has his autobiographical novel of adolescence. Having taken his first big step on this relatively certain ground, he will probably make his later excursions into other fields, or he may decide that the realm of fiction is not the best place for him to travel in. Relatively few decide to settle in the field of fictional adolescence, and cultivate its soil assiduously season after season.

A third fact, and one which is not so easily explained, is that important novels dealing with adolescent males are far more numerous and far franker than those dealing with adolescent females. Over ninety per cent of the best novels about adolescence are centered on boys; and a number of them—notably those by James T. Farrell, William Maxwell, Truman Capote, and J. D. Salinger—are completely frank. It is not until the latter 1950's that novels about girls attain the frankness that novels about boys showed during the 1940's; and the frankest fiction with female protagonists—Grace Metalious' *Peyton Place* and Pamela Moore's *Chocolates for Breakfast* (both published in 1956), and *Love Me Little* (1957) and *The Bright Young Things* (1958), both written by Warren Miller and published under the pseudonym "Amanda Vail"—are not among the best of novels about adolescents. The numerical predominance of novels about boys may be explained partly by the great predominance of male novelists over female, but the excess of masculine protagonists is greater than the excess of masculine writers. The franker treatment of boys may be explained by the fact that the male adolescent hero, as firmly established in Anglo-American literary tradition, was far more readily adaptable to the newer interests in fiction than the female. Leslie Fiedler, in one of a series of articles appearing in the *New Leader* in the spring of 1958, labeled these protagonists respectively as the Good Bad Boy (freckle-faced, sandy-haired, good-hearted but always getting into trouble) and the Good Good Girl (blonde, sexless, sinless, and sickly—ready to be a martyr to the thoughtless transgressions of an older male).[5] Obviously Tom Sawyer and Penrod Schofield are more closely related to the soul-searching modern protagonists than are Little Eva and Elsie Dinsmore. But perhaps it is social custom rather than literary tradition that makes girls less suitable for fictional analysis than boys: perhaps the closer surveillance of girls throughout adolescence gives them less opportunity for the varied adventure that makes good fiction material.

A fourth fact about the novels of adolescents is a natural result of their autobiographical character: the protagonist is almost certain to be unusually sensitive, and is probably looking forward to a career in one of the arts. Generally, of course, he is planning to be a writer; but almost as often he plans to be a musician, a painter, an architect, or an actor. In each case, he is misunderstood by his contemporaries, who do not share his insights and cannot comprehend many of his problems. In most of the novels, the hero is set apart from his contemporaries not only because of his abilities which they do not share, but because he has not the athletic ability which most of them regard as the criterion of excellence. In those striking exceptions where the hero is an athletic star, he is likely to win prominence in track or boxing; his lack of rapport with his fellows prevents him from attaining much success in team play.

RECENT CRITICAL DISCUSSIONS OF FICTIONAL ADOLESCENTS

To complete the background for this study of the problems of adolescents in novels, it only remains necessary to cite some recent critical observations on American fictional adolescents. The first chronologically, but the narrowest in scope, is an article by Frederic I. Carpenter entitled "The Adolescent in American Fiction," which appeared in the *English Journal* for September, 1957. Professor Carpenter concentrates on three recent novels of adolescence—Carson McCullers' *The Heart Is a Lonely Hunter*, J. D. Salinger's *The Catcher in the Rye*, and Jessamyn West's *Cress Delahanty*—but in addition to specific comments on these works, he makes some noteworthy observations on American novels about adolescence in general. After remarking on the great number of recent American works of fiction that emphasize the problems of adolescence —a circumstance which some critics have interpreted as a reflection of the immaturity of American society—Carpenter comments:

> But books about immaturity need not be immature, and a few American novels about adolescence have embodied some of the most adult wisdom that America has produced. . . . The stories about adolescence which have remained merely childish have been those which have described their heroes from the superior point of view of the adult, condescendingly. The adventures of the romantic Tom Sawyer, and of Penrod and Sam, have seemed somewhat ridiculous because they have been motivated by those confusions of adolescence which their adult

19

authors and readers have, of course, outgrown. But the novels which have attained genuine maturity, and sometimes greatness, are those which have entered into the confusions of their adolescents at first hand, and have described them through the eyes of their protagonists. . . . Always the authors have remained objective, respecting their youthful heroes as human individuals and recognizing their problems as real. Indeed, these adolescent problems have often reflected the problems of their parents and elders, as in a distorting mirror. For this reason some of these novels . . . may prove to be the most important fiction produced by our society, whose values are similarly confused.

He then points out that Huckleberry Finn and Salinger's Holden Caulfield, together with the protagonists of most significant novels of adolescence, share a hatred of hypocrisy and a search for integrity, although this search may be confused by their own adolescent daydreaming and love of playacting.

A much more thorough study of the subject is Mrs. Helen White Childers' unpublished doctoral dissertation "American Novels about Adolescents, 1917–1953" (George Peabody College for Teachers, 1958). Although Mrs. Childers' study covers very nearly the same period as the present work, it differs considerably in that her main emphasis is on the techniques of the authors, whereas this volume emphasizes the problems of the adolescent protagonists as they adjust to a more mature station in life. Both are interested in the changes in adolescent problems and in authors' treatments of them throughout the years, but this book also notes differences in the problems and their treatments in different sections of the country. The main body of Mrs. Childers' dissertation devotes one chapter to the techniques used in each of four main types of adolescent novel and a fifth chapter to the techniques used in several minor types, as she explains on page 10:

> The four major types into which the novels fall are as follows: novels representing the life history of the adolescent, the many-area developmental novel, ending in his more or less successful initiation into adulthood; the sociological study, concerned with the adolescent as a victim of society; the psychological study, presenting the adolescent who because of psychological disaster fails in his initiation; and novels in which the adolescent character is mainly a technical device that allows the achievement of special fictional effects. There are also several minor types, kinds of novels which are continuous yet are either not numerous enough or not illustrated by enough novels of high literary merit to be placed in a major category.

Mrs. Childer's very useful appendix lists, with brief summaries, about four hundred novels, some of which, for one reason or another, are outside the scope of this study.

Her observations on the changing scopes, techniques and attitudes of novelists are worth noting here. Many novels of the twenties and thirties, she noted, cover a long span in the life of the central character and show him "in broad social context," often emphasizing some condemnation of society (p. 347). Novels of the forties and fifties, on the other hand, concentrate on a much shorter period of time and a much smaller group of characters, and are more concerned with the psychological processes of the protagonist than with flaws in society (p. 349). Objective, naturalistic narrative was common in the novels of the twenties and thirties, according to Mrs. Childers; some notable exceptions were the strictly limited points of view presented by Sherwood Anderson in *Winesburg, Ohio* and by William Faulkner in *The Sound and the Fury* and *As I Lay Dying*. During the forties and fifties, however, she found the limited point of view to be more usual than the objective narrative, and she attributed this change in technique to the increased interest in the "depths and complexities, and the ambiguities, ironies, and uncertainties" of the human mind (p. 356). Like some other critics, Mrs. Childers noted a new sort of adolescent protagonist emerging in the fiction of the forties and fifties—a pathetic figure, thrust too early into the world of maturity where even the adults are lonely and insecure. "He stands as the symbol of the plight of modern man." (P. 360.)

Mention has already been made of Leslie Fiedler's theory of the Good Good Girl and the Good Bad Boy in American literature, which first appeared in a series of articles in the *New Leader* in the spring of 1958. The series as a whole discusses the place of children (i.e., non-adults) in modern fiction. Although his study is not limited to adolescents or to American novels or to works published since 1920, many of his comments are applicable to this more restricted study. After noting the frequency and importance of children as symbols of innocence and instruments of true insight in books of the last hundred years, Professor Fiedler suggests:

> So ubiquitous and symbolic a figure is, of course, no mere reproduction of a fact of existence; he is a cultural invention, a product of the imagination. But what have we invented him *for*, and out of what stuff have we contrived him? There is something both ambiguous and un-

precedented about the cult of the child: indeed, the notion that a mere falling short of adulthood is a guarantee of insight and even innocence is a sophisticated view. . . .[5]

This concept of childhood, says Fiedler, has been established in our culture only since Rousseau introduced his religion of Romanticism with its doctrine of Original Innocence. The adoration of childish innocence in English and American literature has led to, or has been accompanied by, the near exclusion of adult sexuality. To Fiedler, this preoccupation with and admiration of immature innocence seems unhealthy in adults, and he is encouraged to see signs of reaction against it—a trend which he earlier implied in the very title of his first collection of essays, *An End to Innocence* (Boston, 1955). He notes the frequent recurrence in modern fiction of the theme of initiation into maturity; that such initiation means a loss of innocence is clearly shown, he insists, by the fact that in much recent American fiction the entry into adulthood comes not through sexual experience, but through the taking of a life, either human or animal (see my comments below in Chapter VII, pp. 225–29). In some recent works of literature, even the child becomes a symbol of evil: for example, the child murderess in William March's *The Bad Seed*. (Fiedler also names Eula Varner in Faulkner's *The Hamlet* as a symbol of evil. Faulkner undoubtedly intended her to personify sex, even in her infancy; but she does not seem to be a symbol of evil, although the sight of her arouses men's animal instincts.) An extreme reversal of the traditional symbols of innocence corrupted by experience is found in Vladimir Nabokov's *Lolita:* "it is the naïve child, the female, the American who corrupts the sophisticated adult, the male, the European." Without admiring *Lolita* as literature, Fiedler is pleased to see in it

> a resolve to reassess the innocence of the child, to reveal it as a kind of moral idiocy, a dangerous freedom from the restraints of culture and custom, a threat to order. In the place of the sentimental dream of childhood, writers like Faulkner and Nabokov have been creating for us a nightmare in which the child is no longer raped, strangled or seduced, but is himself (better herself!) rapist, murderer and seducer. . . . Such writers have come to believe that the self can be betrayed by impulse as well as rigor; that an Age of Innocence can be a tyranny no less terrible than an Age of Reason; and that the gods of such an age, if not yet dead, must be killed however snub-nosed, freckle-faced or golden-haired they may be.[6]

The shift of American novelists' interest from innocence to experience was also noted by Ihab H. Hassan in his essay "The Idea of Adolescence in American Fiction," which appeared in the *American Quarterly* for the fall of 1958. Professor Hassan was obviously influenced by some of the ideas expressed by Fiedler in *An End to Innocence;* the increasing emphasis on adolescents rather than children in the American fiction of the last seventy-five years is, according to Hassan, a reflection of writers' interest shifting from innocence to the beginnings of experience. It is also, he says, a reflection of "the American dream, the vision of youth, hope, and the open road." Adolescence is a period of contradictions. "Rejection and affirmation, revolt and conformity, recklessness and sensitivity" characterize the adolescent, who seems "at once innocent and guilty, hopeful and disillusioned, Arcadian and Utopian, empirical and idealistic." These contradictions symbolize "the felt contradictions which history imposed on the American tradition of innocence," and the adolescent made his appearance in American fiction about the time these contradictions began to be felt—shortly after the Civil War. (Pp. 313–15.)

Four European movements, according to Hassan, influenced the American idea of adolescence. First, Romanticism, through such writings as Rousseau's *Confessions* and Goethe's *Sorrows of Young Werther,* contributed such adolescent attitudes as self-conscious introspection, individual rebelliousness, heroic posturing, and disillusioned innocence. Second, Naturalism, reaching Crane and Dreiser through the influence of Taine, Maupassant, and Flaubert in France and Butler, Moore, Hardy, and Bennett in England, contributed a determined candor and an awareness of external facts. Third, Primitivism, as represented by Bergson's subjectivist philosophy and Rimbaud's personal example, influenced the candid revelation of naked emotions in American fictional adolescents from Gertrude Stein's Melanctha to Salinger's Holden Caulfield. Fourth, Freudianism obviously heightened American novelists' awareness of the shaping influences that made the adolescent what he is, and of the importance of adolescent experiences in determining later life.

In the preface to his outstanding psychological study *Adolescence* (New York, 1904), G. Stanley Hall warned of the dangers facing American youth because of changing attitudes toward sex and maturity. Hassan comments that Hall had no way of knowing that even more radical changes would follow and "involve adolescence in a crisis without wholly disrupting its moral economy. . . . These changes can be conveniently regarded in relation to the family, the school, and the battlefields of two wars." In the home, says Hassan, the changes came about as a result of the permissive trend in child-rearing, linked with the crumbling of the patriarchal family structure; in the school, they were the result of so-called "progressive education," with emphasis on freedom of expression, and on guidance rather than compulsion, so that "the adolescent derived his values from his multitudinous peers rather than his teachers, and from his teachers rather than his parents." (Pp. 321–22.) The generation that came to maturity at the time of World War I explored their own adolescence in search of lost innocence and old stable values, and thus gave literature an autobiographical impulse which was likely to be skeptical rather than nostalgic; but those who came to maturity at the time of World War II had not known innocence or stability in childhood or adolescence, and the shadow of the regimentation of war times has produced a "beat" or "silent" or "cool" generation. The newer novelists, when they explore their childhood or adolescence, are likely to find misogyny, Oedipal conflicts, and incipient homosexuality. Even though they do not find innocence and stability in childhood and adolescence, they do find relative simplicity, so that the pleasures and pains found there can serve as a comprehensible symbol for the more complex ones to be found in adult life. Thus their retreat to preadolescence is partly escape and partly judgment.

In "The Adolescent Hero: A Trend in Modern Fiction," appearing in *Twentieth Century Literature* for April, 1959, Professor James William Johnson suggests:

> The emergence, within the past thirty years, of the child and the adolescent as heroes of much important fiction is a phenomenon only recently noted by the critics. . . . The truth seems to be that an entirely new sort of hero has appeared in the fiction of recent years, reflecting a peculiar system of values and effecting important changes in literary technique. The adolescent protagonist, as we have come to know him in the persons of a Holden Caulfield, a Eugene Gant, or a Nick Adams, is a distinctly Twentieth-Century manifestation, virtually without precedent in British or American fiction.

Professor Johnson considers that the sincere and candidly honest depiction of the thoughts and problems of adolescents in novels of the last few decades has produced "the most convincing—perhaps the only convincing —adolescent heroes and heroines to appear in English fiction." Like Hassan, Johnson notes both the paradoxes in the adolescent point of view and the usefulness of the adolescent world as a microcosmic symbol for the adult world. After listing some of the more obvious elements in the "new mythos of man's youth"—tentativeness in tone, ambiguity of attitude, the leitmotif of change, the themes of search and shocking discovery—he points out some subtler elements in specific works that he calls "a half dozen of the most important novels of the past thirty years": James Joyce's *A Portrait of the Artist*, Ernest Hemingway's *In Our Time*, Thomas Wolfe's *Look Homeward, Angel*, Katherine Anne Porter's *Old Mortality*, Carson McCullers' *The Member of the Wedding*, and J. D. Salinger's *The Catcher in the Rye*. He notes that the adolescent protagonist in each of these works is likely to have (1) an inexplicable sense of loss, with no poignancy in the memory of childhood, but only a realization that it is gone and some anxiety about the future; (2) a sharp awareness of strange shapes and sensations in the body; (3) some sexual confusion, particularly when the protagonist is a girl; (4) a sense of isolation and loneliness in a world of similar but alien beings; (5) a desire to escape familiar surroundings, thus not only asserting physical independence but also repudiating emotional dependence on other people and intellectual dependence on the past; (6) the realization (often revealed in a vision) that "there can be no escape from a duty correlative to man's existence in time and his biological connection to others."

After noting that earlier novelists, like the ancient Greeks, recognized only three phases of human life—infancy or childhood, maturity or adulthood, and old age or senility—Johnson attributes the "discovery of the adolescent" to both the psychologist and the sociologist. The wide acceptance of Freud's theories, which stress the influence of childhood and adolescence on later life, has obviously affected the subject matter of fiction; the popularizing of the social scientists' concept of adolescence by such authors as Gesell, Spock, and Kinsey has helped to fix this concept in the mind of the public; and modern living conditions which "prolong youth's apprenticeship to adulthood" have added financial, social, and legal problems to the physical, emotional, and intellectual problems of adolescence, and have thus greatly increased the suitability of this age for the literary treatment of inner and outer conflict. Thus the adolescent has become an archetypal figure for the confusions of our age; and if modern

25

novelists hold out any hope for him to find order in life, it is likely to be the relative order of existentialism.

A final commentary on adolescents in recent fiction may be more briefly noted; it is not a work of criticism, but a sort of annotated anthology of fictional treatments of the problems of adolescents. Professor Norman Kiell, a psychologist at Brooklyn College, appreciates, as Freud did, the novelist's subtle but perceptive insight into the human mind; in his book *The Adolescent Through Fiction: A Psychological Approach* (New York, 1959), Professor Kiell describes the types of problems that are most likely to disturb adolescents, then illustrates each type of problem with one or more rather lengthy passages from American, English, or European novels of the last sixty years, and comments briefly on the psychological significance of each passage. There is little if any attempt to evaluate the various fictional treatments, or to trace changes in the problems presented from one decade to another, or even from one country to another. Although Kiell's book has only a slight connection with the present study, it is worth noting here for the specific examples it gives, many of them taken from novels included in this survey.

It is interesting that all of the critics here mentioned see the adolescent in fiction as a symbol of modern man in a period of doubt and confusion. Professor Carpenter is particularly concerned with adolescent protagonists in novels of the forties and fifties; Mrs. Childers and Professor Johnson place the emergence of this type of literary figure at about the end of World War I, whereas Professor Hassan places it shortly after the Civil War; Professor Fiedler never recognizes a distinction between the child and the adolescent in fiction, but attributes the "invention" of the innocent non-adult to the influence of Rousseau in the eighteenth century. Professors Fiedler and Hassan note decreased emphasis on the innocence of childhood and adolescence in recent fiction, and a growing recognition that there can be wickedness as well as innocence at an early age. Professor Carpenter points out that young people must encounter evil as well as good if they are to advance to a normal maturity. All of these critics call attention to the increased subtlety and psychological insight in the novels of the forties and fifties. Mrs. Childers is most explicit about the differences between novels of adolescence published in the twenties and thirties and those published in the forties and fifties, indicating the greater scope of the earlier novels and their greater emphasis on the need for social reform as at least one answer to the problems which

26

adolescents face. She also shows most specifically and clearly the shift in fictional technique from objective naturalism to subtle and symbolic presentation of inner mental patterns.

With a knowledge of the literary and cultural background, of the fictional trends which took place during the period studied, and of the general observations which critics have made on the recent novels about adolescents, a specific study of the problems presented in these novels should be more meaningful. In the final chapter, some of these critical comments will be reconsidered in the light of the many characters and incidents which will have been analyzed in the intervening chapters.

Chapter II

SEXUAL AWAKENING

The most obvious aspect of adolescence is the growing to sexual maturity. The physical and emotional problems involved in this phase of development are many, varied, and inevitable. It is hard to find a novel of adolescence which does not dwell on the young person's new awareness of sex—although Mark Twain allowed the most famous of American fictional adolescents to remain remarkably unaffected by this powerful force. The genteel novelists treat the romantic manifestations of sex with indulgent smiles for inexperienced puppy love, or sympathetic sighs for the ever recurring, ever new miracle of idyllic love. The naturalists remind us that there are unhumorous and unlovely aspects of sex, and the lure of forbidden mysteries or the sincere desire for hitherto unexplored truth may draw the reader into accounts of the secret, sordid, and shameful with fully as great a fascination as he feels for the funny or the beautiful.

Since this aspect of adolescence is so universal, it would be pointless even to mention all the novels that treat of it. Rather, it seems advisable to select typical examples of four different approaches: the humorous treatment of puppy love, the romantic presentation of idyllic love, the recounting of adolescents' initiation into the mysteries of love and sex with an older, more experienced person, and the exploratory hunting of sex as a thing in itself, detached from the genteelly acceptable stalking-horse of love.

Puppy Love

To view adolescent love as comical and unimportant is a typical adult attitude. Though Booth Tarkington's Penrod Schofield and Willie Baxter still remain for most readers as prime examples of the victims of puppy love, they are by no means the last, despite the tendency for novelists in later decades to view adolescent problems sympathetically. An echo of Penrod is found in Ted Robinson's *Enter Jerry* (1921), and Leona

Dalrymple's treatment of Paul Northrop in *Fool's Hill* (1922) is reminiscent of Tarkington's treatment of Willie Baxter in *Seventeen*. Paul, however, has not one love affair but five.

During the thirties and early forties there was a notable revival of interest in novels with a condescending humorous attitude toward adolescents, particularly toward girls. Often the girl would go through a series of crushes on older men, but usually she would, at the same time, be enjoying or tolerating a fumbling love affair with the boy next door. This boy would usually be red-haired and awkward but devoted; the girl was likely to be much more poised, and to enjoy taking advantage of the power she held over him.

Two husband-and-wife teams at this time produced a series of popular books about adolescent girls in love. Florence Ryerson and her husband, Colin Clements, followed the adventures and amours of Jane Jones and her neighbor Chump Edwards through two volumes. *This Awful Age* (1930) presents Jane between the ages of twelve and fifteen. Jane has successive crushes on a Shakespearean actor, a college boy, and a young Communist organizer, but it is Chump who is her almost constant companion. The authors make it plain that even in "this awful age" of smoking and drinking and jazzing, the average youngster is innocent at heart and can be trusted. When suspicious neighbors point out to the trusting parents that Jane's and Chump's secret meetings in a deserted cottage ought to be investigated, the investigation exposes the fact that the young people are making Christmas presents. Mr. Jones and Mr. Edwards assure each other that, although all children must grow up eventually, Jane and Chump will never cause worry to their parents. *Mild Oats* (1933) takes Jane from the age of fifteen to seventeen; although she dreams of herself in romantic situations, she finds more real pleasure in going fishing with Chump. Ryerson and Clements are not unsympathetic to the problems of adolescence, but they naïvely suggest that well-brought-up boys and girls cannot possibly get themselves into serious difficulties.

Another husband-and-wife team, Graeme and Sarah Lorimer, brought the puppy loves of another adolescent girl, Maudie Mason, to the hearts of American slick-fiction readers through the pages of the *Ladies' Home Journal*, and periodically collected these stories into volumes that might be called episodic novels: *Men Are Like Street Cars* (1932), *Stag Line* (1934), *Heart Specialist* (1935), and *First Love, Farewell* (1940).

From the age of sixteen in the first volume to the age of nineteen in the last, Maudie relates—in wisecracking, subdeb style—her conquests over members of the weaker, more crudely impassioned sex. Though various males of varying ages receive her languishing adoration for varying intervals of time, she never surrenders more than a sweet look, a gentle pressure of the hand, or—at most and very rarely—a chaste kiss, and returns inevitably to her devoted contemporary, Davy Dillon. Many of the situations in which Maudie finds herself seem contrived merely to find opportunities for some of the outrageous puns in which her chronicles abound. By the end of the fourth volume the wisecracks have worn rather thin, but Maudie herself is fresh and unsullied.

Maudie is womanly-wise in the techniques of making herself desirable, but is righteously and naïvely indignant when men approach her with more than properly respectful adoration. More consciously and cruelly tantalizing is the fifteen-year-old heroine of F. Hugh Herbert's *Meet Corliss Archer* (1944), who had appeared earlier in the pages of *Good Housekeeping*. Lovely Corliss takes sadistic delight in showing her power over Dexter Franklin, the clumsy boy from next door, whom she scornfully calls "a ninfant," though he is a year older than she. She loves to make him "grobble" before her until even her amused and devoted father thinks she has gone too far. But the last page of the novel hints that her adolescent love of feminine power is developing into mature womanly tenderness.

Adolescent *femmes fatales* of this period are descended from Penrod's Fanchon and Willie Baxter's Miss Pratt, but they have considerably more character and substance. More common are innocent heroines of the Good Good Girl tradition (see p. 18 above): they appear, for example, not only in the Ryerson-Clements novels but also in Josephine Bentham's *Janie* (1940) and Sylvia Dee's *And Never Been Kissed* (1949), among others. As the progression of the century brought increasing acceptance of equality of the sexes, there understandably developed a new sort of heroine—the Good Bad Girl. In Peggy Goodin's *Clementine* (1946), for example, the red-headed neighbor boy is intermittently devoted to an equally red-headed tomboy. The reader first meets Clem Kelley as a ten-year-old fifth-grader, beating a fat boy in a fist fight and winning a place on Hank Matthews' neighborhood football team. At eleven she attacks Hank with her fists for accidentally breaking her treasured bow; she is shamefully beaten, and cannot understand why she saves in an envelope the tuft of red hair she has managed to pull from his head. But Clem, unlike many of the heroines of puppy-love novels, shows real growth and development. By the time she is fourteen, she has begun to feel jealous of the attention Hank pays to her pretty friend Cathy Simmons, and at sixteen she accepts Hank's treasured Hi-Y pin and begins "going steady" with him. The author, for all her intimation that this is puppy love, shows far more sympathy than Tarkington showed for his young lovers:

> Love, like measles, has nothing to do with age. Most anybody, any time, can catch it. At sixteen you may not know what's the matter with you until you find the spots, but when you do, you're very likely to uncover something that is just as severe as a similar infection at twenty or thirty or forty. The only real difference is that then you stand a better chance of knowing what to do about it. At sixteen you get all wrapped up in your symptoms. (P. 235.)

Not so tomboyish as Clem, but more likable and believable, is the orange-haired protagonist in Jessamyn West's *Cress Delahanty* (1953). Like Clem, Cress shows increasing maturity from one adventure to the next. At twelve, she dreams romantically of the love life that should soon be hers:

> Some day her mother would tell her the secret phrase, the magic sentence—something the other girls already knew. Then the boys would notice her. Then he would come. Joe and Ina and Bernardine already had notes from boys, and candy hearts on Valentine's Day, and a piece of mistletoe at Christmas time. The boys rode them on their handlebars and showed them wrestling holds, and treated them to sodas. "But no one," she mourned "ever looks at me. . . . It's because Mother hasn't told me yet. Something the other girls know. Sometime she'll tell me— some beautiful word I've been waiting a long time to hear. Then I'll be like a lamp lighted, a flower bloomed." (P. 23.)

Of course Cress never learns the magic word, but a little later in the same year she begins to show a keen understanding of and sympathy for clumsy, unpopular Edwin Kibbler, Junior, whose teeth she has knocked out by accident. At thirteen she pathetically tries to arouse the awkward Edwin's interest with an ornate hat and high-heeled shoes. Through her high-school years she has one or two infatuations with older men, but at sixteen, as a freshman in college, she finds that Edwin has taken on a new fascination with the masterfulness of his approaching maturity.

The preponderance of girls over boys as protagonists in the puppy-love novels of this period is no indication that clumsy male adolescent lovers were unpopular. Indeed, the popularity of Henry Aldrich on the Broadway stage and of Andy Hardy in moving pictures, as well as numerous teen-age boys and girls in comic strips and radio series, demonstrates that the public enjoyed laughing at mooning boys as much as at languishing girls. Yet from *Fool's Hill* in 1922 to Max Shulman's *The Many Loves of Dobie Gillis* in 1953, the only noteworthy novels emphasizing the masculine side of puppy love are John Peter Toohey's *Growing Pains* (1929) and Herman Wouk's *The City Boy* (1948). None of these novels are as sincere, sympathetic, or convincing as Miss Goodin's and Miss West's; *Dobie Gillis* and its sequel, *I Was a Teen-Age Dwarf* (1960), are as silly as the television series about their amorous, adolescent hero. Perhaps the more capable novelists felt that Tarkington had gone as far as it was possible to go in the light-hearted treatment of boys in love. In novels giving *serious* treatment to the problems of adolescents, whether sexual or otherwise, male protagonists far outnumber female. The excess of memorable female protagonists in the one field of puppy love is striking enough to deserve some attempt at explanation. Perhaps in the gradual process of abandoning the goody-good concept of the female adolescent in fiction, authors and readers reached a point during the thirties and forties where girls could be laughed at and loved for clean, wholesome naughtiness, as boys were in novels of a hundred to forty years ago. In the middle and late fifties a few girls were given the full, frank, naturalistic treatment in love problems that boys received in novels of the thirties and forties.

Idyllic Love

It is difficult to choose examples of idyllic love from the novels of this period. Although most adolescent love affairs seem idyllic to those involved, writers of the realistic period are well aware, and make it clear to their readers, that few if any loves are as wonderful as they seem, particularly those of adolescents. Except for fiction of the slick-magazine type, novels with lived-happily-ever-afterward endings went out of fashion with the decline of the genteel tradition. A possible exception might be the fiction of Dorothy Canfield Fisher, who belongs as much to the genteel tradition as she does to the realistic. Her novel *Rough-Hewn* (1922), for example, ends with an idyllic and very promising love; but by this time Neale is twenty-six and Marise is twenty-one—both obviously beyond their adolescent stage. Most of the important novels, from the very beginning of the period we are considering, treat adolescent love with some cynicism. Thus Amory Blaine in Scott Fitzgerald's *This Side of Paradise* (1920) experiences his first kiss at thirteen for the sole purpose of proving to himself that he can do it, while Myra is thinking, "What a story this would make to tell Marylyn!" (P. 15.) During his sophomore year at Princeton, Amory has a nearly idyllic love affair with Isabelle Borge, which lasts for several months, although it began simply as the mutual attempt of two handsome and popular young people to impress each other. After a chaste but exalted week end at the Princeton June Prom, Amory visits Isabelle's family on Long Island, convinced that their love will be eternal. But even as he finally enfolds her in a story-book embrace, he is thinking about what an attractive-looking couple they are; and when, a moment later, she complains violently about the visible bruise made on her neck by his shirt stud, he decides that their love is over.

Less obviously cynical, but still pessimistic, are Floyd Dell's presentations of adolescent love experiences in *Moon-Calf* (1920). The first shows eleven-year-old Felix Fay, the author's *alter ego*, meeting secretly in a dusty garret with Rose, a fifteen-year-old girl who, with her strait-laced grandfather, occupies the other side of the two-family house the Fays live in. Their common delight in stories and poems leads the two children to a series of secret meetings, ending with a picnic in the woods at night and a nap in each other's arms. The suspicious grandfather tells Felix that Rose is a shameless harlot to tempt a child. Felix no longer trusts her; he dreams of her erotically, but avoids seeing her again. When Felix is sixteen and working in a candy factory, he and a fellow worker named Margaret are mutually attracted but are both too shy to express their feelings in more than glances. When the candy factory closes, Felix cannot obey his impulse to kiss Margaret good-bye, and a few weeks later he leaves town without having seen her again. A year or so later he has a third romance, which will be discussed later in this chapter.

With characteristic subtlety and indirectness, Ernest Hemingway lets the reader know of the strong emotions Nick Adams experiences when, at the instigation of cynical friends, he breaks off his idyllic romance with Marjorie in one of the episodes of *In Our Time* (1925). The reader never knows the romance at its height, but he can sense its idyllic quality from the hesitation and the pain with which Nick tells Marjorie, on their last fishing trip together to a favorite spot, "It isn't fun any more. Not any of it." (P. 45.) Nick's empty feeling persists in the following episode, and the reason for the break is revealed as his friend Bill compliments him on his ending the romance:

> "It was the only thing to do. . . . If you'd have married her you would have had to marry the whole family. Remember her mother and that guy she married? The fat one? . . . Imagine having them around the house all the time and going to Sunday dinners at their house, and having them over to dinner and her telling Marge all the time what to do and how to act. . . . You can't mix oil and water and you can't mix that sort of thing any more than if I'd marry Ida that works for Strattons." (Pp. 63–65.)

Although Nick admits that Marjorie's mother was "terrible," he is not consoled until Bill reminds him that there is some danger of his becoming involved with Marge again. At the thought that the break is not irrevocable, Nick feels better, even though he knows he will probably never go back to her. Thus Hemingway indirectly suggests that the most idyllic of adolescent love affairs may be ended by social snobbery and be forgotten like a three-day wind storm.

James T. Farrell's Studs Lonigan trilogy is so well remembered for its harsh naturalism that readers are likely to forget the brief idyllic love affair between Studs and Lucy Scanlon during their fifteenth summer. Their afternoon in Washington Park, sitting in the branches of a big tree, affords a delightful and memorable contrast to most of Studs's adventures.

> There he was, and there was Lucy, swinging her legs, singing *The Blue Ridge Moutains of Virginia*, and it was nice, and he told himself that no afternoon in his whole life had been like this one, not even the afternoon after he had licked the stuffings out of Weary Reilley. He had felt sick from the fight then, and the gang had all been around and made things a lot different from now, with himself and Lucy sharing and owning all the niceness themselves. And he had a feeling that this was a turning point in his life, and from now on everything was going to be jake. (*Young Lonigan*, p. 12.)

Ironically, the afternoon does prove to be a turning point in his life, but not in the way Studs anticipated. Two days later he finds that someone has scrawled "Studs loves Lucy" on the sidewalks, buildings, and fences around the part of Indiana Avenue in Chicago where his gang hangs out. Fearing the loss of his reputation as the toughest guy in the gang, he stays away from Indiana Avenue for a while, making himself leader of a gang of bullies and thieves who hang around Fifty-eighth Street and Prairie Avenue. Thus, while he continues to long for Lucy, he becomes more and more deeply involved in activities which make it impossible for him to be acceptable to her.

These presentations of adolescent love from Fitzgerald, Dell, Hemingway, and Farrell may be taken as representative of the attitude of the better novelists in the twenties and thirties: a realization of the seriousness of the love to those participating, and a refusal to take it as a laughing matter; at the same time there is a realization that a very slight thing may abruptly terminate a love affair which the inexperienced youngsters had thought would last forever. In the novels of the forties and fifties idyllic adolescent love is increasingly rare; the emphasis is likely to be placed on sordid circumstances, on sexual experimentation, and even on perversion.

Two novels of the period, however, may be mentioned for the skill with which they convey the sense of newness and wonder that adolescent love may have. The first is *Seventeenth Summer* (1942) by Maureen Daly, who, when she wrote it, was only two or three years beyond her own seventeenth summer. A carefully nurtured small-town Wisconsin girl, Angie Morrow, relates the exciting new experiences of the summer after her graduation from a girl's academy: her steady dating with the high-school basketball star Jack Duluth; her first kiss; her first declaration of love. Her problems are minor ones—whether to send Jack a card or a letter when he goes away for a few days, how to see Jack frequently without worrying her parents, how to tolerate Jack's ignorance of her family's fastidious table manners—and yet the reader shares her concern over them as he shares her delight over the discoveries of first love.

A second novel which successfully communicates the enchantment of adolescent love is Donald Wetzel's oddly titled *The Rain and the Fire and the Will of God* (1957). As in *Seventeenth Summer,* the youthful wonder in the experiences is intensified by the first-person narrative. Jack Haywood, a fourteen-year-old Alabama farm boy, describes his parting from the neighbor girl, Jenny, after their first moonlight walk together:

> We stood there, close, and I reached down and got Jenny's hand again. It sure was small. Like Jenny said, she was hardly full-growed yet.

"Jack," Jenny said, "this was the nicest you ever been to me." I started to say something back, but then she kind of pushed my arm out of the way where I was holding it out in front of me holding her by the hand, and come up against me quick and soft, but then stayed there long enough to reach my head down and get my face mixed up in her hair for a minute and then kiss me. It sure was sudden. (P. 141.)

In a period devoted to realism in fiction and skepticism in life, it is not surprising that such idyllic scenes are comparatively rare. It is perhaps surprising that realistic fiction presents them at all, and yet they are a very real if very transitory part of adolescent love. They seem more appropriate in the fiction of fantasy, and their presence may be noted in two highly imaginative novels that seem anachronistic among many realistic ones. Edwin Granberry, in a symbolic fantasy called *The Erl King* (1930), describes two adolescents who love each other and love romantic adventure more than they love the realities and the practical comforts of life. They sail across dangerous reefs off the southern coast of Florida to explore a sunken Spanish galleon, and they never return alive. Robert Nathan in *Long After Summer* (1948) presents an idyllic romance between two impoverished adolescents in a Cape Cod fishing village. Their summer love ends suddenly and tragically in September, when Johanna sees Jot drown a mile from shore in a sudden storm. Keeping her grief within herself, throughout the following winter she relives in reverse the experiences of the summer, in fancy moving backward through time from her last days with Jot to April, the time of her coming to the Cape Cod village, when she believes everything will end. In an unconvincing Hollywood ending, Johanna, assisted by an elderly Catholic priest and the middle-aged narrator, eventually becomes aware of her illusion and begins to look forward to the time when she will be old enough to take care of the narrator, a man more than twenty-five years her senior. Thus the story shifts from one type of daydream to another, the transition effected by sentimental melodrama.

The tragic endings of the idyllic love affairs in these two fantasies suggest that even in fiction of this type the Victorian idea that love is the solution to all problems no longer is acceptable. In many of the American novels before 1920, the mutual discovery of love was enough to satisfy the young protagonists as it satisfied the readers. In the novels of the twenties and thirties, the young people were likely to think of love as eternal, and the discovery of a reciprocal love seemed to be the finding of a destiny; but authors quickly made it clear that young love is not as indestructible as it seems. A realistic understanding of the nature of love reached intellectual readers through the writings of such men as Sigmund Freud, Havelock Ellis, and Bertrand Russell; and was spread to a wider public by novelists such as Floyd Dell and James T. Farrell. By the forties and fifties, even the characters in the novels are seldom ready to accept love as completely idyllic. Many of them experiment with love with the same detached curiosity they would show in sampling different flavors of ice-cream soda. Jack Kerouac in *Maggie Cassidy* (1959) illustrates the confusion of idyllic love with experimentation as his protagonist, Jack Duluoz, recalls the tiring and painful half-hour-long kisses exchanged with Maggie, his first sweetheart:

> But somehow we were supposed to do this, and what everybody said, the other kids, Maggie and all the others "necking" at skate and post office parties and on porches after dances had learned this was the thing—and did it in spite of how they felt about it personally—the fear of the world, the children clinging in what they think is a mature, secure kiss (challenging and grown-up)—not understanding joy and personal reverence— It's only later you learn to lean your head in the lap of God, and rest in love. Some gigantic sexual drive was behind these futile long smooches, sometimes our teeth'd grind, our mouths burn from interchanged spittle, our lips blister, bleed, chap— We were scared. (P. 38.)

Love for Someone Older

As the experience of adolescence is commonly regarded as an initiation into maturity, it is not surprising that the initiating into the mysteries of love and sex is frequently conducted by an older person. This is by no means a modern discovery; the Old Testament tells of Joseph, who was offered instruction by Potiphar's wife; and his eighteenth-century namesake, Fielding's Joseph Andrews, found both Lady Booby and Mrs. Slipslop only too willing to initiate him. Also in the eighteenth century, Richardson's Pamela narrowly escaped being initiated by Mr. B—— into sex without love or marriage before her persistent clinging to accepted standards of virtue was rewarded by his offer of marriage and, presumably, love. Even an American "genteel" favorite like Jean Webster's *Daddy Long-Legs* (1912) shows an adolescent girl finding love with an older man. Freud gave a new insight into a well-recognized situation by suggesting that the love of an adolescent for an older person is the result of an easy transferral of affection from the parent of the opposite sex. This Freudian interpretation is obviously the basis for John V. A. Weaver's *Her Knight Comes Riding* (1928), in which the Brooklyn stenographer Fanny Williams falls in love with a marine sergeant because his dashing manner and the white patches of hair over his ears remind her of her father, who used to tell her stories of knights before he was killed by a truck.

Less obviously Freudian are two novels of 1923 which portray adolescent love for older people. Willa Cather's *A Lost Lady* relates Niel Herbert's adoration for Mrs. Marian Forrester from the time he is twelve until he is well into maturity. With an adolescent's idealism, Niel has only admiration for the youthful wife's devotion to her elderly husband—until the June morning when, her husband being away on a business trip, Niel goes to place an early-morning bouquet on his lady's bedroom window sill.

> As he bent to place the flowers on the sill, he heard from within a woman's soft laughter; impatient, indulgent, teasing, eager. Then another laugh, very different, a man's. And it was fat and lazy,—ended in something like a yawn.
> Niel found himself at the foot of the hill on the wooden bridge, his face hot, his temples beating, his eyes blind with anger. In his hand he still carried the prickly bunch of wild roses. He threw them over the wire fence into a mudhole the cattle had trampled under the bank of the creek. He did not know whether he had left the house by the driveway or had come down through the shrubbery. In that instant between stooping to the window sill and rising, he had lost one of the most beautiful things in his life. (P. 86.)

But even though Mrs. Forrester, in the years following her husband's death, falls still lower in Niel's regard, he cannot completely lose his affection for her; and when he learns of her death years later, he is grateful to know "that she was well cared for, to the very end." (P. 174.) Like most of Miss Cather's protagonists, Niel has a nobility of spirit that keeps him from impure thoughts or actions even though he recognizes sordidness in the actions of people about him.

Another novel of 1923, Floyd Dell's *Janet March*, presents an adolescent girl's initiation into both love and sex with older men, after boys her own age have failed to arouse her. Janet is nearly twenty, and has been courted and kissed by various boys, when she falls violently in love with a middle-aged artist named Vincent Blatch. By sheer will power, she manages to get her emotions under control; and when, some time later, she becomes his mistress, she admits that she is motivated by curiosity rather than by love. Her experiences with Blatch are part of her growing-up process, and they prepare her for a successful love affair with Roger Leland, who has loved her in his fancy since she was six and he was twenty.

Obviously, the purposes of these two authors are quite different. Miss Cather, without rejecting conventional moral standards, indicates that a person who does reject them can remain kind and likable, but may cause great pain and even permanent psychological harm to a youthful ad-mirer who, without questioning the validity of these standards, discovers that they are sometimes violated. Dell, on the other hand, is obviously condemning the traditional standards of sexual morality. His novel con-trasts the adolescent love experiences of Roger, reared according to rigid conventional standards, with those of Janet, brought up by liberal, under-standing parents, and shows that Janet adjusts much more easily and successfully to mature love.

Ellen Glasgow in *The Sheltered Life* (1932) presents a situation similar to that in *A Lost Lady*, but this time an adolescent girl is in love with a married middle-aged man. Jenny Blair Archbald, unlike Niel Herbert, is as concerned with her own passions as she is with the continuing happi-ness of George and Eva Birdsong; and when she finally confesses her love to George, it is the older couple, rather than the adolescent, who suffer the tragic results of the flouting of convention. Miss Glasgow's title suggests that even "the sheltered life" of a Virginia gentlewoman is no sure protection against the dangers of human passions. Ironically, the novel ends with old General Archbald trying to protect his "innocent" granddaughter from the shock of exposure to the sordid tragedy in the Birdsong family, while Jenny Blair realizes she herself is far from innocent.

> Springing to her feet, Jenny Blair stared at him with eyes that saw nothing. Desperately, as if she were about to run round and round in the same circle, she flung herself into his arms.
> "Oh, Grandfather, I didn't mean anything," she cried as she sank down into blackness. "I didn't mean anything in the world!" (P. 395.)

Much less tragic, but still painfully disturbing, is the love affair between the seventeen-year-old Nebraska farm boy Julian Howard and the young wife of his middle-aged neighbor in Alvin Johnson's *Spring Storm* (1936). Sympathy leads Julian to give companionship to Betty Millsbaugh when she comes from Pennsylvania to be isolated on a Midwestern farm with a coarse, drunken husband considerably older than herself; the natural impulses of his age lead him into a passionate relationship with her; an idealistic streak in his nature leads him to try to rescue her and assume responsibility for his own guilt by eloping with her; but when she treacherously reveals his plan with the hope of raising herself in her husband's esteem, Julian is enough of a realist to accept the bitter disillusionment as a part of growing up, and to leave Dutchman's Bend with the intention of preparing for a new kind of life by attending college in the East. *Spring Storm* is unusual in the history of literature in that it is a first novel by a sixty-two-year-old man who had previously won fame as a classical scholar, an economist, a journalist, and an educator, and who turned to the writing of fiction because he had something to say and fiction seemed the best way to say it. As art, it lacks the psychological subtlety of Miss Cather's and Miss Glasgow's novels and the straightforward realism of Dell's, but it is very convincing in areas that Johnson thoroughly understands—Nebraska farm life, and adolescent problems.

Several novels of the thirties present rather grotesque love affairs between adolescents and older people. The most outstanding of these is Faulkner's *Light in August* (1932), which tells of the initiating love of seventeen-year-old Joe Christmas for the little waitress Bobbie Allen:

> Even a casual adult glance could tell that she would never see thirty again. But to Joe she probably did not look more than seventeen too, because of her smallness. She was not only not tall, she was slight, almost childlike. But the adult look saw that the smallness was not due to any natural slenderness but to some inner corruption of the spirit itself: a slenderness which had never been young, in not one of whose curves anything youthful had ever lived or lingered. . . . It was because of her smallness that he ever attempted her, as if her smallness should have or might have protected her from the roving and predatory eyes of most men, leaving his chances better. (P. 150.)

Even after Joe finds her with another man in her room, he believes that Bobbie truly loves him. Not until after he has stolen money and almost killed his foster father for her sake does he realize that she has no intention of marrying him. Even more grotesque are the love affairs in some

41

of Erskine Caldwell's novels. In *Tobacco Road* (1932), sixteen-year-old Dude Lester marries a sex-starved widow, forty-year-old Bessie Rice, and his hare-lipped eighteen-year-old sister, Ellie May, seduces Lov Benson, the mature husband of her thirteen-year-old sister Pearl. In *God's Little Acre* (1933), the teen-aged nymphomaniac Darling Jill Walden happily gives herself to several older men, including her sister's husband, although she intends to marry fat, middle-aged Pluto Swint.

In contrast to the amoral adolescent sex-cravings in these novels is the idealistic, sentimental love of fourteen-year-old Ellen Pennifer for her grandfather's German Ph.D. secretary in Robert Nathan's *Winter in April* (1938). Although Eric von Siegenfels is nearly twice Ellen's age, she loves him devotedly, craving not so much his embraces or even his attentions as the opportunity to make sacrifices for him. She sells her treasured first sleeveless evening gown to make Eric a Christmas present of enough money to send his younger sister from Paris to Nice. Grandfather Pennifer, melodramatically rescuing the dress in time for Ellen's dancing-school date with Eric, remarks philosophically:

> One must not laugh because the child is in love. It is the last clear moment she will have before the world grows old and shadowy around her, the last time she can say yes with all her heart, without doubt or wonder—the last hour in which to play her games of innocence and joy. She loves for no reason, for a smile, for a glance, and her grief, which is also for no reason, is piercing and sweet. Her world is a simple place of me and thee, of the rose and the briar, of sun and rain. (P. 180.)

Four novels of the forties may be given briefer mention. In Carson McCullers' first novel, *The Heart Is a Lonely Hunter* (1940), the adolescent girl Mick Kelly silently loves the middle-aged deaf-mute John Singer, but she dreads the proprietor of the New York Café, Biff Brannon, who silently loves her. Harry Harrison Kroll's *Waters Over the Dam* (1944) presents "Mr. Danny," the eighteen-year-old hired hand at Paw Jack Dixon's grist mill in Alabama, coming into a variety of love experiences as the mature, determined schoolteacher, Miss Parnell Dees, tries to seduce him, and Paw Jack's fourteen-year-old tomboy daughter Rennie determines she is going to marry Danny herself when she is old enough. George Sklar's *The Two Worlds of Johnny Truro* (1947) is a slickly written book, unconvincing in many respects, but it presents with some understanding a situation which occurs frequently enough in adolescent daydreams, and probably occurs sometimes in fact during wartime—

the solacing of a serviceman's wife by a boy just under the age for enlistment. In Blythe Morley's *The Intemperate Season* (1948), seventeen-year-old Robert Fleming loves Melissa Middleton, a married woman ten years his senior; but his intemperate love affair ends in melodramatic violence when Melissa, with the help of an older paramour, murders her husband and the killers themselves are killed while fleeing.

Mention was made earlier in this chapter (see above, page 32) of a schoolgirl crush on an older man in Jessamyn West's *Cress Delahanty*. Like many girls, in fiction and in life, Cress has amorous dreams concerning males of various ages, and one of these is Mr. Cornelius, the invalid father of the high-school track stars. Unlike most lovesick girls, in fiction or in life, she decides that instead of continuing to suffer in silence, she will go to the dying man and tell him that she loves him. The memorable scene in which she carries out her decision adds another dimension to Miss West's dramatic presentation of a very unusual but quite believable girl.

Such a direct and reasonable approach to a problem is particularly unusual during the fifties, when novels were likely to emphasize the abnormal. Cathy Ames, in John Steinbeck's *East of Eden* (1952), is introduced to the reader as a monster who, from the age of ten, gains sadistic pleasure and material profit from her sexual power over older males. Sixteen-year-old Mick Cargan in Hal Ellson's *Summer Street* (1953) is a rather lustful city boy making normal adolescent passes at Grace Sutton, the girl across the street, until Grace's mother bluntly seduces him, giving him one thoroughly gratifying sexual experience and then refusing him any more. This strange treatment the author seems to regard as beneficial to Mick, helping him to accomplish the difficult adjustment from boyhood to manhood. Similarly, Allison MacKenzie of Grace Metalious' *Peyton Place* (1956), after a prolonged and frigid adolescence, becomes mature and fully alive after her middle-aged literary agent has given her detailed instructions in every phase of seduction, from the proper position of the lips in kissing to the proper position of the heels in bed. The twelve-year-old heroine of Vladimir Nabokov's *Lolita* (Paris 1956, New York 1958) approaches her problem even more directly than does Cress Delahanty, but not so reasonably; she seduces her thirty-eight-year-old would-be lover while he is trying to make up his mind whether or not to seduce her.

In general, although a considerable number of fictional adolescents have brief love affairs with older people, such a love is not likely to be the main theme of a novel. The only exceptions I think of are *Winter in April, Johnny Truro,* and *The Intemperate Season;* and none of these is of great literary significance. Of the novels which I have discussed in connection with such love affairs, the most valuable from a literary standpoint are *Light in August* and *The Heart Is a Lonely Hunter;* and in each of these the mismatched love is only one of a tangle of complexly interwoven themes. Love for an older person seems to be an aspect of adolescent problems that most novelists have neglected. Perhaps, in the mind of the American reading public, such love affairs are either ludicrous or grotesque; yet many serious novels of the forties and fifties give sympathetic treatment to problems which earlier generations would have considered ludicrous or grotesque. It may be that, with the increased public interest in adolescence, authors feel that a novel with two adolescents in a love affair will be twice as appealing as a novel with one adolescent and an older person.

A few general trends may be noted. Dell's *Janet March* was well in advance of the trend in advocating sexual initiation by an older person as a helpful step in growing up; it is not until the fifties that a number of other novelists express a similar idea. More typical of the twenties and thirties are the novels of Miss Cather and Miss Glasgow, contrasting the idealism of the adolescent with a more worldly attitude in the older generation. All three of these authors show a great interest in psychology: Miss Cather and Miss Glasgow emphasize the subtle and complex interplay of character that is typical of Henry James, while Dell combines a naturalistic massing of detail with Freudian psychology. In the early thirties Faulkner and Caldwell presented adolescents with grotesquely inappropriate lovers; the adolescent girl as seducer of older men reappears in the fifties in *East of Eden* and *Lolita.* Adolescent boys have for centuries been courted by older women in fiction, and such situations appear all through the period of this study. *Tobacco Road, Spring Storm, Waters Over the Dam, The Intemperate Season* and *Summer Street* I have mentioned specifically, but there were others. The adolescent girl with an admittedly futile crush on an older man is likewise familiar in literature: *Winter in April, The Heart Is a Lonely Hunter,* and *Cress Delahanty* are just a few of the more outstanding examples from this period. In novels of the late thirties and the forties, there seems to be a feeling of sorrow that love between an adolescent and an old person is unlikely to last, but in many novels of the fifties this kind of experience is accepted as a normal part of the adolescent's initiation into maturity.

In discussing fictional love affairs between adolescents and older people, I have not tried to distinguish hopeless love and Platonic love from consummated love. If the love of an adolescent for an older person is returned at all, it is rather more likely to be physically consummated than is love between two adolescents—especially if the older person is a woman. Apparently the tradition that a young girl should be chaste is so firmly rooted that even in these times of relaxed inhibitions both boys and older men are often reluctant to deprive young sweethearts of virginity. They are not so hesitant with older women, and there is no strong tradition to keep an older woman from seducing an adolescent boy.

Experimenting With Sex—Petting

For most adolescent boys and girls, sex is a new experience; [1] and it is such a powerful one that, despite taboos, it is likely to be sought and investigated, whether accompanied by love or not. It has been noted that in real life, boys are more likely than girls to investigate sexual experience, and in fiction there are far more detailed accounts of psychological sex problems of boys than there are of girls. Of the various kinds of sex experimentation available to adolescents, the most common for girls is petting, or erotic physical contact between a male and a female not involving the genitalia.[2] Among adolescent boys, petting is about as common as it is among girls, but masturbation is even more common.[3] Most of the novels in this study present petting to some extent at least, although petting without love was apparently a sensational and even shocking aspect of the "flaming youth" novels of the twenties. Fitzgerald's *This Side of Paradise* was apparently the first to comment on "that great current American phenomenon, the 'petting party.'" On a trip about the country with a Triangle Club play,

> Amory saw girls doing things that even in his memory would have been impossible: eating three-o'clock, after-dance suppers in impossible cafés, talking of every side of life with an air half of earnestness, half of mockery, yet with a furtive excitement that Amory considered stood for a real moral let-down. But he never realized how widespread it was until he saw the cities between New York and Chicago as one vast juvenile intrigue. (P. 65.)

45

But Fitzgerald gives no description of the petting activities, except for occasional kisses between young people who scarcely know each other, and the flushed faces on girls who disappear from the dance floor with young men. Franker accounts of petting activities appear in Percy Marks' *The Plastic Age* (1924). At his first fraternity dance, Hugh Carver is horrified to find girls drinking, and startled when a half-drunk girl asks him to take her from the dance floor into the dining room.

> He had not been in the dining-room since the dance started, and he was amazed and shocked to find half a dozen couples in the big chairs or on the divans in close embrace. He paused, but Hester led him to an empty chair, shoved him clumsily down into it, and then flopped down on his lap.
> "Le's—le's pet," she wispered. "I wanna pet."
> Again Hugh smelled the whisky fumes as she put her hot mouth to his and kissed him hungrily. He was angry, angry and humiliated. He tried to get up, to force the girl off of his lap, but she clung tenaciously to him, striving insistently to kiss him on the mouth. (P. 214.)

A little later Hugh is completely disgusted when, going into a bedroom to get a girl's coat, he finds a girl and a man lying on the bed. Yet a year later he himself drinks heavily with his girl at the Junior Prom, takes her to a dormitory bedroom, and is saved from something more scandalous only by the appearance of the friend whose room he is using.

As petting has become more and more an accepted aspect of American adolescent social conduct during the last forty years, the novels have described it more casually and fully. Several novels of the forties and fifties describe even the most intimate petting in great detail, and several present bizarre variations, such as the house party described in Robert Gutwillig's *After Long Silence* (1958), in which several couples of college boys and girls lie before an open fireplace licking cinnamon from each other's half-nude bodies.

All through the period of this study, petting was widely enough accepted so that adolescents could, for the most part, indulge in it without much danger of frustration because of conflict with social mores. There are a number of instances, especially in the earlier novels, where petting is psychologically disturbing because it conflicts with the ideals inculcated by strait-laced parents; Hugh Carver in *The Plastic Age,* Roger Bendrow in Irving Fineman's *This Pure Young Man* (1930), and Vridar Hunter in Vardis Fisher's *In Tragic Life* (1932) are some of the boys with this problem, and of course there are a great many more girls. A much more common problem is the frustration that boys usually and girls occasionally feel at being aroused by petting without achieving complete satisfaction. Felix Fay in *Moon-Calf*, Clyde Griffiths in *An American Tragedy*, and Studs Lonigan are just a few of the many boys in fiction who face this problem, and Cassy Kane in C. G. Lumbard's *Senior Spring* (1954) is one of the comparatively few girls who do. Though petting which stops short of intercourse may create problems of frustration, that which does not stop may create greater problems, which will be discussed later in this chapter. A less frequent problem, but still a considerable one, is that of the sexually ardent but rather unattractive adolescent who cannot find a petting partner, like Farrell's Danny O'Neill and Ruth Suckow's Sarah Bonney in *The Bonney Family* (1928).

Masturbation

Although masturbation is almost universal among adolescent boys, and is rather common among girls,[4] it is given very little serious consideration in novels; until the 1950's those novels which did refer to it were likely to treat it as something shameful and abnormal. The forthright Theodore Dreiser does not mention it in his novels, but in the autobiography of his adolescence he speaks of it as "the ridiculous and unsatisfactory practice of masturbation, which finally became a habit that endured—broken, of course, by occasional normal sex relations with passing women and girls —until I married." (*Dawn*, p. 268.) He goes on to describe, vividly and at some length, the delights and terrors of this forbidden practice. There is scarcely a novel that does it so well. Farrell, usually outspoken and detailed, is very brief and indirect in presenting Studs's introduction and reaction to the habit. On a hot night in his fifteenth year, after playing kissing games at a party and after seeing his thirteen-year-old sister in a thin nightgown, Studs cannot control his erotic thoughts.

> He went to the bathroom.
> Kneeling down at his bedside, he tried to make a perfect act of contrition to wash his soul from sin.
> He heard the wind, and was afraid that God might punish him, and make him die in the night. He had found out he was old enough, but

> . . . his soul was black with sin. He lay in bed, worried, suffering, and
> he tossed into a slow, troubled sleep. (*Young Lonigan*, p. 63.)

Concerning the autoerotism of Danny O'Neill, whose preadolescent sex
play and later fumblings with girls are fully reported, Farrell speaks
only slightingly and in retrospect. In his third year of high school, after
hearing a priest talk on the beauty of sex in marriage, Danny recalls:

> Back in his first year, he used to masturbate. He had given it up,
> disgusted with himself. That was not such an intense pleasure. Was
> the real thing so much more than that had been? (*Father and Son*,
> p. 156.)

Meyer Levin in *The Old Bunch* (1937) presents many adolescent problems of a group of Chicago Jews after their graduation from high school.
The sexual practices of most of them are described; the only one who
habitually masturbates is presented as a contemptible weakling.

Despite the contempt with which novelists of the thirties obviously
viewed masturbation, it is a novel of this decade which, alone of all the
novels in this survey, treats the problem at length and sympathetically;
that is Vardis Fisher's *In Tragic Life*.

At the age of twelve Vridar Hunter (whose name is obviously intended
to suggest the author's own) is introduced to the art of masturbation by
his fourteen-year-old cousin Hankie as "somethink [*sic*] to make you
shiver with joy" (p. 338), but as a great threat to the performer's
sanity. Vridar quickly discovers for himself both the joy and the fear.

> Under the first caress, the rapture came in from all sides, moving
> through him in waves of sweet emotion; and these grew in intensity
> and power, like a deepening stream; until he could feel around him
> the vast and imminent flood. His heart, and even his brain, melted into
> infinite tenderness, into a power unspeakably clean and good. Depth
> rose upon depth, height relaxed and fell away, like valley dissolving
> into valley; and from all boundaries, from every remote and alien place,
> the great flood converged and closed in, as if all space and time would
> be distilled into the clear burning rapture of the crisis. Then breath
> left him, an awful sweet pain was riven into his heart, through and
> through his quivering flesh; and the flood burst and he was drowned.
> From these first experiences, when off by himself, he took an intense
> and spiritual cleanness; but this he lost, it became an ugly degradation,
> and his fight to recover it became the epic of his life. (P. 357.)

After three years of this alternate delight and terror, Vridar comes upon
an old pamphlet which pictures vividly the horrible physical and

mental effects of "self-abuse." The effect of the pamphlet is not to cure him of the habit, but to destroy his pleasure and to intensify his agony. In spite of tremendous efforts to free himself through prayer, through physical exercise, and through mental occupation,

> the idea would come, gently insinuating, voluptuously soft and warm; it would grow in his heart, like a lovely fragrant weed, until the small garden of his better life was choked and overrun; and then it would flower upward, pushing its alluring foliage into his mind, sinking caressing roots into his heart. It twined tendrils round his nerves, laid its heavy loamy odor on his breath, and ran down into his hands. And as it grew and ripened in luxuriant sensuous stealth, until all his hunger, accumulated from days of self-denial, was drawn into vivid focus, then the Thing obsessed him again, the dread deepened. (Pp. 388–89.)

In his struggle, he is often convinced that his flesh is rotting and his mind is cracking, just as the pamphlet predicted; until, at the age of nineteen, he visits a wise doctor who tells him that this dreaded practice is almost universal at some time in life, that it is ridiculous for him to fear that it will bring insanity, and that the best prescription for him is to "work and eat a lot and be cheerful." (P. 452.)

Novels of the forties pretty generally ignore this vice; but several novels of the fifties refer briefly to masturbation as a practice which the adolescent protagonists are unable to give up, although in most cases they are disgusted by it and fear the horrible results which older people have told them will follow. In William Demby's *Beetlecreek* (1950), the Pittsburgh Negro boy Johnny Johnson, lonely and unwelcome in a tiny West Virginia mountain community of Negro miners, is at first delighted when a local gang invites him to its secret clubhouse; but when he sees a repulsive boy masturbating in an obscene dance as the other members look at pornographic cartoons, he is filled with shame and disgust, and becomes even more ashamed as he remembers his own secret sins (p. 42). In James Baldwin's *Go Tell It on the Mountain* (1953), the very religious Harlem boy John Grimes fears that he will miss Salvation because, in the school lavatory, "he had sinned with his hands a sin that was hard to forgive" (p. 14). In Peter S. Feibleman's *A Place Without Twilight* (1958), thirteen-year-old Dan Morris, younger brother of the narrator-protagonist Cille Morris, is caught in the act by his mother, who tells him that if he ever does it again she will come with a razor and "cut

49

that part of you right off to stop you from going crazy" (p. 135). In contrast to this reactionary warning of the mother, Cille herself later receives from an older girl friend the advice that she (Cille), if she is unwilling to give up her virginity, ought at least to play with herself, because it "gets you ready for a man; gives you a chance to tone yourself up while you waiting" (p. 195).

One novel of the 1950's casually accepts masturbation as a normal and unimportant aspect of adolescence. Jack Kerouac's *Doctor Sax* (published in 1959 but written in 1952) mentions unemotionally several incidents of self-stimulation, but does note disgust in two members of a group of twelve-year-olds who watch a nineteen-year-old repeatedly masturbate in a living room to entertain his juniors (pp. 68–70).

References to masturbation among adolescent girls are so few and so brief in the novels studied that one could hardly say any novel really treats it as a problem. This is surprising, but even more surprising is the fact that practically no novels of the twenties and forties make reference to the practice among adolescent male protagonists. A few novelists of the thirties touched upon the subject in their increasing attempts to be frank; but apparently after Vardis Fisher had produced his very thorough analysis, most authors felt either that there was little more to say about the problem or that masturbation was too unsavory a practice to attribute to a sympathetic protagonist—until the Kinsey report of 1948 showed that, unsavory or not, it is an all but inevitable step toward male maturity. Indeed, considering its prevalence and the mental anguish it often causes, it could well be treated far more thoroughly in fiction of adolescence than it has yet been.

PREMARITAL COITUS

After petting and masturbation, the most common sort of sexual experimentation among adolescents of both sexes is premarital heterosexual intercourse.[5] Unlike masturbation, this problem appears in a great many novels throughout the period studied, although it is treated more fully and frankly in the last decade or so, with frankness increasing gradually from 1920 until the late 1940's. The intercourse may take place as a business arrangement (prostitution), or for love, or simply for excitement and pleasure. The novels of all four decades give examples of all three classes of intercourse, but examples of intercourse for excitement and pleasure probably increase in frequency more than the other two classes with the increasing frankness of sexual discussion in literature. In the novels of the 1920's, premarital intercourse between adolescents is more likely to take place among relatively uneducated people than it is among college students, and this is in accord with the findings of Kinsey and his associates about adolescents in real life.[6] In the later novels, sexual intercourse among college students is treated about as often as that among the less educated people. This can hardly be taken as an indication that premarital intercourse has become as common among college students as among adolescents of less education, though it does suggest either that college students are less hesitant to enter sexual union before marriage than they were a generation ago, or that the presence of sexual intercourse on campuses is more generally recognized—perhaps both.[7] The high proportion of college students or pre-college adolescents in novels is easily explained by the fact that most novelists have had at least some college experience, and they tend to write about the class of people that they know best.

The chief concern here is not so much in the prevalence of premarital intercourse among adolescents as it is in the problems which it may produce. These are chiefly psychological—feelings of guilt, fear of discovery and consequent social, religious, or legal punishment (although in some cases fornication brings greater prestige than virginity), fear of aftereffects on one's health or one's chances of success in marriage, fear of pregnancy. A girl may have two additional fears that a boy seldom or never has: fear that the boy may leave her if he has once been sexually satisfied, and fear of becoming a prostitute. In some cases, any or all of these fears may be realized; however, greater acceptance of sexual freedom, wider knowledge of contraceptives, and more effective means of combating venereal disease have made the dangers and consequently the fears much less in the last two decades.

One of the early champions of sexual freedom was Floyd Dell. Felix Fay, the protagonist of *Moon-Calf*, is very shy with girls during his early adolescence (see above, p. 34); but after moving to Port Royal (Davenport), Iowa, at the age of sixteen, he learns that many girls of the working class are fully available to him. His first complete love affair is with Joyce Tennant, niece and ward of a prominent lawyer, when both of them are about twenty. Dell does not present the seduction scene itself, but he leaves no doubt as to when it takes place, and he presents rather fully the ideas of both young people concerning their relationship. Before the seduction, Felix expresses himself as strongly opposed to marriage, wanting a physical and spiritual union with Joyce, but wanting it to remain completely free on both sides. Joyce, although she has long rebelled against social conventions and has even experienced sexual intercourse with other men, does not want to give herself to Felix unless it can be forever—a marriage according to conscience if not according to law. After the seduction, their opinions are almost reversed: Joyce fearlessly enjoys sex with Felix while accepting the attentions of another man who hopes to marry her, while Felix considers himself bound to Joyce as sacredly and permanently as if they were married. It is Joyce who finally ends their relationship because she desires conventional security with a home and children. In his later novel *Janet March* (1923), Dell presents more examples of premarital intercourse. Janet herself is not sexually aroused until late in adolescence (see above, p. 39). She is about eighteen when the United States enters World War I, and she is shocked to learn that some of her friends are having affairs with young men who are about to be sent overseas. A year or so later Janet becomes pregnant by a man she does not wish to marry, but she calmly arranges for an abortion, and apparently finds the whole affair not unduly distressful. Roger Leland, the second chief character of the novel, is very puritanical through childhood and adolescence; but when he begins to experiment with a freer kind of living, he encounters girls who have sought premarital sex experience for a variety of reasons: to spite a neglectful lover, to forget a dead lover, to have a last good time before marrying a prosaic lover. In each case the girl is disturbed at the thought of disregarding social conventions, but in only one case—that of his beloved Sally—does this disregard bring such a tragic result as suicide because of unwanted pregnancy.

Another novel of 1923, Homer Croy's *West of the Water Tower*, presents other problems resulting from an unwanted pregnancy. Guy Plummer, son of an impoverished minister in a small Missouri town, is attracted to Bee Chew, daughter of the wealthy village atheist. Guy's parents have refused to answer his questions about sex, and as a result the subject has a special fascination for him. Bee, on the other hand, has been freely given any information she has asked for, and as a result she feels capable of handling any situation that may come up. In the summer following their graduation from high school, they spend some delightful evenings together; but they are unexpectedly carried away by passion, and Bee becomes pregnant. Guy steals several hundred dollars to send her to Kansas City for an abortion; but when she gets there Bee decides to have the baby, and, after a prolonged visit with her aunt, brings the child back to Junction City, causing ostracism to herself and Guy, and great embarrassment and loss to their respective families. Later, Guy is arrested and convicted for the theft of the money; when he is finally released from prison, he learns that Bee has left town with their child. It takes ten years of hard, sincere effort to regain his townspeople's respect and to win Bee back to his side.

Perhaps the most famous American novel of adolescent problems involving unwanted pregnancy is Dreiser's *An American Tragedy* (1925). Clyde Griffiths, like Guy Plummer, has been brought up in poverty by religious, puritanical parents. Reacting against this repressive background, he has an affair with the factory girl Roberta Alden, who becomes pregnant just at the time that Clyde is receiving encouragement from a wealthy society girl, Sondra Finchley. Roberta's reaction to the pregnancy is a firm determination to marry Clyde; Clyde's reaction is an equally firm determination to escape from his entanglement with Roberta so that he can marry Sondra. After trying unsuccessfully to get help from a druggist or a doctor to end the pregnancy, he decides to re-enact an incident he has read about in a newspaper, in which a girl's drowned body is recovered from a lake, with an overturned boat and a man's hat floating nearby. He loses his nerve at the last minute, but through a combination of accident and Clyde's refusal to help her, Roberta is drowned anyway. Most of the last three hundred fifty pages of this long novel are devoted to Clyde's trial, conviction, imprisonment, and execution. Throughout the novel Dreiser thoroughly airs his views on the hypocrisy of society's attitude toward premarital sexual relations, and on the conflict between America's avowed morality and its practiced greed, sensuality, and materialism.

These three novels of the twenties represent a transition between the unquestioning condemnation of premarital intercourse and pregnancy found in novels of the genteel tradition, and the almost casual treatment of these problems in later novels. Dell obviously intends Janet to represent the sane, modern handling of these problems, while Sally represents the tragic, emotional, conventional attitude. Croy shows in Bee a courage, perhaps born of ignorance, to have her illegitimate baby in defiance of convention; in Guy he shows at first a cowardly attempt to evade responsibility through dishonesty and secrecy, but later a successful effort to redeem himself through sincere and consecrated hard work. Dreiser indicates a possible effect of American standards on a very ordinary young couple, implying a condemnation of those standards, and by his very title suggesting that similar tragic results might fall upon any young people of America.

In later novels, the authors are likely to take an unsentimental, matter-of-fact attitude toward premarital pregnancy, but the attitudes of the characters involved vary considerably according to the period and the locale in which the events take place. Faulkner's novels contain a number of adolescent unmarried girls who become pregnant, and in each case the girl herself seems remarkably unconcerned, willing to have the baby and to care for it, while her male relatives are greatly concerned with protecting the family reputation from any suggestion of female unchastity. Caddy Compson in *The Sound and the Fury* (1929) and Eula Varner in *The Hamlet* (1940) are hurriedly married to conveniently willing males as soon as their pregnancies are discovered. When Eupheus Hines, the grandfather of Joe Christmas in *Light in August* (1932), learns his daughter is pregnant, he unerringly finds and kills the dark-skinned lover—Mexican or mulatto—and as soon as possible after Joe's birth he puts Joe into an orphanage. In the same novel, the eighteen-year-old orphan Lena Grove has an unshakable faith that her lover Lucas Burch will marry her, though her older brother calls her a whore and is apparently relieved when she leaves his house to go traveling in search of Lucas.

Away from Faulkner's violent and tradition-bound South, families are more likely to be understanding and helpful than angry. For instance, in Martin Yoseloff's *The Family Members* (1948), the general secretary of the Y.M.C.A. in Rock Center, Iowa, is very understanding when he learns that his seventeen-year-old daughter, Lorraine, is pregnant and that the teen-age boy responsible does not want to marry her. He arranges to have the baby baptized with its mother's family name, and the whole family gives the baby affection and care. A more serious problem appears in Daphne Athas' *The Fourth World* (1956) when two adolescent students in a school for the blind in Pennsylvania discover

54

that their experimental love-making is going to produce results. Feeling that they have no one to turn to in their predicament, they plan to run away and make a life together; but the boy is accidentally killed. Here the girl's problem is not so much the pregnancy as it is the unsympathetic headmaster of the school. In the 1958 novel *The Wheel of Earth* by Helga Sandburg (daughter of Carl Sandburg), Ellen Gaddy's problem as a seventeen-year-old expectant mother without a husband is intensified by an unsympathetic, overstrict father. Under the pretext of a visit to a friend and former servant who lives in another state, Ellen is able to give birth to a son and arrange for his care without her parents' knowing about it. When she does tell her father, a few years later, that he has a little grandson, Anton Gaddy is at first furiously angry, but later accepts the child in lieu of the son he has always wanted.

In Monte Linkletter's *Cricket Smith* (1959), a teen-age pregnancy is further complicated by the facts that the prospective father, Cricket, is only fifteen years old and his uncle and guardian is the strait-laced minister of the Third Reformed Church in their small Iowa town. In Daniel Tamkus' *The Much-Honored Man* (1959), a Nobel-prize-winning professor of physics reveals to a prospective son-in-law that his strictness drove his daughter, during adolescence, into intimate relations with one of his students, who was later killed in an automobile accident, and that the small boy living with them is actually Fredericka's illegitimate son. In Barbara Solomon's *The Beat of Life* (1960), the Jewish girl Natasha lives in Greenwich Village with Timothy, a Gentile student at Columbia University; when she becomes pregnant, marriage seems impractical while Timothy is a student because of his father's violent anti-Semitism, and Natasha fears an abortion, so that at last she chooses suicide as the only solution to her problem. But girls in most recent novels are not likely to consider premarital pregnancy so tragic, especially when the setting is in New York or its environs. Jeannie Childress of Scarsdale, in Vance Bourjaily's *Confessions of a Spent Youth* (1960), expresses some impatience with her lover Quince for using a contraceptive with her. She tells him that she had an abortion when she was barely sixteen, but that now she wishes she had kept the child.

The danger of venereal disease, or the fear of it, was at one time a serious problem in relation to premarital sex relations; but since the discovery of miracle drugs in the 1940's and their effectiveness in controlling venereal infection, this is no longer a disaster. Of course it may still appear as a threat in novels whose action takes place before the discovery of penicillin, or whose characters are members of a class not likely to benefit from advances in medical techniques. The novels of James T. Farrell are especially effective in presenting the problems of venereal disease. Perhaps the most striking example is that of Paulie Haggerty in the Studs Lonigan trilogy. At sixteen, Paulie picks up a disease from a girl his own age. He has no money to go to a doctor, and is afraid to tell his father. The symptoms disappear after he has used something a druggist recommended, and Paulie considers himself cured. At seventeen he suddenly marries a girl five years older than himself, and his friends all wonder whether it was a "shotgun wedding" and whether Paulie will infect his wife with the disease he thinks he has cured. At twenty-one, Paulie is dead. His death has a sobering effect on his friends; it does not curtail their sexual activities, but it does add considerable fear. In general, the boys in Farrell's novels accept venereal disease as one of the hazards of life—something to be avoided if possible by picking clean girls and by using a condom, but something which a doctor can cure if you are willing to go through some pain and expense. Danny O'Neill and his friend Ed Lanson submit to the long and painful treatment then required, but even this does not persuade them to avoid promiscuity. After losing his religious inhibitions, Danny advises his younger brother:

> "Bob, I want to tell you something. Nobody told me. You've reached the age where you are interested in girls. . . . There isn't anything wrong with it. But you have to know how to take care of yourself. If you have anything to do with girls, you have to know how to take care of yourself. You go to a drugstore and ask for a prophylactic, so you don't get any diseases. Don't forget that." (*My Days of Anger*, p. 353.)

So many novels about adolescents present problems of premarital sex relations that it is impossible to comment individually on each of them. A few minor novels have even satirized the eagerness of young people to lose their virtue: Charles Samuels's *The Frantic Young Man* (1929) presents eighteen-year-old Arthur Gordon trying to find sexual adventure in a large city, but being thwarted by his own romantic idealism; *Love Me Little* (1957), which Warren Miller wrote under the pen name "Amanda Vail," shows fifteen-year-old Emily and Amy seeking sex experience at a summer resort, while the boys they pursue suppress their own instincts in order to protect the girls. In a less satirical sequel, *The*

Bright Young Things (1958), Emily and Amy, now seventeen-year-old college freshmen, at last attain the experience they have sought for so long; but neither they nor their author finds much humor in the situation. Amy's affair is treated as an acceptable step toward a very suitable marriage; Emily's, undertaken for curiosity rather than for love, leads to heartaches for both people involved.

Abnormal Sex Experience

Abnormal sexual behavior, such as homosexuality and incest, receives little more than bare mention in the novels of the twenties and thirties. Both Studs Lonigan and Danny O'Neill, Farrell's chief adolescent protagonists, have incestuous thoughts about their sisters; but Danny's thoughts are limited to his preadolescent period, and Studs rejects his thoughts with shame. Both boys are approached by homosexuals in Chicago parks, but neither has any difficulty in repulsing the advances. Faulkner's Quentin Compson has incestuous thoughts about his sister Caddy, but it is clear that no actual incest takes place, and apparently there is not even a strong sexual attraction between them. Incest is avoided only by fratricide in Faulkner's *Absalom, Absalom!* (1936), but Thomas Sutpen, the father of both lovers, seems more disturbed by the miscegenation that would result from their marriage than he does by the thought of incest.

In novels of the forties and fifties, homosexuality and incest are presented more frequently and more fully. In Henry Bellamann's *Kings Row* (1940), the protagonist's friend Jamie Wakefield has homosexual inclinations which are discussed sympathetically and at some length, and the protagonist's mistress, Cassandra Temple, is later shown to have lived incestuously with her physician father for a number of years. One of the chief themes in William Maxwell's *The Folded Leaf* (1945) is the love between Lymie Peters and Spud Latham, which amounts to a homosexual attachment, although their physical contact is apparently limited to holding hands and sleeping in the same bed (see below, pp. 126–27 and 264–65). In Truman Capote's *Other Voices, Other Rooms* (1948), an important theme is the attempt of the obviously homosexual Cousin Randolph to seduce thirteen-year-old Joel Knox, but the ambiguous ending of the novel leaves the reader uncertain about Randolph's success. Joel's best chance to find normal heterosexual love seems to be with twelve-year-old Idabel Thompkins, but Idabel's own homosexual inclinations lead her to repulse him and later to run off with Miss Wisteria, the midget lady who earlier tried to seduce Joel. In Calder Willingham's *End as a Man* (1947), the homosexual sophomore Perrin McKee uses blackmail as well as persuasion to win fellow students at a Southern military academy to follow his practices. Gore Vidal's *The City and the Pillar* (1948) presents fully the problems of its homosexual protagonist during adolescence and later. Lesbianism in a reform school for girls is described with almost scientific detachment in *The Wayward Ones* (1952), by the sociologist-novelist Sara Harris. Meyer Levin's *Compulsion* (1957) fictionalizes the famous Leopold and Loeb murder case of 1924, and makes vivid and understandable the homosexual relation between the two teen-age killers. James Purdy's satiric novel *Malcolm* (1959) allows its protagonist, at ages fourteen and fifteen, to maintain his innocence in spite of several pederastic approaches; but twelve-year-old Warner Sands, in Philip McFarland's *A House Full of Women* (1960), is assaulted by an elderly pervert who boards in his mother's house. Incest is not as common as homosexuality, but William Styron's *Lie Down in Darkness* (1951) has as its main theme the unfulfilled incestuous attraction between the adolescent Peyton Loftis and her father, while an actual coitus in sleep between father and daughter is vividly described in Ralph Ellison's *Invisible Man* (1952).

Rape is a sensational sex problem that is perhaps better suited to treatment in melodrama than in serious fiction; yet it appears in serious novels as well as sensational ones. Sometimes it is not easy to distinguish between rape and seduction, as in Caldwell's *God's Little Acre*, when Will Thompson takes his sister-in-law Griselda, much to the latter's delight, or in Helga Sandburg's *The Wheel of Earth*, when Christian Ay forces himself on Ellen Gaddy, who is somewhat in love with him both before and after the incident. Perhaps the most notorious rape in American literature is the corncob raping of Temple Drake by the impotent Popeye in Faulkner's *Sanctuary* (1931). Some other repulsive cases of rape occur in *The Young Manhood of Studs Lonigan* (1934), in which Weary Reilley violently rapes his New Year's Eve date; Grace Metalious' *Peyton Place* (1956), in which Selina Cross is raped by her own stepfather; and Richard Frede's *Entry E* (1958), in which a group of college boys repeatedly rape an eighteen-year-old girl in a dormitory room, after giving her a mixture of benzedrine and grain alcohol to lower her resistance. Even in such a sentimental novel as Betty Smith's *A Tree Grows in Brooklyn* (1943), Francie Nolan is terrified by a would-be rapist.

Summary—Trends in Fictional Treatment of Sex

The problems of love and sex are so ubiquitous in novels dealing with adolescence, and each problem is so individual in character, that it is hard to make generalizations about them. It is obvious, of course, that sex problems are treated more freely, more fully, and perhaps more sensationally in the later novels than in the earlier ones. This is particularly true of novels presenting the sex problems of girls. The relatively rare presentations of adolescent girls' sex problems in the twenties and thirties were likely to be written by men, such as Floyd Dell, James T. Farrell, and William Faulkner. Beginning with Carson McCullers in 1940, women became franker in writing about the sexual problems of girls, and this frankness reached its height in 1956 with novels by Grace Metalious and Pamela Moore. It is possible that the 1953 publication of the second Kinsey report, *Sexual Behavior in the Human Female*, may have helped to prepare the way for a freer discussion of women's sex problems by feminine authors. Similarly, it seems likely that increasing frankness in discussing sex throughout the period, and increasing attempts to explain its problems psychologically, are at least in part the result of increasing understanding of the mind's hidden motives, brought about by the publication and wide circulation of psychoanalytic works by Freud and his successors. Even without Freud and Kinsey, however, a period of frankness might have been expected as a reaction to the preceding period of repression of the discussion of sexual matters. The writings of Freud, Kinsey, and other scientists might be taken as a part of this reaction, serving not only to stimulate it but to give it greater insight, direction, and balance.

Reviewing by decades the trends in treatment of love and sex in fiction about adolescents, a reader notes in the 1920's a few unimportant imitators of the Booth Tarkington attitude of condescending amusement at puppy love, but more reaction against this. Edgar Lee Masters attempted to revive a sort of Tom Sawyer-Becky Thatcher idyll in *Mitch Miller* (1920), but few if any important American novelists of the time followed his example. Far more typical of the twenties is the trend set by Anderson, Fitzgerald, and especially Dell—the attempt to relate frankly and honestly the kind of love and sex problems that do disturb adolescents, particularly boys. Very few women authors attempted this kind of frankness in novels of the twenties, though there are touches of it in Mildred Gilman's *Fig Leaves* (1926), Martha Ostenso's *Wild Geese* (1925), and Ruth Suckow's *The Bonney Family* (1928). Even in novels by men, the physical details of sexual experiences are likely to be implied rather than fully presented, and the language which adolescent boys actually use in speaking of sex is considerably expurgated.

During the thirties, humorous stories of puppy love were adapted to feminine protagonists and were very popular in slick magazines, from which they were later collected into episodic novels. The detailed autobiographical revelation became even more detailed and considerably franker, both in the physical details presented and in the language used. Such writers as Wolfe, Farrell, and Vardis Fisher extended the autobiographical revelation into thousands of pages, filling two, three, or even four volumes. Grotesque sex experiences began to appear in novels by Faulkner and Erskine Caldwell. Most women writers still avoided frank discussions of sexual problems.

Novels of feminine puppy love and idyllic first love became less condescending and more sympathetic and convincing during the forties. There was frank sentimentality in novels by Robert Nathan and in Betty Smith's very popular *A Tree Grows in Brooklyn*. At the same time, a few women authors, notably Carson McCullers in *The Heart Is a Lonely Hunter* and Daphne Athas in *The Weather of the Heart*, presented the sexual thoughts and experiences of adolescent girls more frankly than women writers had previously done. The frankness of male novelists in presenting the physical details and the typical language of adolescent sex life probably reached its peak during this decade, but surprisingly little attention was given to the nearly universal problem of masturbation. Multivolume autobiographical fiction was somewhat less popular, although Farrell continued the adventures of Danny O'Neill until 1943, and then moved him to New York under the name of Bernard Clare (or Carr). Naturalistic fiction apparently was declining in importance, though it was far from extinct; under the immediate influence of Wolfe and Faulkner and the more remote influence of Hawthorne, Melville, and James, symbolism became increasingly important. The understanding of such authors as Carson McCullers, Jean Stafford, and Truman Capote depends on an understanding of their symbols; and even realistic writers such as William Maxwell in *The Folded Leaf* and Willard Motley in *Knock on Any Door* depend largely on symbols to convey the impact of adolescent experiences with love and sex.

In the novels of the fifties, adolescent love is seldom treated lightly. Even Jessamyn West, who writes with humor and usually with a certain amount of optimism, presents in *The Witch Diggers* (1951) an adolescent love affair whose tragic ending is as fatalistic as any of Thomas Hardy's. Her *Cress Delahanty* (1953), though it includes humorous scenes of puppy love and some rather sentimental scenes of long-established middle-aged love, also contains occasional reminders that love and sex may be sordid or tragic. One of the finest adolescent love novels of the decade, William Humphrey's *Home from the Hill* (1958), has a convincingly inevitable tragic ending. The decade abounds in sordid but usually believable novels of adolescent sex experience, written with complete frankness by both men and women: Calder Willingham's *Geraldine Bradshaw* (1950), Theodora Keogh's *Meg* (1950), Nelson Algren's *A Walk on the Wild Side* (1956), Pamela Moore's *Chocolates for Breakfast* (1956), Grace Metalious' *Peyton Place* (1956), Charles Thompson's *Halfway Down the Stairs* (1957), Richard Frede's *Entry E* (1958), and Vladimir Nabokov's *Lolita* (1958), to name only a few. If there is gaiety in love, it is likely to be a desperate "beat generation" gaiety, as in *A Walk on the Wild Side* and in Robert Gutwillig's *After Long Silence* (1958). If there is faith in anything, it is likely to be not a faith in the ultimate goodness of love or of God, but an existentialist faith in the right and the duty of every person to do what he wants to do, regardless of God or society or reason.

Differences in the fiction of various regions are less striking, on the whole, than differences in various decades; the rapid and wide circulation of both novels and criticism and the interchange of faculty members of various universities and writing schools has tended to standardize the ideals and the techniques of fiction throughout the country. Most of what regional differences there are will be more conveniently discussed in Chapter VI, on adjustment to community environment. However, it is appropriate here to mention some regional differences as they affect the love and sex experiences of adolescents.

The most striking regional differences occur in the novels of the South. Novels with Southern settings, especially in small towns and rural areas, place greater emphasis on the obligation to protect the honor of white women, and to avenge its desecration by personal violence, than do novels about other parts of the country. It is particularly important to protect white women from Negro men. Negro girls, on the other hand, are considered by the general public to be available to any man, white or black. These attitudes may be observed in almost any novel by William Faulkner, in several by Erskine Caldwell—notably *Trouble in July* (1940) and *Place Called Estherville* (1949)—and in several by Negro authors, such as Langston Hughes' *Not Without Laughter* (1930), Ralph Ellison's *Invisible Man* (1952), and James Baldwin's *Go Tell It on the Mountain* (1953). People in small towns anywhere, but especially in the Middle West, are likely to be very conservative in their attitude toward sex—at least outwardly. The small towns of the Middle Atlantic states and southern New England are likely to be more liberal, probably because of the sophisticating influence of New York City. Greenwich Village is a symbol of sexual freedom in a number of novels—Floyd Dell's *Janet March* (1923) and *Souvenir* (1929), Margery Latimer's *This Is My Body* (1930), Peggy Goodin's *Clementine* (1946), Julian Halevy's *Young Lovers* (1955), and others—and all of New York City is usually represented as relatively indifferent to traditional standards of sexual behavior. This is only slightly less true of other large cities, notably Chicago as pictured in the novels of Farrell, Meyer Levin, and others; Reno, of course, as depicted by Walter Van Tilburg Clark in *The City of Trembling Leaves* (1945); Denver, as seen in Willard Motley's *Knock on Any Door* (1947) and Jack Kerouac's *On the Road* (1957); and even New Orleans in Nelson Algren's *A Walk on the Wild Side*. In novels of the lower and middle classes in large cities, there is likely to be competition among the boys in accumulating and bragging about sexual experiences, but the boys generally regard girls of their own religious group as a little purer than girls of other groups. The Irish Catholic boys in Farrell's novels believe that most Catholic girls are unattainable, and the Jewish boys in Meyer Levin's *The Old Bunch* (1937) seek their sexual adventures with *shiksehs*, though they intend to marry Jewish girls. Sexual standards in rural areas are likely to be somewhere between the conservatism of the small towns and the liberalism of the cities. Farm parents often have very strict moral standards, but the young people, lacking opportunities for group entertainment and sometimes stimulated by the sight of copulating farm animals, are very likely to be tempted into sexual experimentation.

For each of the trends mentioned above there are of course numerous exceptions. In fiction, as in real life, love affairs and sex experiences may tend to follow recognizable patterns, but each one has its own distinct characteristics. That is what makes them endlessly challenging to the imagination.

Chapter III

REVOLT FROM THE FAMILY AND JUVENILE DELINQUENCY

Breaking family ties is a normal part of growing up; the adolescent who fails to break them prolongs his period of dependency and thus adds to his problems. Under ideal conditions, the ties are gradually weakened with the knowledge and under the guidance of the parent, so that the adolescent develops strength for the complete independence which he must eventually assume. Sometimes, however, there is violent revolt, perhaps because one or both parents try to prolong parental control or to exercise it in an unreasonable way, or perhaps because of a deep-seated antagonism which is more than just a transitional phase of adolescence. In such cases, of course, the problems of revolt are intensified.

To discuss novels dealing with adolescent rebellion against the family, this chapter considers three main types of revolt: revolt caused by personality clashes, usually with mother or father or both, but sometimes with other members of the family; revolt caused by special problems, such as financial trouble, broken homes, or parental standards of living which conflict with those sought by the adolescent; and revolt caused by or resulting in the delinquency of the adolescent. Juvenile delinquency is perhaps more accurately regarded as a symptom of problems of various sorts rather than a problem in itself; yet it is certainly a cause of further problems, many of which are closely related to the family. At any rate, this seems as logical a place as any to discuss novels of juvenile delinquency as a group.

REBELLION AGAINST MOTHER

Rebellion caused by personality clashes appears more often in male adolescents than in female; novels with boy protagonists are more numerous than those with girl protagonists, and boys are more likely to show open rebellion against parental authority than are girls.[1] In

view of the emphasis given to the Oedipus complex in popular discussions of modern psychology, one might expect to find that contemporary novels show fewer boys than girls rebelling against their
mothers; but a survey of the novels refutes this idea. Still, the rebellion
of a son against a mother is more likely to be characterized by ambivalence than is that of a son against a father or that of a daughter against
a mother. Such ambivalence is seen in the attitude of Clyde Griffiths
in Dreiser's *An American Tragedy*. Clyde has always felt degraded by
the street hymn-singing which his mother has required of him regularly
until he gets his first job as a bellhop at the age of sixteen. As soon
as he begins to have some time and money to spend as he likes, he
takes pleasure in activities that he knows his mother would not approve.
Yet he does not completely reject her. After he has been convicted of
the murder of Roberta Alden (see above, p. 53), and his mother travels
from Denver to visit him in his upstate New York prison, he sees her
with mixed feelings.

> Whatever her faults or defects, after all she was his mother, wasn't
> she? And she had come to his aid. . . . And who knew but that possibly,
> and even in the face of her dire poverty now, she might still be able
> to solve this matter of a new trial for him and to save his life? . . .
> No longer did the shabby coat and the outlandish hat and the broad,
> immobile face and somewhat stolid and crude gestures seem the racking
> and disturbing things they had so little time since. She was his mother
> and she loved him, and believed in him and was struggling to save
> him. (Vol. II, pp. 343–44.)

Eugene Gant in Wolfe's *Look Homeward, Angel* feels a similar ambivalence toward his mother. As the youngest of seven children who
survived infancy, he has been babied by his mother, and slept with her
every night until he was twelve. He feels affection for her, and knows
that she is devoted to him; yet he is constantly embarrassed by her
niggardliness, her whining, her feeble and obvious dissembling. All
through his adolescence he rebels against these petty qualities in her;
after the death of his favorite brother Ben when Eugene is about eighteen, he feels something within him urging him to leave her and to go find
himself "beyond the hills":

> O but I can't go now, said Eugene to it. (Why not? it whispered.)
> Because her face is so white, and her forehead is so broad and high,
> with the black hair drawn back from it, and when she sat there at the
> bed she looked like a little child. I can't go now and leave her here

alone. (She is alone, it said, and so are you.) And when she purses up her mouth and stares, so grave and thoughtful, she is like a little child. (You are alone now, it said. You must escape or you will die.) It is all like death: she fed me at her breast, I slept in the same bed with her, she took me on her trips. All of that is over now, and each time it was like a death. (And like a life, it said to him. Each time that you die, you will be born again. And you will die a hundred times before you become a man.) (Pp. 577–78.)

Although Dreiser's novel and Wolfe's are unlike in almost every respect, both depict their protagonists as drawn to their mothers even after they have rejected all that their mothers stand for.

The relative disinclination of a girl to rebel is well illustrated in Helen Woodbury's *The Misty Flats* (1925). All her life Linda Bradley has made sacrifices to keep her mother happy; at her mother's request she gives up college, marriage, and even writing. When her mother goes to Europe, Linda goes to Greenwich Village and finally experiences freedom, literary success, and love; but by that time her habit of sacrifice has grown so strong that she gives up all these things upon her mother's return. Her brother Tad, on the other hand, is not expected to follow his parents' wishes; though Doctor Bradley has hoped that his son would follow in his footsteps, he readily concurs when Tad expresses a preference for chemistry over medicine. In Grace Zaring Stone's *The Almond Tree* (1931), sixteen-year-old Marise Brune is likewise overshadowed by her mother, although not so completely dominated as is Linda. Marise gets a job in spite of her mother's disapproval; but it is the lovely, middle-aged widow who marries the young naval officer whom she and her daughter both love. Harlow Estes's novel *Hildreth* (1940) presents another demanding mother, but the nineteen-year-old Hildreth Considine is too strong-willed to let herself be knowingly dominated; in fact, with blind though well-intended forcefulness she tries to control the lives of her mother, her young widowed aunt, and everyone else with whom she comes in contact. It takes some harsh setbacks for Hildy to learn that the independent competence she has been acquiring since her father's desertion ten years earlier may be less attractive and even less effective in a young woman than a certain amount of dependence. The first of these three feminine novels is conventional in its attitudes and characterization, although it recognizes the fairly modern concept of the adolescent's need for some freedom of choice; the second very unsentimentally destroys illusions of filial or maternal self-sacrifice; and the third, with astute

67

insight, demonstrates that an adolescent's domination over the family is at least as harmful as the family's domination over an adolescent.

Two novels of 1929, Anne Parrish's *The Methodist Faun* and O. E. Rölvaag's *Peder Victorious*, show boys rebelling against their mothers' domination as they reject the religious and cultural standards to which their mothers cling. Clifford Hunter, filled with a pagan love of beauty and of nature, tries to escape from the influence of his mother's staunch Middle Western Methodism; but, failing first to become an artist in New York and later in his campaign to marry the wealthy and sophisticated Cathleen King, he ends in an unhappy marriage with the dull daughter of a Methodist minister. Peder continually fights his mother's attempts to bring him up in the traditions of her native Norway; his decision to marry a girl of Irish Catholic background is almost the final blow to topple his mother's already tottering mind, but Peder insists that he and Susie are "just two human beings," not Norwegian and Irish (p. 325).

More complex are the motives which lead Farrell's Danny O'Neill to turn away from his mother. Danny has lived with his Grandmother O'Flaherty since he was two or three years old, finding the clean apartment and the adulation of aunts, uncles, and grandparents more appealing to his childish tastes than the filthy, impoverished flat where many brothers and sisters competed for the attention of his weary, discouraged parents. His grandmother becomes a mother-substitute. When he reaches adolescence, his conscience sometimes bothers him for not spending more time with his parents; but when he does visit them he is always uncomfortable. His mother's personal slovenliness and foul-mouthed vindictiveness are especially offensive to him, and her excessive religiosity helps to turn him away from religion. His grandmother also embarrasses him with her frequent drunkenness after her husband's death, but Danny feels toward her the same sort of ambivalence that Clyde Griffiths and Eugene Gant feel toward their mothers, and it is not until his grandmother's death that Danny finally breaks all connections with his family.

Sonie Marburg in Jean Stafford's *Boston Adventure* (1944) rebels partly because of her mother's Russian immigrant ways and the embarrassing family poverty, but more because of personality clashes. These clashes become more frequent and more violent after her German father's desertion places more responsibility on Sonie and shocks Mrs. Marburg into increasing eccentricities. Like Danny O'Neill, Sonie finds a mother-substitute. It is the wealthy spinster Lucy Pride, who, disappointed in the persistent rebelliousness of her niece, Hopestill Mather, whom she has raised as a daughter, takes Sonie into her Boston home as a personal secretary. At first Sonie is delighted that her childhood dream of living with Miss Pride has come true, but at the end of the novel she realizes with despair that she has been trapped by the spinster's motherly possessiveness—the ravenous maternal appetite that the niece committed suicide to escape. There is malign symbolic significance in Miss Pride's summons to Sonie to re-enter the now dreaded mansion:

> Under the lamplight, she appeared vigorous and even youthful, as if her age which she had passed on to her niece were buried along with Hopestill in New Hampshire. She looked again as she had done when I was five years old in Chichester; her flat, omniscient eyes seized mine, grappled with my brain, extracted what was there, and her meager lips said "Sonie, my dear, come out of the cold. You'll never get to be an old lady if you don't take care of yourself." (P. 496.)

In the novels discussed thus far in this chapter, practically all the adolescent rebels, especially the boys, have felt some compunction in opposing the long-established tradition of the sacredness of motherhood. As the popularization of depth psychology made prevalent the concept that repressed emotions may do more harm than those expressed, novelists began to disclose more open antagonism between mothers and their adolescent children, especially girls. William Styron's *Lie Down in Darkness* (1951) shows such an antagonism in a family relationship amounting obviously to an Electra complex. Peyton Loftis has no use for her mother, and openly rebels against her during adolescence; her father she loves with an abiding passion that makes impossible for her any satisfactory adjustment to lover or husband. Mrs. Loftis is repelled by her pretty daughter's increasing sexual attractiveness, and lavishes all her affection on her crippled and mentally retarded daughter Maudie. A less extreme version of the Electra complex appears in Grace Metalious' *Peyton Place* (1956). Allison MacKenzie worships the picture and the mental image of her dead father; her mother she increasingly resents for keeping her from the generally accepted adolescent experiences with boys. But it is neither an innate hatred of her mother as a sexual rival nor a resentment of her strict domination that ultimately destroys Allison's sense of belonging to her; it is the shock of the revelation that her mother, for all her prudish ideals, was never married to her father.

69

Only after Allison has lived away from home for a few years and has had a lover herself does she return to her mother with understanding. In Paule Marshall's *Brown Girl, Brownstones* (1959), Selina Boyce, daughter of Barbadian Negro parents living in Brooklyn, is fondly attached to her gay, irresponsible father and hates her conscientious mother until her father's death and her own increasing maturity bring her to a better understanding and appreciation of her mother; even then, however, she feels toward her mother the sort of ambivalence which the male adolescent protagonists of earlier novels had shown toward their mothers.

Two rather prominent novels of the 1950's present adolescent boys in shocked reaction to discovering their mothers in sin. Cal and Aron, the twin sons of Adam and Cathy Trask in John Steinbeck's *East of Eden* (1952), have been given an idealized picture of the mother who deserted them and her husband soon after they were born. Cal—who represents, in this allegorical novel, Cain, or the potentiality for both good and evil —is fifteen when he learns that their mother is now the owner of the most notorious brothel in town. To him, the discovery is a confirmation of his growing realization that evil can exist anywhere. To Aron—who represents Abel, or undiluted goodness—the discovery comes two years later, and it is so shocking to him that he loses the desire to live. In Irwin Shaw's *Lucy Crown* (1956), thirteen-year-old Tony Crown finds his mother in bed with his tutor-companion, a Dartmouth undergraduate, and, in his great distress and uncertainty, informs his father before he tells Lucy herself of his discovery. Thus he destroys the possibility of a bond of understanding between himself and his mother. Still, it is Lucy rather than Tony who makes the break between them irreparable; in making peace with her husband she stipulates as a condition of their continuing marriage that she should never have to look at Tony again. Two years later Oliver Crown tries fruitlessly to reunite his wife and son; Tony's final note to his mother ends with the sentence, "I repudiate you," but with typical adolescent ambivalence he crosses the last sentence out (p. 235). Thus, although the son rejects his mother as a result of her wrong-doing, the reader is made to feel that the mother could, with a reasonable effort, end or at least minimize this rejection. Less obvious, and more closely related to the modern trend toward depth psychology in fiction, is the hatred which Andrew Wyman, a Colorado college student, feels toward the retired actress whom he believes to be his mother, in Kenneth Flagg's *Andrew* (1958).

Although the adolescent's rebellion against his mother becomes increasingly open and violent in novels between 1920 and 1960, the same can hardly be said of rebellion against the father. Several novels of the twenties show strong rebellion against fathers because of treatment which the adolescents consider unduly demanding or unduly neglectful. As early as *Huckleberry Finn*, American fiction presented a father who provoked rebellion by being both demanding and neglectful, so that this relationship was well established in literary tradition by 1920. Guy Plummer in Homer Croy's *West of the Water Tower* (1923) rebels against his father's overstrict religious and sexual discipline; Edward Patterson, Junior, in Henry Kitchell Webster's *The Innocents* (1924) defends his interest in radio mechanics against his father's attempts to make him a classical scholar. Judith Gare, in Martha Ostenso's *Wild Geese* (1925), is the only one of her father's children with spirit and strength enough to fight back against his cruel domination. Tar Moorehead in Sherwood Anderson's *Tar* (1926) is attracted in childhood by his father's story-telling ability, but in adolescence Tar turns against his father for his improvidence and neglect of his family. In the conventional novel *Rebellion* (1927) Mateel Howe Farnham tells of Jacqueline Burrell blackmailing her tyrannical father into giving her her rightful inheritance so that she can marry the man she loves and help him to get an education. Each of these novels shows the kind of conventional adolescent revolt that might have been found even in fiction of the genteel tradition.

A few novels of the thirties and forties indicate a trend toward subtlety in turning from fathers. Although *Acquittal* (1938) by Graeme and Sarah Lorimer is not a very well written book, it is interesting in its presentation of an unusual problem: an adolescent son's judgment of his father, who has just been acquitted of an unusually sordid murder charge. Jock Rolfe considers his father guilty, in spite of the acquittal; he leaves home, and even considers changing his name, but eventually realizes that his father needs and deserves his family's support. In Flannery Lewis' *Abel Dayton* (1939), the protagonist's admiration for his father gradually turns to contempt as he realizes his father's un-

71

worthiness. In William Maxwell's *The Folded Leaf* (1945), motherless Lymie Peters is pretty much ignored by his father, who seems interested only in liquor and women. After Lymie's attempt at suicide, Mr. Peters asks why Lymie did not at least leave him a note of explanation.

> "I didn't think about it," Lymie said.
> He simply spoke the truth, but for a long time afterward, for nearly a year, Mr. Peters held it against him. With that one remark the distance which had always been between them stretched out and became a vast tract, a desert country. (P. 294.)

A subtle and unusual revolt against a father is presented in Shirley Jackson's psychological novel *Hangsaman* (1951). Throughout her childhood and early adolescence, Natalie Waite is far more sympathetic to her father, a noted literary critic, than she is to her whimsical and rather commonplace mother. She allows her father to dominate and mold her intellectually until she goes away to college, where she falls under the spell of a popular young English professor. Eventually she recognizes that the professor is cruel and domineering to his wife, and that he uses his personal charm rather than intellectual ability to impress his students. This realization enables her to see that her father has some of the same characteristics, and she breaks her father's hold on her by forming a close and almost fatal relationship with a strange but sympathetic college girl named Tony—although it is never entirely clear whether Tony exists or is a product of Natalie's fertile and vivid imagination (see below, p. 128).

Another psychological rebellion of a college girl against her doting father appears in Harvey Swados' *Out Went the Candle* (1955). Jewish war profiteer Herman Felton works and manipulates unceasingly and unscrupulously during World War II to gain wealth and privileges for his wife and children; but his beautiful daughter Betsy, faced with the uninspiring example of her idle, pampered mother, rejects what he has to offer and goes out of her way to embarrass him, explaining to her Gentile friend Joe Burley:

> "Do you want me to go through life paying him back for his sacrifices? I'd rather pay him back for his hypocrisy. He loves it, he loves all the crap. . . . He wants me to be obligated to him for a career, a husband, anything I really want. But I don't want anything I have to get through him. Can't you get that through your head?" (P. 170.)

An interesting contrast to the Lorimers' *Acquittal* is provided by Ruth

Suckow's *The John Wood Case* (1959). Whereas Jock Rolfe in the earlier novel single-mindedly rejects his father in spite of a legal acquittal, Philip Wood has very mixed reactions to the arrest of his father for embezzlement. Philip is valedictorian of his high school class and a boy of high ideals; John is one of the most respected men in their Iowa community; and the two have been brought into an unusually close father-son relationship by the chronic illness of Philip's mother. When John finally admits that he has embezzled from his kindly employer in order to procure for his wife medical help which he could not otherwise afford, Philip's reaction is not rebellion but an agonized disappointment and a realization that the distinction between right and wrong is not as clear-cut as he has hitherto supposed.

Conrad Richter's *The Waters of Kronos* (1960) shows an unusual insight into an adolescent boy's rejection of his father, who is very popular in their Pennsylvania community. John Donner, in his old age, is fantastically enabled to return to a few days in his own boyhood and to observe objectively the relationship between his adolescent self and his father. As he sees his father's resemblance to himself as a man, John begins to understand what caused him, as a boy, to fear and hate his father:

> It was the great deception practiced by man on himself and his fellows, the legend of hate against the father so the son need not face the real and ultimate abomination, might conceal the actual nature of the monster who haunted the shadows of childhood, whose name only the soul knew and who never revealed himself before the end when it was found that all those disturbing things seen and felt in the father, which as a boy had given him an uncomprehending sense of dread and hostility, were only intimations of his older self to come, a self marked with the inescapable dissolution and decay of his youth. (P. 161.)

REBELLION AGAINST THE FAMILY

If adolescent rebellions against mothers in novels become increasingly open and violent during the period of this study, and rebellions against fathers become increasingly subtle and complex, what trends can be observed in rebellions against the family as a whole? In most of the novels of the twenties and thirties the rebellious adolescent is represented as obviously justified in his rebellion; the family is domineering or un-congenial, or in some cases merely too conservative. In novels of the forties and fifties, the adolescent is not so likely to be represented as the innocent victim of an unsympathetic home environment, who revolts when pushed to the limits of endurance; the rebellion is more likely to be the result of a complex interplay of characters, the fault lying as much in the adolescent as it does in the family. If the rebellious adolescent is a girl, she is not likely to break family ties completely or to rebel as overtly as a boy; remaining in the family, she is a constant source of irritation or anguish, a thorn in the flesh, until she is removed by marriage or by her decision to support herself. A rebellious boy is much more likely to run away from home, or to revolt so strongly from the family discipline that he becomes a juvenile delinquent. Since boys are not as closely supervised as girls, a minor rebelliousness in boys may work itself off in acts of disobedience that go undetected or are dismissed with a casual "Boys will be boys." Similar acts in girls may bring strong censure and closer restrictions, resulting in an increased feeling of rebelliousness. Thus, although girls are usually more docile than boys, a number of novels present a girl who is the rebellious member of the family, while her brother is regarded as a model of propriety: for example, Martha Ostenso's *Wild Geese*, mentioned earlier in this chapter; Langston Hughes's *Not Without Laughter* (1930); Ruth Suckow's *The Folks* (1934); and Hope Williams Sykes's *Second Hoeing* (1935).

All through the period of this study there are occasional novels which treat with condescending humor minor acts of rebellion and flouting of authority, as was done earlier in such novels as *Tom Sawyer, Peck's Bad Boy,* and *Penrod.* In earlier novels, the subjects of such humorous treatment were always boys, but in this period—especially after 1930—they were just as likely to be girls. Perhaps the outstanding humorous "bad boys" of the 1920's are Leona Dalrymple's Paul Northrop in *Fool's Hill* (1922) and John Peter Toohey's Wilbur Jones in *Growing Pains* (1929). Booth Tarkington tried to revive an earlier favorite in *Penrod Jashber* (1929), but with no greater success than Mark Twain had in his later books about Tom Sawyer. A feminine rival of the humorous bad boys of literature appears in Ryerson and Clements' Jane Jones of *This Awful Age* (1930), followed by a number of others, such as pudgy Judy Graves in Sally Benson's *Junior Miss* (1941), the red-headed tomboy protagonist of Peggy Goodin's *Clementine* (1946), and the imaginative heroine of

74

Jessamyn West's *Cress Delahanty* (1953). Booth Tarkington in *The Fighting Littles* (1941) presents a seventeen-year-old girl and a fourteen-year-old boy in amusing conflict with their parents. Humorous treatment of a masculine adolescent rebel appears again in Bentz Plagemann's *This is Goggle* (1955). Although Goggle at ten glibly uses four-letter words that Penrod Schofield and Filmer Little apparently never heard of, by the time he is ready for college Goggle has become a socially acceptable young man.

A refreshing change, not only from condescending humor but also from the bitter naturalism found in many novels of rebellious adolescents, appears in Josephine Carson's *Drives My Green Age* (1957). The narrator is a rebellious and remarkably perceptive twelve-year-old orphan, Christine Hamilton, who cheerfully shows her disrespect for the aunt and uncle with whom she lives, the teacher who boards with them, and almost every other adult in the tiny town of Morning Springs, Kansas. Her straightforward contempt of adult hypocrisy, combining a shrewd awareness of duplicity with a naïve disregard for its causes, amuses and delights the reader; but through the development and experiences of her thirteenth year, Chris realistically comes to an increased understanding of the way grownups act, and to the realization that she herself will probably act that way before long.

The great majority of novels of this period which deal with rebellious adolescents are serious in intention, and almost all of them are sympathetic with the young rebels, whether the revolt is occasioned by too strict family domination, by unjust circumstances, by early traumatic experiences, or simply by innate uncongeniality of individuals living together. There are almost as many novels dealing with rebellious girls as there are dealing with rebellious boys; there are considerably fewer novels in which several adolescents of the same family are rebels.

Several novels by Ruth Suckow show varying degrees of rebelliousness in girls. Marjorie Schoessel in *The Odyssey of a Nice Girl* (1925) is the commonplace daughter of rather well-to-do middle-class parents in a small town in Iowa, reasonably content with her home and family until success in school elocution contests begins to stir her ambition for finer things. She longs to get away from her family, her father's business, and all the people of Buena Vista; after a year at the Academy of Expression in Boston, she looks forward to an arty life in New York. But her rebelliousness is not forceful enough to withstand her family's wish that she return to Iowa, where her hopes and ambitions dwindle until she is content with an unromantic marriage which takes her farther than ever from Boston and New York. Sarah Bonney in *The Bonney Family* (1928) is less attractive and popular than Marjorie, and is more weighted down by the care of a younger brother and sister. To her family and friends she seems endlessly complacent and reliable; inwardly she rebels at her family responsibilities, her own docility in accepting them, and the fact that no boy finds her cute or desirable.

> She was healthy, and there was nothing the matter with her, but somehow she did not have the thing that the other girls had—what they called "cute." "All the cute girls . . ." Even she could feel that there was something heavy about her, awkward and downright and big. . . . Coming back to the dresser, she tore savagely at her hair, pulling at the two soft, fair loops until they came down almost to her eyebrows. She yanked down her middy blouse until it showed the hollow between her large white breasts. She felt a weakness go over her, and a terrible, straining longing. All the sturdy strength seemed to melt out of her limbs in a thrill of strange, blissful agony. (P. 186.)

After the death of her mother, it is Sarah who keeps the family going until the children are grown up and her father has married again; then at last she has a chance to leave their home town and see some of the rest of the world. More violently rebellious than either Marjorie or Sarah is Margaret Ferguson in *The Folks* (1934). Her brothers and her sister adapt themselves rather easily and willingly to the family pattern of behavior, but Margaret from early childhood feels that nobody in the family loves or understands her. Thus she feels justified in doing things that she knows will annoy her parents, and is constantly resentful of the things her parents and her older brother say and do to her. Even when the others go out of their way to be nice to her, she senses their insincerity and is resentful of it. Miss Suckow, with great understanding, makes this illogically rebellious adolescent seem both real and sincere.

Rebellious tendencies appear in adolescents of both sexes in the novels of William Faulkner, but for the most part, the rebellious girls are more striking and memorable. In *The Sound and the Fury* (1929), Caddy Compson rebels against her family's attempts to keep her away from men, as does her daughter Quentin a generation later. Caddy's brother Quentin has rebellious impulses, but the only solution he can find is to commit suicide. In *Sanctuary* (1931), Temple Drake has no mother to control her, but she delights in acting against the wishes of her father and her three older brothers. In *Light in August* (1932) Lena Grove slips out the window of her brother's house, where she is living, to meet her lover at night; and adolescent Joe Christmas climbs down a rope from his room in the home of his foster parents, the McEacherns, to attend a forbidden dance. Eula Varner in *The Hamlet* (1940) has little supervision from her parents, and she easily evades the strenuous attempts of her brother Jody to keep her under strict surveillance. Chick Mallison in *Intruder in the Dust* (1948) successfully defies the wishes of his family in going to the aid of a Negro falsely accused of murder.

The later novels are likely to be much more complex as to the causes and the methods of rebellion. Brooke Holly in Mac Gardner's *Mom Counted Six* (1944) belongs to one of the distinguished families in their community, near Seattle; but she does not care for the kind of life distinguished families are supposed to lead. She falls in love with the handsome but disreputable son of the town drunkard and, despite her family's disapproval, has an affair with him. Miss Gardner's novel begins in the light, flippant vein that its title would lead a reader to expect, but before it is over it becomes deadly serious.

One of the most complex and penetrating novels of revolt from the family is Jean Stafford's *The Mountain Lion* (1947). Ralph and Molly Fawcett, aged ten and eight respectively at the beginning of the novel, are repelled by the false gentility of their mother and of their older sisters Leah and Rachel, and are destined by their homely appearance and peculiar manners to be cut off from popularity not only at home but in the world outside. Thus they are drawn strongly toward each other; but as they grow up into adolescence, their attitude toward each other assumes an ambivalence that suggests a guilty sense of incestuous love. Ralph finds some release from his inhibitions in the free life of their uncle's Colorado ranch; but Molly is disturbed by constant reminders of sex, which morbidly frightens her. Increasingly bitter, she uses her superior wit to make hateful and sarcastic remarks to everybody with whom she comes in contact. When Ralph, hunting a mountain lion, accidentally shoots and kills his sister, the accident is given a Freudian significance by his too vehement denial, "I didn't see her! I didn't hear her! I didn't kill her!" (P. 229.) In Miss Stafford's later novel *The Catherine Wheel* (1952), twelve-year-old Andrew Shipley feels rejected by his parents, who leave him in boarding school during the winter and at the Maine coast estate of his mother's beautiful cousin Katherine Congreve during the summer. Andrew feels closer to Katherine than to anyone else in the family (his seventeen-year-old twin sisters Honor and Harriet are lost in a world of dates and clothes), but this particular summer a strangeness has grown up between them which he cannot understand, and which his bewildered behavior only serves to intensify. Nearly half of the novel is devoted to a fine psychological portrayal of the lost and perplexed adolescent boy, although the main interest of the story is in Katherine's relationship not only to the boy but to his parents. Katherine's melodramatic fiery death at the end of the novel seems contrived to give added significance to the Catherine wheel which causes it, and this obvious artificiality detracts somewhat from the sincere and very convincing psychological presentation.

In William Humphrey's *Home from the Hill* (1958), Theron Hunnicutt is a football in the marital scrimmage of his parents. Captain Wade Hunnicutt is admired by the more sporting men of his Texas community for his many successful extramarital amatory conquests, while his wife Hannah is vehemently opposed to infidelity. She delights in discovering and embarrassing his successive mistresses with friendly attention, while she herself refuses any solace to his ardent appetite. She believes she is fulfilling her wifely duty by raising Theron to adore his father—or rather, the false image of a chaste man that she presents to him as his father. Inevitably he must discover the truth in time, and when she feels that the time has come when she must tell him, Theron's reaction is to hate his father for the kind of man he is and his mother for telling him about it.

> He pitied her, yet he could not help despising her as both cowardly and disloyal. In that intolerant, youthful idealism to which he clung more earnestly than ever now that he considered himself judged and condemned by it, he believed it ignoble of her not to go on suffering in silence. He was ashamed of her for having made a claim upon his gratitude by revealing her self-sacrifice. Unselfishness, he believed, should blush to be discovered. These things, however, she being all that was left to him now, he might have been able to suppress. Certainly he had the wish to. It was her campaign in the time following to convince him of his father's guilt that taught him at last to hate her. (P. 190.)

In the novels previously discussed, the causes of the personality clashes resulting in revolt of an adolescent from the family are sometimes obvious and sometimes obscure—usually more subtle and complex in the novels of the forties and fifties than in those of the twenties and thirties. In the next group of novels the causes of revolt are more readily apparent, and for that reason they may perhaps be discussed more briefly.

Rebellion Against Family Status

It is not surprising that inadequate finances in the home frequently cause an adolescent to seek his happiness elsewhere. Not only is the poverty itself distressing, but it usually causes friction and bitterness among members of the household, so that the home is psychologically as well as physically an unpleasant place in which to be. In *Moon-Calf*, the Fays struggle for years to keep together, but when Felix is sixteen, the family dissolves. Felix goes to live with a married brother in Port Royal, but his brother's house is never home to him. In Booth Tarkington's *Alice Adams* (1921), Alice's adolescent brother Walter spends as little time at home as he can, turns to undesirable companions and pastimes, and finally embezzles funds from his employer; Alice herself, though she is twenty-two years old, has an adolescent's dread that her friends will realize her family is not as affluent as it once was. In Sherwood Anderson's *Tar* (1926), young Tar Moorehead resents his home because of the constant poverty there. During his childhood, Tar often imagines himself belonging in the family of a nearby grocer who has many daughters; as the only son in the family, Tar would be treated like a prince, and would have all he wanted to eat. When he is old enough to sell papers at the railroad station, he likes to imagine that he is not really a Moorehead, but the son of a wealthy man who left him in Mrs. Moorehead's care while he traveled abroad. Tar frequently dreams that a well-dressed man getting off the train will say to him, "My son, my son. I am your father. I have been in foreign parts and have accumulated a huge fortune. Now I have come to make you rich." (P. 287.) Sometimes Tar eats at the home of his friend Hal Brown, where he enjoys the rich variety of food and the jovial friendliness of the family; but he never dares ask his friends to eat at his house, where corn meal mush or cabbage soup is often the only dish served at a meal.

Mention has been made (p. 68 above) of the aversion that Farrell's Danny O'Neill feels for the impoverished home of his parents. Mick Kelly in Carson McCullers' *The Heart Is a Lonely Hunter* (1940) dreams of escaping from the family poverty and going to some far-off place where she will become a famous painter or writer or musician; but the poverty traps her into taking a job at Woolworth's before she has a respectable education, and she knows that her dreams of escape will never be realized. Francie Nolan in Betty Smith's *A Tree Grows in Brooklyn* (1943) is more fortunate—or perhaps more determined—than Mick. Although Francie also has to leave school to get a full-time job, as soon as she is put on a night shift she bluffs her way into college. Francie's childhood and early adolescence, in a home with a likable but improvident father, have been very hard; and her later adolescence, after her father's death, has been even harder. Yet she and her brother, as they discuss their mother's forthcoming marriage with a second and rather well-to-do husband, can feel sorry for their baby sister who, if she will never know the hard times they have known, will never know the fun their father brought into the home.

The family background of Mary Millar in *Morning Song* (1948) by Dorshka Raphaelson[2] is remarkably similar to that of Sonie Marburg in *Boston Adventure*, mentioned earlier in this chapter. Sonie is the daughter of a scholarly, improvident German father and grasping Russian mother; they live in a small fishing village near Boston. Mary is the daughter of a scholarly, improvident Austrian father and grasping Russian mother; they live in a part of New York City (near Broadway and 175th Street) which was almost a suburb about the time of World War I, when their story takes place. Sonie's father deserts his family when Sonie is twelve; her mother becomes mentally unbalanced after giving birth to a son, and Sonie devotes her adolescent years to supporting her mother and brother until the child dies and the mother is placed in a mental institution. Mary's parents are divorced when she is eight, and her father dies when the girl is fourteen; Mary soon has to leave school and work full time to support her mother and younger brother. But at this point the resemblance ends. *Boston Adventure* is somber, symbolic, full of hatred and evil: *Morning Song* is humorous and sentimental. In spite of her difficult home life and the greedy amorality of the theater world where she earns her living, Mary remains excitedly happy and naïvely idealistic, overcoming dangers and difficulties as inevitably as Sonie is overcome by them. *Morning Song* is delightful entertainment with little original insight into human nature; *Boston Adventure* is not easy to read, but it presents many believable and memorable characters with penetrating understanding of the somber depths of their minds.

Adolescent boys, especially in novels of the depression era, are likely to react more vehemently than girls to a shortage of money in the family. The feelings of Bigger Thomas, in Richard Wright's *Native Son* (1940), are typical:

> He hated his family because he knew that they were suffering and that he was powerless to help them. He knew that the moment he allowed himself to feel to its fulness how they lived, the shame and misery of their lives, he would be swept out of himself with fear and despair. So he held toward them an attitude of iron reserve; he lived with them, but behind a wall, a curtain. And toward himself he was even more exacting. He knew that the moment he allowed what his life meant to enter fully into his consciousness, he would either kill himself or someone else. So he denied himself and acted tough. (P. 9.)

Like other adolescent boys from impoverished homes, Bigger wavers on the brink of criminality. He and his friends—Gus, Jack, and G. H.— have stolen small amounts from other Negroes and have been sent to reform school, but they are not hardened criminals; after planning with his friends to rob a Jewish delicatessen, Bigger picks a fight with Gus so he won't have to go through the robbing of a white man's store. When Bigger kills the daughter of his white employer, he does so accidentally; the chance discovery that he has power over wealthy white people compels him to claim the crime by trying to make money from it. It is poverty that turns him from his family, but it is mischance and pride that make him a confirmed enemy of society. Other boys who rebel from poor homes and dabble in petty thievery are Soap Dodger Pendleton in Emerson Price's *Inn of That Journey* (1939), Marvin Lang in Walter Karig's *Lower Than Angels* (1945), and the protagonist in Saul Bellow's *The Adventures of Augie March* (1953). In the legal sense, these boys are all juvenile delinquents, since they are minors who have broken the law; yet they are not bad enough to fit the popular concept of juvenile delinquents as hardened young enemies of society whose chief pastimes are vandalism, grand larceny, and murderous gang warfare. Boys of this latter sort appear seldom in novels published before 1930, but they are rather common in novels published after 1945. They will be discussed a little later in this chapter.

81

It may be noted in general of novels dealing with adolescent revolt from impoverished homes that the earlier novels are likely to present their protagonists as almost helpless victims of society or of incapable fathers, dreaming of more affluent homes but unable to escape harsh reality until the girls are old enough to marry and the boys are old enough to earn their own living. In later novels, the protagonists are usually not content to sit and dream; the girls are likely to begin earning money early in adolescence, sometimes with astonishing success, while the boys, most of whom have to begin early to contribute to the family income, may augment their legitimate earnings by petty thievery or worse practices.

Another condition likely to cause revolt from the home is an incomplete family; the parents may be divorced, or the father may be kept from home by his job or by military service, or one or both parents may be dead. Dr. Luella Cole, a recognized authority on adolescent psychology, comments:

> It is highly desirable that a child should grow up in a home composed of a father, a mother, and some brothers and sisters. Both parents are needed, since the two serve somewhat different functions in the rearing of children. A child is more likely to develop normally if there are other children in the family to help him learn the basic lessons of adjustment to the needs and desires of a group and to prevent him from becoming spoiled by too much attention.[3]

Perhaps one-eighth of all the novels dealing with problems of adolescents present families which are incomplete according to Dr. Cole's standards. Few novelists have emphasized the problems caused by lack of brothers and sisters, except as this intensifies the loneliness and neglect of a young person lacking a mother or father or both, but a great many stress the problems resulting from a lack of parents. In the above discussion of novels presenting impoverished homes, there are several in which the father is missing: *Boston Adventure, A Tree Grows in Brooklyn, The Adventures of Augie March.* Fathers are also missing in several of the novels cited early in this chapter as illustrations of revolts against the mother: *Peder Victorious, The Almond Tree, Hildreth, Peyton Place.* When the mother is missing, the problems are likely to be more acute. Lymie Peters of *The Folded Leaf* suffers greatly from neglect; he has no brothers and sisters, his mother is dead, and his father takes little interest in him. In Ruth Suckow's *The Bonney Family* and in Helen Hull's *Candle Indoors* (1936), the oldest girl is left with unwonted responsibilities upon the death of the mother. Several novels present adolescent orphans trying to make their own way in the world—Edgar Lee Masters' *Kit O'Brien* (1927), Paul Horgan's *A Lamp on the Plains* (1937), Irwin Shaw's *The Young Lions* (1948)—or living in uncongenial foster homes— Faulkner's *Light in August*, Helen Martin's *Emmy Untamed* (1937), Josephine Johnson's *Wildwood* (1946), Truman Capote's *Other Voices, Other Rooms* (1948).

Immigrant parents who cling to the ways of the old country almost inevitably come into conflict with children who are brought up in America and who go to school with children of American families. Mention has been made (p. 68 above) of O. E. Rölvaag's novel *Peder Victorious*, in which the mother, Beret Holm, insisted that her children should speak and read Norwegian, but Peder, like his older brothers, considered English a more logical medium of communication for people living in America. Another novel published the same year (1929)— Myron Brinig's *Singermann*—presents a Jewish couple from Romania rearing seven children in Montana and constantly struggling against the children's tendencies to desert the ways of their forefathers. Two novels of 1937 present interesting parallels to these of 1929. In Sophus Keith Winther's *Mortgage Your Heart*, a Danish farmer in Nebraska tries to compel his children to retain Danish language and customs; while Meyer Levin's *The Old Bunch* presents several Jewish families in Chicago, the casual relations in families with American-born parents contrasting sharply with the bitter strife in families with parents born in Europe. Levin enables the reader to sympathize both with the outraged morality of Polish-born Mrs. Greenstein when she hears that Estelle has bobbed her hair, and with the extremes of flapper dress and behavior that Estelle adopts in compensation for her mother's uncouth Polish-peasant appearance and manner. Farrell's Danny O'Neill is sometimes embarrassed at the Irish ways of his substitute mother, Grandmother O'Flaherty, although she is more often in conflict with her own grown-up American-born children. In Harry Mark Petrakis' *Lion at My Heart* (1959), twenty-year-old Tony Verinakis is caught in the middle of a violent conflict between his immigrant father, who wants to keep his sons true to their Greek heritage and religion, and Tony's older brother Mike, who wants to be purely American and to marry an Irish Catholic girl. In Peter Martin's *The Building* (1960), three of the four sons of the Russian Jewish immigrant Aaron Golin (called A.G.) reject their father's plans for them to build up the family business, and each tries in a different way to make a place for himself in American society.

Most of the novels mentioned in the preceding paragraph involve some rebelling against the religious convictions as well as against the national traditions of the parents. Of course, revolt against strict religious teachings of the parents is likely to occur even when both parents and children are American. Earlier pages in this chapter have mentioned rebellion against strict Protestant training in Croy's *West of the Water Tower* and Anne Parrish's *The Methodist Faun,* and Danny O'Neill's reaction to his mother's excessive Catholicism. Isaac Rosenfeld's *Passage from Home* (1946) shows fourteen-year-old Bernie Miller leaving his close-knit Jewish clan in Chicago to live with his "liberated" Aunt Minna and her *goyish* lover. In Herman Wouk's *Marjorie Morningstar* (1955), the stage-struck heroine also abandons her Jewish religious practices and the family name of Morgenstern, but later decides that she can be happier in the Jewish tradition than outside of it.

Adolescents may revolt not only from homes that are too un-American or too narrowly religious, but also from homes that are too staid or genteel. This concept was considered rather new and daring in 1920, although the English novelist Samuel Butler in *The Way of All Flesh* and the American Theodore Dreiser in *Sister Carrie* had set the example about twenty years earlier. The novels of Dell and Fitzgerald were notorious for the young characters who rebelled against genteel families. The rather satirical *Pandora Lifts the Lid* (1924), by Christopher Morley and Don Marquis, seems to poke fun at the eighteen-year-old Pandora Kennedy and her Long Island society-girl friends who plan to convert their wealthy families and neighbors to socialism, using as their club slogan the phrase, "Not debs but Gene Debs." (P. 89.) Some of Ruth Suckow's novels, particularly *The Odyssey of a Nice Girl* and *The Folks,* present girls who turn from the genteel tradition in which they were reared. Dorothy Canfield Fisher's *The Deepening Stream* (1930) shows Matey Gilbert confused and repelled by her parents' highly admired surface culture, which conceals bickering if not deeper conflicts.

After 1930, adolescent revolt from genteel families was no longer a strikingly new fashion in fiction, but the trend did not disappear. In Dan Wickenden's *The Running of the Deer* (1937), fifteen-year-old Mel Trace turns from the surburban gentility of his parents to admire his adventurous Uncle Christopher. In Emerson Price's *Inn of That Journey,* mentioned a few pages back (p. 81 above) for Soap Dodger Pendleton's revolt from his poverty-stricken family, there is also the account of school superintendent Michael Cullen's son Mark, who joins Soapy's gang as a gesture of rebellion against the staid propriety of his own parents. In Daniel Lundberg's *River Rat* (1941), Ralph Blood deserts the fashionable, conservative society life of his family and friends in Dedham, Massachusetts, to join the river rats of Mac's Canoe Club. John Phillips Marquand, Junior, in *The Second Happiest Day* (1953, written under the pen name of "John Phillips") presents an observer-narrator, Augustus Taylor, who breaks away from the gentility of his family and the preparatory-school-Harvard atmosphere in which he was educated; Gus relates the problems of the protagonist, George Marsh, who loses much in life because he fails to break away from that tradition. In *Compulsion* (1956), Meyer Levin's fictional interpretation of the Leopold and Loeb murder case, the crime of the adolescent Jewish boys is explained as due in part to a revolt against the standards of very proper behavior expected by their wealthy and prominent families.

This group of novels of revolt—those in which the revolt is caused by special problems such as financial trouble, a broken home, or conflicting philosophies of living—have not been discussed in detail because merely to mention the problems makes the probable treatment of them rather apparent. However, some general comments on treatments and trends probably should be made. We should expect novels of revolt from impoverished homes to be more prevalent during the depression years; actually, such novels were as common during the forties and fifties as they were during the thirties, but those published during the thirties were more obviously directed toward inspiring social and economic reforms, presenting the young rebels as helpless victims of circumstances which needed changing. Novels on this topic published during the forties and fifties were more likely to be psychological studies of the effects of such environment on the individual; in many cases they presented pictures of hopeless gloom, but others showed an existential faith that an individual may escape from the influence of family and environment. Novels of adolescents revolting from broken homes became particularly common during the forties and fifties, when the subtle interplay of psychological influences replaced the preaching of social doctrine as a popular trend in fiction. Novels of revolt from gentility were very popular during the twenties, as they matched a trend in the interest of leading intellectuals

85

of that time; later novels of such revolt, particularly those of the forties and fifties, present the rebels not as enlightened leaders of a needed reform movement, but as the result of extensive and hidden psychological forces which the novelist brings to the surface, sometimes obviously and didactically, but more often by implication and symbolism. There seems to have been less change in the treatment of revolt from an unacceptable national or religious tradition; in novels published all through the period of this study the parents are presented as trying to compel the children to accept their own conservative standards. Sometimes the parents act with willful obtuseness on the premise that children should obey their parents; more often they act with a sincere though sometimes misguided belief that they are directing the children for the children's own best interests. In most of the novels the psychological motivation and conditioning of the children are fully portrayed, and in many of them, regardless of the date of publication, the psychological processes of the parents are also presented, though usually not so fully as those of the children.

JUVENILE DELINQUENCY

It was earlier mentioned (p. 81 above) that the juvenile delinquent, as conceived in the popular mind today, rarely appears in novels published before 1930. In the decade between 1920 and 1930, the sympathy of novelists was usually with the rebel as a victim of society, and rebellion was held to be a means of reform, not a cause for downfall. Such a conservative writer as Booth Tarkington might present a juvenile delinquent in Walter, the brother of Alice Adams; but Walter is not fully developed in the novel, and he seems to be a holdover from an earlier tradition in fiction rather than a forecast of the switch-blade rebel of post-World War II fiction. Clyde Griffiths in Dreiser's *An American Tragedy* is willing to use criminal means to attain his ends, but he does not prefer crime for its own sake. The flouting of moral standards at college and even at high school parties was pictured in several novels of the twenties, but these will be discussed in the next chapter. An early novel which suggests that rebellion from the family may be carried to the extent of juvenile delinquency is Harold W. Brecht's *Downfall* (1929). Malcolm Campbell is a likable, courageous freshman at Spring City (Pennsylvania) High

School when he gets into some minor difficulty with the school authorities and his parents, is harshly punished, and is sent to work on a farm for the summer under a strict German farmer. With punishment threatening from all sides, Malcolm welcomes the friendliness of the hired man Dick Cain and Dick's advice to "kid 'em along"—pretend to be giving in to those in authority, while actually doing whatever he likes. Adopting this philosophy, Malcolm returns to high school and, although freely indulging in smoking, drinking, gambling, and sex, becomes a popular fraternity member and baseball hero. Eventually he becomes too cock-sure and loses the honors he has won. Malcolm is still far from the modern juvenile delinquent, but his failure to reach an understanding with his parents and his acceptance of obviously immoral advice undermine his chances of successful adjustment to responsible adult life.

Probably the most thorough fictional study of the influences that may lead a boy from a fairly satisfactory family environment into illicit gang activities is James T. Farrell's Studs Lonigan trilogy. The Lonigans are a respectable and fairly well-to-do middle-class family. The parents are fond of their children and wish them well, without expecting impossibly high achievements from them. At the beginning of *Young Lonigan* (1932), Studs is a likable and promising boy of not-quite-fifteen, about to graduate from a parochial grammar school. But the ideals of the street boys of Chicago are opposed to those which his school, church, and family have been trying to instill. Studs's ability as a fighter wins him the adulation of a rough gang of street boys, and the chance incident described in the last preceding chapter of this study (see above, pp. 35–36) deprives him of the potentially salutary influence of a girl like Lucy Scanlon. His sister Fran irritates him by constantly reminding him of his duties, and he has little affection or respect for his parents; but long after he has ceased to care for the opinion of his family, his love for Lucy is the one motive impelling him to strive for respectable citizenship. Studs is never as completely demoralized as some members of his gang—the bully Weary Reilley or the clowning thief Kenny Kilarney, for example—but his way of life is so different from anything acceptable to Lucy that when he tries to return to her five or six years later, they find that they have very little in common (*The Young Manhood of Studs Lonigan*, pp. 239–54).

For a somewhat comparable novel of an adolescent of Italian descent dragged down by a New York City street environment, see Leane Zugsmith's *The Reckoning* (1934). Nelson Algren's *Never Come Morning* (1942) presents a Polish boy in Chicago trapped by his environment. Algren's *Somebody in Boots* (1935) presents, vividly and from firsthand observation, a life typical of that lived by many boys and men and some girls during the depression years—a life "on the road." Actually, it is Cass McKay's home environment rather than the depression that motivates him to wander. Living with an older brother and sister and a half-crazed father in a run-down Mexican section of a little town in Texas, he finds little at home to appeal to him, but comradeship and fascination in the hobo jungle at the edge of town. So at the age of sixteen, two years before the depression was to hit the country, Cass takes to the road, traveling in box cars or riding the rods from west to east and from south to north, spending time in jail, stealing when he can't find work, witnessing all kinds of depravity, constantly hiding from "somebody in boots," the somebody in authority who seems always eager to beat, to imprison, or to banish the underprivileged. The novel is as formless as the wanderings of a hobo; typically of the proletarian novels of the thirties, it presents all men in authority as the enemy, and the contemptible and hopelessly doomed Cass as the victim of social conditions. (See below, page 91, for comments on a later version of this novel.)

A very different road story—more diverse, more optimistic, more poetic—is Frederic Prokosch's *Night of the Poor* (1939). Although seventeen-year-old Tom (last name not given) is on the road only eleven days as compared with four or five years for Cass McKay, and travels only from Wisconsin to Texas as compared to Cass's complete coverage of the country, he experiences more aspects of America than Cass does. Cass sees only the despairing, the downtrodden, though he meets a great variety of these. Tom sees many such people, but he also sees courageous, energetic men who lead reasonably happy lives without homes or regular incomes; optimists who are sure that better times are just ahead; and some nonentities who complain bitterly about hard times without lifting a finger to help themselves. Cass is obviously destined for a life which will never rise above crime and vagabondage; Tom is willing to work, beg, or steal to support himself during his travels, but he maintains high ideals, and there is a fair chance that he will settle down to a steady married life in Texas. In any case, his life on the road means to him growth, not destruction. Algren has some very poetic passages, especially when he describes the innocent adolescence of Cass's sister Nancy, but much of his narrative is ugly and revolting. Prokosch's style is always beautiful, even when the things he describes are repulsive; at times it recalls the styles of Whitman, Wolfe, and Stephen Vincent Benét, and yet it is invariably his own style. It would take a quotation of several paragraphs to convey the full flavor of his prose, but perhaps the following short paragraphs will give a suggestion:

> He was at a troublesome age—awkward, lanky, with a face appealing but unshaped, coarsely-grained, rather ashamed of himself, all in all. But speculative, adventurous, and physically strong, healthy, larger and more developed than other boys of his age. But it didn't mean anything clearly yet—it merely disturbed, it tugged at his blood; that was all.
>
> Still, these recent days had cured him of certain weaknesses—laziness, prevarication, a sense of inferiority and imprisonment. He was beginning to see men for what they were. He was beginning to feel the outside world—bark of trees, world of towns—against the palm of his hands, rather than his own flesh and desire, his secret paradise. (Pp. 127–28.)

Price's *Inn of That Journey* and Karig's *Lower than Angels* have been mentioned as precursors of the post-World War II deluge of novels about juvenile delinquents. By 1947 the deluge had arrived. Among the best of those published in that year are Willard Motley's *Knock on Any Door*, Virgil Scott's *The Dead Tree Gives No Shelter*, and Irving Shulman's *The Amboy Dukes*. At least two novels of that year give memorable pictures of girl delinquents: William Henning's *The Heller* and I. S. Young's *Jadie Greenway*. *The Weather of the Heart* by Daphne Athas presents two adolescent sisters and a French-Canadian boy in a small town in Maine whose activities are legally delinquent, though not as deliberately and ostentatiously law-defying as those of many adolescent protagonists in postwar fiction. *Knock on Any Door* relates the deterioration of Nick Romano, a happy and devout altar boy at twelve, a confirmed enemy of the law at sixteen, and a convicted cop-killer at twenty-one. Motley clearly and convincingly shows the steps in Nick's downward course: the unexpected poverty which forces the family to move to a slum section, the undeserved reform-school sentence accepted to protect a friend, the brutality of reform-school authorities which turns Nick against all authorities, the shamed hostility of his family when his term in reform school is over, the arrests and the brutal handling by Chicago police that make him determine to kill a cop rather than let himself be manhandled by them again. *The Amboy Dukes* tells of sixteen-year-old Frank Goldfarb, who gets no guidance and inspiration from his working parents or from his incompetent teachers at a vocational high school, and all too little from the only two people who are interested in him—his girl and the athletic director at the Jewish Center. His ambition is to be an admired member of the Brooklyn neighborhood social club, the Amboy Dukes, whose members amuse themselves with liquor, dope, zip-guns, knives, and sex. After accidentally killing a teacher, Frank is killed by a moronic member of the club. In *The Dead Tree Gives No Shelter*, Mike Brandon runs a numbers racket in his high school, becomes involved with a bootlegger, and is murdered at twenty-one after murdering the bootlegger for love of the latter's mistress.

The novels about delinquent girls end more optimistically, although Jadie's life, at least, is sordid enough. She is a sixteen-year-old Negro girl living in a crowded section of Brooklyn, where she feeds her younger brother and sister on their mother's earnings as a prostitute. Jadie carries a switch-blade knife to protect herself, uses it in the classroom on a girl who tries to bully her, becomes infected from a casual sex experience with a sailor, tries to seduce a Negro teacher and to frame him when her attempt at seduction fails. Yet despite these shocking experiences, Jadie does not usually seek trouble; she is quiet most of the time, and is able to handle most of her problems without resort to violence and crime. Anne Karlan, protagonist of *The Heller,* is somewhat less involved in illicit activities than Jadie is. Anne is an energetic, bold, attractive high-school girl who is completely uninhibited in her speech and actions. She does not hesitate to cheat in school or to pick up dates on the street or in a bar. When her favorite boy friend, a high-school athlete, is forced to marry her best friend Betsey, Anne proceeds to trap into marriage one of her mother's roomers, a young man already engaged to someone else. But there are indications that, after a few months of marriage, Anne is becoming something less of a heller.

These five novels are representative of the great outpouring of juvenile delinquency novels during the decade or so after World War II. Such novels follow so nearly the same pattern that there is no need to discuss them all individually. Virtually all of them contain much sex and violence —usually gang warfare involving guns and knives. The novels are usually set in crowded sections of large cities, particularly in New York or Chicago, but often in other cities such as Los Angeles or New Orleans, or even in smaller communities. The young people make frequent use of alcohol and marijuana; stronger drugs are not infrequent. The homes are almost invariably comfortless, often impoverished. Parents are ignored by the adolescents if possible; teachers and social workers are considered nuisances; police are considered enemies. If any adult is admired, it is a successful criminal from the neighborhood. In nearly a third of the more important novels, the delinquents are Negroes; in several, they are Mexican *pachucos* or others of foreign background.

Three novelists who have been repeatedly successful with novels of juvenile delinquency are Nelson Algren, Irving Shulman, and Hal Ellson. Earlier in this chapter (page 88 above), Algren's *Somebody in Boots* was discussed; his more recent *A Walk on the Wild Side* (1956) apparently was undertaken as a rewriting of the same novel, but the protagonist is changed from contemptible Cass McKay to amiable Dove Linkhorn, only a few of the original adventures are kept, and the tone of the writing is entirely different. The earlier version is a typical proletarian novel of the thirties, while the second is a typical "beat" novel of the fifties. Cass McKay is the hapless and hopeless victim of capitalists and minor government officials; Dove Linkhorn is favored by fortune in everything, even in his apparent misfortunes. A natural "beat" philosopher, he finds joy in the impractical, unscrupulous, and sometimes unprofitable activities of society's outcasts; and when he is permanently blinded by the legless athlete whose mistress he has stolen, he is fortunate in that he is now linked inescapably with those outcasts. Algren's *Never Come Morning* (1942) follows more closely the typical pattern of juvenile delinquency novels, as Bruno Bicek, a young Polish pugilist in Chicago, performs acts of brutal violence in accordance with the code of the street gangs. Besides *The Amboy Dukes*, Irving Shulman is remembered for *Children of the Dark*, adapted from the story idea of the motion picture *Rebel Without a Cause*, and showing juvenile delinquency in a relatively small city of the Midwest, developing without the awareness of most of the parents. Hal Ellson, a former social worker, has written novels which sound rather like case histories: *Duke* (1949) about a fifteen-year-old Negro boy who is a gang leader and a dope runner; *Tomboy* (1950) about a white girl who is as tough and brutal as any boy in her gang; *Summer Street* (1953), a novel of sex activities which was discussed in Chapter II (see above, p. 43); and *The Golden Spike* (1952), depicting the drug addiction of a sixteen-year-old Puerto Rican boy in New York.

91

From the great mass of juvenile delinquency novels, a few others stand out as superior in literary quality or different in content or technique. Marie Baumer's *The Seeker and the Sought* (1949) is unusual in its point of view; a placid, middle-aged resident of an apartment house at the edge of New York City, making a delayed response to an appeal for help from a desperate teen-ager, comes into firsthand contact with juvenile delinquency in the city. Donald Windham's *The Dog Star* (1950) is exceptionally well written and interesting both for its fresh psychological insight and for its symbolism. Fifteen-year-old Blackie Pride, on his return to his home in Atlanta from a reformatory farm school, strives to emulate Whitey Maddox, whom Blackie admired at the reformatory for the aloof way he lived and the calm way he committed suicide. As the memory of Whitey is the dog star about which Blackie revolves, so Blackie becomes the dog star for his own younger brother. John Bell Clayton's *Six Angels at My Back* (1952) is also effectively written, and it is somewhat unusual in that it presents juvenile delinquency in a rural rather than an urban setting. On a stretch of the Gulf coast of Florida, where large estates of wealthy Northerners are close by the shacks of impoverished natives, three shack-dwellers in late adolescence—the narrator Ed Grever, his friend Turkey Simms, and Turkey's wife Mae—turn to stealing when Mae's cousin Limp comes to them from jail with a grotesque, maniacal giant known as Bible. Douglass Wallop's *Night Light* (1953) is a little like *The Seeker and the Sought* in that a respectable midde-aged man investigates juvenile delinquency, which has not interested him before. Robert Horne in the later book is impelled by a much more personal motive than that of Walter Williams in the earlier book; his six-year-old daughter is wantonly shot by a youth on the roof of a nearby apartment house, who then plunges from the roof to his own death. In investigating the identity and the motives of the killer, Horne learns much about the violent, egocentric personality of the young jazz-drummer Alfie Lambert who shot a strange little girl as a gesture of rebellion before committing suicide. Mark Kennedy's *The Pecking Order* (1953) has been called "the first serious account of Chicago's Black Belt since Richard Wright's *Native Son*." [4] As chickens in a barnyard peck at each other in a certain order established by their respective aggressiveness, boys tend to order each other around in accordance with a similarly established order. Eleven-year-old Bruce Freeman is the leader in his neighborhood until the younger boys are joined by a reform-school graduate named B. J. and a cynical Southerner named Henry. B. J. organizes the younger boys into a gang and leads them in various escapades ranging from cookie-stealing in the A. and P. to car-stealing; the end is a catastrophe of which Bruce is the sole survivor.

Two recent novels are interesting as fictional interpretations of the same notorious adolescent crime of the 1920's—Leopold and Loeb's murder of little Bobby Franks: Meyer Levin's *Compulsion* (1956) and James Yaffe's *Nothing But the Night* (1957). Of the two, Levin's stays much closer to the original facts of the case and has considerably more literary value. Like Sid Silver, the narrator in the novel, Levin was a fellow student of the murderers at the University of Chicago and was also a cub reporter who reported the case for a Chicago newspaper. Besides his personal knowledge of and interest in the case, Levin had the advantage of a longer and more successful career as a novelist than Yaffe had. *Compulsion* certainly does not rank with *Crime and Punishment* as literature, or even with *An American Tragedy* or *Native Son;* but it will probably remain as a significant landmark among literary interpretations of criminal minds. Yaffe's novel is more compact than Levin's; it also sticks fairly close to the original facts, but makes the murderers seventeen-year-old high-school seniors instead of precocious university graduate students, and entirely omits the homosexual relations that played a significant part in the original case and in Levin's novel.

A novel which has had influence far out of proportion to its literary value is Evan Hunter's *The Blackboard Jungle* (1954). The experiences of a young teacher in the fictitious North Manual Trades High School of New York City are based on the author's experiences in a similar school, and are undoubtedly authentic, although probably no one teacher encounters quite so much meanness and violence within so short a span of time. And the novel presents many memorable characters, such as the bright Negro student Gregory Miller and the treacherous Artie West, besides a number of exciting incidents. But characters, incidents, and the general development of the story all seem subordinated to the didactic purpose of revealing an important social problem of today and a possible means of dealing with it. The obvious sincerity of the book and its appearance at a time when uncontrolled violence in public schools was much in the news account for the striking success of a work that is no better written than several other novels of juvenile delinquency.

Three novels published in 1959 give some interesting insights into the problems of juvenile delinquents. Evan Hunter's *A Matter of Conviction* shows three Harlem boys on trial for the murder of a Puerto Rican boy; they are pictured as victims of society, reflecting the resentments of one downtrodden group against the intrusions of another. Warren Miller's *The Cool World* presents the point of view of a fourteen-year-old Harlem boy who takes over the leadership of a fighting gang, is sent to reform school when a member of an opposing gang is killed, and finally shows promise of becoming interested in more constructive things. William Peter McGivern's *Savage Streets* has the respected adult members of a fashionable suburban community resorting to gang methods to combat the supposed threat of a teen-age club from a neighboring under-privileged area.

In spite of the vast number of juvenile delinquency novels since World War II and the great public interest in the subject, none of the postwar novels are equal to the best earlier treatments of this theme—works such as *An American Tragedy,* the Studs Lonigan trilogy, and *Native Son.* *Compulsion* is probably the best of the postwar novels of juvenile de-linquency, unless Saul Bellow's *The Adventures of Augie March* could be counted in that category. A few more may hold a lasting though not very lofty place in American literature: *Knock on Any Door, The Amboy Dukes, Six Angels at My Back,* and perhaps *The Blackboard Jungle.* The others are likely to retain interest only for the special student of the field.

Closely linked to the novel of juvenile delinquency—indeed overlap-ping it to a considerable extent—is the novel of adventures on the road, the modern descendant (usually motorized) of the Spanish picaresque novel, of the novels of Fielding and Smollett, of such earlier American works as the *Leatherstocking Tales, Huckleberry Finn,* and perhaps *Typee* and *Omoo.*[5] Much of Sherwood Anderson belongs in this tradi-tion—the early part of *Poor White* (1920) and most of *Kit Brandon* (1936), his story of a woman outlaw from the Southern hills, as well as numerous short stories. Nick Adams in Hemingway's *In Our Time* (1925) early becomes a wanderer, and so does Mac McCreary in Dos Passos' *The 42nd Parallel* (1930), the first part of his trilogy *U.S.A.* Adolescent wanderers in the early days of the West are Clay Calvert in H. L. Davis' *Honey in the Horn* (1935) and Brazos Bolton in Ross McLaury Taylor's *Brazos* (1938). But probably the first extended account of an adolescent on the road in modern times is Algren's *Somebody in Boots.* This novel and its later version, *A Walk on the Wild Side,* as well as Prokosch's

Night of the Poor, have been discussed earlier in this chapter (above, pages 88–89 and 91). Two very popular road novels of recent years are Jack Kerouac's *On the Road* (1957) and Vladimir Nabokov's *Lolita* (1958). The first is concerned with the pointless "beat" dashes across the country performed by the adolescent Dean Moriarty and his admiring pal, the narrator Sal Paradise, beyond adolescence in years but certainly not in his self-centered, rebel-without-a-cause attitude; and the second tells of a "nymphet" who spends the thirteenth and fourteenth years of her life touring from motel to motel with her middle-aged lover. In James Leo Herlihy's *All Fall Down* (1960), Clinton Williams, from the age of fourteen to sixteen, admires the wild and carefree roamings of his older brother, Berry-berry, and hopes to participate in them; but he realizes at last that his brother's irresponsibility and lack of affection for others give his life an emptiness. Most of the adolescent nomads in all of these novels steal and cheat not merely for the excitement of defying laws and conventions (although this is usually a contributory motive) but as a means of providing the necessities of life. Thus dishonesty is made necessary and hence forgivable.

SUMMARY—TRENDS IN NOVELS OF ADOLESCENT REBELLION

For obvious reasons, the adolescents who form lawless gangs are likely to be in cities. Only a small percentage of all adolescents are rebellious to the extent of complete lawlessness, but in large cities a small percentage can still be a formidable number. Gangs of juvenile delinquents do exist in small towns to a much larger extent than most novels suggest. Novelists seek to present powerful dramatic conflict, and opportunities for such conflict are not as apparent in small towns as they are in large cities, with their concentrations of rebellious youths in slums and in vocational high schools. Still, there is plenty of opportunity for perceptive novelists to write of small-town gangs, as Emerson Price does in *Inn of That Journey* and William Demby does in *Beetlecreek.*

The rebels who take to the road are likely to originate in rural areas or small towns. Anderson's Kit Brandon comes from the mountains between Virginia and Tennessee; she runs away from home when she thinks her father is about to rape her, and she works in cotton mills until she gets the more profitable and glamorous job of driving fast cars for a bootlegger. Nick Adams runs away from a small town in Michigan; Soap Dodger Pendleton begins his wanderings from a tiny hamlet in Ohio. Cass McKay and Dove Linkhorn start out from small towns in Texas; when they do settle down, it is in large cities: Chicago for Cass and New Orleans for Dove. The young people who rebel from their families to the extent of becoming lawless are almost invariably people who crave excitement and violence; they find these more plentifully in large cities than in small towns or in rural areas.

Since the time of Rousseau it has been customary in European and American societies to think of rural families as being much better adjusted within themselves than city families. In general, novels of adolescent rebellion conform to this popular supposition. Although the novels of William Faulkner, Erskine Caldwell, and Jesse Stuart show considerable violence in rural areas of the South, this violence does not usually concern adolescents and their parents. Martha Ostenso, O. E. Rölvaag, Hope Williams Sykes, Sophus Keith Winther, and Helga Sandburg show rural adolescents rebelling from their families, but there are many more authors who present rural families as well adjusted, and rebellion in city families is both more common and more violent in novels than is rebellion in country families. In view of these tendencies, it is interesting to note the results of a survey of adolescent-parent adjustment in cities, towns, and farms conducted by Ivan Nye in preparation for a doctoral dissertation and reported in *Rural Sociology* for December, 1950. Here is a part of Nye's abstract of his article:

> City families were found to be significantly better adjusted than farm families as measured by an adolescent-parent adjustment scale on a sample of 1,456 city, small-town, fringe, village, open country non-farm and farm adolescents. In general, adjustment declined with increased rurality, but town families were found to be an exception, ranking below village and fringe. Socioeconomic level was found to explain a portion of the rural-urban differences, but residence remains a significant variable with socioeconomic factors held constant. Hypotheses are advanced that the poor adjustment of the farm adolescent is associated with rapid rural social change within the space of a generation, increased contact with urban adolescents who enjoy more obvious privileges, and a feeling that society as a whole considers them underprivileged. (P. 334.)

Besides the explanations that Nye offers for increasing frequency of

96

family maladjustment with increasing rurality, another explanation might be that small-town adolescents ordinarily have more home chores to perform than city adolescents, while farm adolescents have considerably more than either town or city youngsters. Since farm parents thus become severe taskmasters as well as guardians of behavior, there are more possible areas for family maladjustment on the farm than in small town or city. The fact that adolescent rebellion on the farm less often goes to the extreme of juvenile delinquency might be explained by commenting that farm youngsters simply do not have time or opportunity for such activities. It is very likely, also, that activities which would bring police interference in the city and hence the official charge of juvenile delinquency, would not attract legal intervention in the country, where law enforcement means are less effective. In Jesse Stuart's *Hie to the Hunters* (1950), sixteen-year-old Jud Sparks chews tobacco constantly, has not attended school in years, and wears a gun as a standard part of his attire for social affairs; Jud is considered a rather respectable boy in his farm community, but such behavior in a city youth would be cause for grave suspicion if not for listing as a juvenile delinquent.

The novels indicate, though not always accurately, a relationship between adolescent rebelliousness and the degree of rurality; they do not show much relation between rebelliousness and the region of the country presented. There is perhaps a little more rebelliousness in novels of the South, where rebelliousness seems to be a more admired quality than in other parts of the country. Novels of the East, particularly those with settings within a hundred miles or so of New York City, show considerable sympathy for the rebels, but not admiration for them. Novels of the Middle West are more likely to show a conservative attitude in most of the characters, but the attitude of the author is likely to be liberal. In fact, the very conservatism of the majority of potential readers in the Middle West is likely to lead to the writing of some outstanding novels of adolescent rebellion, as in the works of Theodore Dreiser, Sherwood Anderson, Ruth Suckow, James T. Farrell, Richard Wright, and Nelson Algren.

The kinds of writing that deal with such problems are extremely varied. As rebellion is one of the most obvious aspects of growing to maturity, and as it provides good opportunity for the dramatic conflict so essential to holding readers' interest, it is popular subject matter for novelists of varied interests and abilities. Traditionally, the rebellion of adolescents has been occasion for tolerant laughter, and such an attitude is maintained in the period of this study by Booth Tarkington, Sally Benson, Ryerson and Clements, and others. At the other extreme, juvenile rebellion is presented as cause for serious alarm in the novels of Dreiser, Richard Wright, Irving Shulman, and others—often to the extent of lurid sensationalism. Sentimental nostalgia for the wild-oats period marks the novels of Edgar Lee Masters and Betty Smith. Perhaps most typical of the best novels in the early decades of this period is the presentation of fresh and challenging ideas, as in the writings of Floyd Dell, James T. Farrell, and most of the other writers of the twenties and thirties; more typical of the best novels in the forties and fifties are subtle psychological studies like those of Jean Stafford, Carson McCullers, J. D. Salinger, William Faulkner, and Shirley Jackson.

Whether adolescent rebellion from the family is laughed at, tolerated, admired, or decried depends very little, apparently, on whether the author is from the South, the East, the West, or the Middle West. It depends somewhat on whether he is writing of the city, the small town, or the country and somewhat on the period when he is writing, but most of all it depends on the individual author and his way of interpreting the things he sees. For in any decade of the period studied, and in any region of the country, we can find some novels of revolt which are humorous, some which are nostalgic, some lurid, some didactic, and some psychological. So each fledgeling comes to the edge of the nest and, each in his own way—with confidence, with tremor, with mockery, with gratitude, with bravado—prepares to undertake his solo flight.

Chapter IV

ADJUSTMENT TO SCHOOL AND COLLEGE

Next to the development of his sexual powers, and the contact with his home and family, nothing has a greater influence on the adolescent than the school he attends. A good many of the adolescent's waking hours are spent in the school building, and his most important duties and pastimes are centered there. Understandably, the college or boarding school exerts more influence on its students than does the public or private day school, and the problems of the student who lives at school are likely to be more complex and interesting than are the school problems of those who live at home.

This discussion of the problems of adjustment to school and college will begin with the problems which are common to all schools below the college level, then take up the problems peculiar to the pre-college boarding school, and will finally present the problems of adjustment to college life.

School Problems—Fellow Students

Most important to the student himself is his adjustment to his schoolmates and to their standards of dress and behavior. The major adjustment comes in the preadolescent period, when the child first enters school; but later adjustments are necessary if he changes schools, and some young people always have difficulty in adjusting to their schoolmates, even though they have been at the same school for years. Such problems in adjustment are due to personality differences or to differences in background between the protagonist and his schoolfellows. The experiences related in the novels are usually autobiographical, and the problems are about what we would expect to find when a young person with an author's temperament tries to adjust himself to the ways of the ordinary adolescent: the unusual sensitivity, imagination, and intelligence of the protagonist serve only to widen the breach between him and his unimaginative schoolmates. Such a basic conflict in personalities and interests is apparent when Felix Fay, in Floyd Dell's *Moon-Calf*, after attending school for seven years in a village, enters the eighth grade [1] in a small city of thirty thousand inhabitants. Through his knowledge of parliamentary procedure, Felix makes an impression on his classmates and is elected president of the newly formed Jefferson School Literary and Athletic Society; but he oversteps the limits of his unexpected power when he leads the club into a program of essays and debates instead of the baseball and basketball the other boys and girls have anticipated. Felix steps out of the presidency, and the organization goes to pieces. There is nothing very striking in this incident or in Dell's way of presenting it; but in contrast to the obviously invented escapades of fictional adolescents in the earlier genteel tradition, its very simplicity and realism were impressive to readers of 1920.

A more striking problem of adjustment resulting from a change of schools appears in Robert S. Carr's *The Rampant Age* (1928). This novel was the first to make it clear that the sinful activities of "flaming youth," which many novels of the decade had described on college campuses, were also becoming prevalent in some high schools. Paul Benton transfers in his junior year from a small-town high school to a big-city one, where he learns that, in order to be accepted in high-school fraternity life, he must learn to handle gin and sex in the approved "collegiate" manner. Paul goes through some very distressing experiences before he graduates and decides to go to a college noted for its learning rather than for its country-club atmosphere. Although the novel does not rank particularly high in literary quality, the author, who was just eighteen years old and still in high school when he wrote it, was able to give authentic touches that make it plausible.

In one of the recognized classics among novels portraying adolescence, Vardis Fisher's *In Tragic Life*, Vridar Hunter has a particularly hard time adjusting to his schoolmates because he spent the first ten years of his life on a remote farm in Idaho where he seldom saw anyone except his immediate family. From his second year in school, when he is eleven, he and his younger brother Mertyl "batch" in a house by themselves, doing their own cooking and house cleaning—a peculiarity which further sets them apart from other students. During his early adolescence, Vridar feels compelled to use his fists to win acceptance among the rough boys of the little rural schools he attends.[2] When he reaches high school, he meets more sophisticated schoolmates; and, like many boys who have kept excessively "pure" during childhood, he undertakes to show that he can drink, smoke, and steal as well as any of them. He also feels that he should match his schoolmates in sexual activities, and finds plenty of girls who are willing to co-operate; but his devotion to his childhood sweetheart and the powerful reflexes conditioned by his early experiences make it psychologically impossible for him to do more than kiss and pet with the girls he meets when he is in high school.

Children of foreign parents find it particularly hard to adjust to their American schoolmates. During World War I there was a tendency to persecute children of German families; this tendency appears in Gordon Friesen's *Flamethrowers* (1936), which tells of Peter Franzman persecuted by schoolmates in a Kansas village because of his German background (see below, p. 178), and Vincent Sheean's *Bird of the Wilderness* (1941), which shows Bill Owen despising his mother's German relatives and cherishing the memory of his Welsh father. Jean Stafford's *Boston Adventure* shows the complex attitude of her schoolmates toward Sonie Marburg, whose father is German and whose mother is Russian. To the children of the small fishing village near Boston, twelve-year-old Sonie is half mystery and half monster:

> Russians, to the children at school, were utterly improbable, though all that was known about them was that they had ludicrous names. A favorite sport was to tease me by saying: "Hisky, Sonivitch, have you got your geographysky homeworkskivitch?" In a way, I was flattered by this, for it had replaced Pig-Latin and was known as Sonie-Latin. On the other hand, Germans were perfectly credible and, because of their reputation for cutting off the hands of sleeping children and of being sired by Kaiser Bill, they enjoyed a certain prestige. (Pp. 71–72.)

Sonie would have been glad to sacrifice some of this dubious prestige to be accepted by her schoolmates for what she was.

Rölvaag's *Peder Victorious* presents the adjustment problems in public schools made up almost entirely of Norwegian Lutherans and Irish Catholics. In spite of completely incompatible backgrounds, the children might adjust to each other fairly well if it were not for the families constantly urging them to keep with their own kind. Peder's best friend at school is the Irish Charles Doheny, whom he continues to play with even after his mother tells him earnestly, "You will have to find another playmate, Peder!" (P. 113.) Even where language and religion are not

barriers, differences in national and cultural backgrounds make for difficulty in adjusting. In Christopher Morley's *Thorofare* (1942), young
Geoff Barton is fairly well accepted by his schoolmates when he comes
from England to live in Chesapeake (apparently Baltimore), Maryland,
but he gets rather tired of always having to be a defeated British general
when the boys play war, and of being called "Thomas G-offerson" or
"G-offerson Davis" even after he changes the spelling of his name to
"Jeff." More serious is the plight of the Negro in a predominantly white
school; in Langston Hughes' *Not Without Laughter* (1930), Sandy Rogers
is kept in Negro classes under Negro teachers through the first four
grades of public school in a small town in Kansas; in fifth grade, which
is predominantly white, he and the two colored girls in the class are
placed in seats at the back of the room, without regard to their scholastic
ability or to the alphabetical order of their last names. Sandy's sixteen-
year-old Aunt Harriet is not allowed to sit with her high-school classmates in the local movie theatre, even though the picture is being shown
especially for school children. Charles Beaumont's *The Intruder* (1959)
shows some of the problems which face both Negro and white students
in a Southern high school integrated by unpopular law, especially when
a rabble-rouser comes to the community to stir emotions.   .

Problems of adjustment among white Americans may result from
differences in regional traditions; in Phil Stong's *The Rebellion of Lennie
Barlow* (1938), a Southern white boy refuses to be dominated by Yankees
when his family moves to Iowa, and consequently he is always at odds
with his schoolmates and his teacher. White Americans from the same
region—even from the same city—may have trouble adjusting to each
other in high school if they have had markedly different earlier training.
George Santayana's *The Last Puritan* (1936) shows Oliver Alden, the
only child of wealthy parents, entering high school in his home town after
having had his earlier schooling from a German governess. He rather likes
his classmates, but finds them puzzling in many ways, particularly in
their language.

> He soon learned their dialect and slang, but it always remained a
> foreign language to him, as did common American speech in general.
> He didn't hate it; sometimes it made him laugh; it all seemed to him
> like a turn on the variety stage, meant to be funny, and really droll,
> though it might become too constant and tiresome. His own natural
> speech was that of ladies and clergymen. . . . Oliver, in spite of his

102

tendency to believe that whatever was natural in himself was right, was rather disturbed and uncertain on this subject. He couldn't be content, in speech any more than in anything else, with what was wrong or inferior, or second best; yet it was most puzzling to decide what the absolutely best was, and so hard, even then, to live up to it. Language, for him, didn't belong to the sunny side of life. (Pp. 124–25.)

The Newcomer (1954), by Clyde Brion Davis, describes the adjustment problems of thirteen-year-old Henry Trotter when he moves to a city not very far from his original home.

William Maxwell's *The Folded Leaf* presents two boys who are drawn to each other partly because they are not readily or completely accepted by other students in their Chicago high school. Lymie Peters is a thin, timid, impoverished boy who admires from a distance the poised, well-dressed young people who dominate the high-school hangouts; while Spud Latham, though handsome and athletic, is a newcomer to Chicago and misses his old gang in Wisconsin. The friendship which these two establish to meet a high-school need causes another problem when they get to college, as will be shown later in this chapter (see below, pp. 126–27).

. Sometimes an exceptionally gifted student, as the protagonist of a school novel usually is, overreaches himself in an effort to attain popularity with the student body as a whole. Jessamyn West's *Cress Delahanty* shows a girl from rural California undertaking a planned campaign, in her first year at a centralized high school, to make herself known to and accepted by both students and faculty as "that crazy freshman." Her campaign is successful, but when her attempt to become freshman editor of the yearbook is greeted with howls of laughter, Cress realizes that she has been accepted as a false personality, not as her true self.

School Problems—Teachers and Studies

Besides adjusting to his schoolmates, the adolescent student must make an adjustment to his teachers. This is often a more difficult adjustment to make, partly because of the greater difference in age and background and partly because the student is not free to choose his teachers for compatibility as he can choose his school companions. Some teachers and administrators may be too domineering; others may be too indecisive.

Some students may feel personal antagonism toward their instructors; other students may be attracted to certain teachers to an embarrassing extent. In Harold Brecht's *Downfall* (1929), it is the homely, enthusiastic teacher Miss Sturges who comes closest to putting the morally wavering Malcolm Campbell on the right path; in Wolfe's *Look Homeward, Angel* (1929) it is the scrawny, tubercular wife of the headmaster who makes Eugene Gant's four years in private school profitable and happy, instead of miserable as his college years are to be; in Leane Zugsmith's *The Reckoning* (1934), the idealistic young teacher Carolyn Muller comes as close as anyone can to saving the New York slum product Castie Petrella from the life of delinquency to which he seems destined.

In contrast to these devoted and sympathetic teachers are others who are indifferent or harmful in their effects on their students. Vridar Hunter goes to high school with great illusions concerning education and educators, and is at a loss when he sees unquestionable human weaknesses in his teachers. Hollis Summers' *City Limit* (1948) reveals the jealous persecutions of a high-school junior, Harriet Shrader, by the dean of girls, Miss Gertrude Bates. The frustrated old maid, just entering her menopause, secretly identifies herself with the ingenuous Harriet, who is discovering the first thrill of "going steady." Sensing the futility of her own love longings for the handsome minister, Miss Bates unjustly accuses Harriet of indecent relations with her popular classmate Ed Webster, hounding the girl into running off with Ed, and high-handedly arranging a speedy marriage when they are inevitably brought back within the city limits a few days later. In Daphne Athas' *The Fourth World* (1956), the dictatorial and ambitious Dr. Maynard August, director of Canopus Institution for the Blind (known as "See-Eye"), is contrasted with the sympathetic new teacher Actia Clewes and with the blind history teacher Theodore Balkan, who replaces Dr. August as director after the latter's harsh methods of discipline have caused rebellion and riot among the students. Varying attitudes of public high school teachers toward their students are shown in Charles Calitri's *Strike Heaven in the Face* (1958), in Ethel Erkkila Tigue's *Betrayal* (1959), and in Mildred Walker's *The Body of a Young Man* (1960). In each of these novels, some teachers favor strict and repressive discipline, some favor easygoing permissiveness, and some favor energetic but sympathetic inquiry into the causes of behavior problems in their respective student bodies.

Racial and cultural differences may affect adjustments between student and teacher as well as between students. In Oliver La Farge's *The Enemy Gods* (1937) the Navajo student Myron Begay is well adjusted at his first Indian school, under the leadership of the missionary Mr. Butler, who understands the Navajos and occasionally speaks to them in their own language; but at the age of twelve, Myron is transferred to another school, where there are more Apache than Navajo students and where the missionary leader is rather contemptuous of the Indians' ability to understand. Mr. Snyder's suspicious attitude impels Myron to wonder whether the Christian ways are really better than Navajo ways, and he is constantly though unwillingly drawn into un-Christian but traditional battles between Navajo and Apache students. (For other comments on this novel, see below, p. 178.) In *Look Homeward, Angel,* Headmaster Leonard has a subconscious tendency to bully the one Jewish student in his Southern private school. Although a number of novels offer examples of such racial or cultural antagonism or misunderstanding between student and teacher, the proportion of such maladjustments in fiction is considerably smaller than the proportion of them in real life. On the other hand, there are examples in fiction of students exploiting a tendency to look for such misunderstandings where they do not exist. In Evan Hunter's *The Blackboard Jungle,* the trouble-maker Artie West stirs up misunderstanding between his teacher Richard Dadier and the intelligent Negro student Greg Miller, and leads the principal to believe that Dadier is showing racial prejudice.

Incidentally, *The Blackboard Jungle,* presented primarily from a teacher's point of view, reveals the attitudes of a number of different teachers toward their work—the impractical idealism of Josh Edwards, the sex-conscious artiness of Lois Hammond, the imperturbable cynicism of Solly Klein who tells Dadier that the vocational schools of the city are garbage cans for the waste product that won't fit into the general high schools. "And you want to know what our job is? Our job is to sit on the lid of the garbage can and see that none of the filth overflows into the streets." (P. 58.) Each of these attitudes presents a different adjustment problem to the students. A more complete picture of the varied faculty personalities in a more typical high school in a more typically American city is presented in Playsted Wood's *The Presence of Everett Marsh* (1937). Marsh is the plain-speaking, hard-working, high-thinking principal of a large city high school in Wisconsin, a man whose spiritual presence, even after his death, is felt by the members of his faculty:

the silly, vain Mr. Wentworth; the tense, nervous Mr. Weldon; the fierce Mr. Melford; the complacent Mr. Gross; even the snobbish young novice Mr. Minot.

Closely related to—and sometimes dependent upon—the adjustment to schoolmates and to teachers is the adjustment to studies. As education is the primary reason for a school's existence, it is rather surprising to find that novels devote much less space to adolescents' adjustment to studies than to their adjustment to schoolmates, teachers, or extracurricular activities. Two possible explanations for this may be offered: first, the struggle to master academic knowledge is not a particularly dramatic conflict and is not likely to hold the novel-reader's enthralled attention; second, the protagonists in novels of adolescence are, as a rule, unusually intelligent young people who are not likely to have difficulty with school subjects. In the last decade or so, since the complex nature of intellectual and spiritual development during adolescence has been better understood, novelists have begun to indicate that even a gifted student may encounter academic difficulties. In the novels of the twenties and thirties, and in most of those of the forties, academic difficulties are usually minor for the protagonist, though minor characters may face major academic problems. Amory Blaine in *This Side of Paradise* annoys the masters at St. Regis' Prep because he does not do as well in his studies as he is intellectually capable of doing. One master tells him that he could get the best marks in school if he wished; Fitzgerald comments that "it was temperamentally impossible for Amory to get the best marks in school." (P. 30.) In Dorothy Canfield Fisher's *Rough-Hewn* (1922), Neale Crittenden in his senior year at Hadley Prep, under increased pressure from both his teachers and his football coach, finds himself slipping below his accustomed high standing in his class; but after football season, by devoting all his waking hours to study, he is able to bring himself up to sixth in his class within a few months. After taking his college entrance examinations, Neale is shocked and disgusted to realize that the high standards required at Hadley were not to help the boys, but "to exalt the name of Hadley throughout the collegiate world." (P. 119.) In Harold Brecht's *Downfall*, which was mentioned a few pages back (see above, p. 104), the problem facing Malcolm Campbell is not so much his inability to master his high-school subjects as it is his temptation to let cheating take the place of study so that he will have more time for sports and for good times.

106

J. D. Salinger's *The Catcher in the Rye* (1951) is unusual in that the protagonist, although obviously of superior mental ability, fails out of one preparatory school after another. Asked by his history teacher to explain his poor academic record, Holden Caulfield is unable to do so; he only knows that he is bored with all his subjects except English, and that he believes most of the teachers and students are "phonies." Psychologists have noted a direct ratio between a student's liking for his teacher and his liking for the subject taught,[3] and they have noted an inverse ratio between emotional disturbance and academic success.[4] Holden's liking for English is due partly to innate aptitude, as his older brother is a professional writer, but it is significant that the one teacher he has liked is an English teacher. It is even more significant that Holden has been very much disturbed emotionally since the death of his favorite brother three years earlier. His experiences at various prep schools, including his academic failures, have increased his emotional disturbance, thus decreasing his chances of success in his studies.

The same sort of vicious circle appears in *I'm Owen Harrison Harding* (1955) by James Whitfield Ellison, a novel obviously influenced by *The Catcher in the Rye*. Owen is failing two subjects near the end of his sophomore year in a large high school in Michigan, although his IQ is over 130 and he was almost always on the honor roll in junior high. In a conference with his home-room teacher, Mr. Harris, Owen can give no reason for his low grades except that he has lost interest in studying. Everything his teachers say or do annoys him; he does not see or admit that his dislike for school is related to the facts that his mother has just died after a long siege of cancer, that his father is drinking heavily, that his brother is on active duty in the Pacific war theater, and that he himself is going through his first important love affair. Although he is almost rude to Mr. Harris, and fights the teacher's offer of extra assistance, he is secretly flattered by the interest shown in him, finally accepts the offer, and manages to pass all his courses.

Schoolboys tend to regard instructors as enemies and to suspect the sincerity of teachers who flatter them. Many novelists point out the hostility of boys, and sometimes that of girls, toward teachers who try to help them. Owen suspects Mr. Harris of giving him "a snow job," but eventually he is won over. Richard Dadier, the inexperienced teacher in *The Blackboard Jungle*, is less successful in a similar attempt to win the co-operation of Greg Miller by complimenting him on his intelligence and leadership ability; a day or so later Greg recalls with scornful laughter, "Man, the snow was knee-deep." (P. 93.) Some weeks after this, Dadier achieves his purpose by paying Greg the tacit compliment of assigning him special responsibilities.

Juvenile delinquents may be as detrimental to a school as to a family, although a school is less hesitant to expel a delinquent member than a family is. Solly Klein's cynical attitude (page 105 above) that his school's chief function is to keep delinquents off the street and under supervision, is more likely to prevail in a vocational school than in a general public or private school, and in a city school more than in a rural school. The task of supervising delinquents is more typically assumed to belong to reform schools, such as the one vividly described in Willard Motley's *Knock on Any Door*. Although state laws usually require school attendance up to a certain level or a certain age, the law may be evaded, especially in rural areas. The juvenile delinquent is likely to be as desirous of avoiding school as the school authorities are desirous of excluding him. Though a few novelists tell of delinquents who use the schools for corrupt purposes —like Mike Brandon in Virgil Scott's *The Dead Tree Gives No Shelter*, who runs a numbers racket in school, or like a number of boys who furtively use the tools in the school shop to make guns for gang wars— most delinquent boys in novels either stay away from school entirely or visit it only occasionally, in the same way that they visit activities supervised by social workers: for the excitement of stirring up trouble. For example, in Farrell's *Young Lonigan*, three boys who have been expelled from St. Patrick's parochial grammar school attend commencement exercises in order to heckle and cause a commotion. In the comparatively few novels that give much attention to delinquent girls, the girls are much more likely to remain in school, presumably because they are less venturesome than boys.

Juvenile-delinquent elements in otherwise admirable high schools are given considerable attention in Charles Calitri's *Strike Heaven on the Face* (1958) and John Farris' *Harrison High* (1959). Calitri describes a sex club of about fifteen or twenty girls and boys in a medium-sized New Hampshire school; and Farris presents sexual delinquents, brawling, and stealing among a few students in the most respected of the several high schools in a rather large Midwestern city. He indicates that conditions are much worse in one of the city's other high schools. A central character in *Harrison High* is Griff Rimer, a tall and handsome young hoodlum whose pastimes include reckless driving in a borrowed car, casual seduction of many girls, beating up of smaller students, open defiance of teachers, and occasional robbery. He unintentionally causes the death of one of the school's star athletes, and deliberately tries to kill another by beating him on the head with a Coke bottle.

SCHOOL ATHLETICS

Although rather little space in novels is devoted to academic adjustment, considerable space is devoted to adjustment to extracurricular activities, including athletics. Athletic competitions have captured men's imaginations for thousands of years, and spectators are almost always interested in learning how the ordinary human being develops into a champion. Athletic champions, by the way, are found more frequently in the earlier novels of this period than in the later ones; perhaps the popularity of the Frank Merriwell books during the first two decades of the twentieth century (see above, p. 10) persuaded novelists that the public wanted successful athletes in novels of school and college life. Fitzgerald's *This Side of Paradise* shows Amory Blaine, playing quarterback for St. Regis', making the only touchdown in the game against Groton in his senior year. Mrs. Fisher's *Rough-Hewn* shows Neale Crittenden making the football team at Hadley almost without competition and going on with the sport at Columbia to become a star player. In Percy Marks's *The Plastic Age* (1924) Hugh Carver becomes a campus hero at fictitious Sanford College because of his high scoring in a track meet against a traditional rival. On the other hand, two novels of 1953 which present football heroes in their respective prep schools—*The Second Happiest Day* by John Phillips and *Scotland's Burning* by Nathaniel Burt—sound rather old-fashioned for their time in this respect.[5] More will be said about these two novels a little later (see below, pp. 111–12 and 116–17).

But the concern of this study is not so much with champions as it is with those who have adjustments to make, problems to solve. In Farrell's *Father and Son,* Danny O'Neill, who has tried various means to make himself popular and respected, becomes an effective player on his high-school football, basketball, and baseball teams through the same sort of patient, painstaking study and practice that he applies to his school subjects. His motive in playing is not love of the game or pride in his school, but the hope for personal recognition, and he is frequently rebuked for playing to the grandstand rather than working with the team. At last he is elected basketball captain and has his picture and an article about him in a Chicago newspaper; he thinks that at last he is "on the road to being somebody." (P. 433.) But he finds that his success has not brought him the respect he sought. When the coach leaves him in charge of basketball practice, the players laugh at Danny and refuse to do what he tells them to. He asks his friend Marty Mulligan to help him enforce discipline, but Marty says, "They think you're a goof. And you act like one. If you can't make them respect you, what can I do? You're to blame yourself, O'Neill." (P. 478.)

One of the most familiar and amusing happenings in school athletics to be found in modern American fiction is Aram Garoghlanian's heroic attempt to win the fifty-yard dash in William Saroyan's *My Name Is Aram* (1940). After a very brief attempt to grow powerful through Mr. Lionel Strongfort's correspondence course in physical culture, Aram abandons it for his own method—sheer will power, without trouble or muscular exercise. Convinced that his method has made him superhumanly fast and strong, Aram enters the race against three other boys, starting with shut-eyed concentration "in a blind rush of speed which I knew had never before occurred in the history of athletics."

> It seemed to me that never before had any living man moved so swiftly. Within myself I ran the fifty yards fifty times before I so much as opened my eyes to find out how far back I had left the other runners. I was very much amazed at what I saw.
> *Three boys were four yards ahead of me and going away.* (P. 77.)

The outcome of the race is obvious. Ridiculous as this incident seems, it is disturbingly close to the method used by many adolescents to achieve glory on the school athletic fields. The story is far more true to human nature than is the more seriously intended account of Homer Macauley's remarkable performance in the two-twenty hurdles, related in Saroyan's later novel *The Human Comedy* (1943).

A very different sort of school athletics problem is presented in John R. Tunis' *All-American* (1942), an unusually mature book by America's most popular author of sports stories for boys. A preparatory-school football player, Ronald Perry, is remorseful when Meyer Goldman, a local high-school player whom Perry and his teammates have deliberately "roughed up" on the playing field, is sent to the hospital with a broken neck. Disturbed by the scornful anti-Semitism of many of the academy boys, Ron decides to transfer to the high school, where he has some difficulty in adjusting to the crowded conditions, the lower academic standards, the distractions of coeducation, and the violent antagonism shown to him as an "outsider" by some of the high-school boys. When the high-school team is invited to play an intersectional game in a Southern city on condition that its Negro left end be excluded, Ron leads the team in refusing to play unless the Negro boy is allowed to participate. Thus the need to work for justice and understanding between races and cultures becomes a problem of school athletics as well as one of education in general.

Two novels of 1953 were mentioned a few pages back as being rather old-fashioned in their presentation of preparatory-school football heroes; yet both these novels are very modern in the psychological entanglements that involve the athletes and their friends. In each case the story is narrated by a less athletic friend of the champion. The tragedy of George Warwick Marsh III, as presented by his friend Gus Taylor in *The Second Happiest Day*, is that he never grows beyond being a prep-school football hero. The only twice-elected football captain in the history of Emmanuel Academy in Massachusetts, George is told, at a banquet following Emmanuel's defeat of its rarely beaten rival Middlesex, that he will always remember this as the first happiest day of his life, the second happiest to be the day he is married. Through his years of Harvard and World War II and his many attempts to find a suitable profession, George remains the perpetual idealistic, dependent schoolboy, always remembering that first happiest day and never attaining the second. An adult life similar to George's seems to await Dan ("Breck") Breckenridge, the football hero in *Scotland's Burning;* but he is saved from this anticlimactic destiny by being killed, heroically but quite unnecessarily, in trying to rescue some phonograph records from a burning school building. The new building which replaces it is dedicated to him, and Breck is canonized as the incarnation of all the lofty but rather meaningless ideals of the private school and its athletic program. So these ideals which the genteel tradition in literature admired without question, and which the more rebellious literature of the twenties still represented as worth while, are condemned by the new iconoclasm of the fifties as empty or even harmful.

Three novels of 1959 present varying problems of school athletes. In John Knowles's *A Separate Peace* the narrator, Gene Forrester, an excellent student and a fair athlete, suddenly realizes that he is completely dominated by his friend and roommate Phineas, probably the best athlete in the history of the private school they attend but a rather weak student. Gene suspects Finny of constant maneuvering to keep the two roommates in situations where his own athletic superiority will be apparent and Gene's scholastic superiority will not. Gene's resentment at this supposed maneuvering finds expression in an underhanded maneuver of his own, which destroys Finny's athletic career, and leads indirectly to the star athlete's death. In Jack Kerouac's *Maggie Cassidy* the narrator is a valued performer on his high school's track and football teams; his best girl, while she professes admiration for his athletic achievements, seldom attends the competitions in which he stars, and she dates other boys on evenings when he has to attend team practice. In John Farris' *Harrison High* the members of a school football team are so provoked by the dirty playing of a rival team that they are tempted to try some underhanded brutality of their own in retaliation. The problems presented by Kerouac and Ferris are, of course, by no means unusual in stories of school athletics; but Knowles provides fresh and subtle insight into a problem of the playing field.

In novels about schoolgirls there is little emphasis on athletics, except in a few books obviously intended for immature readers. There are some athletic girls in more adult novels, but they play little if any part in a school athletic program. Helen Shires, a minor character in Farrell's *Young Lonigan,* practices basketball and football with Studs in the Chicago streets; Peggy Goodin's Clementine Kelley plays quarterback for Hank Matthews' neighborhood football team. Jessamyn West's Cress Delahanty comes as close to being a school athlete as any of the girls; she leads cheers at the track meets. But she is more interested in the father of two of the track stars than she is in the school athletic program.

Many of the protagonists of school novels write for or edit school publications, and a considerable number participate in school dramatics and musical organizations. But any problem arising from these extra-curricular activities are usually caused either by misunderstandings between students or between teachers and students, which have been discussed earlier in this chapter, or by questions regarding the adolescent's artistic ability, which will be discussed in the next chapter.

Although far more Americans go to public school than to private school, there seem to be more novels devoted to private-school life than there are to public-school life. This may be because a great many American novelists are graduates of private schools, but it is hardly possible that a majority of American novelists are. A more likely explanation is that private-school graduates find in their school days more that seems suitable material for fiction than do public-school graduates. In the first place, private-school students spend much more of their time at school; in the second place, the absence of parents and the presence of many other adolescents necessitates a more rapid adjustment to one's contemporaries than public-school students must make; in the third place, the problems of private school are more readily recognized because of the long fictional tradition stemming from English novels of boarding-school life. In those novels which present adolescents attending private school but living at home—Wolfe's *Look Homeward, Angel,* Miss Benson's *Junior Miss,* Morley's *Thorofare,* Miss Suckow's *The Bonney Family,* Nora Johnson's *The World of Henry Orient*—the school problems encountered are not likely to be any greater than those found in a public school, and will probably be less because of the greater homogeneity of the student body and the greater individual attention which each teacher can give his students. There are, however, some problems peculiar to the private boarding school, and these merit some attention.

Boarding School—Teachers in Place of Parents

The most obvious problem facing the adolescent in boarding school is to learn to get along without his parents. This problem is shared by public-school students in one or two novels—Vardis Fisher's *In Tragic Life* and Robert P. Tristram Coffin's *Lost Paradise* [6]—when the nearest public school is too far from home for walking or commuting. In Coffin's *Lost Paradise* (1934) and in Mabel Robinson's *Bright Island* (1937) the protagonists miss not only the close family relationship but also the distinctive and independent way of life they have known on the Maine coastal islands where they have always lived before. In a great many of the novels of boarding-school life, the protagonists come from broken homes, and in some they are wanted by neither parent; yet they long for home and family, even though they realize that many of their school-mates are also from broken homes. Perhaps the most striking account of the boarding-school "orphan" is *Early Frost* (1952) by Jane Mayer and Clara Spiegel, writing jointly under the pseudonym of "Clare Jaynes." Lann Saunders has lived almost all of her life in expensive schools and summer camps; her parents have been divorced since she was in her early teens, but even before that they quarreled constantly and had little time for her. Now in her last year at a fashionable California boarding school, she invents stories to make herself and her schoolmates believe that her parents do care for her. In the secret society at school known as the Multiple Parents Club, Lann boasts of the wonderful wedding her mother is soon to have and the real home that Lann will have; but when the wedding takes place Lann is excluded, and the prospect of a new baby leaves no room for her in the home. The early frost in Lann's family has forced an early maturing of the fruit, even though it is not as fully developed as it might have become in a full season of ripening adolescence. A younger girl, forced from child-hood into early adolescence by a similar experience with parents and boarding school, is Christie Warren in Ruth Harnden's *I, a Stranger* (1950).

Since teachers and administrators in boarding schools stand *in loco parentis,* cruelty or incompetence in them has a more devastating effect on the students than would the same qualities in public school teachers. In Stephen Vincenet Benét's *The Beginning of Wisdom* (1921), young Philip Sellaby thoroughly despises the headmaster at Kitchell Military Academy, Dr. Ward Erastus Kitchell, who calmly lies to the parents of prospective students about the benefits of his school and who hypo-critically speaks in assembly about the great purposes of the school while he is trying to make as much money as he can from the students and parents. Philip Stevenson's *The Gospel According to St. Luke's* (1931) presents the headmaster of an exclusive New England boarding school as a conscientious snob. Robert H. Newman's *Fling Out the Banner* (1941) shows among the faculty of another New England school the kind of psychological abnormalities that appear frequently in fiction of the forties: a German teacher who approaches the boys homosexually, and a football coach who sadistically urges his heavy first-string team to maul an elusive second-string quarterback in practice scrimmage. J. D. Salinger's *The Catcher in the Rye* reveals, through the perceptive though somewhat prejudiced eyes of Holden Caulfield, the "phoniness" of masters at various Eastern private schools he has attended—especially of Dr. Thurmer, the headmaster at Pencey Prep, and of Mr. Haas, the headmaster of Elkton Hills, who was

> the phoniest bastard I ever met in my life. Ten times worse than old Thurmer. On Sundays for instance, old Haas went around shaking hands with everybody's parents when they drove up to school. He'd be charming as hell and all. Except if some boy had little old funny-looking parents. You should have seen the way he did with my room-mate's parents. I mean if a boy's mother was sort of fat or corny-looking or something, and if somebody's father was one of those guys that wear those suits with very big shoulders and corny black-and-white shoes, then old Haas would just shake hands with them and give them a phony smile and then he'd go talk, for maybe half an *hour*, with somebody else's parents. I can't stand that stuff. It drives me crazy. (P. 16.)

An even more jaundiced view of the headmistress of a fashionable finishing school for girls is presented by a senior, Alida Grant, in Betsey Barton's *Shadow of the Bridge* (1950). The headmistress of Cragmere, whom the students sarcastically call the "Old Understander," makes a pretense of democratic government through a student council, but actually she maintains harsh discipline by packing the council with girls who will carry out her wishes.

BOARDING SCHOOL BULLIES

Another serious problem in boarding schools is that of bullying or corrupting of weaker students by stronger ones who enjoy a display of domination. There is no way for the weaker students to escape the stronger ones in a boarding school, and disinterested students usually make it a point of honor not to inform the school authorities of any malpractices. Novels of the twenties were usually rather mild in describing students' mistreatment of each other. Benét describes briefly but vividly, in *The Beginning of Wisdom*, an encounter between the new

115

student Philip Sellaby and the bullies Butch Draper and Star Hawes; a year later, in advancing Philip to the rank of cadet sergeant, the faculty drill major compliments him on his improved relations with other boys, while Pihlip silently recalls how the "improvement" has come about:

> He sees himself as he was when he first came to Kitchell, a scared atom of an "only child," to be kicked around and chucked into corners like Froggy Stillman's books. Now he has improved—he has the age and the muscles and the bag of dirty stories that will keep him from being bullied at all, that may even permit him to bully some one else. A fierce cramped hatred runs through him at the bullies and his new chevrons and Major Stelly and the whole air of uniformed stupidity and disciplined nastiness that hangs over the school like gas above a marsh. Lord! If he could only get out of the place! (Pp. 37–38.)

Sometimes religious differences provide an excuse for student bullying. Two novels of the early thirties reveal Jew-baiting among the students of predominantly Protestant boarding schools: *The Gospel According to St. Luke's* and Lincoln Kirstein's *Flesh Is Heir* (1932). John Harriman's *Winter Term* (1940) offers further refinements on the evils that fashionable New England prep-school boys can and do perpetrate on each other, especially during that very restless period between Christmas and Easter. Fourteen-year-old Sturgis Trumbull, a rather likable but strongly prejudiced third-former, instigates other members of his form to a serious but ill-organized attempt to crucify a supposed Jew in the group, and starts a rumor that another unpopular, non-athletic member of the form is illegitimate. These mischiefs are subtle compared with those of the previous year, when a boy returned from Christmas vacation with a burglar kit, and when a bomb exploded in the quadrangle at three in the morning, destroying much of the highly prized turf which had been imported from Oxford. The one sympathetic master on the faculty of twenty is powerless to control the boys' energy and conduct, defeated partly by the prejudices of the boys, partly by the wearied indifference of the other masters, and partly by the traditions of the school.

Scotland's Burning presents several boys who symbolize or typify the various character traits most frequently found in prep-school students, though not ordinarily so artificially concentrated in separate individuals as they are in this novel. Mention was made earlier (p. 111 above) of Dan Breckenridge, who personifies the prep-school ideals of

116

loyalty, heroic self-sacrifice, and athletic ability—admirable qualities, but meaningless when there is no discrimination regarding their application; and Tony Comstock, the narrator and observer, who represents the sensitive, discriminating, unpopular nonconformist. In addition there are Lassiter Camp, the personification of exciting and fascinating evil, an arsonist and an amused instigator of wrong-doing in others, who is finally described in terms clearly implying Satan (pp. 281–88); Sam Petrie, who epitomizes all the baser impulses of the adolescent schoolboy with none of the compensating charm and intelligence; Liggett, the football captain, lionized for his atheltic ability but lacking in moral and mental power; and Alan, Tony's closest friend, the conservative intellectual.

A few novels of the fifties tell of boarding-school students who, plagued by fellow students and finding no comfort or affection in faculty or family, gain their release by taking their own lives. In *Shadow of the Bridge,* Alida's friend Deborah Lane is beautiful and lovable; but her pretty, widowed mother finds that having an adolescent daughter in the house interferes with her own rather copious love life, and the other students at Cragmere ostracize both Dee and the lanky, awkward Alida, hinting that the close friendship of the two girls is Lesbian. Dee finds brief happiness with a young man, who takes what he can get from her without assuming any responsibilities. She learns that she is pregnant, and is condemned for immorality by the devoted Alida. When the student council votes for the expulsion of both girls, the complete rejection is more than Dee can stand, and she commits suicide. Holden Caulfield in *The Catcher in the Rye* recalls James Castle, a thin, unpopular boy at Elkton Hills, who refused to retract his statement that the athletic Phil Stabile was conceited, although Phil and six friends tortured James in a locked dormitory room. To escape his tormentors without retracting, James leaped from the upper-story window to his death on the stone steps of the building. In Herbert Gutterson's *The Last Autumn* (1958), sensitive, undersized Tommy Conway is intolerably miserable after only a few weeks in Carver School in Massachusetts. Tommy's father had attended Carver thirty years earlier, the brawny son of a Pennsylvania coal miner, and was cheered for his athletic prowess but snubbed for his family connections; now a wealthy widower, Roger Conway bull-headedly insists that his son must be among the school leaders in athletics, scholarship, and opulence. None of these roles suit the quiet

Tommy, who misses his sympathetic mother, fears his overbearing father, and detests his coarse, sex-conscious roommate. A science field trip to a high rock ledge in the nearby hills gives Tommy an opportunity for escape from his incompatible schoolmates and a hope of reunion with his mother. The suicide occurs very early in the book, which reveals much of Tommy's personality and problems as it presents the opinions of various faculty members concerning the best way to break the news to his father.

A few novels show private schools influencing students' religious beliefs, as public schools seldom do. The anti-Semitic activities in Protestant New England schools, mentioned above, are usually social rather than religious influences, even though they may pretend a religious motivation. More genuinely religiously is the impact of a Protestant school environment on a Catholic student; thus in Newman's *Fling Out the Banner* the protagonist, Boss Mackenzie, whose father has died during the preceding summer, fears that he is losing his Catholic religion among his Protestant schoolmates and masters. Parochial schools are, of course, intended to influence the religious beliefs of the students who attend them; Danny O'Neill in Farrell's *Father and Son* is told by Sister Magdalen, his eighth-grade teacher, that he may have a call to the priesthood, and he seriously considers going to seminary instead of to high school. He decides that he does not have a call, and he attends St. Stanislaus High School; but in his third year, at the annual retreat, he again wonders whether he should become a priest. The possibility of a call seems fainter now than it did three years earlier, but Danny decides that at least he will make a good confession of his whole life.

> Danny came out of the confessional box, feeling as if he had actually lost weight. Yes, it was over—his soul was in the state of grace. He wished that he could take wings and fly. (P. 164.)

Probably the best account in American fiction of a spiritual experience at school is in James Agee's very short novel *The Morning Watch* (1951), telling of a Good Friday experience at a Catholic boarding school in Tennessee. A twelve-year-old boy's sincere struggle for grace as he commemorates the disciples' watch in the garden at Gethsemane, and the catalytic effect of this spiritual struggle on the mundane schoolboy activities which follow, elevate the reader with the same kind of spiritual exaltation as that which results from a reading of James Joyce's famous

account of a schoolboy retreat in *A Portrait of the Artist as a Young Man.*
Since boarding schools are almost never coeducational,[7] it is rather surprising that homosexuality does not more often appear as a featured problem in boarding-school novels. The existence of the problem is barely suggested in a few novels about boys' boarding schools, and it is featured in Sara Harris' novel of a girls' reform school, *The Wayward Ones* (1952). Justin O'Brien, in his excellent study *The Novel of Adolescence in France* (New York, 1937), comments that French novels of the 1890's sometimes blamed boarding schools for creating sexual tensions and problems in adolescent boys, but that this discussion in novels led to a relaxing of certain school rules so that older students could leave school for their sexual experiences rather than corrupt the younger students. American boarding-school students probably have never been as closely confined to school as were the French students of the 1890's; also, public opinion in America is more violently opposed to homosexuality than is public opinion in most European countries, and adolescents are strongly influenced by the opinions of their peers, at least in outward appearances.

PROBLEMS OF COLLEGE STUDENTS

In many ways, the problems that adolescents face in college are like those which they face in boarding schools, but there are a number of important differences. Some of these differences result from the different stages in the process of adolescence. Most students have reached full physical maturity by the time they begin college, and many have reached their peak of innate mental ability by that time.[8] But the powers of imagination, reason, and judgment are dependent on learning and experience as well as on innate intelligence, and are likely to continue developing until the age of twenty-five or later.[9] Most states set twenty-one as the age of legal responsibility or adulthood, but under our present American system of training and apprenticeship, a professional person or artist is not ready to assume full financial responsibility until several years after he has finished college—seldom before the age of twenty-five. During his college years the adolescent does not have to adjust himself to his rapidly changing body and mind, as he did in public school or private school, but he does have to acquire new skills and adjust to new responsibilities, while he may realize that financial independence and full adult status may not be his for several years after graduation.

Problems in college differ from those in public or private school not only because of the different stages of development in the students, but also because of differences in the nature of the institutions. Colleges place much more responsibility on the students in their course work, their extracurricular program, and their social conduct. Colleges are more likely to be coeducational than are private preparatory schools; and this fact, combined with the full physical development of the students, the reduction or absence of parental and teacher supervision, and the remoteness of financial independence that would make marriage feasible, makes problems of sexual adjustment more prevalent in college than on the lower levels of education or among young people who go to work instead of going to college. Colleges are more cosmoplitan than boarding schools, and far more so than public schools; the protagonist of a college novel is certain to encounter students and faculty from various parts of the country and even from foreign countries, and he himself may come from a region with culture patterns far different from those which predominate in the college. All of these conditions add to the problems of adjustment.

Neale Crittenden in Mrs. Fisher's novel *Rough-Hewn* seems at first to be a person who would have little difficulty in adjusting himself to college life. He is an outstanding athlete, a better-than-average student, and one who has lived most of his life just across the Hudson from Columbia University. But this combination is not one that is likely to bring him into close friendship with other students; he is too much a student to enjoy conversation with his relatively illiterate football team-mates, too busy with football to have time for discussion with serious students, and so close to home that for the first year and a half he lives with his parents, thus eliminating other possible contacts with fellow students. Even after moving into a fraternity house in the middle of his sophomore year, and learning to smoke, drink, and play poker with his fraternity brothers, he realizes that he is not completely at ease with the group. "Neale felt for them the amused scorn of the native-born great-city dweller for the uneasy provincial who thinks he can hide his provincialism best by assuming a boisterous nastiness." (P. 247.)

A very full account of Hugh Carver's problems of adjustment to life at fictional Sanford College is presented in Percy Marks's *The Plastic Age*. An earlier chapter of this study (page 46 above) mentioned Hugh's gradual adjustment to the college parties with their petting and drinking; Marks presents just as fully the problems relating to studies, athletics, religion, and fraternity life. Late in his senior year, Hugh sums up his impressions of college in a talk with some of his fellow students:

> "College is bunk," said Hugh sternly, "pure bunk. They tell us that we learn to think. Rot! I haven't learned to think; a child can solve a simple human problem as well as I can. College has played hell with me. I came here four years ago a darned nice kid, if I do say so myself. I was chock-full of ideals and illusions. Well, college has smashed most of those ideals and knocked the illusions plumb to hell." (Pp. 294–95.)

Hugh's friends, all honor students, agree that college has made them coarser but not wiser. In a seminar with a favorite English professor, they raise the question of the value of a college education; and Professor Henley's answer, extending through a ten-page chapter of the novel, seems to express the author's opinion. In brief, Henley points out that it is not college that coarsens a man and destroys his illusions; it is life. With all their faults, colleges do teach something, and the years spent in earning a degree are well spent.

A much more bitter attack on colleges, especially women's colleges, is made by Kathleen Millay, younger sister of Edna St. Vincent Millay, in *Against the Wall* (1929). Rebecca Brewster, living in a small town in Maine, receives a scholarship for Matthew College (Miss Millay attended Vassar College, which was named for Matthew Vassar) and anticipates a wonderful experience. She tries to participate fully in the college activities, but finds herself so hampered by rules, traditions, and prejudices that she is unable to learn anything really significant. In sharp contrast to this picture of a conservative Eastern campus is the remarkably full presentation of a Midwestern state university—unnamed, but obviously the University of Illinois—in Olive Deane Hormel's *Co-Ed* (1926). Lucia Leigh has been accepted as a student at Vassar, but a week-end visit to the state university, her parents' alma mater, persuades her that three years in boarding school have given her enough of life in a "hennery." At first she is interested primarily in the social opportunities of a large coeducational campus; but after a year devoted to dating, dancing, and sorority activities, she becomes aware that "about ninety per cent" of the students are more interested in preparing for future careers than they are in present good times. And so, in the course of her sophomore year, Lucia effects a transition from campus butterfly to campus leader and student. It is a rather hackneyed story, without suspense or excitement, but it gives effectively the atmosphere of the large Midwestern university.

The attacks on colleges in *The Plastic Age* and *Against the Wall* suggest a commonly-held belief regarding college novels of the twenties—that they were more concerned with sensational revelations of the wrongs in higher education than with truthful presentations of American young people. It is true that novelists of that decade were eager to show phases of life which had been concealed by earlier writers, and that the accounts of drinking and petting parties, the distorted value placed on election to clubs and fraternities, the occasional incompetence of professors and the great resistance to learning in students who were accepting their parents' support were all very startling to readers whose ideas of college life had been formed by the Frank Merriwell books and *Stover at Yale*. But most of the novels made it clear to unprejudiced readers that higher education was not a continual orgy of gin and free love, and that the blame for maladjustment in students could not always be placed on the colleges. In *This Side of Paradise*, the novel generally credited with beginning the fictional flood of campus confessions, Amory Blaine makes frequent jaunts from the Princeton campus to New York City or to New Jersey seashore resorts, enjoying himself with liquor and girls; but he preserves his virginity, makes a name for himself in literary and dramatic activities, and does reasonably well in his studies—until his junior year, when he carelessly fails a mathematics examination and becomes ineligible for extracurricular activities. In *The Beginning of Wisdom*, Philip Sellaby also makes a name for himself by writing for the Yale undergraduate publications. Although he visits rather frequently the tables down at Mory's, he does not get thoroughly drunk until the end of his junior year. He has little to do with girls and he makes good grades until his senior year, when he falls in love with a rather insignificant New Haven girl and secretly marries her. His wife dies suddenly just before examination time, and Philip leaves Yale without taking his examinations or his degree. Although Hugh Carver in *The Plastic Age* gradually succumbs to the college pastimes of drinking and petting, he has time to win a letter in track and to maintain unusually high grades for an athlete. In Robert Wolf's *Springboard*

(1927), Brian Hart, the son of a Middle Western railroad magnate, goes to Harvard with a good deal of naïveté regarding sex and "collegiate" wildness. There he learns to pet with girls of various social levels, but in his junior year he becomes engaged to a thoroughly acceptable girl who is a member of the Boston aristocracy. Meanwhile, he learns a great deal about economics, his major subject.

The novels discussed in the above paragraph all present Eastern colleges, where social life was considered to be wilder and academic life more decadent than in other parts of the country. Miss Hormel's *Co-Ed* suggests that "about ninety per cent" of the students in a large Middle Western university are interested in getting a practical as well as a cultural education, although the other ten per cent may be as wild and as thoughtlessly irresponsible as students at any Eastern college. Ruth Suckow in *The Bonney Family* gives a picture of life at a small Midwestern college, but she shows nothing at all of wild college parties. Among college novels of the twenties apparently none describes Western colleges, and the only one that presents a Southern college is Wolfe's *Look Homeward, Angel*. Though Wolfe makes it clear that the boys of the state university at "Pulpit Hill" (actually Chapel Hill, the seat of the University of North Carolina) pay frequent visits to a nearby town for drinks and women, and though he reveals the imperceptiveness of some faculty members, he places his chief emphasis not on the weaknesses of the institution but on the problems of Eugene Gant which arise from his own personality and his earlier background.

This shift of emphasis from the weaknesses of the institution to the peculiar problems of the individual is typical of the general trend in college novels beginning about 1929. In that year appeared William Faulkner's first great artistic success, *The Sound and the Fury*, in which Quentin Compson of Mississippi tries to adjust himself to New England ways at Harvard University. Faulkner suggests nothing wrong with Harvard, but brings out the difficulties faced by Quentin: the knowledge of his sister's promiscuity and her marriage to an undesirable Harvard man; his own virginity, which led some coarser Harvard classmates to speculate that he was having an affair with his roommate, Shreve; his concern over the way he should act toward Negroes in the North, and over the Northerner's opinion of a Southerner's attitude toward Negroes. In Faulkner's later novel *Absalom, Absalom!* (1936), Quentin explains to Shreve the background for some of his feeling toward the South;

123

when Shreve asks him, finally, why he hates the South, Quentin exclaims, too vehemently, that he does not hate it. This suggests that an ambivalent attitude toward his native region contributes to Quentin's difficulty in adjusting to college life: he tries to escape the South and its problems by going to a New England university, and yet he is inevitably drawn to his home state and to its indigenous attitudes which are causing him distress.

A much more comprehensive picture of Harvard students and their problems of adjustment is presented in George Anthony Weller's *Not to Eat, Not for Love* (1933). Weller uses an impressionistic technique, rather like that of Dos Passos with overtones of James Joyce and Virginia Woolf, to show a cross-section of the Harvard student body. The most fully realized character is Epes Todd, a football player who, in his junior year, is a not-quite-good-enough athlete to make the varsity and a not-quite-good-enough student to have much hope of earning his degree with distinction. He has typical student difficulties with his tutor, his roommate, and his girl friend, and settles each difficulty in a way which is neither highly satisfactory nor highly unsatisfactory. About the story of Epes Todd are woven other narratives, descriptions, and glimpses of various undergraduates, graduate assistants, faculty members, and non-academic employees of the university as they busy themselves with typical activities of the classroom, the various athletic competitions, the student publications, the clubs, and the informal social life about the Yard. The novel gives a remarkably complete picture of Harvard life, but the pointlessness of all this busy-ness in the opinion of the author is indicated by his title, taken from Emerson's *Journal*, the entry for April 11, 1834:

> Went yesterday to Cambridge and spent most of the day at Mount Auburn. . . . After much wandering and seeing many things, four snakes gliding up and down a hollow for no purpose that I could see—not to eat, not for love, but only gliding. . . .

Especially full in their treatment of individual problems at college are Vardis Fisher's *Passions Spin the Plot* (1934) and James T. Farrell's *My Days of Anger* (1943). Both novels present boys who are a little older than the average college student; Vridar Hunter is nineteen when he starts at Wasatch College in Salt Lake City, and Danny O'Neill is twenty-one when he begins attending the University of Chicago. Vridar's chief problems are his poverty and his complete ignorance of worldly ways. Because he has never had the time or the money to spend on the simplest pastimes of young people, he does not know the small talk or the social manners that would put him at ease with boys and especially girls of his own age. Seeking companionship, he is attracted to a well-dressed, good-looking sophomore who is always at ease with girls, a boy named A. M. McClintock, but known to Vridar as "Forenoon." McClintock makes use of Vridar's studiousness to save himself the trouble of doing his own assignments, and the two become close companions. Impelled partly by Forenoon's taunts and partly by his own youthful desires, Vridar is driven into stealing, drinking, brawling, and going after women—all activities which contrast strongly with the puritanical training he received on a remote Idaho farm, and all, except the last, activities which he practices with more success than misgivings. His awkwardness of appearance and manner, his ignorance of social behavior, his remnant of chivalrous idealism, and his love for a girl in Idaho all combine to thwart his efforts to make free with the girls at college, while his strong sexual impulses keep urging him on. The novel centers on Vridar's problems to such an extent that it tells nothing about the college itself, except for descriptions of a few of the professors in the second chapter; but the fact that Vridar and Forenoon can live as they do, even in a city as large as Salt Lake, without being dropped for academic or disciplinary reasons, suggests a small, struggling institution which cannot afford to lose many students.

Although the University of Chicago is a far cry from Wasatch College, and Danny O'Neill's background is as different from Vridar's as could be imagined, the problems which the two young men encounter in college are remarkably similar. Both boys have known poverty—Vridar far more than Danny—and both compensate for this to some extent by petty stealing from their employers (as also does Augie March in Saul Bellow's *The Adventures of Augie March* (1952) when he goes to the University of Chicago). Both are awkward and ill at ease with girls and are looked down upon by boys, and in compensation for their unpopularity both make fools of themselves by drinking, fighting, and otherwise conspicuous behavior. But whereas Vridar finds himself psychologically incapable of sexual intercourse with any girl but Neloa, even when the opportunity presents itself, so that he finds release through masturbation until his marriage at the age of twenty-one (see above, pp. 48–49), Danny has no particular sweetheart, and finds his sexual release with prostitutes. Both boys have had religious and puritanical upbringing, and feel qualms of conscience when they engage in discussions and activities which are common among college boys but which would bring distress to their families. Both boys find pleasure in their studies, but particularly in their composition assignments. Vridar wins some local fame from the appearance of his writings in the college paper, but he does not learn much from the experience; Danny deluges his conscientious instructor with realistic sketches of Chicago life, and after two years he feels ready to earn a living as a writer in New York.

Novels of college life published between 1920 and 1945 usually presented the sort of problems faced by normal (if somewhat unusual) students in typical college situations. Beginning about 1945, a considerable number of novels presented psychological problems of students who were abnormal in one way or another, and college situations that were far from typical. Earlier in this chapter (see p. 103 above) there was mention of *The Folded Leaf* as a novel which shows two high-school boys drawn to each other because they are not completely accepted by their fellow students. As Lymie and Spud go on to college, their attachment to each other grows stronger and becomes a latent homosexual love (see p. 57 above). Then both boys fall in love with Sally Forbes, a gay, unconventional classmate who is the daughter of one of their professors. Lymie soon realizes that Sally's love is all for Spud, but in his self-effacing way he is content to be with them and watch their happiness.

> It didn't seem to bother Spud or Sally that Lymie was with them a great deal of the time. They felt that in a way he was responsible for their happiness, and out of gratitude they included him in it. . . . Sometimes all three of them sat in a booth in the back of the Ship's Lantern, and Spud and Sally talked about the home they were going to build as soon as they got married. . . . When they grew tired of arranging the future, Spud measured his hand against Sally's . . . and was amazed each time at how much bigger a boy's hand is than a girl's. Or they sat and looked at each other and smiled and were sometimes pleased with the silence, or drove it away by talking a silly, meaningless language that they had invented between them. Because they felt free to say anything they wanted to in front of Lymie, they didn't realize that he was there, much of the time. But if he got up to go, they would get up and go with him. (Pp. 168–69.)

This strange but idyllic triangle continues for some time; but at last Spud grows jealous of Lymie over Sally's affections, and Lymie grows desperate as he finds Spud slipping away from him. When Lymie realizes that jealousy has caused Spud's former affection for him to turn to hatred, he tries to kill himself; and in the course of his long convalescence the relation between the two boys becomes a normal friendship, while the folded leaf of their undeveloped manhood unfolds into maturity.

Calder Willingham's *End as a Man* presents a normal youth in an abnormal college situation. Robert Marquales attends a college-level military academy in a Southern state which borders the Mississippi River, and is assigned to a room with an over-religious, over-sensitive, maladjusted fool known as "Sow-belly" Simmons. Sow-belly's appearance is as grotesquely offensive as his manner:

> He looked like a mule. A pale mule wearing spectacles. He had a long nose that was rounded off at the end in a remarkable way. His ears were huge and he could wiggle them. His lips were thin; he had the habit of going around with his mouth open. This was bad because his teeth were always dirty. They were large teeth, the bottom row as big as the top; they slanted outward. Simmons' voice was thick and he usually spat forth flecks of saliva when talking. His body was emaciated; the bones stuck out all over him. (Pp. 4–5.)

Sow-belly wets his bed every night, and vehemently denies that he does, despite obvious evidence to the contrary. He never bathes, because he is ashamed of being seen naked in the shower room. He ostentatiously kisses the picture of an ugly younger sister who died several years earlier, and the other cadets take delight in obscenely mutilating this photograph. Fortunately for his sanity, Marquales is not forced to continue rooming with this freak; but his contacts with less obviously abnormal fellow students are far more damaging to his developing character because their deviations are accepted and, to some extent, admired and imitated. Among the student leaders are sadists, aggressive homosexuals, dishonest gamblers; apparently the chief ambition of many of the cadets is to be admitted to the Hair of the Hound Club, whose avowed purposes are drinking, gambling, and the breaking of other academy rules; yet the faculty members seem almost completely unaware of the corrupt practices going on, and the old retired army general in command of the school insists emotionally:

> "I will not hesitate to say that I do not know of any other institution in America that can give you a more solid basis on which to construct your life. . . . No youth can pass through four years of The Academy and not end as a man." (P. 350.)

127

One of the strangest and most perplexing of college novels is Shirley Jackson's *Hangsaman*. Natalie Waite attends a small, progressive college for women, probably modeled on Bennington, Miss Jackson's own alma mater. At this unnamed institution, where all of the faculty members are men, informal and slangy conversation between faculty and students is encouraged both within and outside the classroom, and drinking and gambling are freely permitted on the campus as long as a faculty member or his wife is present. Thus it is common, and regarded as educational experience, for students and faculty to entertain each other with cocktails, sometimes in very small and intimate groups. It was mentioned in Chapter III (page 72 above) that Natalie finds in her English professor a father substitute, that she recognizes both in the professor and in her own father domineering cruelty and a pose of intellectual superiority, and that she forms a strange relationship with a perhaps nonexistent fellow student named Tony. It is this relationship that makes the novel so perplexing. From the beginning of the story Natalie holds frequent conversations with creatures of her own invention; just before going to college she experiences with one of her father's cocktail-party guests either an actual seduction or an imagined one which she herself later believes to have been real; when she finally meets Tony, it is after she has been made to feel rather gauche and unwanted by other girls in her dormitory, and it would be natural for her to invent a companion who is even less popular than herself. However, some of the things that Natalie and Tony say and do together seem too complex and too closely related to the words and actions of other characters to be purely imaginary. Toward the end of the story, Tony tries to seduce Natalie—whether to Lesbianism, to suicide, or to complete retreat from reality is not clear; but Natalie successfully resists and, walking away from Tony and the lonely wood where their night-wandering has taken them,

> she thought theatrically, I will never see Tony any more; she is gone, and knew that, theatrical or not, it was true. She had defeated her own enemy, she thought, and she would never be required to fight again, and she put her feet down tiredly in the mud and thought, What did I do wrong? (P. 276.)

Whatever it is that actually happens, it is clear that an intelligent and sensitive girl experiences something of a retreat from life as a result of disturbing contacts at college after an unsatisfactory family relationship, and that she narrowly escapes complete insanity or death.

Ralph Ellison's *Invisible Man* (1952) presents a situation which may be familiar to Negroes in segregated colleges, but it is not often encountered by white people either in fiction or in real life. The unnamed narrator-protagonist, upon his graduation from a Southern high school, receives a scholarship to a Negro college; at first he is impressed by the beautiful buildings, the inspirational talks in chapel, the opportunities that are supposedly offered here for Negroes to better themselves; but in his junior year he learns that the talks are designed to mislead both the students and the wealthy white men who support the school, and that the alumni, rather than benefiting from their education, find themselves persecuted for it unless they can learn to accept the artificial limitations traditionally assigned to them and to feign inferiority to the most ignorant of white people. He is dismissed from college when he inadvertently allows a Northern white trustee to discover how ineffective the college is in raising the standards of Negroes in the area, and it seems to the boy that the impressive statue of the revered founder lifting the veil from the eyes of a kneeling slave could just as well symbolize a lowering of the veil more firmly into place.

Two novels of the fifties, with settings on opposite coasts and presenting very different aspects of college life, are alike in that they both feature undergraduate love affairs leading to unwanted pregnancies, with mental instability in the girls. Against a realistic background of academic perplexities and fraternity informalities, C. G. Lumbard's *Senior Spring* (1954) describes the love of Steve Burnett and Cassy Kane in their senior year on a California campus—presumably that of the University of California at Berkeley. Though Steve is fascinated by Cassy's "sexy" appearance and amorous appetite, he is reluctant to go beyond heavy petting with her; and when, at Cassy's urging, they do spend a week end together, he is very careful to obtain and use contraceptive devices. Thus he is greatly perturbed and somewhat skeptical to learn, a few weeks before commencement, that Cassy is pregnant. He feels strongly that they should not marry until he is established in his profession; and when he learns some of the startling facts about her past, he stops seeing her and concentrates on his studies. But he cannot forget her, and when he tries to get in touch with her again, he finds that she has left college because of a nervous breakdown and has tried to commit suicide. Pamela Oldenburg, in Julian Halevy's *The Young Lovers* (1955), reveals her mental disturbance very early in the novel. Eddie Slocum, appropriately known as "the Groper," finds her suffering from amnesia in a New York subway and brings her to the Greenwich Village studio apartment that he shares with two fellow sophomores of Washington Square College, New York University. With the help of Eddie's practical roommate Doc, Pam recalls her name and her New York address, the fact that she is a student at an uptown art institute, and that her amnesia was caused by the shock of receiving a suicide letter from her mother in California. The fumbling but tender love affair of the two pathetically impractical young students is presented against a varied background, which includes the "campus" activities of a campus-less college, wild parties of Greenwich Village bohemians, an idyllic week end in the country, and the strangely-assorted, well-meaning friends of both Pam and Eddie. Faced with uncertainty about his future career, with the danger of failing college courses, and with the very pressing threat of compulsory military service, the Groper can only suggest an abortion when Pam proudly announces her pregnancy, and this shock again sends her into amnesia. But he faces his problems with new-found maturity, and the novel ends, a little too neatly and easily, with reasonable prospects for a happy future.

Charles Thompson's *Halfway Down the Stairs* (1957) is somewhat reminiscent of *Senior Spring* in that it presents an attractive, sex-hungry coed in an affair with a relatively inexperienced college boy, this time at Cornell University. Dave Pope, the narrator-protagonist, looks back from a few years after graduation, recalling his undergraduate days about the time of the Korean War, the insecurity and irresponsibility of the students in general, and his own particular sense of inferiority as a small-town boy on a sophisticated campus. The picture of college life is wilder, more desperate, and more "beat" than those drawn by Lumbard and Halevy; Thompson explains in a foreword that his description of Cornell "was true, at one time in the past, for one small element of students. The element has no counterpart there now."

Two recent novelists reveal close-ups of "beat generation" college life by detailing each a single wild week end at universities which probably represent Ohio State and Yale, respectively. In Nolan Miller's *Why I Am So Beat* (1954), eighteen-year-old Mark Gillis and a more experienced friend, Marty Feldman, spend their week end with Monica, the forward female editor of the college magazine, and Jane, a young streetwalker who takes her baby with her. Mark worries about the draft and about his inability to sublimate sex into poetry. The style suggests an older and somewhat more sophisticated Holden Caulfield, and the total effect is comical but not especially convincing. Much more realistic and disturbing is Richard Frede's *Entry E* (1958). Ed Bogard is a junior at "Hayden University," and he prides himself on maintaining a dispassionate attitude toward life while conforming outwardly to the standards of behavior that are expected of him. On the week end of the Princeton football game he tries to catch up on his back work in architecture courses while the other residents of his entry (that is, his section of a dormitory) engage in exorbitant drinking, ending with the drugging and mass raping of an over-willing but underaged girl from New York. Ed tries to keep the party from getting out of hand, but he does not want to get himself involved, and he believes that to call the campus police would be contrary to the code of undergraduate behavior. When the other men of Entry E are expelled because of the week-end activities, Ed is asked to withdraw. The dean of the Undergraduate College tells him:

> "I maintain that your inability to keep up with your assignments is much the same sort of inability you exhibited Saturday night to take what I assume was the proper course. . . . They were both matters of lack of concern." (Pp. 242–43.)

Later in the interview, the dean adds:

> "You don't seem to have a single conviction to your name—just a book of etiquette, or a book of parliamentary procedures. . . . By the way, *Time* called you 'The Silent Generation.' I prefer, The Indifferent Generation." (P. 245.)

A few other college novels of the fifties deserve brief comment. Glenn Scott wrote his unusually perceptive first novel, *A Sound of Voices Dying* (1954), while he was still an undergraduate at Washington and Lee—apparently the institution that he calls "Philips-Whitehead" in his story. Reid Carrington, the central figure, matures greatly during his freshman year, under the stimulus of liberal arts courses, intellectual conversations with boys from other parts of the country, and a love affair with the disillusioned wife of a self-centered fraternity brother. Two novels deal with the problems of students of foreign background in adjusting to American college life: Irving Shulman's *Good Deeds Must Be Punished* (1956) shows an American army veteran of Italian parentage experiencing social discrimination on the campus of a small coed college in West Virginia; and Peter Sourian's *Miri* (1957) tells of the complex, interwoven relationships of three college students, revealed through a narrative by each—the Greek immigrant girl and war orphan Miri who attends college in Boston, her wealthy cousin Lexy, and Lexy's Harvard roommate Josh Bigelow. Robert Gutwillig's *After Long Silence* (1958) pictures very fully the unconventional actions of two boys in a large coed university in Connecticut who try to find the good life in freedom of intellect, alcohol, and sex. Speaking of his experiences with his friend Chris Hunt, who somewhat resembles Dean Moriarty in Jack Kerouac's famous "beat" novel *On the Road*, the narrator Tom Freeman says:

> Arden is a big university, and as in other large universities I know of, what you make of yourself is pretty much up to you. Chris and I thought we knew what we were doing there. We thought we could get a good education, if only by the process of osmosis, and have a good time. Everything in its proper perspective, we thought—good classes, good teachers, good books, good parties, good girls, good times. Somehow it didn't work out that way. . . . I used to operate on the theory that "something would always turn up." But now I know that things will never turn out unless you make them turn out, and nothing will ever really "turn up" by itself. To have learned just this at the cost of multiple personal disappointments does not seem to me much of an achievement. (Pp. 5–6.)

This theory of getting a college education through osmosis, with plenty of good parties and good times, appears also in two novels of 1960: Vance Bourjaily's *Confessions of a Spent Youth* and Glendon Swarthout's *Where the Boys Are*. The former tells how its narrator-protagonist, U.S. D. Quincy, spends two years in a New England college modeled on the ivy-league school, joins a fashionable fraternity, devotes most of his time to drinking, gambling, and wild escapades, and studies just enough to be allowed to stay in classes. Swarthout's novel describes the recent college custom of spending spring vacation in Fort Lauderdale, Florida. The narrator is a freshman girl from a Midwestern university, participating for the first time in the annual student pilgrimage.

The above comments on various novels selected from the large mass of contemporary college fiction have cited specific examples of the kinds of problems that arise from the conditions mentioned at the beginning of this discussion (above, pp. 119–20). There has been little attempt to classify the novels according to the type of problems treated because these problems are so diverse in each novel. In a few works the problems are more specialized: Mildred Gilman's *Fig Leaves* (1925) and Peggy Goodin's *Take Care of My Little Girl* (1950) both show college girls fighting against the evils of the sorority system; John R. Tunis' *The Iron Duke* (1938) and Millard Lampell's *The Hero* (1949) present problems of big-time college athletics; Michael Amrine's *All Sons Must Say Goodbye* (1942), LaMar Warrick's *Yesterday's Children* (1943), and William Kehoe's *A Sweep of Dusk* (1945) emphasize the college student's break with his home and family and the development of his own individuality. But even in these novels the problems are far more varied and complex than this classification seems to indicate.

One rather striking fact about the college novels in this study is that almost none of them show college life earlier than 1910. A considerable number of them describe campus activities just prior to World War I, and many of these indicate the drastic effect which the sudden departure of thousands of men had upon the students who remained. But among all the recent novelists who have portrayed adolescents at the turn of the century or earlier, there are none who give more than brief mention of college life of these times. This study revealed only two novels, both published in 1923, which make any reference to college days before 1910: in Floyd Dell's *Janet March*, Roger Leland progresses studiously through a small denominational college in Minnesota, scorning all college activities and spending what free time he has selling books in a department store; in Edgar Lee Masters' *Skeeters Kirby*, the narrator-protagonist spends one very studious year at the University of Illinois without any noteworthy incident other than a landlady's futile attempt to seduce him. It is hard to account for this neglect of early campus life in modern American fiction; it is possible, though it hardly seems

133

probable, that the great success of Fitzgerald's *This Side of Paradise* discouraged competition from older writers who might have recalled college activities of a decade or more prior to World War I.

The relative frequency of college novels set in various regions corresponds roughly with the relative importance placed on higher education by the people of those regions. According to a survey made in 1952, 36 per cent of all American college graduates come from the East (New England and the Middle Atlantic states), which contains about 26 per cent of the total United States population; 34 per cent of the college graduates come from the Midwest, containing 30 per cent of the total population; 20 per cent of college graduates come from the South, containing 31 per cent of the population; and 10 per cent of the college graduates are from the West, which contains 13 per cent of the population.[10] Almost half of the college novels are set on Eastern campuses, a considerable number are set on Midwestern campuses, comparatively few on Southern campuses, and very few on Western—mostly in California. Harvard provides the setting for far more novels than does any other campus, with Yale and Princeton, in that order, following in popularity. Much the same sort of activities and problems are presented in the colleges of all regions, but women's colleges do not place nearly as much stress on athletics as do men's and coeducational institutions. Midwestern colleges, especially the smaller ones, do not tolerate wild parties as much as those of the other regions, while the Eastern colleges seem to stress higher academic standards, keener competition for extracurricular honors, and greater emphasis on social prestige than do those of other regions.

The novels of private-school life, like private schools in actuality, are almost entirely concentrated in the East; boarding schools are most likely to be in Massachusetts or Connecticut, whereas private day schools are frequently in New York City. A few novels show private schools in the South, the Midwest, or California. Public schools, of course, are plentiful all over the country, but the majority of novels emphasizing problems in public schools seem to have settings in the Midwest, while a considerable number are in the East. Adolescents who leave school early or avoid it entirely are most likely to be in rural areas of the South.

Grouped according to decades, both school and college novels show about the same trends that have been noted in other novels of adolescence: those of the twenties seem to stress a new frankness in discussing school problems which the genteel tradition had preferred to ignore; those of the thirties either present these problems still more frankly and in fuller detail, or return to the humorous, condescending attitude of the *Penrod* period; novels of the forties are still more frank, but symbolism and depth psychology appear as frequently as naturalism; and the novels of the fifties are likely to stress abnormal situations and "beat" attitudes. Throughout the entire period, college novels show greater extremes of individual behavior than do the high-school and preparatory-school novels, with more frequent and more serious decisions depending on the adolescent himself, and considerably less guidance from parents and teachers. Progressively throughout the period the novels tend to treat smaller aspects of school and college life in greater detail: early school-and-college novels, like *This Side of Paradise* and *The Beginning of Wisdom,* devote only a chapter or so to school and only a few chapters to college, with about half the book devoted to postgraduate years; but novels of the fifties usually present anything from two or three days to eight or nine months in their protagonists' academic careers. Yet some novels of the late fifties, like John O'Hara's *From the Terrace* (1958) and Herbert Gold's *The Optimist* (1959), return to the Fitzgerald pattern, devoting a chapter or two to prep school and a few chapters to college in an extended account of the protagonist's life. Since school and college play a large part in the life of almost any adolescent, it is not surprising that approximately three-quarters of the novels of adolescence in each decade of this study devote considerable attention to student problems.

Chapter V

FACING THE FUTURE: VOCATION AND *WELTANSCHAUUNG*

One of the great problem areas of adolescents is that of preparation for assuming full responsibility as adults. This involves both the finding of a vocation or means of earning a livelihood and the developing of some acceptable concept of what life is all about. In the first category, it is not surprising that the protagonists in most of the novels of adolescence have a calling to follow one or more of the fine arts; since these novels have a tendency to be autobiographical, it is also predictable that more of the protagonists are planning to be writers than to be any one other kind of artist. It is somewhat surprising that music, the visual arts (painting, architecture, pottery and sculpture), and acting, in that order, follow so closely behind writing in popularity that, taken all together, they appeal to almost twice as many protagonists as does literature. Of course a great many protagonists prepare for other professions or occupations—business, law, medicine, teaching, and farming seem to be most common—and some who want to be artists find it necessary or advisable to have another occupation which will supplement their income.

In the second category—the finding of a meaning for life—a number of fictional adolescents are content with a life purpose which they create or discover in their own dreams. They may in time discard such personal ontologies for concepts more conformable with reality or with the ideas accepted by society, or they may reject the evidences of the senses and popular opinions in order to cling to their dream concepts. In some cases, of course, the conflict between incompatible metaphysical ideas leads to serious mental disturbances. Very often the doctrines of an established religion may aid an adolescent in working out an acceptable meaning for life, but just as often the conflict between different religious doctrines or between the teachings of religion and those of science may bring additional problems. Many adolescents in twentieth-century novels work out an agnostic or atheistic *weltanschauung* which fits observable facts as well as personal ideals.

Two of the earliest novels considered in this study—*Moon-Calf* and *This Side of Paradise*—present protagonists who seem destined to be writers. Felix Fay of *Moon-Calf* writes his first story and begins to write a novel when he is ten years old. His interest in such activities sets him apart from other boys, in his own mind even more than in reality. When his school principal catches him designing a brass plate for his birthplace—"Felix Fay, the Great Novelist, was born here, May 10, 1886" (p. 60)—and exposes his egotism to the class, Felix is so angry and embarrassed that he resolves never to write another line; but his literary urge is too strong to be thus easily quelled, and he is motivated by its drive throughout the rest of this novel and its sequel, *The Briary-Bush*. Amory Blaine in *This Side of Paradise* is much less dedicated to establishing himself in a literary career than is Felix; Fitzgerald describes his literary activities at Princeton and afterward, but these are dilettantish, and at the end of the novel, a year and a half after he has left Princeton, Amory is still uncertain about his future. More interesting than the poetic juvenilia attributed to Felix and Amory are those which Stephen Vincent Benét offers in *The Beginning of Wisdom* (1921) as the early work of his protagonist, Philip Sellaby; for Benét is a far better poet than either Dell or Fitzgerald. Philip, like Felix, is driven by impulses of poetic creativity and by the desire to correct social injustices, both through direct action and through the use of his literary talents. Benét's account covers a slightly longer expanse of years than does either Dell's or Fitzgerald's; Philip is in his late twenties when he finally finds himself both as a poet and as an adult.

In *Souvenir* (1929), a sequel to both *Moon-Calf* and *The Briary-Bush*, Dell again treats of the adolescent who aspires to become a writer. The events take place a generation later than those in the earlier novels: Felix Fay, a successful, middle-aged playwright living happily with his second wife in a New York suburb, is unexpectedly reunited with his nineteen-year-old son Prentiss, the offspring of the ill-fated marriage described in *The Briary-Bush*, and tries to help the young man realize his own literary aspirations. Again and again Felix sees in Prentiss' problems "souvenirs"

138

of the problems he himself faced; but each time he is forced to recognize, and at last with finality, that his own hard-won wisdom is of little value to his son—that each adolescent must discover again the meaning of life and the application of his talents.

Wolfe in *Look Homeward, Angel* attributes to Eugene Gant a precocious passion for letters beginning in infancy. Even as he lay helpless in his crib, Eugene

> was in agony because he was poverty-stricken in symbols: his mind was caught in a net because he had no words to work with. He had not even names for the objects around him: he probably defined them for himself by some jargon, reinforced by some mangling of the speech that roared about him, to which he listened intently day after day, realizing that his first escape must come through language. He indicated as quickly as he could his ravenous hunger for pictures and print: sometimes they brought him great books profusely illustrated, and he bribed them desperately by cooing, shrieking with delight, making extravagant faces, and doing all the other things they understood in him. He wondered savagely how they would feel if they knew what he really thought. . . . (P. 37.)

When he was old enough to crawl about on the floor, his favorite toys were letter blocks, which he loved to study and handle, "knowing that he had here the stones of the temple of language." (P. 39). Whether this amazingly early devotion to language is meant to be taken literally or symbolically, it foreshadows one of the great passions of his adolescence. When, at the age of twelve, he transfers to a new private school in his home town, Headmaster Leonard's wife guides him through the masterpieces of English poetry; and his study of German, Latin, and Greek introduces him to some of the great works of foreign literature. All of these, Wolfe implies, Eugene understands with far keener insight than do his teachers, with the possible exception of Mrs. Leonard. At the state university he continues his voracious reading of English, Latin, and Greek classics, but the novel tells very little of his creative impulses and efforts. Brief mention is made of his participation in various campus literary activities, of his editing the college paper in his senior year and writing the class poem for commencement, but he seems far more interested in studying literature than in producing it. When he graduates, at the age of nineteen, he is unable to make any decisions regarding his life's work beyond rejecting his father's plan that he make a career in law and politics and his mother's ambition for his success in business or journalism. He welcomes a professor's suggestion that he take a year of graduate work at Harvard, which Mrs. Gant is willing to finance; and it is only in Wolfe's next novel, *Of Time and the River* (1937) that Eugene seriously undertakes a writing career.

Vridar Hunter, of Vardis Fisher's *In Tragic Life* (1932), resembles Felix Fay in his youthful desire to use his writing ability to help usher in the socialistic millenium. Since his energy far exceeds his discrimination, he produces during his seventeenth year—his first year of high school—hundreds of typewritten pages of verse and a complete novel, all strongly influenced by his strangely mixed and very limited reading: religious tracts, Socialistic periodicals, and third-rate sentimental literature. For several weeks he makes a daily practice of hanging an unsigned copy of one of his poems on the blackboard before the students enter; but he stops when the principal, who knows of Vridar's secret ambition, kindly warns him that the whole school is ridiculing the anonymous but persistent poet. In Fisher's next novel, *Passions Spin the Plot*, Vridar is a college student; as he becomes familiar with classics of literature, he begins to question his own power to produce work of value, and decides that he will be a college professor rather than a writer. It is not until the final volume of the tetralogy (*No Villain Need Be*, 1936), when Vridar is well past adolescence, that he becomes both a writer and a professor.

The novels of the twenties and thirties which present female literary aspirants are not nearly as original or as impressive as those which present males. Among the more important accounts of girls who want to write are Helen Woodbury's *The Misty Flats* (1925) and Margery Latimer's *This Is My Body* (1930). In the former, Linda Bradley's problems in trying to become a writer are related to and subordinated to the problems presented by her demanding mother, which have already been described in Chapter III (above, p. 67). In Miss Latimer's novel, Megan Foster finds in writing a release for the emotional intensity that brings her into conflict with her own family and with fellow students and authorities at college. Like Linda Bradley, Megan has a love affair in Greenwich Village, where she goes to establish herself as a writer; but whereas Linda sacrifices both a suitable love and a promising career for the sake of filial duty, Megan defies society's various calls to duty for the sake of love and literary success, and she fails in every respect.

In contrast to the somber earnestness of the novels just discussed, several novels of the thirties and early forties presented optimistic and rather light-hearted pictures of literary adolescents. Florence Ryerson and Colin Clements' *This Awful Age* (1930) and its sequel, *Mild Oats* (1933), describe Jane Jones, who at fifteen undertakes to write a tragic problem novel and at sixteen decides to write great poetry which will rival that of Ella Wheeler Wilcox. The authors, who are hubsand and wife, treat Jane's efforts with the same sort of amused and tolerant affection that Booth Tarkington showed toward his Willie Baxter in *Seventeen*. William Saroyan in *My Name Is Aram* (1940) humorously hints at his protagonist's literary aspirations when Aram's third-grade teacher refers to him as "one of our future poets." A less humorous but more sentimental treatment of a would-be author appears in Betty Smith's *A Tree Grows in Brooklyn* (1943). Francie Nolan at fourteen receives excellent grades on her eighth-grade compositions and is encouraged to write the graduation play for her class; but when Francie begins to write compositions based on the poverty and drunkenness she has seen in her own family, the teacher tells her that ugly subjects are not suitable for writers, and that her play cannot be used because it mentions an ash can.

> Miss Garnder handed her the "sordid" compositions and the play, saying, "When you get home, burn these in the stove. Apply the match to them yourself. And as the flames rise, keep saying: 'I am burning ugliness. I am burning ugliness.'" (P. 278.)

When Francie gets home, instead of burning the offending papers she begins to write a novel full of the kind of fanciful beauty Miss Garnder admires. But after writing twenty pages, she realizes that she is simply inverting her true thoughts about poverty and making them into lies. Saving out her four realistic compositions, she burns all her "A" papers and her just-started novel, saying, "I am burning ugliness." (P. 282.)

Most of the novels of the forties and fifties treat young would-be writers seriously and sympathetically; they differ from most novels of the twenties and thirties in placing less emphasis on the sociological aims and more on the psychological struggles of the aspirant artists. Farrell's *My Days of Anger* (1943) is a striking exception; this last of the Danny O'Neill tetralogy is more typical of novels of the thirties, when the series was begun. Encouraged by a sympathetic professor at the University of Chicago, and driven both by a tireless creative urge and a rage at social conditions that have damaged or destroyed many of his family and friends in the city, Danny pours out hundreds of pages of naturalistic writing, and at last feels confidence enough in his ability to try to make a new life for himself in New York. Forrest Rosaire's *East of Midnight* (1945) presents a rather lurid tale of psychological traumata of adolescent artists resulting in tragedy in their adult lives. From childhood, Grey Manning dreams and writes of knights in armor rescuing damsels in distress; but at sixteen he accidentally causes the permanent crippling of a potentially great young dancer, Dru Praynor, whom he worships as the embodiment of all the romantic qualities of womanhood. Some years later, as a successful novelist, he is amazed at her generosity in being willing to marry him; but Dru, half crazed by a sense of Grey's wrong to her and by a sense of her own guilt for her mother's accidental death, uses the marriage to wreck her husband's career. Two less important novels of the forties present milder psychological problems: Phillis Whitney's *Willow Hill* (1947) shows a white girl, Val Coleman, in a formerly all-white high school, losing the treasured editorship of the school paper to Mary Evans, one of the newly admitted Negro students; and Charles Norman's *The Well of the Past* (1949) tells of poetic young David Gerald revolting against the Philistine attitudes of the Manhattan neighborhood where he grows up, and particularly that of his narrow-minded clergyman father.

Earlier chapters of this study have told about two outstanding novels of the early fifties dealing with adolescent girls who want to write: Shirley Jackson's *Hangsaman* (see above, pages 72 and 128), in which Natalie Waite's writing talent is so closely supervised by her literary-critic father that she escapes by retiring more and more into the world of her own imagination; and Jessamyn West's *Cress Delahanty* (see above, pp. 32, 43, and 103), in which Cress goes through her own distinctive versions of the typical stages of budding authorship, from romantic daydreams and avant-garde poetry at thirteen through earnest high-school journalism to the affected preciosity of a talented college freshman. Three novels of considerably less literary merit also stress psychological problems of incipient writers: William DuBois' *A Season to Beware* (1956) tells of Dave Story and Tony Cole alternately helping each other to become established writers and competing with each other for the love of Julia Peck; Grace Metalious' *Peyton Place* (1956) describes Allison MacKenzie's adolescent ventures into fiction-writing, which she combines with reactions against her mother's over-protectiveness against sexual experience; and Jack Kerouac's *On the Road* (1957) narrates the auctorial, amatory, and anti-social adventures of the literary juvenile delinquent Dean Moriarty and his older but still adolescent-behaving friend, the narrator Sal Paradise. A strange psychological compulsion to write appears in Clinton Williams, the adolescent narrator of James Leo Herlihy's *All Fall Down* (1960). At the age of fourteen Clint stops going to school and spends all his days recording in notebooks the conversations that he hears and incidents and thoughts that occur to him. He fills hundreds of notebooks, not with fiction or poetry, but with details of his own life and the lives of those about him.

The shift of emphasis from sociology to psychology is the most striking trend in the novels of would-be writers throughout the years covered by this study; but it is by no means the only observable trend, nor is it without notable exceptions. Early novels like *Moon-Calf* and *The Misty Flats* show strong influence of Freudian psychology, and late novels like *Peyton Place* and *On the Road* show awareness of social problems. Other trends include a slight decrease in strictly autobiographical elements, increasing intensity of analysis of problems and motives covering decreasing periods of time in the lives presented, and an increase in the proportion of serious and original novels by women in comparison to those by men. All of these trends reflect the general trends of the times and the constant search for fresh fictional material. During the decade following World War I and the decade of the Great Depression, intellectuals of America were consecrated to a frank investigation of incidents in childhood and adolescence, and the conditions of society in general, which produced various problems of adult life. Most convenient for them to investigate were the incidents of their own early years and the social conditions that surrounded them. Since they were interested in both causes and effects, the novelists of the twenties tried to cover a considerable span of years, reaching from childhood well into maturity. But by 1930 the autobiographical novel of a developing writer had become a commonplace in American literature; and the multivolume works of Wolfe, Farrell, and Fisher, published mostly during the thirties, made even full and rather detailed studies of such lives a familiar formula by the early 1940's. To find fresh fictional material from their own limited experience, young novelists could then either limit their studies to shorter intervals of life, giving even greater detail and exploring deeper psychological levels, or they could vary the auto-

143

biographical formula by mixing a larger proportion of invention with their facts, often replacing the young writer with another kind of artist of equal sensitivity. Actually, both methods were used. The number of novels featuring young writers remains fairly constant through the period, while the total number of novels of adolescence increases almost steadily, and the number featuring young artists in other fields increases greatly after 1930, and still more after 1940.

WOULD-BE MUSICIANS

Novels about young musicians appear early and frequently. Heywood Broun's *The Boy Grew Older* (1922) tells of Pat Neale, who is brought up by his sports-writer father because his musical-comedy-star mother left family responsibilities to return to the stage immediately after Pat's birth. Peter is determined to make his son into an athlete and a newspaperman, but Pat shares his mother's love of music and her talent for singing, and of course it is the natural ability rather than the paternal influence that finally determines the boy's career. Broun, a newspaperman himself, presented the conflict from the father's point of view, but the son's problems are apparent.

In Ruth Suckow's *The Bonney Family* (1928), musical talent helps one adolescent to solve his greatest problem but contributes to another's tragic end. Warren Bonney, throughout high school and his first years of college, is tremendously self-conscious about his tall, thin figure, his conspicuous red hair, and his general awkwardness of appearance; but his genuine ability as a violin soloist and as a member of the much-respected college glee club gives him prestige and poise to help him withstand and overcome the teasing of his classmates until his figure fills out and he gains enough mature dignity to become an object of admiration and envy rather than one of ridicule. Warren's friend Donald Satterley, however, torn between the exacting demands of his Latin-professor father and the pampering of his erratically brilliant mother, finds that his undisciplined talent as a pianist brings him an unhealthy and somewhat undeserved adulation and makes it almost impossible for him to undergo the rigorous drilling on fundamentals which would be required before his talent could be fully realized. This conflict, both inner and outer, between the impulses of genius and the demands of discipline, makes Donald's life intolerable and drives him eventually to suicide.

Since music and acting both involve performances before the public, it is not unusual for both to be treated in the same novel, and often both arts appeal to the same individual. In Helen Carlisle's *The Merry, Merry Maidens* (1937), a mother tells her high-school-age daughter about her own high-school days with a club of six girls, and about the problems each girl faced; one sought a career as a concert musician, and another became an actress. In Anne Miller Downes's *Until the Shearing* (1940), Felix Thorpe inherits from his mother an aptitude for music and acting; but after the early deaths of both parents, he is brought up by his grandfather Thorpe, who instills in him a sense of practical realism and of family loyalty. After working his way through college by playing in a dance orchestra, Felix goes to work in his Uncle Henry's bank; but, like Pat Neale in Heywood Broun's novel, he finds that the call of talent is stronger than the call of duty, and he leaves the bank to go on the stage. In Madeleine L'Engle's *The Small Rain* (1945), Katherine Forrester grows up in a world of stage people and musicians. At the beginning of her career as a concert pianist, she falls in love with the actor Pete Burns, but the hours that each of them must spend in practice keep them apart so much that eventually she loses Pete to an actress.

Frances Frost's *Yoke of Stars* (1939) presents seven-year intervals in the life of Judith York, a composer, and at each interval Judith is torn between the impulses of her artistic nature and the common sense of her Vermont heritage and environment. At the ages of seven and fourteen, Judy has to fight the exacting demands of her neurotic mother in order to find time for music; at twenty-one, she is torn between love of music and love for a young man; after marrying the wrong man, she finds that her family and her neighbors conflict with her career as a composer. Thus, as in most of the novels about young artists, the protagonist is faced repeatedly if not continuously with strong forces that oppose her artistic impulses.

Carson McCullers' *The Heart Is a Lonely Hunter* (1940) shows Mick Kelly at twelve, undecided whether she will be a famous author, a great musician, a successful painter, or a resourceful inventor. With great earnestness but with little help or understanding, she pursues each of these ambitions, but decides at last, "Nothing was really as good as music." (P. 44). Having almost no money, she tries to make herself a violin out of an old cracked ukulele, goes without lunches in order to pay a classmate fifty cents a week for piano lessons, and creeps through the twilight to hide in the shrubbery near houses whose inhabitants have radios tuned to symphony broadcasts.

Walter Van Tilburg Clark's *The City of Trembling Leaves* (1945) traces the adolescent years of two young artists in Reno, Nevada: Tim Hazard, the protagonist, becomes a composer, and his closest friend, Lawrence Black, seeks the fulfillment of his artistic passion through painting. The narrator is their mutual friend Walter Clark, a novelist, who makes no mention of his own early struggles, but concentrates on those of Tim and Lawrence; yet the creative pangs are so thoroughly and so feelingly described that the reader strongly suspects Clark of transcribing his own artistic growth into terms of music and painting. Like Mrs. McCullers' Mick Kelly, Tim shows early interest and aptitude in art, literature, and music, but finds music the most satisfying. Until he is about thirteen, his musical instruction comes only from his public-school teachers, who give him extra attention in recognition of his ability; but his hobby leads him at last into friendship with a classmate who is the son of a music-loving Jewish pawnbroker, and the father gives Timmy both expert instruction and an excellent violin. But the boy's chief interests throughout high school are in girls and sports; though music remains one of his favorite pastimes and a means of earning money through playing the trumpet at dances, it is only in his adult years that the urge to compose becomes one of the most powerful forces in his life. The novel is reminiscent of the fiction of Thomas Wolfe in that it is long and diffuse, and it presents a young protagonist hounded by many compelling passions.

A young person of varied artistic talents also appears in *Sarah* (1949), by Margueritte Harmon Bro. When Sarah is eleven, her father dies after urging her to make a career of her talent for painting. She tries hard to fulfill his ambition for her, but realizes at last that music rather than art is her forte. For a while she studies singing, but when it becomes apparent that her voice is not good enough to assure her conspicuous success, she becomes a concert pianist. Like Judith York in Miss Frost's *Yoke of Stars*, Mrs. Bro's heroine finds that marriage, though it answers her needs as a person, prevents her becoming as successful in her career as her talent promises.

It has been noted (pp. 143–44 above) that after a number of novelists of the twenties and thirties have represented the normal development of young people in any area of experience, novelists of the forties and fifties are likely to show deeper psychological levels or abnormal psychological development of adolescents in the same area. Some of the deeper psychological levels in an adolescent musician appear in Jane Mayhall's *Cousin to Human* (1960), wherein a fifteen-year-old Louisville girl, Lacy Cole, is faced with the double problem of developing her talent and overcoming misunderstandings. Two novels of the fifties present the abnormal psychological development of two young musicians: Douglass Wallop's *Night Light* (1953), which was mentioned in Chapter III of this study (see p. 92 above), and Evan Hunter's *Second Ending* (1958). The former tells of Alfie Lambert, who, his home life destroyed by an unsympathetic stepmother, finds some measure of self-realization in progressive jazz. At sixteen he is drummer for a band of bop musicians; but his failure to find satisfaction through this outlet leads him to senseless murder and suicide. *Second Ending* tells of four young people, one of whom is a jazz trumpet player. At fifteen, Andy Silvera is a shy boy, finding his greatest excitement in the wild, heady music of the dance band for which he plays. Then he turns to drugs to help create in himself the mood for the music he must play; by the time he is eighteen he is a hopeless addict, and at twenty he dies from the effects of his drug habit. Neither of these novels is an outstanding literary achievement, but both of them, in describing the lives of young musicians, present aspects which better novels omit.

WOULD-BE PAINTERS, ARCHITECTS, ETC.

Painters, like writers but unlike musicians and actors, produce their work in private and let the public see only the results. Thus they do not have the knowledge of the public's approval and encouragement while they are working, and they are likely to be discouraged by this uncertainty as well as by their inability to achieve the effects they have envisioned for themselves. Like artists of all kinds, they run constantly into conflict with the prosaic and unimaginative standards of most of the people about them. In Anne Parrish's *The Methodist Faun* (1929), young Cliff Hunter lacks the ability to become a really successful painter, but he has enough artistic sense to rebel against his mother's unaesthetic, narrow-minded, small-town Methodism, finding some satisfaction by working in his father's photographic shop, and actually going to New York to study painting before marriage brings him back to the very kind of narrow life he has been trying to escape. Similarly, Richard Melville in Alexander Laing's *An End of Roaming* (1930) has enough of the aesthetic creative impulse to rebel against the pragmatic ideals of his businessman father and to reject the career in science which his love of chemistry might make feasible. Adopting a bohemian way of life, he is expelled from college, attends art school, goes to sea to escape amatory entanglements and find true aesthetic experience, and paints enough pictures to have one successful exhibit before he decides to abandon the uncertainties of an artist's life and takes a job in a chemistry laboratory.

A more consecrated artist is Neil Glass in Harry Lee's *Fox in the Cloak* (1938). The title comes from the Greek fable of the Spartan boy who kept a stolen fox concealed in his cloak, not daring to reveal its presence though it constantly gnawed at his body. Of course the fox is represented in the novel by the desire to paint, which Neil keeps hidden, in spite of pain, because such an interest is incongruous both with the Southern aristocratic tradition of his family and the plutocratic tradition of boom-time Atlanta, where his father is a talented though erratic automobile salesman. The father's increasing drunkenness leads the family into poverty, which first the mother and then Neil himself must struggle to overcome. Neil sees a talented artist friend give up art to work in a butcher shop, and he himself is offered work as a department-store window-dresser; but still the fox in his cloak keeps him painting and enables him to succeed in spite of the hostility of his environment, his need for financial security, the rather overpowering devotion of his mother, and his youthful desire to marry a pretty but shallow girl. The author of the novel is a painter who grew up in Atlanta, and he is able to present such a character more fully, convincingly, and sympathetically than is either Miss Parrish or Mr. Laing.

The problems of the painter Lawrence Black in Clark's *The City of Trembling Leaves* are presented much less fully than those of the musician Tim Hazard, though they seem to be at least as great. The two become close friends during one summer of their adolescence, but Lawrence goes away to school, and the reader does not encounter him again until he is a man. As he wanders in and out of the story, he shows anguish of frustration because his pictures do not fully realize his visions, and he is acutely sensitive because his low earning power forces him to live off the wealth of his beautiful and devoted wife. It is safe to assume that such torments have also marked his adolescence, but they can only be imagined. The hopes and despairs of a young artist are more fully described in George Sklar's *The Two Worlds of Johnny Truro* (1947), but here the presentation is not thoroughly convincing (see p. 42 above for other comments on this novel).

In Gore Vidal's *The Season of Comfort* (1949), young Bill Giraud's devotion to painting is one of the many points of contention between the youth and his mother, but it is also one of the means by which he finally succeeds in severing the silver cord. Bill's father, Stephen Giraud, had abandoned painting many years earlier because his domineering wife and her prominent-statesman father had considered it an unworthy occupation. When Bill, during adolescence, shows great interest and talent in painting, his mother tries to compel him also to give it up. Though Bill is abnormally distressed by his own defiance of his mother's wishes, he refuses to forsake this talent; and eventually his success in the forbidden art, added to a promising love affair after a prolonged period of mother-fixation and sexual inversion, gives him the courage to cast off his mother's domination.

Beatrice Ann Wright, under the pseudonym "Martin Kramer," presented in *Sons of the Fathers* (1960) the development of six young artists—one poet and five painters—by showing them first as students at the University of California and then at two different periods of their adult lives. Each of the five painters faces problems resulting not only from his own aesthetic yearnings but also from the conflicting personality of his father. Terrence Collin is an extremely handsome, shy, and sensitive youth who is scoffed at by his coarse and brutal family. Robb Nixon, an albino, is regarded as a freak by his father, and eventually becomes a homosexual. Johnny Rue is a talented, hard-working Negro trying to rise above the level of his father, a porter. George Morley III, on the other hand, reacts against the ostentatious wealth of his millionaire father and turns Communist. Virgil Benthwick is completely dominated and psychologically crippled by the personality of his father, an English aristocrat who insists on a strict adherence to standards which are beyond his present means and sometimes inappropriate to American customs.

The novels which treat of the problems of adolescent painters are rather disappointing on the whole. Apparently *The Fox in the Cloak* is the only one which was written by a painter, and it comes the closest to giving a full and convincing presentation of the problems of young painters. In most of the other novels, painting seems to be used as a substitute for the creative writing which the novelist presumably struggled with in his own adolescence, and the problems peculiar to painting are not understood well enough to be presented in convincing detail.

This survey revealed no novels featuring adolescents whose main interest was sculpture, although some painters and architects show a certain amount of interest in sculpture—notably Joe Freedman in Meyer Levin's *The Old Bunch* and Lawrence Black in *The City of Trembling Leaves*. The father of Eugene Gant in Wolfe's *Look Homeward, Angel* is a sculptor and stone-cutter, but none of his many children seem to share this interest. Ceramics, somewhat related to sculpture, is featured in Rollo Walter Brown's *The Firemakers* (1931) and in Margaret Thomsen Raymond's *Sylvia, Inc.* (1938). The former tells of Luke Dabney, an artistic youth who has grown up in a coal-mining community and who seeks in pottery an aesthetic escape from his drab surroundings and an economic escape from soul-destroying labor. The novel follows Luke well into maturity and indicates that he never completely escapes the mines; but a sequel, *Toward Romance* (1932), shows Luke's son Giles escaping through knowledge of the building trade and a talent for architecture. Mrs. Raymond's book also stresses economic problems as well as artistic creativeness: as the mass-production techniques in the Linton Pottery prove unsatisfactory for depression times, Sylvia Linton, an art student who is daughter of the owner, and her friend Julianna Goodheart, a company typist whose grandfather is a master potter, save the company from financial disaster by establishing within it "Sylvia, Inc.," a small business specializing in handmade, high-quality ceramics. Like most of Mrs. Raymond's novels, the book is intended for youthful readers, but it is realistic and mature in its presentation of both economic and personal problems.

Several novels, all of them published either in the thirties or the fifties, present the problems of young men who are planning to be architects. Irving Fineman's *This Pure Young Man* (1930) contrasts the training and early development of Roger Bendrow, who takes up architecture because he has a talent for it, with that of Harry Jaris, whose father has ordered him to choose architecture as a career promising prosperity and prestige. Throughout the novel Harry, admitting he has no talent, does whatever is expected of him, and eventually becomes a popular architect by giving his clients the kind of trite designs they expect. Roger, on the other hand, remains the "pure young man," not only in his personal life (see p. 46 above), but also in his devotion to his own artistic standards. His plans are too unorthodox to have wide appeal, and he refuses to design the "papier-mâché fortresses" that most wealthy people want to live in. The novel ironically points out the triumph of mediocrity over the high ideals of pure art.

The architectural ambition of Gardiner Sitwell in Mary Austin's *Starry Adventure* (1931) is rather incidental. When family expenses prevent Gard from going to college immediately after graduating from high school, he goes into partnership with an architect; but this venture proves to be just one of Gardiner's various abortive attempts to find the starry adventure of life. After he gets to college, he realizes that he has not yet discovered his true calling. Giles Dabney in Brown's *Toward Romance* seems to have a genuine talent for architecture, but the novel ends before this talent has been realized or fully developed. Joe Freedman, one of the most sympathetically portrayed of the twenty young Chicago Jews in Meyer Levin's *The Old Bunch*, has a creative aesthetic urge which drives him restlessly and relentlessly from one enterprise to another and even from one country to another until he is far beyond the age of normal adolescence and has exhausted the patient fidelity of the girl who was willing to wait until he found himself. Asked by Mrs. Freedman whether Joe is really getting anything out of his extended wanderings through Europe to study architecture, Sylvia answers, "It's very important for him,"

> but how could she explain to his mother the alternate exultation and despondency of his moods, as he tried to swallow at one gulp the entire art tradition of Europe, and how could she explain that other theme of his letters, the sense of a quest for he knew not what, only that his

151

instinct would tell him when he found it? How pitiful it seemed to Sylvia in that moment, that Joe was already so far away from his simple mother that it was impossible to explain to his parents the complicated motives, about art, and tradition, and styles, that were actuating his journey. And at the same moment Sylvia felt a compression of fear for herself, for wasn't he gradually working himself away from her, too? Wouldn't he be another person, a foreigner, when he returned? (P. 355.)

Sylvia's thoughts reflect the attitude of the sweethearts, mothers, teachers, and friends of many talented fictional young artists who are on vague, urgent quests similar to Joe's.

Two college novels of the fifties show students torn between the exacting demands of architectural study and the temptations of campus social life. In C. G. Lumbard's *Senior Spring* (1954), Steve Burnett becomes involved in his first great love affair (see page 129 above) at the same time that he is engaged in the Senior Competition at the School of Architecture. It is his visit with Cassy Kane to her family's summer cottage at Pebble Beach that inspires the designs for a seaside hideaway which he submits for the competition; but the hours he spends with her cut deeply into the time he really needs to spend in drawing, not only for the competition but even for his required courses. After weeks of arduous effort to complete satisfactory drawings before the deadlines, Steve is no longer sure whether he wants to be an architect; but a talk with the famous old Mr. Devereux (apparently modeled after Frank Lloyd Wright), who has come to judge the Senior Competition, restores his confidence in his ability and his convictions. In Richard Frede's *Entry E* (1958), Ed Bogard falls behind in doing the assignments for his architecture courses and has to spend the exciting week end of the Princeton football game drawing diligently in his room, in spite of the distracting activities taking place in adjoining rooms of his dormitory (see p. 131 above). Both Lumbard and Frede represent architecture as a mistress who demands long, painstaking hours rather than frenzied moments of inspired service.

A number of adolescent protagonists, mostly girls, aspire to the stage; and a few, mostly boys, follow the art of public speaking. Amory Blaine in *This Side of Paradise* tours the country with the Princeton Triangle Club, but his interest is always more in writing than in acting. Guy Plummer in Croy's *West of the Water Tower* discovers that he has the ability to move people greatly by his speaking; he works hard at the study of elocution, and believes that in some vague way, after he has spent four years at the state university, his talent will bring him worldly success. Meanwhile it gives him confidence to woo his lovely and wealthy classmate Bee Chew, and this leads to the downfall of both of them (see pp. 52–53 above). But after he has done full penance for the wrongs resulting from his amatory entanglement, it is his speaking ability that enables him to raise himself from the lowest depths of public opinion to a place of some prominence in his home town.

Ellen Glasgow in *The Sheltered Life* dwells rather briefly on the thespian ambitions of Jenny Blair Archbald, but in Jenny Blair the hope to become an actress in New York, or even Paris, results not so much from artistic creative impulses as from the desire to escape the social formalities of Queenborough, Virginia, and perhaps to escape her long-felt passion for the charming middle-aged profligate Mr. Birdsong, whose wife Jenny Blair sincerely likes and admires. A more genuine interest in dramatic art is shown by Marjorie Schoessel in Ruth Suckow's *The Odyssey of a Nice Girl*. Marjorie wins many high-school speaking contests in her native Iowa, and then studies dramatic reading at the Academy of Expression in Boston. After two years at the Academy, Marjorie experiences the greatest artistic fulfillment of her life at the final recital, where she reads the part of Titania in a scene from *A Midsummer Night's Dream*. With a talented fellow student she plans exciting dramatic ventures in New York and later in London—as soon as she has spent a few months with her devoted and beloved family, and has saved a few hundred dollars. But family problems and her own loyalties ensnare her in the drab, small-town activities she has promised herself to avoid; and when she finally does escape, it is not to a dramatic career in glamorous

Eastern cities, but to a job as accountant for a garage in Denver, and eventually to marriage with a fruit farmer in the mountains. Thus she is no more successful than Jenny Blair in realizing a life of artistry on the stage.

Stage-struck girls are a tempting target for those novelists who aim at adolescents their silvery arrows of condescending laughter. Jane Jones in Ryerson and Clements' *Mild Oats* dreams of being a great actress as well as a great poet. Her hopes soar when a visiting motion-picture celebrity asks her and Chump Edwards to appear in a film he is making—but it soon becomes evident that he wants them only for comic relief. In Lillian Day's *The Youngest Profession* (1940), fifteen-year-old Jane Lyons does not particularly want an acting career for herself, but she and her plump friend Barbara consider themselves professional movie fans. Besides seeing favorite pictures four or five times, they inflict themselves on such stars as Edward G. Robinson, Basil Rathbone, Madeleine Carroll, and Olivia de Haviland, and even imagine melodramatic movie plots in their own family situations. Jane has some of the bright, half-wise-half-naïve enthusiasm that made Graeme and Sarah Lorimer's Maudie Mason so popular in the thirties, but Maudie is more sympathetically portrayed than Jane. More sympathetically presented than either of these or the Clementses' Jane Jones is the heroine of Peggy Goodin's *Clementine* (1946). The pretty dramatics teacher from New York, Ann McNeil, changes Clem's required Saturday morning acting lessons from an ordeal to a delight, and helps the tomboy discover other interests in life than football and fist-fighting. Perhaps her devotion to Miss McNeil, rather than any innate histrionic impulse, is responsible for Clem's growing interest and ability in acting and public speaking; but by the end of the novel Clem, now sixteen and almost thoroughly feminized, thinks seriously of being an actress during the long years until she and Hank are old enough to get married—at the age of twenty.

Earlier in this chapter (p. 145 above) there was some discussion of two novels in which adolescent stage ambitions are later realized—Helen Carlisle's *The Merry, Merry Maidens* and Anne Miller Downes's *Until the Shearing*—as well as one novel in which a promising career is tragically broken off in adolescence—Forrest Rosaire's *East of Midnight*. In Chapter III (pp. 80–81 above) there was a summary of Dorshka Raphaelson's *Morning Song*, in which Mary Millar unexpectedly tumbles into a stage career before she is fifteen. Mention should be made here

154

of two other popular novels in which girls find at least some success upon the stage. Sinclair Lewis' *Bethel Merriday* (1940), with the author's usual minute attention to realistic detail, and with more sentiment and less satire than he usually displays, follows its heroine's single-minded ambition from the age of six, when she startles her mother with her conscientious imitation of an old woman, through her first introduction to professional actors at the age of fifteen, her mild success as Ibsen's Nora in her senior play in college, a season of learning through summer stock and a short tour with a road company playing *Romeo and Juliet,* to marriage and her first Broadway role when she is twenty-two. Though Lewis' own stage experience enabled him to understand the problems facing aspirant legitimate actors and actresses in an age when movies dominated the entertainment world, and though Bethel is represented to be a girl of ordinary talent rather than a neglected genius, she is never quite real enough and her problems are never quite engrossing enough to capture the reader's deep concern. Herman Wouk's *Marjorie Morningstar* (1955) gives a far more convincing study of the ambitions and frustrations of its protagonist, who is fully as determined as Bethel to be a successful stage actress, but is apparently less talented. Marjorie has some striking successes in amateur productions—*The Mikado* and *Pygmalion* at Hunter College and *A Doll's House* with a theatrical group of the Young Men's Hebrew Association—but in three years of diligently soliciting Broadway parts, she is given only two, and both of these are taken away from her before opening night. The explanation of her composer-playwright lover, Noel Airman, seems reasonably accurate:

> "Marjorie, my sweet, you're not an actress. You're not built to take the strain and smut and general rattiness of a stage life. You're a good little Jewish beauty, with a gift for amateur theatricals. Take my advice, direct all the temple plays in New Rochelle, and be the star in them, and let it go at that—" (P. 345.)

Although she suffers both heartaches and physical exhaustion in her persistent attempts to become a professional actress, the glamorous ideal vanishes with the abrupt awakening that ends her prolonged dream of a happy marriage with Noel, and at last she becomes the "Shirley"—the contented, commonplace suburban housewife—that Noel always predicted she would be.

Two unscrupulous adolescent girls with Hollywood ambitions appear in Blair Treynor's *She Ate Her Cake* (1946) and Steve Fisher's *Giveaway*

(1954). In each of these novels, a fundamentally decent boy is the half-willing accomplice and unwitting victim of ruthless feminine ambition. Mrs. Treynor tells of Danny Miller, an Iowa farm boy, who goes with the lovely but frivolous neighbor girl Pinkie to Hollywood, where she hopes to get into pictures. For the expenses of her campaign, Danny helps Pinkie get money from the Los Angeles gang leader Al Moyse, and helps her flee to a distant California ranch when she murders Moyse; but his misplaced loyalty ends when she tries to have him take the blame for the murder and, when this attempt fails, tries to murder him. Fisher's exposé of television giveaway shows, which antedated the great scandal of "rigged" shows by several years, reveals the mixed feelings of Eddie Shelton of Gary, Indiana, when he is picked up by beautiful Jane Sutton in Hollywood and introduced to the ranks of professional television contestants. Though he is flattered by Jane's apparent attraction to him, Eddie is disturbed at her callous cheating to win contests; and when he discovers that she plans to use him as a temporary partner in the highly-paying "Man and Wife" TV show because this may help her get started on a film career, he promptly hitchhikes back to the family he has run away from in Gary. Neither of these two novels is important as literature, but they show an interesting aspect of the widespread feminine craving for an acting career.

The lure of Hollywood tempts even a "nice" girl to overcome her moral scruples in John Farris' *Harrison High* (1959). Anne Gregor submits to amatory advances from her high-school dramatics teacher and even considers marrying him temporarily because he plans to move to Los Angeles, where his brother knows some studio officials. To earn money for a start in films, Anne allows the lecherous assistant in her uncle's photographic studio to use her as a model for erotic and even obscene pictures.

It is evident that adolescent aspirants for stage success are not often regarded by novelists as dedicated artistic geniuses seeking realization of their inspirations, as writers, musicians, and painters are likely to be. Rather, success on stage or screen is likely to symbolize success in finding personal glory and the adulation of the masses. Few of the would-be actors and actresses in novels have the talent to attain success in a profession of such limited opportunity, and most of them seem contented at last to find a secure but commonplace niche in society.

In general, the problems of any adolescent with creative artistic impulses and aspirations are likely to result from the conflict between the ideals and actions of the talented young person on the one hand and the attitudes and customs of society on the other. The incipient artist is often distressed by things he sees and hears which other people take for granted, and he may do and say things which are important to him but which other people cannot understand or accept. He may, moreover, like Joe Freedman in *The Old Bunch* and Lawrence Black in *The City of Trembling Leaves,* be hounded by the creative urge within him, which will not let him rest until he is able to give it satisfactory expression. Seldom is such expression realized until some time after adolescence. In novels, as in real life, adolescents may feel the creative urge and may give it some expression, but complete artistic success is very seldom achieved during the formative years. Of the rather numerous adolescents who aspire to artistic careers, only a very few ever will be fully successful, even in their mature years. A greater number will be moderately success-ful, but the majority will decide at last that they are better fitted for routine tasks and will give up their artistic ambitions. Some will come to realize that they have overestimated their own artistic ability, and others will simply give in to opposing forces before success is attained.

No particular section of the country is more or less productive of artistic adolescents in fiction than other sections. Artists may originate in North, South, East, Middle West, and West. Most of them eventually seek the cities, particularly New York with its Greenwich Village, its art exhibits, its concert and dramatic stages, its publishing houses, its museums and libraries, and its architectural masterpieces; but writers, composers, and painters are likely to return to small-town or even rural environments to work once they have established themselves. A majority of the artists originate in small towns and small cities, a smaller number come from large cities, and still fewer come from rural areas; these proportions are about what one would expect from the relative proportions of population and the relative availability of cultural influences in these various kinds of environment, if one keeps in mind the fact that poverty and the presence of many conflicting interests excludes many city people from the cultural influences which would otherwise be available to them. There seems to be little change in the kinds of problems faced by artistic adolescents in novels of various decades, except that, as was mentioned in regard to aspiring writers, the novelists of the twenties and thirties are somewhat more concerned with problems of social reform and those of the forties and fifties place more stress on psychological subtleties.

157

It is not so easy to detect patterns among the novels which treat of non-artistic young people preparing for their vocations. The problems are as varied as the professions. Some youths seek to overcome obstacles in the paths to definite goals; some are uncertain how they want to spend their lives; some are willing to accept any occupation which will assure them a livelihood; some are averse to any kind of employment, and to the accompanying responsibilities. Within each of these groups, many kinds of work are represented, and many individual problems.

Of the young people who merely want a livelihood, many go into business. Some novels treat the acquiring of business techniques and employment as a simple, semiconscious process, while others indicate many obstacles, both psychological and economical. The protagonist of Booth Tarkington's *Alice Adams* (1921) is disturbed mainly at the thought that she must admit publicly that her family is not as affluent as it once was. Several of the books of Margaret Thomsen Raymond are designed to present teen-age readers with a realistic picture of the economic problems that girls of their own age may have to face in trying to supplement the family income: *Linnet on the Threshold* (1930) shows a girl of fourteen and fifteen struggling to advance, first in a department store and then in a millinery shop, until the family finances are secure enough to permit her return to high school; *A Bend in the Road* (1934) tells of sixteen-year-old Martha Richards leaving home and trying to support herself on her $8.50-a-week salary as a worker in a greeting-card factory while she learns the harsh facts of busines life during the early years of the Great Depression; this chapter earlier mentioned *Sylvia, Inc.* and its presentation of the financial as well as the artistic problems of the pottery business (p. 150 above). Christopher Morley's *Kitty Foyle*, in the novel of that name (1939), finds problems in a business career that begins in 1929, but Kitty's problems have little to do with the stock-market crash. When her father's ill health interrupts Kitty's formal education after only ten days of college, she goes to business school in her native Philadelphia and gets her first job with Philadelphia socialite Wyn Strafford, who later becomes her lover. Wyn's business project is to launch a Philadelphia magazine that will rival *The New Yorker*. Though Kitty works hard and shows herself very capable both as a businesswoman and as an editor's secretary, the periodical expires with its fourth issue, partly because of the stock-market crash and partly because of Philadelphians' unwillingness to laugh at themselves. She rejects Wyn's proposal of marriage because it is accompanied by a rather insulting Strafford family offer of a year in college and a year abroad to qualify her as a Main Line wife; instead, she enters the cosmetic business in New York with a French chemist and his wife. Thus, as she grows out of adolescence, Kitty's quick imagination and down-to-earth practicality make her a successful businesswoman, but she is constantly aware of the problems that beset the White Collar Girl. In a frustrating nightmare, she tries to make a speech on their behalf at one of F.D.R.'s press conferences, but finds herself unable to speak.

> I really did want to say something for them, the W.C.G.'s that is, your poor damn sharecroppers in the Dust Bowl of business. I see them on subways and on busses, putting up a good fight in their pretty clothes and keeping their heebyjeebies to themselves. There's something so courageous about it, it hurts me inside. . . . If they try to escape by marrying a good provider maybe he's got no brains or he don't talk her language. If they marry a man who's smart he may be more interested in his work than he is in her. How are you going to find a man that's both dumb enough and sweet enough? (P. 334.)

A spherical glass paperweight containing a miniature child coasting downhill amid swirling snow becomes for Kitty the symbol of the young girl in business—"a girl on a sleighride."

Men are less likely than women to obtain white-collar jobs while they are still adolescent, but many novels show adolescent boys who aspire to attain or maintain social position through wealth acquired in business. This is particularly true of the novels of John P. Marquand. In one of his early novels—*Warning Hill* (1930), which has rather trite characters and plot—young Tommy Michael, of a respected but impoverished family in a small New Jersey town, feels inferior to the girl he loves because her father is a wealthy self-made man. Through his job at the bank, Tommy hopes to raise himself eventually to Marianne's level; and he feels degraded when, through her father's interference, he loses his white-collar job and has to work as assistant to the professional at the country club. In one of Marquand's better novels—*Point of No Return* (1949)

—twelve-year-old Charles Gray and his best friend, Jackie Mason, are determined that when they grow up they will make more money than their fathers and will live on the best street in town, not the second best. But Charles is a twenty-three-year-old college graduate before he begins his actual struggle in the business world. Marquand's son, writing as "John Phillips," presents in *The Second Happiest Day* (1953) a more tragic study of a young businessman. Throughout his years at Emmanuel Academy and Harvard, George Marsh is constantly aware of the financial empire, established by his grandfather, that he will be asked to administer at some time in the future. But a period of military service delays his entrance into the business world, and he is well past the usual age of adolescence before it becomes apparent that his long-treasured ideals of preparatory school athletics have left him as unfitted for business as for life.

Innumerable novels, especially during the twenties and thirties, discuss the problems of boys and girls employed in business and industry below the white-collar level. Almost from the beginning of the Industrial Revolution, the exploitation of children and adolescents by industrialists has been a favorite theme of liberal authors. Sentimental treatment of the theme appeared in Victorian novels by Charles Dickens, Charles Reade, and Elizabeth Gaskell; more realistic treatment was offered about the turn of the century in English novels by George Moore and Arnold Bennett and American by William Dean Howells, Stephen Crane, Frank Norris, and Theodore Dreiser. Some noteworthy novels which come within the scope of this study and treat of problems of adolescents in industry include John Dos Passos' *Manhattan Transfer* (1925) and *The Forty-Second Parallel* (1930), Dreiser's *An American Tragedy* (1925), Albert Halper's *The Chute* (1937), Robert Mende's *Spit and the Stars* (1949), and Ralph Ellison's *Invisible Man* (1952). Dos Passos' novels do little more than state the presence of the problems in the lives of the individuals presented; his panoramic method is not conducive to detailed analysis of psychological effects. Dreiser, on the other hand, goes into great detail regarding the aspirations, the frustrations, the minor triumphs and the major defeats of both Clyde Griffiths and Roberta Alden as they work in a shirt factory in upstate New York. *The Chute*, like many other social-protest novels of the thirties, meticulously lists, in a sincere but awkward style, an amazing variety of problems in industry and their effects on an individual—in this case the problems of seventeen-year-old Paul Sussman in a large Chicago mail-order house. *Spit and the Stars* introduces some touches of humor into its study of another young Jewish boy in industry—Gregg Haber in the garment industry in Brooklyn and Manhattan. *Invisible Man* combines problems of race with those of industrial working conditions as the unnamed narrator-protagonist tells of his struggles to make a living in New York after being expelled from a Negro college in the South. Though the specific details vary from one novel to the next, the basic problems remain about the same: comfortless and sometimes dangerous working conditions, exhausting but ever increasing demands, starvation wages, ruthless foremen, inaccessible and indifferent administrators, and battles between management and labor unions, with the laborer helpless to oppose either force.

PREPARING FOR LEARNED PROFESSIONS

A rather remarkable number of adolescent boys in fiction plan to study law, either from their own choice or because of pressure from parents. One of those urged to law by ambitious parents is Skeeters Kirby, in a novel of the same name by Edgar Lee Masters, relating Skeeters' growth and development from the death of Mitch Miller (narrated by Skeeters in an earlier novel by Masters) until Skeeters himself is mature and well established. Skeeters' father, who is state's attorney, wants his son to follow in his steps; but Skeeters is devoted to literature and languages. He is allowed to go to the University of Illinois only on condition that he concentrate on the study of law, discontinuing his literary studies. If he does not accept this condition, he must start working in his father's law office immediately after graduation from high school.

> I looked at my father and a thousand thoughts whirled at once through my brain. Why did I have to be a lawyer? Why did I have to take up the study of it now? Why could I not indulge my present taste for classical studies? Why could I not prepare to be what I wanted to be? As he had disobeyed his father in becoming a lawyer, why could he not applaud me for choosing another way from the way he had taken? (P. 98.)

He grasps the opportunity to go to Champaign, where, besides taking a law course, he secretly registers for a course in Greek and reads Latin

161

and German with a friend in the classical course. During his year at the university and the following year in his father's law office, Skeeters writes articles and verse for various newspapers; at the age of twenty-two, when he passes his bar examinations, he feels well equipped to make his own way in Chicago either as a lawyer or as a journalist. He experiences the problems of a beginner in both these professions, and in business as well, before he achieves the goal he has always sought: success as a writer.

Meyer Levin's *The Old Bunch* describes the problems of adolescents in preparing for and getting started in a variety of professions, especially two which seem to be favorites for intellectual Jews: law and medicine. Sam Eisen is an idealist who would like to be another Clarence Darrow; he deserts the club which "the bunch" has formed because the members seem more interested in dances than in serious discussions, and he allows himself to be expelled from the University of Illinois rather than submit to compulsory R.O.T.C. When Lil Klein seduces him, he is conscientious enough to marry her, delaying his law studies and going into business in order to support her. Quick-witted, humorous Lou Margolis, known as "The Sharpshooter," progresses rapidly, partly by luck and partly by cleverness. Celia Moscowitz, who secretly loves Lou, has her politician father arrange a part-time job for him in a law office, and Lou is able to help the firm win an important case because he is studying similar cases in school at the time. Lou's shadow, Lou Green, is not very bright, but he achieves some success by sticking close to the other Lou. And unscrupulous Runt Plotkin is enough of an opportunist to get through his bar examination and establish some practice, even though he cannot get through law school. The two medical students in the group, Rudy Stone and Mitch Wilner, are both hard-working and conscientious. Rudy works long hours in a drug store while attending college and medical school; Mitch has no need of extra income, but his devoted interest and his quick mind keep him in the laboratory far more than his courses require. Levin deftly enables the reader to feel personally the varied problems of the many young people in this novel.

Another memorable adolescent in fiction who is preparing for a medical career is Parris Mitchell in Henry Bellamann's *Kings Row* (1940). Most of Parris' problems are not peculiar to medical students, but are typical for exceptionally gifted children and adolescents in provincial small towns; as such, they will be discussed more fully in the next chapter.

Two aspects of his community environment have a direct relation to his plans to become a doctor: one is the presence of a state mental hospital, which suggests an opportunity for service in psychiatric medicine; and the other is his frequent contact with two most unusual doctors, the brilliant recluse Dr. Tower and the popular but sadistic Dr. Gordon. Parris has neither the financial nor the intellectual difficulties that many young people experience in preparing for a medical career, but his keen mind and his medical and psychological training give him distressing insight into the problems of people about him even before he reaches what is usually considered to be the age of maturity.

Mention should probably be made here of Richard Frede's popular novel *The Interns* (1960). Interns can hardly be considered adolescents, but the group which Frede presents do face some of the problems which are likely to bother adolescents.

Although many novels describe the early experiences of teachers, not many describe the ambitions and preparation of young people who particularly want to be teachers. Sometimes young people who aspire to another profession, such as writing or music, find it expedient to spend a few years in teaching. Many of the novels which feature the experiences of beginning teachers—Evan Hunter's *Blackboard Jungle*, Daphne Athas' *The Fourth World* and Josephine Carson's *Drives My Green Age*, for example—say little or nothing about the teachers' adolescent problems. This survey found no serious, important novel which has a setting in a teachers college. Two novels that follow their protagonists from adolescence into the teaching profession are Winifred Van Etten's *I Am the Fox* (1936) and Mildred Walker's *Winter Wheat* (1944). In seventh grade Selma Temple, the protagonist of *I Am the Fox*, admires and envies her beautiful music instructor, who fails as a teacher but marries handsome Kirby Townsend. Her own "homely" appearance, Selma believes, dooms her to become a successor to "Old Dewey," the ugly but efficient seventh-grade home-room teacher. As the girl grows older, she learns that her slender figure, white skin, and red curls are attractive rather than homely; but a series of experiences, culminating in the discovery of misery and despair in Mrs. Kirby Townsend's outwardly ideal marriage, turns Selma strongly against domesticity and confirms her conviction that, despite her lack of inclination, teaching is the only career open to her. Her actual teaching experience she finds not only uninteresting but increasingly intolerable, so that she leaves her job after two years to take secretarial training in New York, despite her parents' vigorous contention that "teaching school was the only really respectable profession for a young lady of good family." (p. 209.) Ellen Webb in *Winter Wheat* is not so positively antagonistic to teaching, but her experience with it is not much happier than Selma's. After a year at the University of Minnesota, where she has gone to study languages with the hope of making a career as a translator, Ellen is forced to drop out of college for a year because of the failure of the wheat crop at her Montana home. Still an adolescent herself, she takes a temporary teaching position in a tiny prairie school in Montana. Though she takes on the work only as a temporary alternative to her language study, she learns in time to love her eight pupils and even the loneliness of the "teacherage" after they have left for the day. But she also learns the bitter lesson that a teacher's good intentions and earnest efforts are no guarantee against the anger of narrow-minded parents. Because a feeble-minded boy slips out of school during a blizzard and is frozen to death; because she has a foreign mother, and speaks against war during the superpatriotic weeks that follow Pearl Harbor Day; and because the father of one pupil is found at the teacherage with her early one morning, the members of the school board decide she is not morally fit to teach their children. Ellen knows that she is innocent of the charges against her and could probably insist on the fulfillment of her contract if she chose; but rather than continue to work in an atmosphere of suspicion, she leaves the job at the end of one term and returns to her parents' wheat ranch.

Novels intended for adolescent readers are rather more likely to give the beginning experiences in any profession than are novels intended for adults. A recent juvenile novel about the teaching profession is Margaret Hill's *Really, Miss Hillsbro!* (1960), in which Anne Hillsbro, during her first year of teaching, finds her life complicated by a number of problem children, an ultraconservative principal, and her own love affair with a handsome young forest ranger.

164

Adolescents who look forward to farming careers face problems of two main sorts: adverse conditions of nature, which affect adults as well as adolescents, and conflicts between the lonely, rigorous farm life and the desire for social or cultural advantages. Ellen Webb in *Winter Wheat* loves a rich boy whom she meets in Minneapolis; but when she finds that he cannot share her appreciation of rural pleasures, she gives him up, even though she expects her career to take her away from the farm. Similarly, in Phil Stong's *State Fair* (1932), Margy and Wayne Frake end their love affairs with city people when the fair ends because the city people would not fit into the farm life that the Frakes both want. In a later and somewhat inferior novel, *The Long Lane* (1939), Stong tells of Kenneth Brubaker, whose faith in the steadfastness of his Iowa farm home is destroyed when his mother elopes with his father's sophisticated younger brother, and his father becomes a successful businessman in Des Moines, where he has an affair with a younger woman. In Percy Marks's *What's a Heaven For?* (1938), Nat Wayne—inspired by his father's ambitions for him and by Browning's line "A man's reach should exceed his grasp, or what's a heaven for?"—leaves his ancestral California farm and goes to the University of California at Berkeley, hoping first that he may become a mechanical engineer and later that he may be a successful banker. After years of reaching, he decides that his grasp extends no farther than farming, and that he would be wise to reach no farther. John R. Tunis in *Son of the Valley* (1949), one of his few ventures beyond the school athletic field, shows Johnny Heiskell solving both natural and social problems to build up a farm in the Tennessee River Valley. After six generations of Heiskells have depleted the soil on their old family farm, the TVA engineers condemn this and many other farms to be flooded. Johnny moves with his father and sister to a new farm, which proves no more productive. The father, discouraged, leaves the farm to work on the new dam; but Johnny, despite the opposition of neighbors, adopts suggestions of the county farm agent and succeeds in restoring the vitality of the soil. He even succeeds in interesting his formerly antagonistic neighbors in a co-operative soil program. Ralph Moody

165

in his three-volume fictionalized autobiography shows himself as an adolescent devoted to ranching and farming but faced with problems posed by nature and by economics. The first volume in the trilogy, *Little Britches* (1950), shows Ralph between the ages of eight and eleven, the second oldest child and the oldest son of five children, forced into an early adolescence by a heavy burden of responsibilities as he and his father struggle valiantly but vainly to make a success of an impoverished ranch in an arid section of Colorado. The second volume, *Man of the Family* (1951), begins just after the father's death; it tells how Ralph, between the ages of eleven and thirteen, helps to support the family in a small Colorado town by gardening, raising rabbits, herding cattle, and distributing the products of his mother's New England cooking—never losing sight of his ambition to become a ranch hand. In the third volume, *The Fields of Home* (1953), Ralph, between the ages of thirteen and fifteen, helps his cantankerous grandfather Thomas Gould on a run-down farm in Maine. Ralph's interests and experiences have made him alert to new methods of farming, and he strongly resents the old man's constant criticism of everything he does. But Uncle Levi Gould contrives a sort of reconciliation between them, and Grandpa even takes pride in Ralph's ingenuity when he sees that new crops have been added, a new barn has been planned, and an untrustworthy old horse has been made docile.

Among noteworthy novels that deal with adolescents preparing for special vocational fields are William Wister Haines's *Slim* (1934), Jay McCormick's *November Storm* (1943), and Mary-Elizabeth Witherspoon's *Somebody Speak for Katy* (1950). *Slim* tells of a Southern mountain boy who is fascinated by a company of linemen stringing high-tension wires near a field he is plowing and who goes off with them to learn the various phases of their dangerous occupation. *November Storm* presents the bewildered teen-age Sean Riley, having lost both of his parents, taking a job on the Great Lakes freighter *Blackfoot* and finding himself in maturity as a November storm drives the ship upon rocky shoals. In *Somebody Speak for Katy*, Mrs. Witherspoon describes a naïve Florida girl who goes to New York in order to help people through social work, but who first must learn to accept unpleasantness as reality.

Though business and industry often—and law, teaching, and farming sometimes—are second-choice professions and may be chosen simply as means of livelihood, medicine is almost always—and law, teaching, and farming are sometimes—true vocations, to which some young people are

impelled as others are to the arts. The only other vocation which sometimes matches the arts in the fascination or even compulsion it has for
youthful protagonists in novels is the clergy; examples of such young
people will be discussed later in this chapter, among other problems of
religion. The choice of a vocation seems to bear very little relation to the
locale of the novel; the majority of adolescents in fiction seek to establish
themselves in occupations in or near the regions where they grew up,
but many are anxious to get into new regions. Where there is movement,
it is likely to be toward centers of denser population: country people may
want to move to small towns, and young people from both farms and
villages may want to move to the city. Some city people want to move
to villages, although not very often; still less often do either city people
or villagers want to move to farms.

It is easier to see a relationship between the year of publication and
the kind of vocational problems discussed in a novel. Novels published
during the twenties and thirties are likely to emphasize flaws in society,
with the implication that young people could adjust to their life work
much more successfully and easily if society were more reasonable in its
demands—if factories and mail-order houses were not constantly trying
to increase speed without increasing wages; if patients, clients, and the
parents of school children would realize that doctors, lawyers, and
teachers are human beings with human feelings and limitations. Novels
published during the forties and fifties tend to emphasize psychological
difficulties within the young person preparing for a vocation, so that
different people preparing for the same profession in the same locality
may have entirely different problems. This latter sort of treatment makes
possible far more variety and individuality than does the earlier sort.

The Meaning of Life Through Dreaming

Besides finding a way of earning a living and exercising his talents, the
youth approaching adulthood must find a meaning in life or else he must
persuade himself that he can be satisfied with a meaningless existence.
It is in the nature of human beings to question ultimate goals and to
want to be aware of progress toward these goals. Traditionally, the novel
of adolescence presents a sensitive, often impractical youth surrounded

by people who cannot understand his responses to stimuli that do not affect the majority of people, nor his failure to respond in ways that the majority consider natural if not inevitable. This difference tends to make the young protagonist more withdrawn from reality, and he is likely to find his pleasures in a dream world, from which he may or may not eventually emerge.

Edgar Lee Masters' Mitch Miller is an early example of such a dreamer. Mitch finds satisfaction in noting similarities between his own life and that of Tom Sawyer. He even writes letters addressed to Tom Sawyer in Hannibal, Missouri, and is elated when they are answered. Mitch suffers some disillusioning experiences, especially when his Tom Sawyer turns out to be a middle-aged butcher, but the boy continues to find his greatest pleasure in daydreams until his death in early adolescence. Sherwood Anderson's novels and short stories are full of dreamers, both adolescent and adult. Hugh McVey in *Poor White* (1920) dreams through his adolescence and early maturity; but the precepts of his energetic foster mother impel him to keep active, and at last he makes practical use of his dreams by becoming an inventor. Other sections of the present survey describe the fantasies of Anderson's Tar Moorehead, compensating for his impoverished and unhappy home life (p. 79 above), and the daydream-inspired love affair of Fanny Williams in John Weaver's *Her Knight Comes Riding* (p. 39 above). The adolescent romances in the novels of Robert Nathan and Barry Benefield are half dream and half reality (see pp. 37 and 42 above and 245 below). In Fowler Hill's *Plundered Host* (1929) the dreamy adolescent Peter Brush is gradually brought to a realization of reality through college life, several love affairs, and summer work in a factory. Thomas Wolfe's protagonists, Eugene Gant in *Look Homeward, Angel* and George Webber in *The Web and the Rock* (1939), are incorrigible dreamers during adolescence and even afterward. In fact, this sort of figure is so common in fiction of the forty years here considered, that it would be tiresome and meaningless to try to make a complete list of examples.

Some of the more unusual treatments of dreamy adolescents do merit consideration. One such is Michael Fraenkl's *Werther's Younger Brother,* first published anonymously in a limited edition in 1931. This short novel purports to be the notebook of a schoolboy named Alfred, who constantly compares himself with Shakespeare's Hamlet and Goethe's

Werther. As in some of the novels of Virginia Woolf, the outer world is seen only through the mind of the protagonist; and the reader, following Alfred's daydreams of an affair with his brother's wife, cannot always tell which incidents are supposed to be actual and which are merely fantasy. Similarly, in Shirley Jackson's *Hangsaman* the mind of Natalie Waite slips so easily from reality to imagination and back again that the reader is never sure whether Natalie's friend Tony is a classmate or a dream companion, and whether the thief in the dormitory is Natalie herself, another girl, or Natalie's invention (see above, pp. 72, 128, and 142). Anne Chamberlain's *The Tall Dark Man* (1955) presents the peculiar problem of thirteen-year-old Sarah Lou Gross, who is so addicted to telling tall stories that nobody will believe her when she announces that she has witnessed a murder while gazing dreamily out the schoolroom window. Laura Beheler's *The Paper Dolls* (1956) describes the dream life of Ida Erickson, peopled with paper dolls whose behavior she can control, while she avoids the real problems of adolescence and early adulthood, retreating at last into alcoholism.

Several novels show imaginative adolescents being roughly awakened from their dream worlds into an awareness of reality and responsibility. Carson McCullers' *The Member of the Wedding* (1946) tells how twelve-year-old Frankie Addams, who has long wanted to be a member of something, dreams that her brother and his bride will take her along on their honeymoon.

> "We mean to keep moving, the three of us. Here today and gone tomorrow. Alaska, China, Iceland, South America. Traveling on trains. Letting her rip on motorcycles. Flying around all over the world in aeroplanes. . . . Things will happen so fast we won't hardly have time to realize them. Captain Jarvis Addams sinks twelve Jap battleships and decorated by the President. Miss F. Jasmine Addams breaks all records. Mrs. Janice Addams elected Miss United Nations in a beauty contest. One thing after another happening so fast we don't hardly notice them." (*The Member of the Wedding*, in *The Ballad of the Sad Cafe*, 1951, pp. 737–38.)

When the bride and groom drive off together, leaving Frankie screaming, "Take me!" to the retreating cloud of dust, the reality seems like a dream to her; but the reader senses, through the events that follow, that she is gradually coming to accept reality and responsibility. In Roger Eddy's

169

The Rimless Wheel (1947) the narrator-protagonist, Eben Osborne, is content to dream on his remote New England farm until he is twenty, when the red-haired summer visitor he has fallen in love with gives him a shocking picture of himself:

> "I think you're a disease I had once that I'm rid of now. You need more repair than all your walls or your doors. There's no more shape to you than . . . that fog down in the valley. And some day you'll dissolve, too. . . . Just sit there and say nothing. That's the way I'll remember you best, anyway. Saying nothing and sitting. Smoke your pipe until it's empty. Watch the fire burn down. Get cold, and then go to bed." (Pp. 322–23.)

Eben lets Rusty walk out of his house while he says nothing. Then he sits and smokes his pipe until it is empty, and watches the fire burn down; but before he goes to bed he smashes the pipe in the fireplace, and the next day he makes arrangements to leave his valley of stagnation forever.

The dream life is championed in Truman Capote's *The Grass Harp* (1951). Collin Fenwick, living with his father's cousins Verena and Dolly Talbo from the time he is orphaned at the age of eleven, prefers the dreamy Dolly to the businesslike Verena. When Collin is sixteen, the sisters quarrel over a business plan of Verena's, and Dolly takes refuge in a tree house with the boy and her old Negro companion, Catherine Crook. Various people of the community become involved in the controversy, the kind and dreamy ones sympathizing with the group in the tree house while the hard and practical ones side with Verena. Verena is at last won over to Dolly's impracticality; and though Dolly later dies as a result of exposure in the tree house, both she and the tree house in its field of singing grass are symbolic guides to Collin in recurrent dreams as he grows out of adolescence.

A very unusual presentation of adolescent dreams is Jack Kerouac's *Doctor Sax* (1959), subtitled *Faust Part Three*. The novel presents the childhood and early adolescence of French-Canadian Jack Duluoz (obviously the author himself) in the Little Canada section of Lowell, Massachusetts, and it mingles realistic scenes of boyhood experience with typical boyhood fantasies stimulated by comic books, radio programs, and horror movies. The most prominent inhabitant of Jack's dream world is Doctor Sax, who wanders about the woods in a large cape and a slouch hat that conceals an inflatable rubber boat.

170

He went around having himself a ball searching mysterious lumps of earth around the world for a reason so fantastic—for the boiling point of evil (which, in his—, was a volcanic thing . . . like a boil)—in South America, in North America, Doctor Sax had labored to find the enigma of the New World—the snake of evil whose home is in the depths of Ecuador and the Amazonian jungle—where he lived a considerable time searching for the perfect dove . . . a white jungle variety as delicate as a little white bat, an Albino bat really, but a dove with a snaky beak, and habiting close to Snake Head. (Pp. 28–29.)

In a striking apocalyptic vision when Jack is fourteen years old, Doctor Sax succeeds in bringing the Bird of Paradise to destroy the snake of evil. Jack sees Doctor Sax a few times afterward, but the presence is always joyful, never sinister as before; "—he only deals in glee now." (P. 245.)

The problem of the adolescent dreamer almost necessitates a psychological approach by the novelist. Such early novels as *Moon-Calf* and *Her Knight Comes Riding* show unmistakable Freudian influence. The novels of the twenties usually present adolescent dreamers sympathetically, implying a greater awareness in them than in the practical people who misunderstand them. In 1930 appeared several novels showing dreamers as self-deceivers who need to be awakened before they can really cope with life (Nelson Crawford's *Unhappy Wind,* Irving Fineman's *This Pure Young Man,* William Rollins' *The Obelisk*). The theme of adolescence as an awakening to reality appears in a number of novels of the forties and fifties (Marquis Childs's *The Cabin,* Roger Eddy's *The Rimless Wheel,* John Bell Clayton's *Wait, Son, October Is Near*). Psychopathic dreamers appeared in novels of the fifties (*Hangsaman* and *The Paper Dolls*), but in the same decade came novels paying sentimental tribute to dreamers both old and young (*The Grass Harp* and Ray Bradbury's *Dandelion Wine*). It is apparent that, throughout the period of this study, novelists have sympathized with dreamy adolescents, but this fact has not kept some from believing that dreaminess is not a satisfactory preparation for life.

Intellectual searching for the meaning of life is not as common among fictional adolescents as is dreaming about it. Philosophical novels are in danger of being dull or trite or both. Glenway Wescott's *The Apple of the Eye* (1924) aroused interest by combining a fifteen-year-old boy's search for life's meaning with his growing understanding of sexual impulses and of narrow moral standards in his rural Wisconsin community. Dan Strane is at first strongly influenced by his mother, who tells him solemnly of the importance of chastity, both for strength and for happiness. Later he visits his strait-laced Aunt Selma and her more liberal husband, Jule Bier; while with them he learns that his lovely but uninformed cousin Rosalia is having an affair with the hired man, Mike, who tells Dan, "Well, suppose a man makes love to a girl. I call that good, not wrong. But suppose he gets her with child, then runs off and leaves her. That's pretty rotten. Do you see?" (P. 147.) Mike does leave Rosalia, not knowing she is pregnant; and she, not knowing that help might be possible for her, commits suicide. In the atmosphere of tragedy, while Dan is groping for a meaning in such apparent injustice, Uncle Jule helps him by telling of his own former mistress, "Bad Han" Madoc, whose uninhibited love for Jule dominates the novel:

> "Hannah was different. She took what came. She never worried about what she'd done that she hadn't ought to. She never blamed anybody; she knew everybody did what they had to. She never thought things ought to be better than they were. When things went wrong she stood it. . . . Hannah was just a common woman; she never went to school. But I see all the fine people, the people with brains—they all go to pieces. I guess it's the kind of religion they've got here. Something's wrong; such things don't have to be. (Pp. 274–75.)

At the end of the novel, as Dan leaves for college, his mother reiterates her plea for chastity, and urges him to associate only with "good, clean boy and girls"; but her son has already been won over to Han's more natural philosophy.

Dorothy Canfield Fisher usually shows her adolescents thinking, searching, and experimenting to find a satisfactory meaning for life; what they come up with is likely to be commendable, but is seldom very striking or new. Neale Crittenden in *Rough-Hewn* is exposed to the same kinds of temptations and false values as those that lure other city boys and college students in novels from *This Side of Paradise* to *Entry E;* but his understanding parents, his devotion to sports and fair play, his rigorous summers in a New England lumber mill, and his reading of Emerson all lead him to the conclusion that he can best find happiness in life by keeping healthy, showing consideration to others, and indulging his appetites only moderately. Matey Gilbert in *The Deepening Stream* grows up with apparently uncongenial parents who bicker in public and hide their true feelings behind a facade of brilliance and polite manners, moving from one college town to another as Professor Gilbert receives offers of higher salaries. Her brother is an egotistical show-off like their father, and her older sister is so afraid of anything "not nice" that Matey can never talk to her about the things that really bother her. In spite of this unpromising background, her youthful marriage is successful because it is based on mutual respect and dedicated to service for others. Mrs. Fisher's protagonists are so clear-sighted and sane that they never seem to be in serious danger of being overwhelmed by the problems of adolescence, or even by those of adulthood.

Thomas Wolfe's protagonists are much more subject to appetites and emotions, but they are thinkers as well as dreamers. Eugene Gant in *Look Homeward, Angel* indulges in wild fantasies as he wanders about Altamont or strides his lonely way from Pulpit Hill to nearby villages, but he also reads avidly in the classics of various languages, and struggles titanically within his own mind to understand why Ben should die, why Laura should deceive him, why Galileo and Martin Luther should have risked torture and death to challenge the leading minds of their times. His classmates nickname him "Hegel Gant." George Webber in *The Web and the Rock* also puzzles over the meaning of life. At Pine Rock College he is one of a group of students who cluster about fat, motherly, sentimental Gerald Alsop; but unlike Jerry's other disciples he does not blindly accept the master's statement that Dickens is the greatest and most understanding of all novelists. George dares to read and admire Dostoevski. Although his chief interest at college is in literature, he is also interested in philosophy and logic, and gets good grades in those subjects. But the childhood and adolescence of George are not so fully treated as those of Eugene, and the reader is given little specific knowledge about young Webber's philosophical ideas.

173

One of the most philosophical of fictional adolescents of this period is Oliver Alden in *The Last Puritan* (1936), the one novel by the philosopher George Santayana. His quick mind, his careful training by his German governess Irma, and his puritan conscience all impel Oliver to try to understand the meaning of his life. He comes to the conclusion that it is wrong for him to be a puritan, and yet he cannot stop being one. Santayana reveals thoroughly how various people influenced Oliver's thinking about life at different stages of his development: his parents and his governess during his childhood, the amoral Englishman Jim Darnley ("Lord Jim" to Oliver and his father) and Jim's sister Rose from middle adolescence into maturity, and Oliver's cousins Mario and Edith during his college years at Williams and Harvard. Of Oliver's inability to find a philosophy that is both livable and intellectually satisfying, Santayana says in the Epilogue to the novel:

> I think there is no great truth that sensitive Nordics don't sometimes discover: only they don't stick to their best insights. They don't recognize the difference between a great truth and a speculative whim, and they wander off again into the mist, empty-handed and puzzle-headed. As to moral complications in Oliver, . . . he was the child of an elderly and weary man and of a thin-spun race; from his mother he got only his bigness and athleticism, which notoriously don't wear well. A moral nature burdened and over-strung and a critical faculty fearless but helplessly subjective—isn't that the true tragedy of your ultimate Puritan? (P. 602.)

Percy Marks's *What's a Heaven For?*, mentioned earlier in this chapter (p. 165 above), also presents a young man who finds at last that the philosophy which satisfied his adolescence is untenable—or at least inapplicable—during his adult life. In Farrell's *Father and Son*, Danny O'Neill finds himself torn among the various views of life that have been impressed upon him: his father's gospel of simplicity and hard work, his mother's slovenly religiosity, his Uncle Al's respect for the appearance of culture, his Aunt Margaret's dedication to love and pleasure, his grandmother's irrational and raging desire to reform the world and its people, the church-centered conscientiousness urged by the nuns and priests who guide him at church and at school, and the tough rebelliousness of his companions on the streets of Chicago. It is not until Danny attends the University of Chicago in *My Days of Anger*, the final volume of the series, that he is able to resolve the confusion and find a satisfactory system for his own life.

With less specific detail, but more subtly and symbolically, Katherine Anne Porter in "Old Mortality" indicates the inadequacy of a Catholic education to supply a satisfactory philosophy of life for a questioning and rebellious adolescent. The protagonist Miranda and her older sister Maria are educated in a Catholic boarding school in New Orleans, where they like to think of themselves as "immured." Miranda runs away and marries at seventeen in order to escape the confining patterns of her religion and her family. A year later, visiting her parents to attend the funeral of an uncle, she meditates on her future plans and the meaning of her life:

> She did not want any more ties with this house, she was going to leave it, and she was not going back to her husband's family either. She would have no more bonds that smothered her in love and hatred. She knew now why she had run away to marriage, and she knew that she was going to run away from marriage, and she was not going to stay in any place, with anyone that threatened to forbid her making her own discoveries, that said "No" to her. . . . Oh, what is life, she asked herself in desperate seriousness, in those childish unanswerable words, and what shall I do with it? It is something of my own, she thought in a fury of jealous possessiveness, what shall I make of it? . . . Her mind closed stubbornly against remembering, not the past but the legend of the past, at which she had spent her life peering in wonder like a child in a magic-lantern show. Ah, but there is my own life to come yet, she thought, my own life now and beyond. I don't want any promises, I won't have false hopes, I won't be romantic about myself. . . . Let them tell their stories to each other. Let them go on explaining how things happened. I don't care. At least I can know the truth about what happens to me, she assured herself silently, making a promise to herself in her hopefulness, her ignorance. ("Old Mortality" in *Pale Horse Pale Rider*, pp. 87–89 *passim*.)

Complete failure to find meaning and purpose in life is illustrated in Josephine Johnson's *Wildwood* (1946). Timid and bewildered at the age of thirteen, when she is left an orphan, Edith Andrews is adopted by her mother's elderly cousin Valerie and Valerie's ornithologist husband, Matthew Pierre. Burdened in their old age with an adolescent girl who never behaves quite as they think an adolescent girl should behave, the Pierres unintentionally thwart all her impulses to be like other girls: to visit and be visited, to learn to dance, to have boy friends. Within ten years the old people are dead, leaving Edith Pierre, who was to "be as our own child," in possession of a large estate, but without the experience or the understanding to face adult life.

175

Two girls, one in early adolescence and one in late, seek an understanding of life in Jessamyn West's *The Witch Diggers* (1951). Eighteen-year-old Cate Conboy holds the more central position in the story, but her thirteen-year-old sister Em is more original and likable. Their problem is similar to that of Dan Strane in *The Apple of the Eye*—the reconciling of natural sexual impulses, in themselves and others, with the rigid standards of religion and morality prevalent in rural areas during the early years of the twentieth century. Wescott's scene is laid in rural southern Wisconsin and Miss West's in rural southern Indiana. Mrs. Conboy has a sensual nature which she understands and is able to control, but she reacts violently to any suggestion of sensuality in the behavior of her daughters. Cate is acquiescent and idealistic; the recognition of sexual desires in herself and in members of her family causes her to break off a promising romance, with tragic results. Em is more inclined to act on impulse and to feel no regrets for actions that *seem* right at the time of action. Her innocent revealing of her naked body as a kindness to a peeping Tom brings quick and violent punishment; but the reader senses that Em will learn to adapt her impulses to social conventions, as her mother has done.

Many of the adolescents in novels of the late fifties have a "beat" philosophy, either explicit or implicit. The classic example is Dean Moriarty in Kerouac's *On the Road*, who mates and separates (sometimes even marries and divorces), writes, travels, indulges in drugs and alcohol—all entirely on impulse, without regard for responsibility or convention. Dean's older friend and admirer, the narrator Sal Paradise, shows through his thoughts and actions that such a philosophy results in permanent adolescence. "The world is beyond our control," the beatniks seem to say, in contrast to the reform novelists of the twenties and thirties. "There is no purpose in the universe, no meaning in life beyond what we choose to find in it. Therefore let us live it up, experiencing what we can of life. Death may come at any moment; let us not have to face it with the knowledge that we have never truly lived." Thus Thoreau, distorted through the existentialists of France and Italy and through the constant threat of total destruction by nuclear explosion, finds voice in the American beat generation of the mid-twentieth century.

176

Several novels of the late twenties show the importance of various religious traditions in the struggles of adolescents to attain a satisfactory outlook on life. In Dorothy Coursen's *Fire of Spring* (1928), thirteen-year-old Alma, a Philadelphia girl visiting her aunt and uncle in rural Indiana, experiences religious ecstasy at a revival meeting and declares herself for Christ; but she soon finds a similar ecstasy in her first love affair, when a charming man returns her love. In Myron Brinig's *Singermann* (1929), the seven children of a Jewish couple from Romania grow up in Montana, where they experience conflicts between the orthodox Jewish traditions of the family and the various *goyish* traditions of their neighbors. An earlier chapter of this study mentioned two other novels of 1929 (Anne Parrish's *The Methodist Faun* and O. E. Rölvaag's *Peder Victorious*) in which the respective protagonists, Clifford Hunter and Peder Holm, as they outgrow their mothers' influence, also outgrow the intense dedication to Protestant sects which their mothers have instilled in them (see page 68 above).

During the 1930's a greater number of novels, representing a greater variety of religious traditions, presented in greater detail the religious struggles of adolescent protagonists. Nelson Antrim Crawford's *Unhappy Wind* (1930) traces the development of Winfrid Cartwright from boyhood almost to manhood, through a complexity of religious, sensual, and sensuous conflicts. The sensuous confusion is represented by Winfrid's thinking of sounds in terms of colors; the sensual is shown by his preoccupation with girls' bodies; and the aesthetic and spiritual appeal of High Church ritual appears in his conversion from his family's indifferent Congregationalism to Anglo-Catholicism and in his eventual decision to become a priest. Rollo Walter Brown's *Toward Romance* (see above, pp. 150 and 151, and below, p. 195) depicts the problems of Giles Dabney in the same areas: Giles finds sensuous and aesthetic satisfaction through architecture; he escapes from the sensual entanglement which threatens him with an unsuitable marriage and from the stultifying religious terrors of small-town revival meetings, and moves toward romance and the broader horizons outside the drab little mining town of Wiggams Glory,

177

Ohio. Joseph Gollomb's *Unquiet* (1935) and Meyer Levin's *The Old Bunch* both describe young Jews in American cities (the former in New York, the latter in Chicago) breaking away from the religious patterns which their families have followed for centuries in European ghettos. Ethel Cook Eliot's *Angels' Mirth* (1936) shows sixteen-year-old Mary Stevens, a girl brought up without any religious faith, being won to Roman Catholicism by the nearly grown children of the sophisticated Mrs. Violet Sands, who plans to divorce her husband and marry Mary's father; on the other hand, the last three books of Farrell's Danny O'Neill tetralogy show Danny gradually turning from a complete acceptance of Catholicism to a complete rejection of all religion. Gordon Friesen's *Flamethrowers* (1936) tells of the German immigrant boy Peter Franzman, seared by flames of hatred and intolerance which are thrown in the name of religion and patriotism—hatred of material progress in the Kansas Mennonite village where he spends his first years in America, hatred of anything or anyone German in the high school he attends during World War I, hatred of liberal religion in the Oklahoma denominational college he attends for two years—and rejecting all these bigotries to work out his own philosophy with the help of a woman professor of history. In Wolfe's *The Web and the Rock*, George Webber attends a Southern Baptist college which prides itself on its liberalism, and he spends many evenings there in company with a pipe-smoking Episcopal clergyman who affects a sporty, virile way of talking to male students; but George detects the insincerity of these poses and the religious intolerance behind them. Don Marquis' unfinished novel *Sons of the Puritans* (1939) relates how Jack Stevens, whose father had been a minister, grew up in a small town in Illinois which was dominated by two Protestant churches. As a small boy, Jack shakes the whole community by asking in Sunday school the heretical question "Who made God?" As he grows to maturity, he appears to be one of the few people in town who realize that puritanism grown stagnant becomes impure and even vicious.

Probably the most difficult religious adjustment made by an adolescent protagonist in the fiction of the thirties, and the one described in most detail, is that of Myron Begay, the young Navajo in Oliver La Farge's *The Enemy Gods* (see p. 105 above). From early childhood, when he is placed in a mission school by an unsympathetic stepfather, until his early twenties, when he finally decides what his place in society will be, Myron vacillates between "the Jesus trail" and the pagan rituals of his

178

forefathers. The older he gets, the more painful the struggle becomes; and it is at last love, rather than faith, that leads him to a decision.

Several novels of the forties discuss adolescents' acceptance or rejection of Catholic doctrines. Besides Farrell's *Father and Son* and *My Days of Anger,* which have been discussed earlier in this chapter, there are Robert H. Newman's *Fling Out the Banner* (1941), in which Boss Mackenzie clings to his Catholic faith in a New England Protestant boarding school; August Derleth's *Evening in Spring* (1941), in which Steve Grendon's Catholic faith is tested by his love for Protestant Margery Estabrook and the resultant antagonism of both families; Bentz Plagemann's *Into the Labyrinth* (1948), in which Robert Vandermeer falls into sin after a quarrel with his girl but is brought to repentance by his Catholic faith and his love for Laura; Dorothy Fremont Grant's *Devil's Food* (1949), in which Betsy Lyman, rebellious daughter of a Catholic family, attends a non-Catholic junior college on a scholarship, is seduced by a professor, and returns to her family and her faith; and E. J. Edwards' *The Chosen* (1949), in which five boys from Brooklyn enter a Catholic seminary in the Midwest, but only Marty Manning has the spiritual tenacity to complete the course and be ordained. None of these last five books is outstanding. More unusual and memorable is Ann George Leslie's *Dancing Saints* (1943), which preesnts a sympathetic picture of an adolescent Shaker boy. Orville Thatcher admires the Shakers, who teach him to be an excellent carpenter and prepare the way for his becoming an architect; but their strict laws of celibacy are too much for his normal adolescent desires, as he loves a Shaker girl and has an affair with a carnival girl. Althought he returns from these lapses to the austere life of the Shaker community and helps to defend the group from its enemies, Orville decides, soon after reaching manhood, that his place is in the outer world.

Novels of the 1950's include both intensive and extensive studies of adolescents facing religious problems—some Catholic, some Protestant, some Jewish. The shortest of these, but perhaps the most artistic and convincing, is James Agee's *The Morning Watch.* The twelve-year-old protagonist, participating in an early-morning service on Good Friday at a Catholic boarding school in Tennessee, tries sincerely to capture and maintain the spirit of Christ in Gethsemane, but finds that worldly thoughts and vanities constantly intrude (see p. 118 above). A less admirable Catholic protagonist in a more hackneyed story is Chris Weed in

179

Joseph Weeks's *All Our Yesterdays* (1955). Chris's Catholicism serves him mainly as an excuse not to marry a wealthy Protestant girl whom he makes pregnant; his glib self-assurance apparently is enough to rescue him from his family's poverty by enabling him to get a series of jobs as a radio announcer. Greater depth of psychological penetration is shown by William Kelley in *Gemini* (1959), which tells of a New York slum boy, Bascomb McGoslin, entering a Catholic seminary to atone for past sexual sins and to avoid the lustful urges which still beset him. As he finds that he cannot forget the image of sexy June Cyzmanski, he begins to question the teachings of his church; eventually he gives up not only his intended life of celibacy but even his Catholic religion.

Two novels of mid-century present problems of the sons of Protestant ministers: in Paul Ader's *The Leaf Against the Sky* (1948), John Perry rebels against the austere morality of his parents' religious tradition, especially since his high-school friend and college roommate, Milton Silverstein, has abandoned the Jewish faith and now believes only in science; and in *Go Home and Tell Your Mother* (1950), by Max Wylie,[1] twelve-year-old Gil Ilverson hates his tyrannical, sadistic clergyman father, who campaigns vigorously against sex and liquor but is himself basically carnal. Gil loves the pretty girl next door, Mary Saunders, but allows himself to be seduced by his twenty-three-year-old seventh-grade teacher, Miss Bannerman. In Thomas Hal Phillips' *The Golden Lie* (1951), on the other hand, it is the mother who hides her carnal and unloving nature under the cloak of religion, while her son, Foster Lloyd, shares the truly compassionate nature of his father. In his early years, naturally, Foster was under the influence of his mother and her formal but empty religion; in his middle adolescence, his love of football, his affection for a Negro friend in his Mississippi community, and his tolerance for nonreligious neighbors of both white and colored races all link him more closely with his father and exclude him from "the golden lie" of the Primitive Church.

A more sympathetic presentation of a boy's relation to an emotional Protestant sect appears in James Baldwin's *Go Tell It on the Mountain* (1953). John Grimes, a fourteen-year-old Harlem boy, is active in the Temple of the Fire Baptized, the storefront church of which his mother, stepfather, and aunt are pillars; and Elizabeth Grimes prays that this illegitimate first child of hers will experience conversion and the call to preach. Gabriel Grimes, like the Reverend Mr. Ilverson in Max Wylie's novel, is a vigorous preacher who expresses his resentment against his own lustful urges by brutality to others, especially to his wife's bastard son. As the Grimeses participate in the Seventh Day services, John's heart is torn between hatred of his preacher stepfather and admiration for the athletic young preacher Brother Elisha, the seventeen-year-old nephew of their pastor; between emotional conviction that the Holy Ghost is speaking to him and intellectual rejection of the groveling self-abasement of the Negro penitent. Yet the boy does feel himself suffering the anguish and humiliation of all human sufferers, the baptism by the fire of the Holy Spirit, opposed by Gabriel but sustained by Elisha; and he feels within himself a new spiritual strength.

The extreme teachings of a primitive Protestant sect also play an important part in the growth of fourteen-year-old Francis Marion Tarwater in Flannery O'Connor's *The Violent Bear It Away* (1960). After the death of his fanatically religious great-uncle, with whom he has grown up in the hills of Tennessee, young Tarwater carries out the old man's intention of baptizing, by total immersion, the idiot son of worldly Uncle Rayben, even though the child is drowned in the process.

Two fairly important novels of the fifties show Jewish adolescents trying to adjust themselves to traditional religious doctrine. Through the immediate religious and racial problems of Jews, both of these books symbolize the spiritual problems of modern man. Hilde Abel's *The Guests of Summer* (1951) tells of Julie Dreyfuss, a seventeen-year-old girl spending August of 1939 with her mother at a Jewish summer resort in the Adirondacks. The charms of natural beauty and the liveliness of her own youth are at variance with the constant reminders of anti-Semitic activities in Europe. Julie longs to escape from the tragic destiny of her race and the confines of its religion, to the freedom of young America, represented by Roger, the handsome Anglo-Saxon counselor of a nearby camp who comes to woo her. Yet she is also drawn to the young Polish Jew Friedrich Grocz, who has just come from Europe and is determined to return there, to live or die in the ghetto. Herman Wouk's *Marjorie Morningstar* (discussed also above, pp. 84, 155) shows both the protagonist and her lover, Noel Airman, as renegades from the dietary, sexual, and religious codes of their families, though Marjorie seems to attain at least partial redemption by returning to these three traditions—indeed, she never was very comfortable without them.[2]

It is obvious that most novelists of the last forty years have not regarded religion as a satisfactory key to the meaning of life for sophisti-

181

cated adolescents. In an age dominated by science, a search for fundamental causes and principles is more likely to lead to physical laws than to God. Where there is much religious influence, it almost always comes through tradition, custom, or family indoctrination—almost never as an epiphany of divine power or plan. The important novels of adolescence published in the early twenties usually expressed rejection of religion or indifference to it: Felix Fay in *Moon-Calf* gives little thought to religion, but when he does he signifies his atheism by wearing a red carnation on the birthday of Robert Ingersoll (p. 130); Amory Blaine in *This Side of Paradise* remains curiously indifferent to religion, in spite of his mother's dallyings with Catholicism, his close friendship with Monsignor Darcy, and his attendance at an Episcopal preparatory school and a Presbyterian university. It seems likely that the revolt against the genteel tradition in literature resulted in a disregard of religious problems in fiction for the first decade of the revolt; but the eternal presence of such problems, especially in adolescence, demanded the attention of novelists in the late twenties and thirties when full, multivolume treatments of adolescent personalities became popular. Simultaneously with the novelists' revived interest in this phase of personal development, psychologists produced more studies of religious experiences in adolescence than had appeared in any other decade since the pioneer works about the turn of the century: *The Varieties of Religious Experience* (1902) by William James and *Adolescence* (2 vols., 1904) by G. Stanley Hall; but there was no special peak of interest by psychologists to match the revival of interest by novelists in the fifties, when there appeared what are probably the two best American novels of adolescent religious experience, *The Morning Watch* and *Go Tell It on the Mountain.*

On the whole, it seems that novelists of the period studied have not done justice to the importance of religious adjustment during the adolescent years. Hall showed that throughout history, lives of the saints have reached a high point of religious fervor during the adolescent years.[3] Several surveys conducted during the thirties indicated that college students at that time were doing a great deal of re-evaluating of religious doctrines, but that over 90 per cent of them believed in God, and over 60 per cent held some sort of orthodox religious views.[4] The high proportion of religious skepticism represented in novels may be at least partly explained by the inquiring and analytical minds of the authors, who invent or adapt incidents and feelings based on their own experience. And as intellect without faith in something seldom leads to a satisfactory explanation of the purpose of life, either for adolescents who must plan to live it or for novelists who must interpret and represent it, there should be small wonder that authors who try to replace faith with intellect have led us into a period when a "beat" attitude is considered the most observable literary characteristic.

Chapter VI

COMMUNITY ENVIRONMENT

As a child grows older he becomes more and more subject to the influence of cultural standards in the community in which he lives. During his preschool years, his own family exerts the chief external influence upon him, but the pressures of the community begin to be felt through teachers and schoolmates, and by the time he reaches adolescence the community influence is likely to be greater than that of the family.

Community influences differ, of course, in different regions and in different types of community within each region. This chapter will discuss in order the three main types of community—rural, small-town, and city—noting regional differences within each type, and will then comment on novels where problems of adjustment are increased by striking racial or cultural differences between the adolescent's immediate family and the surrounding community.

RURAL ENVIRONMENT

Of the three types of communities, the rural is least likely to have any sort of planned community program for adolescents, partly because of distance between homes and lack of large, central meeting places, and partly because farm chores are likely to leave the adolescents with comparatively little time for community activities. What community activities there are, usually center in school, church, or Grange; but there is also community influence through neighborhood co-operation in large undertakings, such as harvesting or barn-raising. In the absence of strong human community influences, the land itself exerts more influence on rural youngsters than on city or small-town adolescents.

Well over half of the novels depicting adolescents influenced by rural environment are set in the Midwest or in the South. The harshness of Midwest farm life which Hamlin Garland made famous in *Main-Travelled Roads* (1891) appears in most twentieth-century novels as an occasional

185

danger rather than a constant condition. In Glenway Wescott's *The Apple of the Eye,* Hannah Madoc lives through a rather wretched adolescence on a Wisconsin farm, but her wretchedness is due rather to her father's drunken brutality than to the heavy demands of farm work or the censoriousness of her neighbors, both of which she is able to take in her stride. Dan Strane and Rosalie Bier, adolescents of a later generation in the same novel, suffer in varying degrees because of the narrow moral standards of the community, but they also find beauty in their environment. (For a fuller discussion of this novel, see above, page 172.) Martha Ostenso in *Wild Geese* and O. E. Rölvaag in *Peder Victorious* describe hardships in adolescent adjustment caused by the rigors of climate in the North Central states and by the unappeasable stubbornness of the inhabitants. Judith Gare and Peder Holm are adolescent protagonists of sufficient strength and spirit to overcome these difficulties, as Willa Cather's Midwestern heroines do; but other characters in these novels succumb to the harshness of the country and of its people, as do Wescott's Rosalia Bier and most of Hamlin Garland's protagonists. Phil Stong wrote of Iowa farm life (*State Fair,* 1932; *The Long Lane,* 1939) and Herman Fetzer, under the pen name "Jake Falstaff," wrote of Ohio farm life (*Jacoby's Corners,* 1940; *The Big Snow,* 1941; *Come Back to Wayne County,* 1942) as having irresistible charm for certain adolescents, in spite of the hardships involved. Alvin Johnson's *Spring Storm* (1936) and Katherine Carson's *Mrs. Pennington* (1939) show the coarseness in farm communities, in Nebraska and Kansas, respectively, which is offensive to adolescents whose sensitivity and temperament make them better suited to Eastern city life. But Marquis Childs's *The Cabin* (1944) presents an equally sensitive adolescent who, after longing to escape the annual Iowa farm vacation which he associates with childhood, and to join a more sophisticated contemporary in a visit to Milwaukee, decides at last that the farm experience has more genuine value for him than the trip to the city would have. Mildred Walker's *Winter Wheat* (1944) and Dorothy James Roberts' *A Durable Fire* (1945) both tell of girls in late adolescence who find on Midwestern farms a certain peace of mind that they are afraid of losing if they move away, even though they know, through long experience, that clashes of wills and personalities are more obvious and less avoidable in rural loneliness than in town activity. E. R. Zietlow's *These Same Hills* (1960) tells of eighteen-year-old Jim Heiss in the Badlands of South Dakota torn between the desire to cling to rustic ways by remaining a trapper and the logic of adapting himself to more sophisticated life by getting a college education. Farms in the border region between Midwest and South provide settings for Louis Bromfield's *The Wild Country* (1948), set in Missouri, and Helga Sandburg's *The Wheel of Earth* (1958), set in Kentucky and Illinois; and both these novels show some of the lawlessness and violence characteristic of Southern fiction as well as the narrow conservatism characteristic of much Midwest fiction.

Unthinking mob violence, hatred of outsiders and law enforcement agents, stubborn pride in prejudice and resistance to change—all these have long been characteristic of rural Southerners as depicted in novels. Mark Twain noted them in *The Adventures of Huckleberry Finn* (1885), and they appear, together with the extreme poverty that has become another hallmark of the rural Southerner, in Elizabeth Madox Roberts' *The Time of Man* (1926). The violence and degradation of Southern farmers are described in extreme, even in grotesque, degree in novels by William Faulkner (*As I Lay Dying*, 1930; *Light in August*, 1932; *The Hamlet*, 1940) and by Erskine Caldwell (*Tobacco Road*, 1932; *God's Little Acre*, 1933; *Trouble in July*, 1940). In contrast to these modern novels, there appears to be little if any bitterness in Twain's account of the feud between the Grangerfords and the Shepherdsons, although the author clearly disapproves of the archaic, inhumane code of honor that keeps the feud active. Ellen Chesser in *The Time of Man* has a simple heroism that enables her to find some beauty and goodness in life despite her family's extreme poverty, the casual faithlessness of her first lover, and, in her mature life, the unreasoning hatred and violence of neighbors against her husband. There is no such heroism in the rural adolescents of Caldwell, and if any appears in those of Faulkner it is in such minor characters as Lucy Pate and Jack Houston of *The Hamlet*. The Lesters of *Tobacco Road* and the Waldens of *God's Little Acre* are content with poverty; rather than make an intelligent and sustained effort to rise above it, they intensify it by their misdirected efforts. Sonny Clark of *Trouble in July* is a pathetic Negro youth who knows that, once he has been accused of raping a white girl, there is no hope for him except in flight, and very little even in that; his accuser, Katy Barlow, is a spineless young voluptuary who makes the accusation simply because it is expected of her, and does not deny it until Sonny has been hanged by an angry mob.[1] The young Bundrens of *As I Lay Dying* are as hopelessly doomed to

187

poverty as are the Lesters and the Waldens, although they show a little more insight, initiative, and individuality. Lena Grove of *Light in August* is a rather characterless symbol of the dogged persistence to be found in rural Southern poor whites, as Eula Varner in *The Hamlet* is the symbol of pure sex and the young Snopeses in the same novel are symbols of the increasing influence of the poor white farmer through sheer proliferation.

The Southern code of honor in conflict with natural inclinations brings tragedy to an adolescent couple in James Street's novel *In My Father's House* (1941). Although sixteen-year-old Teenie Abernathy wants to marry Woody Martin, whom all her family like, her father insists that she must first attend Agricultural High School for a year. When Little Hob, Teenie's fourteen-year-old brother, innocently tells his father of the Negro report that Woody has been "planting his crop before fencing it in," Big Hob feels required to kill Woody. Another fourteen-year-old Mississippi farm boy, the title figure of *Piney* (1950) by Zachary Ball (the pen name of Kelly R. Masters), tells of his harsh life on the farm of a brutal cousin after Piney's father has been executed for murder.

Violence and poverty on Kentucky farms are treated matter-of-factly, even humorously, in novels by Jesse Stuart. In *Taps for Private Tussie* (1943) the narrator, Sid Tussie, is apparently in early adolescence when a report of his Uncle Kim's death leaves the family with ten thousand dollars of insurance to put a temporary end to the Tussies' poverty and to stir up bitter rivalry among male members of the family for the hand of the supposed widow. In *Hie to the Hunters* (1950), the fourteen-year-old town boy Did Hargis goes to live with his sixteen-year-old friend Jud Sparks in the mountains, where he takes part in the feud between the farmers and the hunters, and learns to wear a gun when he goes to dances, but never learns to spit tobacco juice with Sparkie's unerring accuracy. Both these novels are written with tall-tale humor and a sprinkling of sentimentality.

A prolonged and violent hatred between Vance Acroft, a Mississippi planter's son, and Max Harper, a sharecropper's son, is the subject of Thomas Hal Phillips' *The Loved and the Unloved* (1955). The feud begins when the Harpers move to the Acroft farm, when the boys are fourteen, and ends with Max's killing of Vance about eight years later. Flannery O'Connor's *The Violent Bear It Away* (1960) indicates violence in the life of young Tarwater in the mountains of Tennessee. But most novels of the rural South published between 1950 and 1960 were more

188

likely to stress the beauties of nature and the fascination of hunting than poverty, injustice, and violence. This trend had appeared as early as 1938 with Marjorie Kinnan Rawlings' *The Yearling,* set in the wild country of Florida, and some of the same atmosphere is found in Faulkner's "The Bear" (1942). During the fifties, novels describing the influence of Southern woods and hunting on adolescent boys became quite common: Stuart's *Hie to the Hunters,* set in Kentucky; Reuben Davis' *Shim* (1953) and James Street's *Goodbye, My Lady* (1954), in Mississippi; Fred Gipson's *Hound-Dog Man* (1949) and *Old Yeller* (1956) and William Humphrey's *Home from the Hill* (1958), in Texas; Donald Wetzel's *The Rain and the Fire and the Will of God* (1957) and Paul Boles's *Parton's Island* (1958), in Alabama; and Wesley Ford Davis' *The Time of the Panther* (1958) in Florida. The novels dealing with adolescents in relation to animals will be discussed further in Chapter VII.

Problems of rural adolescents in novels of the West are as varied as the Western terrain. Vardis Fisher's *In Tragic Life* emphasizes the loneliness of the remote Idaho farm where Vridar Hunter spends his childhood and much of his adolescence; the novel also shows how the coarse words and actions of the country people offend Vridar's natural sensitivity and the prudishness which his mother has firmly implanted in him. Colorado provides the setting for Hope Williams Sykes's *Second Hoeing* (1935), for the latter part of Jean Stafford's *The Mountain Lion* (1947), and for the first two volumes of Ralph Moody's somewhat autobiographical trilogy, *Little Britches* (1950) and *Man of the Family* (1951), briefly described in the last preceding chapter (pp. 165–66 above). Hannah Schreissmiller in *Second Hoeing* faces a double problem of adjustment to community environment: that of an ambitious, intelligent girl doomed to arduous labor in the beet fields, and that of a rebel against her father's Old World tyranny when she sees the freedom and opportunities available to neighboring adolescents of older American families. Miss Stafford's Ralph and Molly Fawcett, closer than most brothers and sisters because of a similar feeling of alienation from both family and community in their California home, react very differently to the new environment of their Uncle Claude's Colorado ranch. Ralph finds freedom, new insights into life, and challenges to his approaching manhood; Molly finds only reminders of her own inadequacy and estrangement from the one person to whom she had been close. *Little Britches* describes the natural hardships on a Colorado ranch—the droughts, the cloudbursts, the tornadoes—and their effect in turning a little boy into a responsible young man at the age of eleven. *Man of the Family* shows the Moody family on the brink of destitution after the father's death places even more responsibility on young Ralph; they have moved to the edge of town, where there is less threat from natural calamities, but they are still able to carry on some of the farming and cattle-driving that the boy loves. All of these novels of rural Colorado indicate that the land either destroys or toughens the young people who grow up on it, and that the neighbors are rough but kindly and helpful.

Both land and people of an unidentified Western state help bring maturity to an adolescent boy in Edmund Ware's *Rider in the Sun* (1935). At the age of fifteen, inspired by his father's romantic cowboy stories, Dan runs away from his Eastern home and gets a job on a cattle ranch. For many months he works hard, always hoping to find his cherished idol, "a gallant, invincible horseman"; but his most likely candidate proves to be a horse thief who is fleeing from justice. Though he never finds what he is searching for, Dan does learn much about human nature and about himself before he returns to his home in the East.

Oregon in the early years of the twentieth century appears in two novels by H. L. Davis: *Honey in the Horn* (1935) and *Winds of Morning* (1952). In the earlier novel, sixteen-year-old Clay Calvert, an embittered orphan, wanders for two years in a vague, unfriendly way through scenic but unfriendly country, encountering violence, murder, and an unsatisfying kind of love affair with Luce, the adolescent daughter of a wandering horse-trader. H. L. Mencken said of the book:

> It would be an error to think of Clay and Luce as its hero and heroine, or even as its principal figures. . . . Its real hero is the sempiternal pioneer, half knave and half child, and its heroine is the uncomely and irrational female who followed him on his witless peregrinations. The wanderers are pretty much the same at the end as they were at the beginning. They have sweated and panted through a series of hostile deserts, and panted and sweated over a series of even more hostile hills, but they have learned nothing useful and forgotten none of their cherished principles, all of them palpably untrue. Sinking down exhausted like so many badly used mules, . . . they hang to the theory that milk and honey must be gurgling from great casks and carboys over the skyline.[2]

And Basil Davenport described Davis' Oregon pioneers as

a set of stupid rowdies whose vocations were, in one way or another, to get rich quick by spoiling the country or each other, and their avocations wenching and murder.[3]

Winds of Morning also presents unprincipled, selfish, distrustful people in adverse natural surroundings as Amos Clarke, a cynical twenty-year-old deputy sheriff, travels about the wilderness with the veteran pioneer Old Hendricks, trying to solve a murder, to mete out justice, and to find the fifteen-year-old Calanthe Busick, with whom he has reluctantly fallen in love. Despite Davis' naturalistic description of a bleak, hostile environment, the novels contain rough, ironic humor and the leading characters are motivated by a shame-faced altruism.

Two novels of the desert region in and around Arizona—Oliver La-Farge's *The Enemy Gods* (1937) and Charles McNichols' *Crazy Weather* (1944)—indicate influences of human and natural environment on adolescent boys; but since both these novels emphasize especially the effects of ethnic conflicts between white and Indian cultures, they will be discussed more fully later in this chapter.

A number of novels published in the thirties, forties, and fifties show adolescents in rural California. Flannery Lewis' *Abel Dayton* (1939) tells of a boy growing to maturity in a tiny railroad junction on the edge of a desert, where his father is telegraph operator. Their only companion in the little yellow building is his father's rather rebellious assistant, Charley Jackson. Abel's adoration of his father decreases as his understanding of Charley grows, and as his freight-train commuting to a nearby small-town high school brings him into contact with other people; but his lonely years on the desert with two men have made him frank, observant, and self-sufficient beyond his years. Steinbeck's novelette "The Red Pony" (1938) also shows the maturing effect of lonely rural life on a California boy (see below, p. 221); his *East of Eden* (1952) is interesting in that it presents contrasting effects of the same rural environment on twin brothers (see above, page 70), but the novel is more strained and less convincing than the novelette. In *The Canyon* (1940) by nineteen-year-old Peter Viertel, the narrator-protagonist George Rivers sees adult prejudices and ambitions and vices gradually penetrating and breaking up his old gang—a girl and three boys besides himself—in their lonely canyon near the coast of southern California. An adolescence almost as limited in human companionship as Able Dayton's is that of Agnes, the protagonist of Judy Van der Veer's *November Grass* (1940). Agnes has

191

her cattle-ranching father's love of outdoors and animals and her Eastern mother's love of books and ideas. She is interested in the people she meets occasionally—the ranchers, the Indians, the sentimental but realistic Gonzales family—but she is more interested in the creatures of nature— her cow pony Pete, her golden bull Joseph, the cows, calves, and goats, the fawns and chipmunks, even the little blind creatures beneath the earth that nibble the roots of the grass and make it quiver. She decides that nature is neither cruel nor kind, but that each living thing, as the center of its own world, is disturbed when death enters that world. This philosophy helps her to adjust maturely when her own love affair ends in tragedy. The loneliness that seems to characterize novels of rural California adolescents is not so apparent in Jessamyn West's *Cress Delahanty;* though Cress lives on an orange ranch, her school activities bring her into frequent and lively contact with other young people and with adults. When she is alone in the country, she lives so much within her own imagination that she seems little affected by her physical environment.

Since the Northeast is more densely populated than other sections of the country, it is not surprising that it provides the setting for fewer novels of rural adolescence. A number of the books about this section that are here classified as novels are closer to autobiography than to fiction. For example, Robert P. Tristram Coffin's *Lost Paradise* (1934) purports to be the nostalgic reminiscences of young Peter Winship, attending school and living in town with a brother and a sister only slightly more advanced in adolescence, as he recalls the typical down-East sights, sounds, and smells of their Maine-coast farm; but it is apparent that Peter is Robert Coffin as a boy, and that many of the experiences and the thoughts described in the book were once the author's. Coffin's first real novel, *Red Sky in the Morning* (1935), has more romantic and sensational elements: a fifteen-year-old boy living with his lovely but unhappy mother, his jealous father, and his favored older brother on a rocky little island off the coast of Maine. Rural Maine, about thirty miles inland, provides the setting for the third volume of Ralph Moody's autobiographical trilogy, *The Fields of Home* (1953), where fourteen-year-old Ralph tries to introduce his Colorado farming methods, much to the scorn of his cantankerous grandfather. A very remote New England farm intensifies the dreamy inertia of Eben Osborne in Roger W. Eddy's *The Rimless Wheel* (for fuller comments on this novel, see pp. 169–70 above); the same author gives a rather ribald, Peck's-Bad-Boy version of his own adolescent years on a farm outside New Haven in *The Bulls and the Bees* (1956). Another Connecticut farm is the scene of action in Victoria Lincoln's *Out from Eden* (1950); but Todd and Topsy Davenport, the adolescent brother and sister in the novel, have moved about the country so much with their restless artist-father that rural New England is only one of a long series of environments to which they have had to adjust. Besides, each member of the Davenport family is so individualistic and independent that only minor concessions to environment are made in this most unorthodox household. Walter D. Edmonds' *The Boyds of Black River* (1953) provides a striking contrast to most novels of farm life in that its adolescent narrator-protagonist, Teddy Armond, spends his summers with a family of New York State gentlemen farmers who are more concerned with training and caring for race horses than with wresting a living from the soil.

Arranged chronologically according to publication dates, the novels discussed above tend toward increasing mellowness and sympathy toward the influence of farm environment and increasing complexity and subtlety of the adolescent characters thus influenced. Novels of the twenties generally revealed both the people and the physical surroundings as offering relatively little inspiration or comfort to the sensitive adolescent, who was usually represented as the victim of his environment. Novels of the fifties were more likely to show a mixture of good and bad in the environment, with the beauties of nature especially emphasized; the adolescent protagonist of the fifties usually responds to his social and natural environment with a maturing attitude that helps him in facing his problems and sometimes even in solving them. Arranged chronologically according to the occurrence of the events described, the novels show a noticeable encroachment of civilization in rural areas of the Middle West and the West, but not much in those of the South and the East. Farm youngsters in the Middle West are likely to be fairly prosperous but hard working, always conscious of the potential disaster of crop failure, and plagued by narrow-minded, meddling neighbors. Those of the South are likely to be impoverished in spite of the productivity of the soil and climate, devoting energies to traditional fruitless pastimes and affairs of "honor" rather than to improving their status in life, or finding their progress destroyed by prejudiced actions of neighbors. Young people on the more spacious farms of the West are usually faced with more physical toil and more loneliness than those in other areas; the neighbors are not so likely to be antagonistic, but they do not have time to be very helpful. On the much smaller and often run-down farms of the East, some source of income other than farming is usually necessary; there is little interference from neighbors, but the reserved New England character often develops annoying eccentricities within members of the immediate family.

SMALL-TOWN ENVIRONMENT

So many American novels describe adolescents in small-town environment that it would be confusing to discuss more than a representative sample of them. Except for some rather slight regional differences, small towns are pretty much alike all over the country, and adolescents seem to face pretty much the same kind of problems in all of them. There have been two characteristic attitudes of authors toward small-town environment in the period studied: one is the nostalgic attitude which has been traditional in English and American literature since Oliver Goldsmith wrote *The Deserted Village*, and the other is the iconoclastic attitude which began in American literature with E. W. Howe's *The Story of a Country Town* (1882) and reached popular heights with Sinclair Lewis' *Main Street* (1920). Many American small-town novels express attitudes somewhere between these extremes.[4]

Sentimental, nostalgic descriptions of Midwestern small towns appear in Rose Wilder Lane's *Old Home Town* (1935), Madeline Babcock Smith's *The Lemon Jelly Cake* (1952),[5] and Ray Bradbury's *Dandelion Wine* (1957). Each of these consists of loosely related episodes revealing the characters and atmosphere of a small town as seen by a youngster at the beginning of adolescence. Mrs. Lane's Ernestine Blake, just growing into long skirts and an interest in boys during the first decade of the twentieth century, gives her impressions of the old-maid school teacher, Miss Sarah; the hired girl, Almantha; the traveling man who secretly dates the rather wild daughter of wealthy parents; the "country jake" who wins the heart of the well-bred Leila Barbrook—all the memorable eccentrics of a typical small town, but none of them as grotesque and tragic as those which Sherwood Anderson presents in *Winesburg, Ohio*.

Mrs. Smith's Helene Bradford, eleven years old in 1900, has unusually intimate contact with adult personalities and problems through her father's activities as town physician, but her understanding of these is amusingly distorted by her own immaturity. Bradbury's twelve-year-old Douglas Spaulding wanders through an Illinois town in the summer of 1928, enjoying the wonders of new sneakers, a carnival fortune-telling machine, the reminiscences of a Civil War veteran, the electric runabout of two elderly sisters, and the annual ritual of making dandelion wine, seeing all these things with the unspoiled eyes of a boy on the threshold of a new phase of life, so that the commonplace small-town environment becomes as strange and marvelous to him as the new worlds of the author's better-known science fiction. Doug learns so many new things about his family, his neighbors, and his town that he keeps a notebook of "Discoveries and Revelations":

> Grandpa or Dad don't know everything in the world. . . . But it's no crime. That I discovered, too. (P. 41.)
> Here's what I got on the wine: Every time you bottle it, you got a whole chunk of 1928 put away, safe. (P. 42.)
> The reason why grownups and kids fight is because they belong to separate races. Look at them, different from us. Look at us, different from them. Separate races, and "never the twain shall meet." (P. 42.)

Very unflattering pictures of Midwestern small towns appear in Rollo Walter Brown's *The Firemakers* (1931) and *Toward Romance* (1932), in Emerson Price's *Inn of That Journey* (1939), and in Henry Bellamann's *Kings Row* (1940). Brown's novels present an ugly Ohio coal-mining town from which two generations of the Dabney family struggle to escape, during adolescence and afterward (see above, pp. 150, 151, and 177). Price's novel shows an equally ugly Ohio town, located among dreary cornfields and inhabited by ignorant, prejudiced, apathetic clods. Though Mark Cullen is depressed by the town when his family first moves there, he comes gradually to accept its ways, and never realizes the potential intellectual superiority which might have enabled him to escape it or to raise its standards (see above, pp. 84-85). Kings Row, apparently located in or near Missouri, is considerably larger than the Ohio towns described by Brown and Price; but it is small enough for Parris Mitchell and his friends to find the formative years of their adolescence inextricably woven into the complex web of personal relationships that involves all the prominent citizens and many that are not prominent.

Thus Cassandra Tower keeps her beauty and ardor in frustrated loneliness, not only because her father is a recluse, but also because the sadistic and influential Dr. Gordon has a daughter of Cassie's age but less attractive. Jamie Wakefield is equally lonely because his poetic interests and mild homosexual tendencies seem repulsive to almost everybody in town. Drake McHugh is confirmed in sensual indulgence by his reaction to the town gossip that censures his choice of girls to go riding with. And Parris himself is regarded as strange and unacceptable by many because he lives with a foreign-looking grandmother, speaks French and German fluently, and befriends the social outcasts (see above, pp. 162–63).

Nostalgic descriptions of New England towns appear in Elizabeth Jordan's *Daddy and I* (1935), R. L. Duffus' *That Was Alderbury* (1941) and *The Waterbury Record* (1959), and Ruth Moore's *The Fire Balloon* (1948) and *Candlemas Bay* (1951). *Daddy and I* purports to be fifteen-year-old June Drew's written account of small-town incidents involving her friends, her teachers, and her father's friends as she searches for a suitable wife for her widower father. *That Was Alderbury* shows how the rugged life in a Vermont town in 1898 molds the character of its inhabitants, especially of four thirteen-year-old boys. Some of the adventures of Phil Burns and his friends are reminiscent of those of Tom Sawyer—especially the searching for buried treasure in a cave—but they are also influenced by some adult activities which they do not quite understand, such as the meetings of their pretty new teacher with the young married minister. Similar scenes and experiences, but somewhat more autobiographical, are presented in *The Waterbury Record*. Still more rugged is the life and more stalwartly independent are the characters in the Maine fishing villages of Miss Moore's novels: Scratch Corner, where Theoline Sewell has a disappointing love affair but learns to take heart from the example of her grandmother, and Candlemas Bay, where Jeb Ellis combines the fearless seamanship of his ancestors with knowledge of new inventions, like diesel engines and ship-to-shore telephones, to aid his widowed mother and his aged grandfather in supporting a large family.

But New England villages, too, may receive very unflattering treatment in novels of adolescence. Two such novels are Daphne Athas' *The Weather of the Heart* (1947) and Grace Metalious' *Peyton Place* (1956). The former shows how the Wall sisters, Eliza and Hetty, in the Maine fishing village of Kittery Point, have their personalities badly warped in adolescence by the town's stiff-necked reaction to Eliza's love affair with the one-eyed French-Canadian outcast boy Claw Moreau. *Peyton Place* shows the devastating effect of small-town bigots on the lives of a number of adolescents in a New Hampshire village: on Allison Mackenzie, whose mother rears her on lies for fear of scandal; on Selena Cross, whose shack home condemns her to the town's contempt; on Ted Carter, whose long devotion to Selena is destroyed when public opinion turns violently against her; and on Rodney Harrington, Betty Anderson, and Norman Page, who are equally trapped by the influence of gossip.

Southern novels of small-town adolescents are far more likely to be critical of the community environment than sentimental about it. Thomas Wolfe's Altamont, William Faulkner's Jefferson, and the small Georgia towns of Carson McCullers' novels—all show more hostility than friendliness, but there is enough of both to make the descriptions credible. Unbelievably hostile are the towns in Erskine Caldwell's novels; his *Place Called Estherville* (1949) shows a town so uniformly cruel to the handsome mulatto brother and sister, Ganus and Kathyanne Bazemore, that the reader finds himself muttering, "Oh, come now!" at each new incident of abuse. Caldwell's poor-white farm families, like the Lesters of *Tobacco Road* and the Waldens of *God's Little Acre*, are sure to be cheated when they go into town. Jesse Stuart's *Hie to the Hunters*, as might be expected, shows a Kentucky town to be much less suitable than the mountains as an environment for growing boys. In Truman Capote's *The Grass Harp*, a small Louisiana town represents unsympathetic practicality and selfishness as opposed to the lovable romanticism of young Collin Fenwick and his elderly cousin Dolly Talbo, taking refuge from the town's encroachments in a tree house among fields where the wind strums music on dry autumn grass.

Western novels of adolescence usually feature great open spaces rather than small-town environments; but in the twentieth century the most remote of ranches maintains some regular contact with town, and farm youngsters attend school in town. Vardis Fisher's Vridar Hunter comes from an isolated Idaho valley to live in town while attending school, but his introspective tendencies and his need to keep house for himself and his brother prevent his joining many town activities. The general effect of the town, however, is to counteract some of his mother's excessive puritanism and to make him aware of normal tendencies among boys of his own age. A more continual influence of small-town environment is apparent in Mac Gardner's *Mom Counted Six* (1944), which describes a large family living in a small town in Washington, across the bay from Seattle. But the Holly family is not one to be influenced by small-town prejudices; Mom and Pop have brought up their children to be extremely liberal, and Brooke in her adolescence does not question the propriety of her love affair with Kip Toby, son of the town drunkard. Although the Hollys represent an extreme case of indifference to town pressures, it is generally true that Western novels show less influence of community prejudices on the adolescent than do novels set in other parts of the country. William Saroyan's *The Human Comedy* (1943) gives a sentimental and unconvincing presentation of a fourteen-year-old boy's abrupt introduction to adult problems through his job as a telegraph messenger boy in a small town in California. The pose of cosmic significance suggested by the novel's title and by its homespun philosophy becomes rather nauseating, but Homer Macauley's awkward attempts to express his newly discovered insights are certainly typical of one aspect of adolescence. In response to an old telegrapher's remarks about the great changes in Homer during his first three days on the job, the boy muses:

> "Yeah, I've changed all right. I guess I've grown up. And I guess it was *time* for me to grow up. I didn't know *anything* until I got this job. Oh, I knew a lot of things, but I didn't know the half of it, and I guess I never will, either. I guess nobody ever will." (P. 140.)

The insights which Homer gains might come to him anywhere, but they come with greater impact because the problems of life and death are perceived in a small town, where he feels a kinship with the people involved.

Although the first part of Jean Stafford's *The Mountain Lion* and a considerable portion of Jessamyn West's *Cress Delahanty* are set in California ranch country, the ease of transportation and communication, the centralization of schools, and the conviviality of neighbors makes the modern farm community almost as closely knit as the small-town community of the nineteenth century, and the problems faced by adolescents in these novels are approximately those faced by adolescents in small towns. Thus Ralph and Molly Fawcett in *The Mountain Lion* are lonely, not because they live in the country, but because they are different from others of their age: they are thin and unattractive, wear glasses, and have frequent nosebleeds besides having the extreme sensitivity that is almost standard in adolescent protagonists. Their two sisters, a few years farther advanced in adolescence, have become typical small-town snobs, concerned primarily with the impression they are making on other people. Cress, too, is conscious of social protocol; as an orange-grower's daughter visiting a school friend in an oil-well area, she feels the way a small-town merchant's daughter would in visiting a friend on the wrong side of the tracks.

LOWER-CLASS CITY ENVIRONMENT

Novels of adjustment to city environment need to be divided into novels of lower-class environment and those of upper-class, since the problems are entirely different. Any such division into classes is of course arbitrary, and it would be as easy to find six classes as it is to find two; but two categories are enough to indicate the differences in environmental influence. Novels of the lower class seem far more common, and certainly they are more striking. Probably at least half of all novels of adolescents in cities are set in New York; Chicago undoubtedly ranks second in popularity, and there are a good many novels set in Philadelphia, Boston, and Los Angeles. Other American cities appear only occasionally, although San Francisco, as the home of "beat" literature, is found rather often in novels of the fifties.

In contrast to small towns, which often present problems because of the prying interest of many people outside the immediate family, cities often present problems because of indifference. It is possible for a city youngster, especially a shy one, to spend days without seeing anyone who cares what he does, outside his immediate family, and city families are likely to spend less time together than families in small towns or rural areas. Lower-class city families are often kept apart by job responsibilities, and upper-class families are often separated by social activities.

The problems of lower-class adolescents living in cities were not new to American fiction readers in 1920. Two of the earliest novels in American naturalism had emphasized such problems: Stephen Crane's *Maggie* (1893) had told of a girl growing up in a New York slum with

199

very little help or sympathy from her family and none from anybody outside the family; and Dreiser's *Sister Carrie* (1900) showed a young girl trying to support herself in Chicago without previous knowledge of the city and its ways. The novels of the 1920's did not add much to what had previously been written of such girls and their difficulties, although John Dos Passos' *Manhattan Transfer* (1925) reminded readers of the great range of city influences on adolescents of all classes,[6] and Dreiser's *American Tragedy* showed the effect of Kansas City on Clyde Griffiths in much more detail than the author's first novel had showed the effect of Chicago on Carrie Meeber. Dreiser shows how the sordid drabness of Clyde's home and family, in sharp contrast to the luxury of the hotel where he works and the fine clothes of the men and women he serves there, make him determined to acquire wealth and social standing by whatever means he can find; but Dreiser also attributes human motives and actions to "chemisms" in the body which apparently are not influenced by environment.

During the thirties, novels about lower-class adolescents in cities were published more frequently. Most famous of these are James T. Farrell's Studs Lonigan and Danny O'Neill books, although both Studs and Danny belong to the lower middle class rather than to the impoverished group which produced Crane's Maggie and Jimmie Johnson and Dreiser's Clyde and Esta Griffiths. While Studs's sister Fran and Danny's Uncle Al strive to raise themselves and their families to a higher social level, both Studs and Danny find that most of their street companions place little value on cultural achievements, admiring instead the boy who can fight, win athletic contests, defy authority, steal without being caught, and boast of his sexual conquests. As Studs is successful in attaining these goals, he is trapped by his own popularity into a life of dissipation that leads to an early death; as Danny is never popular with the street gangs, he seeks satisfaction in study and writing, and presumably escapes to a higher social level when he leaves his family and Chicago to seek a writing career in New York.

New York slums affect the development of adolescent boys in Leane Zugsmith's *The Reckoning* (1934) and Joseph Gollomb's *Unquiet* (1935). The first of these tells of fifteen-year-old Castie Petrello, who, like Studs Lonigan, realizes that he can gain more respect from his peers by daring outlawry than by scholastic achievement. Therefore he steals a car belonging to the rich Jewish manufacturer Arthur Turk, and when he is caught he lies about his age so that he will be sent to Welfare Island instead of to reform school. Through the combined efforts of the sentimental Mrs. Turk, of an idealistic young lawyer from Oneida, New York, and of Castie's sympathetic school teacher, the boy is released; but there is little indication that Castie will gratefully repay these efforts by leading a better life. *Unquiet* tells of a Jewish immigrant boy, David Levitt, who is too spirited and unquiet to accept passively the belligerent contempt which is all that the Irish boys of the neighborhood are ready to offer him. Like Farrell's Danny O'Neill, David has an interest in study and writing, so that his lack of acceptance by the street gangs only supplies him with an additional incentive to rise above his environment.

A number of rather important novels of the thirties and forties present lower-class adolescents in Chicago. Besides Farrell's Studs Lonigan and Danny O'Neill books, there are Nelson Algren's *Never Come Morning* (1941) and the latter part of his *Somebody in Boots* (1935), Richard Wright's *Native Son* (1940), and the latter part of Willard Motley's *Knock on Any Door* (1947). Somewhat less important is Albert Halper's *The Chute* (1936). Since each of these novels is discussed elsewhere in this study (see Index), it is only necessary here to mention that each of them shows the corrupting influence of a city whose gangland activities during the prohibition era made it a world-wide symbol for crime and vice. In contrast to these naturalistic novels of the thirties and forties, Halper's *The Golden Watch* (1953) gives a sentimental and nostalgic picture of lower-class Chicago.

Betty Smith's very popular *A Tree Grows in Brooklyn* combines sentimentalism with realism in depicting the adolescence of Francie Nolan. From her Austrian grandmother, Francie has inherited a great resilience, which enables her to live through poverty, hard work, and the influence of a slum environment with high spirits and a loyal affection for her neighborhood and her family. Even more nostalgic and sentimental than Francie's chronicle is *Transfer Point* (1947) by Kathryn Forbes (the pen name of Kathryn McLean), who is better known for her earlier novel *Mama's Bank Account*. In *Transfer Point* Alice Barton, between her eleventh and thirteenth years in San Francisco shortly after World War I, experiences the separation of her parents, and a divided life which alternates between the boardinghouse that her mother opens as a means of support and the disreputable part of town where her improvident but cherished father is dying. Alice is no angel; she delights in playing pranks, some of which are rather cruel. But neither is she the delinquent youngster who appears as the almost inevitable result of lower-class city life in many novels published after World War II.

Chapter III of this study discussed the wave of juvenile-delinquency novels that began about 1947 and has scarcely yet begun to recede (see above, pp. 89–95). Most of these novels are set in lower-class sections of large cities, particularly New York and Chicago; but other cities come in for a share of the attention: Denver in the first part of Motley's *Knock on Any Door,* an unnamed Ohio city in Virgil Scott's *The Dead Tree Gives No Shelter* (1947), another unnamed Midwestern city in Martin Yoseloff's *The Girl in the Spike-Heeled Shoes* (1949), Atlanta in Donald Windham's *The Dog Star* (1950), Birmingham in John Lee Weldon's *The Naked Heart* (1953), New Orleans in the latter part of Nelson Algren's *A Walk on the Wild Side,* and Saint Louis in Herbert Simmons' *Corner Boy* (1957). In each of these, the adolescent suffers from lack of understanding and appreciation and is impelled to win power and esteem by illegal means, often by peddling drugs and sometimes by prostitution, pandering, and armed violence. Comparatively few recent novels about lower-class city adolescents allow their protagonists to preserve ideals in such a community environment, but two novels published in 1958 indicate their authors' recognition of the fact that this environment does not inevitably produce corruption. Betty Smith's *Maggie-Now* relates how a young tomboy in Brooklyn, left motherless at fourteen, becomes a tender and responsible guardian of her baby brother and housekeeper for her dour and demanding father; and Jerome Weidman's *The Enemy Camp* tells how the Jewish orphan George Hurst develops into a respected and honorable businessman, despite the demoralizing influence of his East Side New York pal Danny Schorr and the implacable "hate gentiles" preaching of his foster mother, "Aunt Tessie."

UPPER-CLASS CITY ENVIRONMENT

Novels of more well-to-do city adolescents are less likely to follow a stereotyped pattern. Ethel May Kelley's *Beauty and Mary Blair* (1921) is the story of the eighteen-year-old daughter of a sophisticated New

York couple who dabble openly in extramarital affairs and allow their three children to live just about as they please. The novel has an unconvincing happy ending; the parents are reconciled to each other, forsaking the temptations of gay city life, and Mary Blair is saved from a "ruined life" partly by coincidence and partly by a sudden instinctive insight into the difference between sordidness and beauty. No such *deus ex machina* rescues Gloria Wandrous in John O'Hara's *Butterfield 8* (1935); Gloria's wealthy widowed mother and her devoted bachelor uncle are unable to keep the lovely girl from being sexually molested at eleven years of age by a middle-aged friend of the family in Pittsburgh, or from being seduced in a New York hotel at fifteen by a respectable-looking school principal, or from becoming a heavy drinker at eighteen and a casual bed-companion of New York college boys at nineteen. A more active desire for precocious sampling of the forbidden pleasures of sophisticated society is the motive for Courtney Farrell and her friend Janet Parker in Pamela Moore's *Chocolates for Breakfast* (1956) in their alcoholic and sexual orgies in New York and Hollywood; and the same motive impels the two New York girls Emily and Amy as they plan campaigns to experience premarital sex, unsuccessfully at fifteen in *Love Me Little* (1957) and successfully but not entirely happily at seventeen in *The Bright Young Things* (1958), both written by Warren Miller under the pen name "Amanda Vail." But other novels about affluent urban adolescents show other reactions to the city's influence. Helen Carlisle in *The Merry, Merry Maidens* (1937) traces a variety of careers for her six New York high-school girls, including a happy, commonplace home life for the narrator, Ruth. Meyer Levin's *The Old Bunch* (1937) shows a group of adolescent Jews in Chicago, most of them from well-to-do families but some of limited means, developing in as many different ways as there are different personalities among them; and the same author's *Compulsion* (see above, page 93) shows two brilliant Jewish boys of very wealthy Chicago families finding their pleasure not only in intellectual discussions and reading, but also in homosexuality, in larceny, and eventually in murder. Two novels by Herman Wouk present very different problems of upper-class Jewish adolescents in New York: *The City Boy* (1948) introduces in eleven-year-old Herbie Bookbinder a fat, urbanized, semitized Penrod who blunders into both difficulties and triumphs; and *Marjorie Morningstar* (1955) studies an intelligent girl who is torn by her respective devotions to her conservative Jewish family, to her apostate, free-living lover, and to her theatrical ambitions. Sonie Marburg in Jean Stafford's *Boston Adventure* indicates that the daughter of poor immigrant parents in a Massachusetts fishing village may find, when her dream of living in a wealthy Boston home is realized, that the honors of city society life are hollow and that the problems which such life imposes are severe. Theodora Keogh's *Meg* (1950) describes a twelve-year-old girl who lives in a fashionable apartment overlooking New York's East River and attends an exclusive day school; but in roller-skating home from school (certainly an unusual practice for a wealthy Manhattan girl!) Meg makes friends with a gang of slum boys, who introduce her to an unsavory world of prostitutes and Lesbians, and to personal experience with sex. Yet these slum experiences are no more horrible than some that are hinted at in Meg's own upper-class world. If Mrs. Keogh's picture of New York's influence on its adolescents is unconvincing, J. D. Salinger's *Catcher in the Rye* demonstrates much more convincingly that sordidness and insincerity at all social levels in the city can be so apparent to a boy of the upper class that his faith in humanity is strained and almost destroyed.

In contrast to the perceptiveness of Salinger's Holden Caulfield, two works by James Purdy show adolescent boys facing corruption in upper-class city life with incredible naïveté. The novella "63: Dream Palace" (1957) presents nineteen-year-old Fenton Riddleway, an impoverished orphan from West Virginia, picked up and richly entertained by wealthy strangers in a large city,[7] so that he murders his beloved invalid brother Claire in order to avoid losing the material pleasures that have suddenly come to him. A still less realistic character, and one apparently intended satirically and allegorically, is the title figure of *Malcolm* (1959), a fourteen-year-old boy left by his father in a luxurious metropolitan hotel, where he is found by the astrologer Mr. Cox and introduced to a series of grotesque individuals representing various aspects of corrupt modern society. Throughout his adventures, Malcolm maintains a strange and attractive innocence, even though he is physically destroyed by excesses of alcohol and sex.

A portion of one chapter can only suggest the great variety of problems which face city-bred adolescents in fiction. In general, the problems of well-to-do city youngsters are likely to be more subtle than those of lower-class boys and girls, but they can be just as important to the adolescents themselves, and even more interesting to novelists and their readers. Blanche Gelfant in *The American City Novel* points out that the city epitomizes the chief concerns of the modern novelist in depicting the plight of man in the twentieth century:

> a concern over man's aloneness and alienation, over the collapse of his community and the breakdown of tradition, the ineffectuality of love and religion, the impact of mechanization, the materialism of modern life, and the conflict between artist and society. (P. 21.)

Since these concerns involve the responsiveness of a perceptive protagonist, and since members of the upper class are, on the whole, likely to be more perceptive than members of the lower class, problems of adolescents in the upper class present more interesting variety and complexity than do those of the lower class, which tend to fall into stereotyped patterns in fiction. Thus a fairly clear pattern can be traced for the development of the lower-class city novel: during the twenties, comparatively few such novels featured adolescents; during the thirties, adolescents appeared as the helpless victims of the economic system; during the forties, these novels increasingly showed adolescents edged into delinquency by their community environment; during the fifties, the output of juvenile delinquency novels remained high, but also during the forties and fifties occasional novels depicted impoverished city life with sentiment and nostalgia. No such pattern appears for the upper-class city novel, however; throughout the period of this study, such novels are notable for their variety and complexity.

Adjustment to any sort of community environment is difficult for an adolescent who has been accustomed to an entirely different environment or who is strikingly set off from others in the community by appearance or manner. The difficulty is likely to be greatest when the young person has come from another country, or shows obvious influence of parents from another country. Members of different races are likely to have difficulty in adjusting to each other, even though both races may have lived in the same community for a long time. And there is difficulty when a boy or a girl moves to a part of the country where customs are different, as from the North to the South, or from the country to the city.

Before 1920, some of Willa Cather's novels, such as *My Ántonia* and *The Song of the Lark,* had presented difficulties experienced by children of immigrant families—Bohemian, Scandinavian, Irish—in adjusting to each other and to native American families in rural communities in the Middle West. Rural communities and cities both tend to maintain distinctions of national origin more than small towns do. On farms, families work together a great deal of the time, and children tend to pick up the speech patterns and the customs of their parents. In cities, large concentrations of people from any particular foreign country are likely to form communities of their own within the American community, and to encourage each other to continue the speech and customs of the old country. In small towns, however, foreign families are brought constantly in contact wtih native families and quickly adapt themselves to native culture, although the process is sometimes painful and humiliating.

Rölvaag's *Peder Victorious* is reminiscent of Willa Cather's novels in that it shows an adolescent child of foreign parents growing up in a Midwestern rural community that is part Norwegian Lutheran and part Irish Catholic. The differences in religion as well as language tend to keep these elements in the community distinct from each other and from being absorbed by the native population. This study has mentioned earlier the mother's attempts to keep her children from becoming Americanized (pp. 68, 83, and 177 above), but Peder finds his closest friend and his sweetheart among the Irish and feels that it is wrong of both groups to place their older national loyalties above their loyalty to the United States. Religious difference delays the assimilation of a Romanian Jewish family into a Montana community in Myron Brinig's *Singermann;* the parents try to maintain their seven children in the traditional old-country manner, and every impulse that draws the children closer to American ways causes pain to the parents and divided loyalty in the children. Similar problems with immigrant Jewish families appear in Gollomb's *Unquiet,* Levin's *The Old Bunch,* and Weidman's *The Enemy Camp.*

A number of novels present German or German-Russian families with

206

children going through adolescence during the violently anti-German years of World War I. In Gordon Friesen's *Flamethrowers,* the German-Russian immigrant boy Peter Franzman is rejected by his Kansas schoolmates because of his German name, while his devout Mennonite mother objects to every concession that he makes to the non-Mennonite world. As a result, Peter is forced to live more and more within himself. In Vincent Sheean's *Bird of the Wilderness,* seventeen-year-old Bill Owens, half Welsh and half German, turns against his German relatives and the Lutheran church in an Illinois town which is largely pro-German during the early years of the war. In Jean Stafford's *Boston Adventure,* Sonia Marburg is plagued by her schoolmates in a Massachusetts fishing village because she is half German and half Russian. Even without the background of war hysteria, German-Russian Hannah Schreissmiller finds herself rejected by American neighbors in the beet-growing country of Colorado in Hope Williams Sykes's *Second Hoeing.*

An immigrant from England has less difficulty in adjusting to an American community, since language and religion do not present barriers. Geoff Barton in Christopher Morley's *Thorofare* is readily accepted in an American community, but he is constantly reminded that he is British, and must always play the part of the defeated enemy when the boys want to re-enact the Revolutionary War. Mario Van de Weyer in Santayana's *The Last Puritan,* half American and half Italian by parentage but almost wholly English by education, is readily accepted by fellow students at Williams and Harvard, but he retains a European attitude toward life.

A variety of novels about immigrant adolescents appeared in the fifties. David Cornel DeJong's *Two Sofas in the Parlor* (1952) tells of the Kegel family, who moved from Holland to Grand Rapids in 1913 with six children, the two oldest of whom—Johannes and Renzel—are in early adolescence at the time. The parents want their children to keep the rigid standards of cleanliness and morality that they enforced in Holland, but American ways are much freer and more untidy. Johannes changes his name to John and tries to adopt the ways of American young people; but Renzel, the protagonist, is more sensitive, introspective, and conscientious and feels that he cannot completely accept American customs any more than he can persistently follow those of Holland. Irving Shulman's *The Square Trap* (1953) shows a young *pachuco* in Los Angeles trying to break out of the Mexican ghetto

207

by means of his boxing ability. He changes his name from Tomas Cantanios to Tommy Kansas, and wins some money and fame as a fighter of preliminary bouts; but his father is contemptuous of anyone who will fight merely for money and for the pleasure of *Anglos,* and Tommy's ring career and brief period of glory come to an end when his overconfidence prompts him to try to win a fight his manager has arranged for him to throw. In a later novel, *Good Deeds Must Be Punished* (1956), Shulman presents an Italian-American college student who finds that prejudices on both sides tend to keep his ethnic group from associating freely with Americans of older native stock, either on his West Virginia campus or in his New York City home neighborhood. Although there is undoubtedly much truth in this discovery, the author, by concentrating his attention on the unmasking of prejudice rather than on the development of character, produced a much less convincing and less artistic piece of fiction than he did in *The Square Trap.* The Greek-Americans and the Greek immigrant girl who appear in Peter Sourian's *Miri* (1957) capture the reader's belief and affection much more readily than do the characters in *Good Deeds;* again the settings are American campuses and cities, but the feelings expressed are individual rather than typical. Miri is confused by American ways, but feels superior to her American admirer Josh Bigelow; her American-born cousin Lexy, Josh's roommate, is alternately proud and resentful of his Greek heritage, which he has partially rejected in running away from home; Josh is enchanted, amazed, and awed by the exotic qualities he finds in Miri, Lexy, and Lexy's family. Harry Mark Petrakis' *Lion at My Heart* (1959) also shows children of Greek parents in America torn between the culture of their ancestors and the American ways of living. *Pocho* (1959), by José Antonio Villarreal, is like Shulman's *The Square Trap* in that it tells of the difficulties experienced by the American-born children of Mexicans in gaining acceptance by *Anglos* in California; but Villarreal, a Mexican-American himself, presents a more typical situation than does Shulman in that his Richard Rubio grows up among the migratory workers on California farms.

All of these novels emphasize the confusion and ambivalence experienced by the American-born children of immigrant parents, especially when the children are brought into close contact with wholly American neighbors.

Two memorable novels present, from opposing points of view, the conflict between Indian's and white man's ways of living, especially to adolescents who are familiar with both ways. Oliver La Farge's *The Enemy Gods* (1937) describes Myron Begay's long struggle, from the age of six to twenty-two, to choose between the Navajo customs to which his inclinations and his sense of identity impel him and the mission-school ideals to which ambition and gratitude urge him. Charles McNichols' *Crazy Weather* (1944), on the other hand, depicts the fourteen-year-old white South Boy, growing up on a Mojave reservation and torn between his admiration for Indian skills and lore and his desire to please his mother by accepting her program of "Cultural Advancement and Christian Instruction." In both these novels the complex interplay of attractions and fears is convincingly presented; and each boy characteristically decides, at last, to conform to the established pattern of his own race. In Peter Viertel's *The Canyon* (1940), a similar conflict of cultures occupies a less central place in the novel and produces less hopeful results: the Mexican-Navajo half-breed Keetcheye, strong and courageous leader of a gang of adolescent boys in rural California, finds that prejudices and his own inclinations almost destroy all hope of his success in adult white American society, and he seeks consolation in drinking and thieving. Jack Thomas Leahy's *Shadow on the Waters* (1960) also presents harmful effects of contact between white and Indian cultures: sixteen-year-old Jerrod Tobin and his half-breed friend Buckety have some innocent Tom Sawyer-ish adventures in and near the Indian coastal village of Teawhit, Washington; but white traders such as Jerrod's father have long been weakening the Indians' self-reliance, and when a woman reporter tries to exploit the quaintness of Teawhit as a tourist attraction with a cheap imitation of a rodeo, the consequences are fatal for Buckety.

Understandably more common are the novels which show the problems of Negro adolescents in white communities. Although the problem of the Indian's adjustment to white man's ways may be acute in parts of the Southwest, in most parts of the country it demands and gets little attention, whereas the problem of Negro adjustment and acceptance is apparent all over our nation. All Negro novelists and many white novelists have had firsthand experience with difficulties in Negro-white adjustment, but very few novelists have had much experience with Indian-white relations.

Most American Negro novelists have emphasized the difficulty of adjusting to a community where white people are dominant, in power if not in numbers. Although this problem must be prominent in a Negro's mind at all periods of his life, it may well have a special significance during adolescence, when the individual is turning from the relative security and the ethnic homogeneity of his family and begins to stand as an individual in a mixed society. Yet no important Negro novel before 1920 stressed the importance of such an adjustment to a Negro adolescent. Robert A. Bone in *The Negro Novel in America* (p. 50) gives "honorable mention" to only two earlier novels by Negroes: *The Uncalled* (1898) by Paul Laurence Dunbar and *The Autobiography of an Ex-Colored Man* (1912) by James Weldon Johnson. The first has a white protagonist and ignores the question of racial relationships; the second moves quickly from the shock of the protagonist's childhood discovery that he belongs to a despised race to the prolonged conflict between his ambitions and the varied adversities of his adult life. Bone points out that during the 1920's there was for the first time an American Negro intelligentsia, producing such literary figures as Langston Hughes, Jean Toomer, Claude McKay, and Countee Cullen (Bone, pp. 55–56), and that at the same time white authors showed an increased interest in Negro life and culture (Bone, pp. 58–61).

The most important novels by Negroes in that period concerned older protagonists or were set in foreign cities; Langston Hughes's *Not Without Laughter* (1930) is not among the best Negro novels, but it is the first noteworthy full-length description of Negro adolescence by a Negro novelist. This study mentioned in an earlier chapter (p. 102 above) the experiences of the protagonist Sandy Rogers and his Aunt Hariett as colored students in the nearly all-white upper grades in a Kansas small-town school system. Even more difficult is the problem of Sandy's friend Buster; this white-skinned, golden-haired son of a mulatto mother and an anonymous father cannot understand why he should not give flowers to white girls. The novel is permeated by the unfair treatment of Negroes by white people; Harriet's reaction is to hate the whole white race intensely, but Sandy tends to agree with his grandmother, Aunt Hager:

> "White peoples maybe mistreats you and hates you, but when you hates 'em back, you's de one what's hurted, 'cause hate makes yo' heart ugly—that's all it does. It closes up de sweet door to life an' makes ever'thing small an' mean an' dirty. Honey, there ain't no room in de world fo' hate, white folks hatin' niggers, an' niggers hatin' white folks." (P. 194.)

Among white authors' novels about Negro intelligentsia, the earliest to give much attention to the problem of interracial community adjustment in adolescence was *Mamba's Daughters* (1929) by Du Bose Heyward. This novel features two adolescents in Charleston, South Carolina, who see the problem from opposite sides of the color line. In the first half, Saint Julien Wentworth, impoverished scion of Charleston aristocrats, keeps a company store for Negro employees of a phosphate mining company and attacks the unfair treatment of Negroes which has been the accepted pattern in the store; in the second half, the lovely mulatto Lissa Atkinson experiences more difficulty in adjustment among different shades of darkness than she does between dark and white.

Since 1930 there have been at least twenty noteworthy novels about Negro adolescents, written by white and Negro authors, and all of them emphasize the difficulty of adjustment between members of the two races, or between mulatto and Negro, or both. The best of these novels are *Light in August* and *Intruder in the Dust*, both written by William Faulkner, and Richard Wright's *Native Son*, Ralph Ellison's *Invisible Man*, and James Baldwin's *Go Tell It on the Mountain*—the last three written by Negroes. Each of these deserves special comment.[8]

Light in August describes at some length the adolescent years of Joe Christmas, who looks perfectly white and may very likely have no Negro blood at all, but who frequently speaks of himself as a "nigger" and is so considered by his grandfather. In early childhood Joe is taunted with the epithet by other children in the orphanage; in traumatic moments of childhood and adolescence the term is thrown at him as an insult. At fourteen Joe reacts violently to his first attempt at sexual experience, partly because the girl is a member of the despised race and partly because her odor revives the subconscious memory of the orphanage dietitian whom he once overheard in furtive copulation and who was the first adult to call him "nigger" as a label of shame. At seventeen he proposes marriage to a white prostitute and is violently rejected, again with the reminder that he is not as white as he appears. Then, for over fifteen years—the rest of his life—he travels restlessly about the country, living sometimes with white women and sometimes with Negro women, fighting white men who call him Negro and Negroes who call him white, unable to accept himself as a member of either race.

Intruder in the Dust tells of two sixteen-year-old boys, the white Chick Mallison and the Negro Aleck Sander, who, reluctantly but persistently, undertake to prove the innocence of an older Negro accused of murdering a white man. In their region of the South, custom demands that the family and friends of the murdered man lynch the Negro before he can be brought to trial; and both Chick and Aleck Sander, far from boldly defying tradition, resent the stronger motives that compel them to go against it. Chick resents the indebtedness he has felt toward old Lucas Beauchamp since the winter day, four years earlier, when Lucas rescued him from a frozen creek and warmed and fed him in the Beauchamp cabin; Aleck Sander resents his own loyalty to Chick, which makes him follow Chick's lead even against his own better judgment. And both boys, like almost everybody else in Jefferson, resent the fact that Lucas will not dress, speak, or act with the humility considered appropriate for a Negro. "It's the ones like Lucas makes trouble for everybody," Aleck Sander says (p. 85). In spite of the reluctance with which Chick and Aleck Sander join the elderly Miss Habersham in seeking the evidence that will clear an innocent Negro, and in spite of everybody else's refusal to consider the possibility of Lucas' innocence before the evidence has been discovered, Faulkner suggests, through the long, moral preaching of Chick's Uncle Gavin, that the best hope for improving race relations in the South lies in such voluntary actions by adolescents and older women, rather than in civil-rights legislation imposed by other sections of the country.

The cities of the North produce different problems of race relationships from those found in small towns and rural areas in the South. Richard Wright comments in his introductory article for the Grossett and Dunlap edition of *Native Son:*

> The urban environment of Chicago, affording a more stimulating life, made the Negro Bigger Thomases react more violently than even in the South. More than ever I began to see and understand the environmental

212

factors which made for this extreme conduct. It was not that Chicago segregated Negroes more than the South, but that Chicago had more to offer, that Chicago's physical aspect—noisy, crowded, filled with the sense of power and fulfillment—did so much more to dazzle the mind with a taunting sense of possible achievement that the segregation it did impose brought forth from Bigger a reaction more obstreperous than in the South. (P. xxv.)

Thus Bigger and his friends feel an intense hatred and resentment of "white folks," who seem engaged in an active conspiracy to keep Negroes from having any privileges.

> "I just can't get used to it," Bigger said. "I swear to God I can't. I know I oughtn't think about it, but I can't help it. Every time I think about it I feel like somebody's poking a red-hot iron down my throat. God-dammit, look! We live here and they live there. We black and they white. They got things and we ain't. They do things and we can't. It's just like living in jail. Half the time I feel like I'm on the outside of the world peeping in through a knothole in the fence. . . ." (P. 17.)

Because of this hatred, Bigger cannot understand the white family which tries to help him. In panic and confusion, he smothers the daughter of the family, and his terror and hatred are intensified during his flight, his capture, and his trial.

Invisible Man presents the problems of its Negro protagonist-narrator in both a Southern and a Northern environment. The novel begins about the time of his graduation from a Negro high school in a medium-sized Southern community; he is asked to repeat his commencement oration before a group of leading white citizens. He feels honored by the invitation, and even after he finds that the occasion is a smoker with a coarse and degrading program of entertainment, he tries to make his address as moving and inspiring as possible. He soon realizes that most of the white leaders regard a serious speech by a Negro as a ludicrous burlesque of intellectual achievement. However, his wounded self-esteem is nearly healed when, at the end of the program, he is given a new leather brief case containing a scholarship to a Negro college. At the college he feels that he is preparing for a life of service to his country for the betterment of his race, and believes that the white trustees and Negro faculty are sincerely interested in helping the students; but he learns by chance that the whole institution is an elaborate pretense of progress and benevolence, concealing an acceptance of the *status quo* (see page 129 above). He travels to Harlem with the hope of absorbing New York culture while earning money for his senior year. Equipped with "letters of recommendation" from the president of his college, he goes hopefully to one prospective employer after another, until one white man is kind enough to let him read a copy of the president's letter, which states that the youth has been permanently expelled from college because he

> threatens to upset certain delicate relationships between certain interested individuals and the school. Thus, while the bearer is no longer a member of our scholastic family, it is highly important that his severance with the college be executed as painlessly as possible. I beg of you, sir, to help him continue in the direction of that promise which, like the horizon, recedes ever brightly and distantly beyond the hopeful traveler. (P. 145.)

He seems for a while to find acceptance by members of the Communist party, both white and black; but he learns eventually that the party accepts him, not as an individual, but as a gifted speaker and as a symbol of the victims of capitalism. Thus his progress from adolescence to maturity is marked by his discovery that he is an invisible man— that people simply refuse to see him as a person.

Go Tell It on the Mountain also presents race-adjustment problems in the South and in the North, but for different generations. The protagonist, fourteen-year-old John Grimes, has lived all his life in Harlem, and his problem of adjustment to the white world surrounding Harlem is mild compared to those of his adjustment to his family and his religion. As a bright student he has been praised by his white teachers and principal, and his gentle ways win smiles from the white people he meets on his rambles to Central Park, Fifth Avenue, and Forty-second Street; but his stepfather has frequently warned him of the treachery and cruelty of white people, and he knows that his dreams of being at home in a white world could never be realized. John stays out of trouble by staying in Harlem; he would never, like his brother Roy, go over to the West Side to seek gang warfare with white boys. The problems of interracial relationships are shown most vividly in this book through the reminiscences of his parents and his Aunt Florence. Florence recalls that when she was thirteen, living in the South, her sixteen-year-old friend Deborah was raped by white men, who later terrorized the Negro section of town to prevent vengeance by Deborah's father and friends. Her younger brother Gabriel, John's stepfather, also recalls the rape, and especially does he remember its effect on his later marriage to Deborah. He recalls, too, an unexplained murder and mutilation of a Negro by white men and the subsequent terrorizing of the Negro community, when Gabriel feared for the safety of his adolescent, unclaimed, illegitimate son. John's mother, Elizabeth, recalls her migration in late adolescence from Maryland to New York so that she and her lover Richard might find better opportunities for advancement and financial security on which to base a marriage; but the opportunities which New York promised to Negroes proved elusive.

> There was not, after all, a great difference between the world of the North and that of the South which she had fled; there was only this difference: the North promised more. And this similarity: what it promised it did not give, and what it gave, at length and grudgingly with one hand, it took back with the other. (P. 220.)

Most bitter in Elizabeth's memory is Richard's arrest and abuse by white policemen for a robbery with which he had no connection—an unwarranted disgrace which led to Richard's despairing suicide. Though Baldwin's novel concentrates on relationships between Negroes, the ever-present menace of the power and treachery of white men strongly influences these relationships.

If the fictional treatment of adolescents facing Negro-white adjustment seems to be given undue space in this study, it is because the period covered far surpasses earlier periods in the quality and variety of such novels. The problem has long been and will probably continue to be one of the most difficult problems of community adjustment. Children of white immigrant families may in time be wholly assimilated by native white communities. Indians and Orientals are more easily assimilable than Negroes, and have the alternative of retaining a good part of their traditional culture. Negroes are completely cut off from the ancient traditions of their race, but in no part of the United States are they fully accepted as members of white communities.

MOVING TO A NEW COMMUNITY

A move from one part of the country to another does not require such a difficult adjustment to the new community; but it may be difficult enough to cause rather serious disturbance, especially to a sensitive person in early adolescence. Such a problem is fully described in Clyde Brion Davis' *The Newcomer* (1954), in which thirteen-year-old Chick Trotter finds difficulty in making friends in a town which is obviously not very far from the town where he previously lived. In William Demby's *Beetlecreek* (1950), the fourteen-year-old Negro Johnny Johnson, after moving from Pittsburgh to a Negro mining community in West Virginia, is so eager to be accepted by the teen-age boys of Beetlecreek that he forsakes his earlier training and his personal inclinations, even committing a serious crime to win approval of boys he cannot really respect. The difficulty experienced by a white boy in moving from a city to a nearby rural community appears in Daniel Doan's *The Crystal Years* (1952), in which twelve-year-old Ray Martin and his family move from Boston to a farm in New Hampshire. In Jesse Stuart's *Hie to the Hunters* (1950), fourteen-year-old Did Hargis forsakes his home and family in a Kentucky town and runs off to live with a mountain family; but he finds the experience so challenging and exciting that he willingly overlooks the hardships that the change involves. Two rather unsatisfying novels of the forties show older adolescents moving in the opposite direction, from mountain farms to town: Mary Elizabeth Osborn's *Days Beyond Recall* tells of sixteen-year-old Gwennie Hewitt leaving a Catskill Mountain farm to work in the home of a middle-aged roué and face the risk of seduction that seems inevitable in novels of this sort; John Pleasant McCoy's *Swing the Big-Eyed Rabbit* tells of sixteen-year-old Artemis Collins leaving a Blue Ridge Mountain farm for education in a mission school and, after learning assorted facts of life from faculty members and fellow students, feeling ready to face the greater challenge of life in the towns beyond the mountains.

When an adolescent moves with his family to a section of the country with very different cultural traditions from those he has known in earlier life, of course the adjustment to the new community is likely to present

216

problems. Such family moves from East to West are described in Mary Austin's *Starry Adventure* (1931) and Katherine Carson's *Mrs. Pennington* (1939): in the former, Gardiner Sitwell learns to adjust to a variety of neighbors in New Mexico, both white and Indian, after having lived in an intellectual, conservative atmosphere in Waterbury, Connecticut; and in the latter, the four adolescent Pennington children find Kansas farm life very different from what they had known in New England. Earlier in this chapter I mentioned Edmund Ware's *Rider in the Sun* (1935), in which a fifteen-year-old Eastern boy goes west and discovers that the cowboys in real life are much less charming than those in stories (see p. 190 above); and Ralph Moody's *The Fields of Home*, in which the protagonist, having moved from New England to Colorado in his childhood, has to readjust to New England farm life at the age of fourteen (see p. 192 above).

Moves from North to South or from South to North involve greater changes than eastward or westward shifts, for the South has kept its distinctive character more tenaciously than other regions have kept theirs. Phil Stong's *The Rebellion of Lenny Barlow* describes a Southern boy who has trouble accepting and being accepted by the small Iowa community to which his family moves. Both Donald Wetzel's *The Rain and the Fire and the Will of God* and Paul Boles's *Parton's Island* describe boys from Northern cities (New York and Cincinnati, respectively) who try to adjust to life in rural Alabama. Bill Temple in Boles's novel finds the adjustment fairly easy, but Rod Blankhard in Wetzel's story repeatedly makes himself conspicuous and uncomfortable by behavior which is inappropriate for his new environment. Even more difficult is the adjustment of Harriet Freeman, the Negro protagonist of Florence Means's *Shuttered Windows* (1938), who leaves an integrated high school in Minneapolis to live with her grandmother in a Negro community on an island off the coast of South Carolina.

SUMMARY—TRENDS IN NOVELS OF COMMUNITY ADJUSTMENT

The problems of adjustment to community environment, like the problems discussed in earlier chapters, become increasingly complex and subtle throughout the period studied. In novels of the twenties, the serious and realistic presentation of the problems of adolescence was new enough that it could command the attention of American readers without being complicated by any added conflict between the character and his environment; therefore most of the early novels show adolescents learning to look at familiar environments in new, adult ways. Some novels of 1929 add the conflict between traditions of the home and those of the community: Brinig's *Singermann* and Rölvaag's *Peder Victorious* show immigrant families in American neighborhoods which differ in religion and in customs, while Faulkner's *The Sound and the Fury* describes a Mississippi student in a Massachusetts town where he always feels like an outsider. During the thirties, the various possible combinations of racial, national, and regional contrasts between adolescent and environment were presented, although there were not many examples of each combination. During the forties and fifties, each of these combinations was represented by a number of novels; yet each novel made its characters and its settings distinctly individual, so that the problems of adjustment are considerably different in the different novels. The increasing emphasis on subconscious and symbolic motives has added to the complexity and subtlety of the problems.

Almost all regions of the country have been used as settings for novels which stress a cultural clash between adolescent and community. Novels about immigrant families are most likely to be set in Midwestern farming regions or in large cities; but they sometimes are set in small towns, especially in the East or the Middle West. Novels about Negroes in white communities are most likely to have Southern locales, but New York and Chicago have provided backgrounds for the best works by Negro novelists. The Southwest is almost inevitably the setting for novels dealing with clashes between the culture of Indians or Mexicans and that of white Americans. One would expect to find problems of Orientals in white communities discussed in novels set in the Pacific states or in various metropolitan areas; rather strangely, there seem to be no important fictional treatments of such problems. Although a number of American novels have characters of Chinese, Japanese, or Korean ancestry, these characters are almost invariably well beyond the age of adolescence. James A. Michener's *Hawaii* (1959) briefly presents a number of problems of Oriental adolescents in white society, but does not treat them in detail.

Probably the two most striking trends in the fictional treatment of the adolescent in relation to community environment during the forty-one years covered by this paper have been the emphasis on Negro-white relationships and the great increase in novels on juvenile delinquency. The former trend may be partly the result and partly the cause of increased public attention to discrimination against Negroes in schools, residential areas, employment offices, eating places, and transportation systems. Emphasis on juvenile delinquency is undoubtedly a result of the great increase in juvenile crime which followed the excitement and the disrupted family life of World War II. Although recent novels are not as obviously intended to bring about social reforms as were the proletarian novels of the thirties, it seems likely that these novels may contribute to a general awareness of some of the problems of growing up, and thus may help to bring about a solution to the more acute of these problems. It is unfashionable to commend novels for their utilitarian and sociological value, but fiction which is artistically successful can hardly be condemned for incidental benefits to society. The more thorough and accurate accounts of the relationship between adolescents and their community environments are likely to be both aesthetically pleasing and socially significant, while stories written to convey a social message may lack both the poetic truth necessary for art and the conviction needed to bring about social reform.

Chapter VII

SPECIAL PROBLEMS

Earlier chapters have discussed problems which, in one form or another, virtually all adolescents face. This chapter will consider problems which affect a limited number of young people, but may affect them very powerfully during the transition from childhood to maturity. Animals, for example, are important in the lives of some boys and girls, whose emotional growth may be strongly influenced by attachment to a certain pet (usually a dog or a horse, but sometimes a more unusual creature) or by the desire to kill or capture a certain game animal. A number of novels in the period of this study show adolescents greatly affected by war—if not through direct participation then through the involvement of loved ones or through the excitement and changed attitudes pervading the atmosphere. Again death or some other disaster may strike down a person very close to the youngster, who is thus forced to change radically his concept of life and its purpose. The adolescent protagonist himself may suffer from a physical or mental handicap. In some novels the adolescent is addicted to drugs or to alcohol, but just as often his problem is that of dependency on an alcoholic older person. For any of these problems, and for various combinations of them, there are fictional adolescents seeking solutions.

Pet Animals

In 1938 appeared two memorable works of fiction involving boys in early adolescence who were deeply disturbed at the death of pets— John Steinbeck's novelette "The Red Pony" and Marjorie Kinnan Rawling's *The Yearling*. Steinbeck's Jody Tiflin has to witness the sick suffering and slow dying of the red pony he affectionately raised and trained but never had a chance to ride; when he is later promised another colt to replace the first, he is with the dam and cares for her from breeding until the birth of the colt, which causes its mother's

221

death. Thus, in the first years of his adolescence, but already given the realism and responsibilities of an adult, the boy is exposed to the mysteries of life and death and birth. Mrs. Rawling's Jody Baxter is only a year or so older than Steinbeck's Jody when he finds a fawn in the Florida scrub near his home and makes it his inseparable companion. When the little deer is a year old, despite all Jody's precautions it twice destroys the Baxters' vital corn crop, and Jody is compelled to destroy his pet. Mrs. Rawlings manages to convey the full emotional effect of this act of adult responsibility without making it seem oversentimental.

During the 1940's a series of novels about an adolescent boy and his horses, written by Mrs. Mary Sture-Vasa under the name of "Mary O'Hara," won great popularity. In the first of the series, *My Friend Flicka* (1941), Ken McLaughlin develops from a dreamy, absent-minded child into a dependable adolescent by breaking and training the nearly wild filly that he calls Flicka. As Ken's father explains upon giving the colt to his son:

> "You're going to train the yearling. I'll give you a little help just with the first breaking, but you'll train her, and she'll train you. I want you to make a good pony out of her. I want her to make a man out of you." (P. 101.)

In the sequel, *Thunderhead* (1943), Ken is in middle adolescence, trying to raise and train Flicka's son, a throwback to the wild white stallion that was Flicka's grandsire. In his recognition of Thunderhead's great abilities that cannot be controlled by man, Ken further matures in his respect for nature and for individuality. The third of the trilogy, *The Green Grass of Wyoming* (1946), presents Ken, now in late adolescence, in conflict with Thunderhead, now the leader of a wild herd, to recapture valuable mares which the stallion has lured from ranchers and to prevent further depredations. And as Thunderhead allows his love for the boy to overcome his love for freedom. Ken also learns that love is as important as dependability and capability in the fulfillment of his own human maturity.

The interrelation of adolescent boys with favorite horses is featured in a number of novels published during the forties and fifties: George Chamberlain's *The Phantom Filly* (1942), Roger Eddy's *The Rimless Wheel* (1947), Dana Faralla's *The Magnificant Barb* (1947) and *Black Renegade* (1954), and Walter Edmonds' *The Boyds of Black River*

(1953), to name only a few. Stories of boys and dogs are even more common. Although it would be impossible to discuss all of them, a few of them merit particular attention.

In Charles Cooke's *The Big Show* (1938), Bob Boulton from upstate New York trains his dwarf collie Skipper to do enough tricks to get him a job with a small circus. Bob marries one of his fellow performers and moves with her and Skipper to the "Big Show" at Madison Square Garden, where he learns to perform on the high wire. But the huge crowds of spectators are too impersonal and too insistent on spectacular entertainment, so the trio retreat to a small-time circus, where the hearts of audiences are won by the human-interest appeal of their animal act. The relationship between the boy and his dog helps him to find both a wife and a satisfactory career, but the real value of the novel is not so much in its characterization or its plot as in its authenticity of circus atmosphere.

Two novels by Fred Gipson present memorable boy-and-dog relationships in Texas. *Hound-Dog Man* (1949) tells how twelve-year-old Cotton Kinney yearns for a dog of his own until he goes on a coon-hunting trip with his pal Spud Sessums and the hunter Blackie Scantling; at one of the farm houses where they stop for meals, a stub-tailed puppy makes it plain that Cotton is the one person he will accept as his master, and the puppy's pretty mistress shows that she feels the same way about Blackie. *Old Yeller* (1956) relates how a fourteen-year-old boy, with the help of his dog, takes charge of the farm, his mother, and his five-year-old brother while his father is off driving cattle to Kansas. Both of these novels abound in situations that could be oversentimentalized, but Gipson treats them with realism and humor. In each novel, the relationship with a dog brings the boy increased understanding of the disappointments and responsibilities that are a part of growing up.

Somewhat more sentimental are the accounts of Teddy Armond and his white bull terrier Leonidas in Walter Edmonds' *The Boyds of Black River;* of young Skeeter and the valuable basenji—a rare, non-barking breed of dog—that he finds in a Mississippi swamp and reluctantly returns when its owner is discovered, as related in James Street's *Goodbye, My Lady* (1954); of Ray Macky and his dog Dingy on their Ozark farm, described by Clancy Carlile in *As I Was Young and Easy* (1958); of Kimmie and his gun-shy English setter in Havilah Babcock's *The Education of Pretty Boy* (1960).

An unusual pet appears in Theodore Pratt's *Valley Boy* (1946). Eleven-year-old Johnny Birch lives in the San Fernando Valley in a community of eccentrics, among whom his own parents must be included. They believe they are encouraging Johnny's individuality by requiring him to live in a home built in imitation of a ruined Mexican hacienda, to wear flamboyant Mexican cowboy clothes, to speak Spanish instead of English, and to find his own recreation while they devote their time and attention to each other. Johnny naturally avoids the laughter of children his own age; he lives in a dream world, from which he emerges only when he plays with Oscar, a trained seal that lives across the street from him. An even more unusual pet is Tom Jeff, the three-legged wildcat in Wesley Ford Davis' *The Time of the Panther* (1958). The protagonist, Tom Jarrad, is nearly fifteen at the time of the story; he and his two brothers have kept Tom Jeff in a cage for many years, feeding it live birds. The wildcat seems to symbolize the interests and activities of childhood; when Tom realizes that the new interests of the three brothers are causing them to neglect their old pet, he kills it rather than allow it to suffer helplessly a forlorn old age.

It is understandable that the strongest relationships between adolescents and their pets appear in novels with rural settings, where children spend more time with animals and less with human beings. Some novels featuring the influence of pets are set in small towns, but almost none are set in cities. There seem to be almost no regional differences in novels about pets; a boy and his dog or horse experience the same sort of mutual devotion whether they live in Wyoming or Florida, in New England or California. Very few novels, and probably none of importance, show a similar devotion between a girl and a pet. The novels which come closest to it are Judy Van der Veer's *November Grass,* in which the California ranch girl Agnes loves all living creatures, and Helga Sandburg's *The Wheel of Earth,* in which the Kentucky farm girl Ellen Gaddy shows a brief devotion to her pet goats.

A chronological survey of novels about adolescents and their pets shows a shifting attitude on the part of the authors. The few novels of the twenties and early thirties that presented such a relationship almost invariably treated it with the sentiment and humor that Booth Tarkington showed in discussing the relationship between Penrod and his dog Duke. From 1938 on, the topic is treated more realistically, and the boy is likely to learn that his love for his pet must be painfully subordinated to his duties as a human being.

Novels which tell about an adolescent seeking to kill or capture a particular animal are rather rare, but some of them are important. Much more common are those which feature a love of hunting in general. In fact, Leslie Fiedler has suggested that learning to kill is now considered an essential part of initiation into maturity:

> In the United States, it is through murder rather than sex, death rather than love, that the child enters the fallen world. He is not asked, to be sure, to kill a fellow human being, only an animal, deer or bear, or even fish, some woodland totem, in slaying whom he enters a communion of guilt with the natural world in which hitherto he has led the privileged existence of an outsider.[1]

Fiedler obviously has in mind the young boy in Hemingway's *The Old Man and the Sea* and Ike McCaslin in Faulkner's "The Bear"; he might have mentioned just as appropriately Ralph Fawcett in Jean Stafford's *The Mountain Lion* and Theron Hunnicutt in William Humphrey's *Home from the Hill* and a number of other adolescent protagonists.

Novels of adolescence published during the first two decades of the period covered by this study place little emphasis on hunting. Even Hemingway, a hunting enthusiast, makes only casual mention of the sport in describing the adolescent experiences of Nick Adams. If the killing of game is to be interpreted as a symbolic induction into a "communion of guilt," the symbol has apparently been recognized only in the last twenty years, and then almost exclusively by writers about the South and the Far West. Nick Adams first senses blood guilt when he encounters gangland killers in a lunchroom and is unable to save their intended victim, as told in "The Killers," a short story which appeared in *Men Without Women* (1927). Winifred Van Etten's *I Am the Fox* (1936) emphasizes a fox hunt in Pennsylvania, with the protagonist, Selma Temple, identifying herself with the victim; but the hunt takes place when Selma is a mature woman, and it is only in reminiscence that she sees her childhood and adolescence as a continual fox hunt. There are some good hunting scenes in Mrs. Rawlings' *The Yearling*, but they do not have the symbolic impact of such scenes in later novels.

It is apparent that in "The Bear," at any rate, Faulkner regards hunting

225

as a part of the initiation of a male into maturity. In "The Old People," the story which immediately precedes "The Bear" in his collection *Go Down, Moses* (1942), Faulkner tells how Ike McCaslin, at the age of twelve, shoots his first deer and has his face marked with the hot blood, "and he ceased to be a child and became a hunter and a man." (*Go Down, Moses*, p. 178.) Having been initiated, Ike can now love the very life he spills, and is able to see the huge buck which is visible only to true hunters. (*Ibid.*, pp. 181–87.) It is this love of wild life, together with a renunciation of the values of civilization, that characterizes Ike's growing into manhood. Old Ben, the huge beast from which "The Bear" takes its title, is a more tangible symbol for the spirit of the wilderness than the big buck in "The Old People," but Ike's relations with it are just as mystical. Sam Fathers, the old hunter who is part Indian and part Negro and who initiates Ike into wilderness lore, tells the boy, now aged ten, that he will not see the bear until he leaves behind his gun, the symbol of civilization invading the wilderness. After searching vainly for half a day without his gun, Ike decides that he is still tainted by his watch and his compass; he leaves these hanging on a bush, and then is able to see the bear for the first time. During the six years that follow Ike's first sight of Old Ben, the boy sees the bear a number of times and has several opportunities to shoot it, but by this time he realizes that he never will shoot it. When Ben finally is caught by the big dog Lion and killed by the knife of the part-Indian Boon Hogganbeck, the wilderness itself seems to succumb to invading forces. But Ike himself, in the fourth part of the story, which seems a loosely-related aftermath to the account of the hunt, shows in his adult life that he has learned the lesson of Sam Fathers and the bear, because he renounces his inheritance of the plantation land that should have remained wilderness in the first place and he spends the rest of his long life as a hunter and carpenter and kindly, impoverished "uncle to half a county and still father to none." (*Ibid.*, p. 300.) [2]

In Peirson Ricks's *The Hunter's Horn* (1947), the hunted fox is symbolic of the illusion of carefree childhood which hunters try to recapture. In a North Carolina plantation house a generation after the Civil War, Conway Tally finds it hard to accept the increasing responsibility of growing up. He has a constant awareness of guilt as a result of frequent conflicts with his father, who finds that hard work is his own best remedy for mental disturbances and is self-righteously intolerant of those who seek relief in other ways. The boy is more sympathetic with his Uncle Benjamin, a Confederate veteran who tries to follow the fox back to his own innocent childhood; but after going on one hunt with his uncle, Conway recognizes the illusion and accepts the responsibility of growing up.

Panthers appear occasionally in stories of adolescence, but never very prominently. The novel which gives most emphasis to a panther is Jean Stafford's *The Mountain Lion;* although the animal appears only at the very end of the novel, and then very briefly, its destruction seems to be symbolic of the growing up of Ralph Fawcett and of his separation from his sister Molly, who fails to adapt herself to her changing condition. In her lonely antagonism to the rest of the world, Molly might even be said to be the mountain lion. Cougars supply exciting moments in Reuben Davis' *Shim* (1953) and Clancy Carlile's *As I Was Young and Easy* (1958); but in both these books, as in Jesse Stuart's *Hie to the Hunters,* the adolescent protagonists find joy and escape from the curse of civilization through hunting in general, not in hunting any particular animal. In Wesley Ford Davis' *The Time of the Panther,* the big cat is seen only once and very briefly, about seven years before the main events of the novel take place; but since the sight was impressive and was concurrent with crucial events in the life of the protagonist, he tends to think of that decisive period as the time of the panther. He is far more interested in watching birds than in hunting beasts; his search for an ivory-billed woodpecker becomes symbolic of his hope for success in life, and the ornithological quest of this Florida boy is as earnest and diligent as that of the Maine girl in Sarah Orne Jewett's story of a half-century earlier, "The White Heron."

The novels that ranks closest to "The Bear" as a memorable story of an adolescent hunter is William Humphrey's *Home from the Hill.* The style and the subject matter were obviously influenced by Faulkner; the Hunnicutt family and the loafers in the square of the Texas town would have been equally at home in Jefferson, and the long, involved sentences are nearly as confusing on first reading and as rewarding on second and third readings as Faulkner's own. Captain Wade Hunnicutt lives for the thrill of the chase, either in the forest or in the bedroom; his son Theron has been carefully trained to emulate his father's skill in the first sort of hunt, and as carefully protected from knowledge of his father's accomplishments in the second. The greatest single event in

Wade's almost legendary life was his shooting of a huge boar in a large stretch of woods known as Sulphur Bottom; Theron's greatest moment of triumph comes when he shoots an equally large boar in the same stretch of forest. Unlike Ike McCaslin's bear, Theron's boar does not symbolize the spirit of the wilderness, but rather the great and ugly envy that has been hidden in the jungle of his subconscious mind.

> Now he knew what longing had so possessed him lately. He recognized the game he had pursued into the deep woods, into the swamp. He had hunted down, he had cornered the beast of his own secret desire, and it had turned. It had shown its face to him in all its bristling ugliness. It had charged, tearing through the disguises with which he had kept it at bay as the live boar had torn through the dancing dogs. There had been no delay, no indecision. As if it recognized him, it charged, squealing with murderous glee.
>
> Yet even as he shrank from the charge, he heard in his mind a gladdening explosion. He felt the recoil. He felt no need of a second shot. His envy of his father's prowess lay stretched out, mud of the swamp caked upon its tick-infested hide, shuddering, peacefully sighing its life away, at his feet. (P. 92.)

Shortly after conquering this envy of his father, he learns to hate him for his promiscuity (see p. 78 above), and to interpret his own natural sexual impulses as evidence that he will resemble his father in this respect also. This beast, too, is at last symbolically slain in Sulphur Bottom, with a more horrible kind of kill that destroys Theron's last hope for happiness.

Two recent novels set in the North Central states feature the hunting experiences of adolescents. Richard B. Erno's *The Hunt* (1959) presents a teen-age boy taken by his father on a deer hunt in Upper Michigan, in company with three other high-school teachers and a native guide. The boy's killing of his first deer is given symbolic overtones both by the boy's guilty reaction and by the realization that one of the men is more eager to shoot the companion who has wronged him than he is to kill a deer. There is less apparent symbolism in E. R. Zietlow's *These Same Hills* (1960); here the trapping of coyote in the Badlands of South Dakota is offered to eighteen-year-old Jim Heiss as a way of life, in contrast to the more civilized way he might enter if he chose to go to college.

Since the memorable modern novels of adolescents devoted to hunting have been written during the time when symbolism was a major technique in fiction, it is not surprising that the hunted animal almost always takes on symbolic significance. The symbolic value varies considerably, however, from one author to another. Fiedler is certainly oversimplifying and overgeneralizing when he interprets the killing of an animal as the usual initiation ceremony by which a modern American youngster "enters a communion of guilt with the natural world." The hunt is featured in too few of the novels of adolescence to be considered representative; it is found almost exclusively in rural novels of the South and West, and even if the gang killings of city novels are counted as variations of the same initiation ceremony, the total number of such killings is not large enough to be considered the usual American substitute for initiation by sex. Girls are almost never involved directly with the killing of either animals or people, and the two or three girls who are involved (such as Idabel Thompkins in Capote's *Other Voices,* who kills the water moccasin Joel Knox cannot bring himself to kill; or Pinkie in Blair Treynor's *She Ate Her Cake,* who murders a Los Angeles gang leader and tries to get the devoted farm boy Danny Miller to take the blame) are rather masculine girls. If killing can be said to have a general symbolic significance to adolescents in American novels, it is more likely to symbolize the initiation of a certain kind of boy into a certain kind of manhood rather than typical American youth into typical American maturity.

EFFECTS OF WAR

As it is boys rather than girls who are affected by the violence of hunting, so it is boys rather than girls who are usually most affected by the violence of war. Boys in late adolescence have been liable to be drafted in time of war, and boys a little younger than draft age or enlistment age may look forward to future military service with dread or with eagerness. But girls as well as boys are likely to lose loved ones to the war, and to suffer from the disruption of civilian life that accompanies war.

Novels of the twenties and thirties, as well as some later novels, are likely to show the effects of World War I on adolescent protagonists. Amory Blaine in *This Side of Paradise* leaves Princeton to enlist and

229

goes overseas, but his military experiences are hardly mentioned. Wolfe's Eugene Gant is also in college in wartime, but is too young to enlist. Floyd Dell's Janet March is eighteen when the United States enters World War I; she wishes she were old enough to go overseas as a nurse or an ambulance driver, but she feels that she is doing what she can for the war effort by entertaining young officers on leave and letting them kiss her good-by.

> When she came home each night, she scrubbed out her mouth with a strong solution of peroxide of hydrogen. In her imagination, she was risking her health, her glorious health, the precious cleanliness and strength of her young body, with every sloppy farewell kiss. She wasn't doing it for her country—nothing so grandiose as that; and not exactly for them, either; she was doing it for the sake of her self-respect. If this sort of thing was all that the world asked of her—why, take it! (P. 124.)

Farrell's Studs Lonigan and his friends are not quite sixteen when President Wilson declares war on Germany. Like Eugene Gant and Janet March, they are swept up by the war hysteria and feel they should do something, but are not sure what they can do. They torture a little Jewish boy because his name is Stein, which indicates that he may be a German spy; they eat quantities of bananas and drink water to add to their weight in hopes of convincing a marine recruiting officer that they are old enough to enlist; when Armistice Day finally comes, they participate in the street celebrations as enthusiastically as they would have liked to participate in the war. But Studs eventually realizes that the real veterans consider him a mere "punk."

Adolescents with German names and German families suffered much more during World War I than during World War II. Earlier chapters of this study have mentioned the schoolfellows' tormenting of Peter Franzman in Gordon Friesen's *Flamethrowers* and of Sonie Marburg in Jean Stafford's *Boston Adventure* (see pp. 101 and 178 above); Walter Karig's *Lower Than Angels* (1945) satirically describes the very unadmirable Marvin Lang, with a German father and an Irish mother, reacting to the increasing anti-German sentiment between 1914 and 1917, and becoming a most unheroic soldier when his ammunition-factory job will no longer save him from the draft.

World War II brought another crop of war novels, many of them featuring the war's influence on adolescents. William Saroyan's *The Human Comedy*, George Sklar's *The Two Worlds of Johnny Truro*, and

James Whitfield Ellison's *I'm Owen Harrison Harding* all feature adolescent boys who face new responsibilities because their older brothers are in military service. The entire way of life changes for Sid Tussie and his family in Jesse Stuart's *Taps for Private Tussie* when the supposed death of "Uncle Kim" in the war brings a large insurance payment to the impoverished mountain family.

In some novels, the problems of adolescents are partially solved by the coming of war. In Arnold Manoff's *Telegram from Heaven* (1942), the Bronx stenographer Sylvia Singer has two main problems: she cannot find work to help support her widowed mother, and her pessimistic boy friend Paul is too honorable to make promises for their future, telling her they cannot expect "telegrams from heaven." But the coming of war is like a telegram from heaven, for it makes jobs plentiful for Sylvia, and prompts Paul into action before he must leave for military duty. In Peter Feibleman's *A Place Without Twilight* (1958), the New Orleans mulatto Lucille Morris has three problems: a widowed mother to help support; a handsome but embittered older brother who has found that prostitution to homosexuals is the most profitable occupation for an attractive "twilight-colored" person; and a lover to whose advances she cannot sexually respond. Both the brother and the lover are drafted; the brother is killed, and his insurance provides for the mother, while the departure of Cille's lover for army service helps to ease the break-up of an unsatisfactory relationship.

One of the best novels showing the effects of war on boys who are close to draft age is John Knowles's *A Separate Peace* (1959). Knowles conveys, at several levels of meaning, the emotional and intellectual reactions of seniors in a New Hampshire preparatory school during the first year of America's participation in World War II—particularly the reactions of Finny, the school's most popular athlete, and of Gene, Finny's friend and roommate. Finny, when he learns that a fall has deprived him of any chance of active military service, decides to ignore the war, to make his own separate peace. Gene, as a result of experiences with Finny and other classmates, is able to make his separate peace in a deeper sense, even before enlisting in the Navy.

> I never killed anybody and I never developed an intense level of hatred for the enemy. Because my war ended before I ever put on a uniform; I was on active duty all my time at school; I killed my enemy there.
> Only Phineas never was afraid, only Phineas never hated anyone.

Other people experienced this fearful shock somewhere, this sighting of the enemy, and so began an obsessive labor of defense. . . . All of them, all except Phineas, constructed at infinite cost to themselves these Maginot Lines against this enemy they thought they saw across the frontier, this enemy who never attacked that way—if he ever attacked at all; if he was indeed the enemy. (Pp. 185–86.)

Several novels show boys in late adolescence experiencing active duty in World War II. Tommy Wadelton's *Silver Buckles on His Knee* (1945) describes the school days and the Navy experiences of an Indiana boy, Peter McCarthy. Gore Vidal's *The Season of Comfort* (1949) tells how Bill Giraud grows up in Washington, D.C., attends preparatory school in New England, enlists in the army at a young age to escape from an excessively possessive mother, and is wounded in the Battle of the Bulge when he is only eighteen. Irwin Shaw's *The Young Lions* (1948) concentrates on three soldiers of World War II, one of whom is the adolescent American Jew Noah Ackerman. In both his training-camp and his battlefront experiences, Noah learns about a great many different American attitudes toward Jews, and how a Jew can manage to live among these attitudes while preserving his own ideals. Another novel about a young Jewish enlisted man encountering prejudice in an army training camp is Mark Harris' *Something About a Soldier* (1957). Seventeen-year-old Jacob Epp (born Epstein) has high ideals and a reputation as a star high-school debater when he enters the army, but he finds that these qualities are not assets in the Georgia camp he is sent to. After a few months, he is discharged as psychologically unsound, and thus escapes the total destruction which meets the rest of his platoon when it goes overseas. In Thomas Hal Phillips' *The Loved and the Unloved* (1955) a Mississippi sharecropper's son carries his feud with the boss's son through adolescence, through their period of military service, and into later life, with tragic results. James Whitfield Ellison's *The Freest Man on Earth* (1958) is not about actual military duty, but it tells how Roger Boswell evades the draft during the Korean War for reasons of conscience, as his father had evaded the draft during World War I. Quince in Vance Bourjaily's *Confessions of a Spent Youth* (1960) sees service with the Ambulance Corps in Asia Minor, North Africa, and Italy during World War II; he resigns to join the infantry and is assigned to the Pacific theater, but never sees as much action there as he did in Europe as a noncombatant.

The novels presenting adolescents affected by World War I are in general far more romantic than those of World War II. Amory Blaine, Eugene Gant, and Studs Lonigan are all eager to take part in the great adventure; they see it as a wonderful experience and as an unquestionable duty. Walter Karig's Marvin Lang is a striking exception to this trend, but *Lower Than Angels,* although it concerns World War I, was written during the later world conflict. By that time America had had much experience on foreign battlefields, and Americans had developed a variety of attitudes toward war, very few of them romantic. Johnny Truro shows some of the old eagerness to enlist, and Randy Weaver in LaMar Warrick's *Yesterday's Children* (1943) conscientiously joins the Army Air Corps before he is old enough to be drafted, but this desire to see active service is by no means unanimous among adolescent boys in novels of World War II. The attitude toward war and military service displayed by most adolescent protagonists in recent novels is likely to be that of Eddie Slocum in Julian Halevy's *The Young Lovers* (1955). Eddie tries hard to avoid the draft by all legitimate means, but accepts it as a necessary though undesirable obligation when it catches up with him (see above, pp. 129–30).

WITNESSING DEATH

Most war novels are likely to contain some adolescent characters, but adolescents in many other novels observe death or disaster through some other medium than battle. It may be through illness, through accident, or through criminal violence. Since matters of life and death are a novelist's stock in trade for holding his readers' interest, few young protagonists reach maturity in serious novels without close observance of death or the near threat of it. Often the young people are resilient enough to recover readily from such experience, but many novels show that recovering may be a long and difficult struggle.

In the novels of the twenties, a rather sentimental emphasis is placed on the prolonged suffering of an adolescent when illness or accident takes the life of a person near to him. This emphasis does not take the form of overplaying emotional appeal, as was common in novels of the genteel tradition, but is made more acceptable and even more effective by depicting the adolescents' unsuccessful attempts to accept death in a matter-of-fact way. In Edgar Lee Masters' novels *Mitch Miller* and *Skeeters Kirby,* the death of Mitch as the result of an accidental injury incurred while stealing a ride on a train has a long-lasting effect on Skeeters, the narrator of both novels. In the earlier novel, Skeeters tries to relate calmly the return to normal activities after Mitch's death:

> Grandma and Grandpa came in to see us, cheerful and kind as they always were. . . . They had lost a lot of children, two little girls the same summer, a daughter who was grown, a grown son who was drowned. They seemed to take Mitchie's death . . . as natural and to be stood. And they said it wouldn't be long before we'd all be together, never to be separated; and then we'd all be really happy. . . .
>
> And then Christmas came and in the evening I went up to the Millers'. The girls were playing about the same as before. . . . The girls rushed into the room laughing and chasing each other. And then I went home.
>
> I had presents, but what was presents? My chum was gone. (*Mitch Miller,* pp. 257–58.)

The second novel takes its narrator-protagonist from early adolescence to middle age, and occasional references to Mitch's death throughout the book indicate that Skeeters never gets over it. During his high-school days Skeeters falls in love with Winifred Hervey, a tubercular girl who loves him but tells him they can never marry because of her poor health. After a year at the University of Illinois, Skeeters learns that Winifred has died in Europe, where she had gone to seek medical assistance. Her death, like that of Mitch, gives him a traumatic shock from which he never completely recovers.

The death of a beloved girl also interrupts the college career of the protagonist of Stephen Vincent Benét's *The Beginning of Wisdom.* During his senior year at Yale, Phil Sellaby falls in love with a rather common New Haven girl and secretly marries her; but after a few weeks of marriage Milly dies of pneumonia. Phil leaves Yale without taking his final examinations. He wants to enlist in the Canadian Royal Flying Corps with the hope of going overseas to participate in World War I, but learns that he has symptoms of tuberculosis. For a few days he is torn between a fear of dying and a desire to join Milly in death; but a vivid dream of her induces a violent fit of weeping that leaves him exhausted but calm enough to face life realistically in another part of the country.

234

In Glenway Wescott's *The Apple of the Eye*, fifteen-year-old Dan Strane is very much disturbed at the suicide of his beautiful cousin Rosalia Bier when she is deserted by her lover, whom Dan has liked and admired. This tragic ending of something beautiful makes life seem meaningless to Dan, until Rosalia's father helps him to find a meaning (see page 172 above). Nick Adams of Hemingway's *In Our Time* is suddenly introduced to suicide in the midst of another shocking experience: when Nick is about twelve years old he assists his doctor father in performing, without anaesthetic, a caesarean operation in an Indian camp, and later learns that the husband has cut his own throat while his wife was screaming. Since he did not know the people, Nick is not overwhelmed by the disaster. Returning to their own camp at sunrise, Nick asks his father a number of questions about death; but, intensely aware of the living world and of himself as a part of it, "he felt quite sure that he would never die." (*In Our Time*, p. 25.) Clyde Griffiths in Dreiser's *An American Tragedy* is exposed to sudden death twice during his adolescence, and each time he feels at least partly responsible. When he is about seventeen he rides with nine other half-drunken young people in a borrowed car which, traveling too fast through the streets of Kansas City, strikes and kills a little girl. When he is twenty-two he watches the drowning of his pregnant sweetheart, which takes place just as he planned it except that an accident causes the capsizing which he has not had the courage to bring about for himself. By running away he is able to escape the consequences of the first death, but not those of the second.

Deaths in the immediate family affect a number of adolescent protagonists in novels of the twenties. Sherwood Anderson's Tar Moorehouse is about fourteen when his mother dies; his father is out of town on a house-painting job, and Tar and his brothers and sister have to meet people and make arrangements for the funeral. After the funeral Tar shocks himself and his friends by playing baseball noisily and ostentatiously—for a few minutes. Then he goes and hides in an empty grain car where he can cry and meditate in solitude. But he soon realizes that he is old enough to have some responsibility for adding to the family income, and that work will make his sorrow easier to bear. So he crawls out of the box car and begins to peddle his newspapers. In Ruth Suckow's *The Bonney Family*, Sarah is an unattractive girl in late adolescence when the death of her very understanding mother forces Sarah, overcome with grief herself, to take the mother's place as the unifying bond in a diverse family. Rölvaag's Peder Holm is hardly more than a child when his father is lost in a blizzard, and throughout the weeks that follow Peder shows a touching faith that God will bring Father back:

> God wanted to do only that which was good; God was almighty; no finer man than Father had ever lived: God could see that they couldn't get along without Father, consequently, he must come back! (*Peder Victorious*, pp. 7–8.)

But when Father's body is discovered at last, Peder's attitude toward God changes completely:

> And thus it happened that from now on God became to Peder another being. He was treacherous, sly, cunning, and because He was invisible and always lay in wait to pounce down on people and strike a blow at them, He was One you had to look out for. . . . Henceforth no power on earth could make him believe that God, who had killed his father in this way, could be only goodness. (*Ibid.*, p. 9.)

Thomas Wolfe's Eugene Gant is one of the most tortured adolescents in the American novels of the twenties, and his contacts with death are proportionately overwhelming. When his brother Grover dies, Eugene is only three years old—too young to feel the full impact; but Ben, Grover's twin and Eugene's favorite, dies when Gene is eighteen and extremely sensitive both to the complex relationships between members of his family and to his own emotional experiences. All of these things Wolfe describes at considerable length, and the feelings of all members of the family reach almost unbearable tension during Ben's prolonged death scene; therefore there is a sense of relief when the struggle is over and there is nothing more anyone can do. This reaction is shared by the other Gants:

> They were tired, but they all felt an enormous relief. For over a day, each had known that death was inevitable, and after the horror of the incessant strangling gasp, this peace, this end of pain touched them all with a profound, a weary joy. . . .
> Eugene thought of death now, with love, with joy. Death was like a lovely and tender woman, Ben's friend and lover, who had come to free him, to heal him, to save him from the torture of life.
> They stood there together without speaking, in Eliza's littered kitchen, and their eyes were blind with tears, because they thought of lovely and delicate death, and because they loved one another. (*Look Homeward, Angel*, p. 560.)

But when the elaborate funeral begins, Gene feels that the body is not really Ben, that Ben is lost to him forever, and that Gene himself is trapped with an insane, ghoulish family at an obscene burial service.

William Faulkner's *As I Lay Dying* (1930) is almost wholly concerned with the reaction of children to their mother's death. Of the five children of Anse and Addie Bundren, only the seventeen-year-old Dewey Dell is definitely adolescent. The novel consists of the streams of consciousness of various members of the family and a few outsiders from a few hours before Addie's death until her body is brought to Jefferson for burial almost a week later. Dewey Dell does not seem greatly concerned with the thought of losing her mother; she is much more concerned with her own pregnancy and the problem of how to get rid of it. When the doctor comes from Jefferson just in time to see Addie die, Dewey Dell's chief thought is that she herself needs the doctor more than her mother does, but cannot ask him for aid. To the girl, the family excursion to Jefferson for the burial means a chance to go to a drug store for help. Her attitude cannot be considered typical of adolescents on the occasion of a mother's death, but it illustrates the trend away from the sentimental emphasis on mourning over death found in many novels of the twenties, and suggests the newer emphasis on the individual personalities of adolescent protagonists which cause them to react to death in a variety of ways.

Other novels of the thirties which include deaths in the family resulting from illness are Langston Hughes's *Not Without Laughter*, Robert P. Tristram Coffin's *Red Sky in the Morning*, and William Maxwell's *They Came Like Swallows*. In the first of these, the colored boy Sandy Rogers is nearly fourteen years old at the death of his grandmother, who has been like a mother to him; his first thought is that he will no longer have to collect laundry from white families, because now there is nobody to wash it. The most difficult problem Sandy faces after his grandmother's death is adjusting to the white people's standards affected by his Aunt Tempy; but the boy's quiet and studious nature makes this adjustment relatively easy. Fifteen-year-old Will Prince in Coffin's novel is forced abruptly into maturity when his older brother David dies of diphtheria in the isolated family home on a small island off the coast of Maine. The father, who much preferred David to Will and was extremely jealous of his wife's attractiveness to other men, returns to the small island alone, while Will, who loves both his parents and wants to bring

237

them together, stays with his mother on a larger and more accessible island and sacrifices himself to save her from the charms of his father's Cousin Rupert. Fourteen-year-old Robert Morison of *They Came Like Swallows* suffers on two accounts when his mother dies of influenza: he feels responsible for her exposure to the disease, and he is hurt by his father's sudden unwonted harshness, not realizing that his father also feels responsible and doubts his own qualifications for bringing up two motherless boys.

In novels of the thirties adolescents react as variously to deaths due to violence as they do to more peaceful demises. Temple Drake in Faulkner's *Sanctuary* is brought abruptly into contact with violence when she sees the good-natured imbecile Tommy shot by the gang leader Popeye, who then proceeds to violate her with a corncob. A few weeks later Popeye jealously has her lover, Red, killed. Perhaps out of fear of further reprisals, Temple subsequently testifies in court that Tommy was killed by the innocent Lee Goodwin. Jenny Blair Archbald, of Ellen Glasgow's *The Sheltered Life,* experiences a great traumatic shock when the middle-aged roué George Birdsong, whom she has secretly loved for years, is shot by his wife, whom Jenny Blair also devotedly admires. But the adolescents in Erskine Caldwell's *Tobacco Road* are as unconcerned as the adults when old Grandmother Lester is run over by an automobile and dies slowly in the Lester farmyard. The fatal shooting of Will Thompson during a mill strike in Caldwell's *God's Little Acre* is distressing to the adolescent girls in the novel primarily because Will was the only man who could satisfy them all sexually. Cass McKay in Nelson Algren's *Somebody in Boots* is permanently traumatized on a sunny day in March of his sixteenth year when he sees a boy hobo dying beside a railroad track where he has been hit by a freight train—one arm cut off, one eye knocked out, the jaw broken, and the chest heaving spasmodically.

> There never came, in later years, a sunny, windy day in March, but Cass would be faintly sickened and half uneasy and somewhat afraid. (P. 19.)

Seventeen-year-old Tommy in Frederic Prokosch's *Night of the Poor,* hitch-hiking from Wisconsin to Texas, sees a Negro hobo lynched and a sickly, impoverished child die of exposure; but he arrives in Texas with a healthy desire for normal life. In Paul Horgan's *A Lamp on the*

Plains Danny Milford has the overpowering task of reconstructing his life alone in a strange part of the country after seeing his evangelistic mother stoned to death for preaching peace during the closing days of World War I.

In the novels of the forties, this trend toward a variety of reaction increases as does the tendency to suggest psychological causes and effects of the varied reactions. In Bellamann's *Kings Row*, Parris Mitchell is fourteen when he hears with terror the news of a schoolmate's father dying of shock after an operation without any anesthetic. Though he admires the doctor who performed the operation, and decides to become a doctor himself, Parris also conceives a long-lasting fear of the doctor. At the age of nineteen, when the boy is ready to study medicine in Vienna, he has a triple encounter with death. His grandmother, who has been his only family since his infancy, dies of cancer; and Dr. Tower, who is both Parris' tutor and the father of his mistress, kills the daughter and himself. To lose at the same time three people who have been so close to him is a nearly overwhelming experience, especially as the reason for Dr. Tower's behavior becomes clear to him; but the challenge of facing new problems in another part of the world helps to keep him from brooding over his loss, and forces him into reaching adult status.

Two novels of 1943 treat with restrained sentiment the reactions of their adolescent protagonists to the loss of beloved members of their families. Homer Macauley is a fifteen-year-old telegraph messenger in Saroyan's *The Human Comedy*, the man of the family since the death of his father and his older brother's induction into the army in World War II. His unpleasant task of delivering death messages to mothers of servicemen makes him well aware that news may come at any time telling of his brother's death; but when that news does come, his reaction is one of futile anger. He tells the manager of the telegraph office:

> "Nothing like this has ever happened to me before. When my father died it was different. He had lived a good life. He had raised a good family. We were sad because he was dead, but we weren't sore. Now I'm sore and I haven't got anybody to be sore at. Who's the enemy? Do you know, Mr. Spangler?" (P. 283.)

Fourteen-year-old Francie Nolan of Betty Smith's *A Tree Grows in Brooklyn* has known for some time that her gay and irresponsible father was drinking himself to death; but when he finally dies, of alcoholism

239

and pneumonia, she is stunned and numb for several days. After the funeral, when she discusses her father's death with her thirteen-year-old brother, both youngsters are able to cry for the first time, and Francie confesses that she cannot believe in a God who "made papa the way he was" and then punished him for being that way. But Jesus was a living man once and knew what it meant to suffer. "Jesus wouldn't go around punishing people. He *knew* about people. So I will always believe in Jesus Christ." (Pp. 252–53.)

Homer's reaction to death recalls that of Skeeters Kirby and Francie's recalls that of Peder Holm, but other adolescent protagonists of the forties are less reminiscent of the fiction of the twenties. Sonie Marburg of Jean Stafford's *Boston Adventure* is about eighteen when her five-year-old brother dies, and his death brings out an amazingly complex tangle of emotions: despair at the loss of the one person in her family who showed some affection for her, relief at the end of the child's suffering from epilepsy and his bitter enmity with his mother, shame at her inability to provide anything more than a pauper's burial, horror at the realization that her mother tried to arrange a sea-burial as the most loathsome way of disposing of the remains of a hated child, and other emotions more subtly related to Ivan's death. Thirteen-year-old Joel Knox in Capote's *Other Voices, Other Rooms,* feeling the need for love after the death of his long-divorced mother, comes to Skully's Landing in search of his father, but finds the decayed Southern estate and its inhabitants pervaded by the macabre atmosphere which its name suggests. His father is a paralyzed wreck, seemingly dead except for his eyes; his stepmother, Amy, lives only in her memories of the past; and Amy's Cousin Randolph, whose schemes to get and keep Joel for his own perverted pleasure motivate most of the action in the novel, suggests that his own life has been a death (p. 139). The book abounds in symbols of death and suspended time, and memories of his mother's funeral and the weird home burial service for the ancient Negro Jesus Fever come repeatedly to Joel's mind. Even his tomboy friend Idabel Thompkins prefers the static world of other voices, other rooms, to the real world about her.

> Now at thirteen Joel was nearer a knowledge of death than in any other year to come: a flower was blooming inside him, and soon, when all tight leaves unfurled, when the noon of youth burned whitest, he would turn and look, as others had, for the opening of another door. . . . Amy, Randolph, his father, they were all outside time, all circling the

present like spirits: was this why they seemed to him so like a dream? Idabel reached back and jerked his hand. "Wake up," she said. He looked at her, his eyes wide with alarm. "But I can't. I can't." (P. 127.)

It is Joel's struggle to "wake up," to escape from the death world of Skully's Landing and move on toward a world of normal maturity, that forms the main conflict of this fascinatingly symbolic novel.

The novels of the fifties show an even greater range of adolescent reactions to deaths of people close to them. In Capote's *The Grass Harp*, after the death of his beloved elderly cousin Dolly Talbo, who had been both a mother and a companion to him since his parents' death five years earlier, sixteen-year-old Collin Fenwick tries to occupy his mind and his time with amusement "because I didn't want to spend a waking moment in the Talbo house." (P. 175.) In Salinger's *The Catcher in the Rye*, Holden Caulfield reacts to the death of a favorite brother by spending the night in the family's garage and breaking the garage windows with his fist; but this physical manifestation of the kind of futile rage that had been expressed vocally by Saroyan's Homer Macauley is mild compared to the psychological distress that keeps Holden from adjusting to his environment for several years and sends him at last to a sanitarium. In Richard B. Erno's *My Old Man*, Joe Burns is bitter and resentful toward his drunken father, holding him chiefly responsible for the death of Joe's mother; but when the old man dies a year or so later, Joe finally begins to understand his father. In Peter S. Feibleman's *A Place Without Twilight*, the light mulatto girl Cille Morris blames her strait-laced mother for the alcoholic death of her book-loving father; and when the mother herself dies some years later, Cille fanatically cleans from the house every vestige of her mother's personality before she will consent to live in it. The "nymphet" protagonist of Nabokov's *Lolita* is curiously undisturbed at the sudden death of her widowed mother; but her years spent with two demanding middle-aged lovers, and the melodramatic murder of the second lover by the first, leave the girl emotionally worn out at an age when she should be at the peak of adolescence.

Many novels of the fifties show varied effects of murder or suicide on perceptive adolescents, who may or may not be responsible for the deaths. To mention only a few: John Bell Clayton's *Wait, Son, October Is Near* vividly presents the response of Tucker English to the near-murder of his father by Staples Milroy, brother of the father's mistress, and the subsequent suicide of Staples; Anne Chamberlain's *The Tall Dark Man* describes the terror of Sarah Lou Gross after seeing, from the schoolroom window, the murder of one stranger by another, who knows that Sarah Lou is the only witness; Grace Metalious' *Peyton Place* shows the devastating effect on Selena Cross of the town's discovery that she has killed her stepfather, even though the killing is found to have been in self-defense; Pamela Moore's *Chocolates for Breakfast* tells of Janet Parker's suicide after being assaulted by her own father, and her friend Courtney Farrell's shocked recognition of the futility of their adolescent experiments with alcohol and sex; Meyer Levin's *Compulsion* and James Yaffe's *Nothing But the Night*, both based on the Leopold and Loeb murder of Bobby Franks in 1924, depict the consequences of a killing for excitement by two highly intellectual adolescent boys. The horrors of death are multiplied for Warren Sands in Philip McFarland's *A House Full of Women* (1960); during his thirteenth year he loses his brother through illness, his father through war, and his mother through suicide.

It is easy enough to trace a chronological trend in the novels which show adolescents witnessing death and disaster. From the excessive sentimentality of the genteel tradition and the restrained sentiment of the 1920's, novelists turned to increasingly complex probings of varied and individual reactions during the 1930's and 1940's, frequently reaching extremes of the lurid and melodramatic in novels of the 1950's. To trace geographical trends is not so easy. Deaths, especially violent ones, are accepted more casually by characters in novels set in the South than in those presenting other parts of the country, and seem to be taken more as a matter of course in the West than in the Middle West or the East, but there is not a great deal of difference in this respect. In rural areas, where killing of both wild and domesticated animals is a part of regular routine, human death is likely to seem less shocking than in small towns and cities; but such novels as Glenway Wescott's *Apple of the Eye* and Vardis Fisher's *In Tragic Life* indicate that adolescents of the sensitivity usually found in fictional protagonists are keenly affected by human death even when they have become accustomed to animal deaths on a farm. And some adolescent characters who live in small towns or cities are likely to be remarkably callous toward human death. Geographical variations in attitude toward death are observable, but are neither great nor entirely predictable.

242

Although adolescents in many novels observe death and may be greatly affected by the observation, relatively few novels show adolescent protagonists suffering from physical handicaps. Edgar Lee Masters' *Mitch Miller* has a numbness in one foot from having had it badly cut when he was four or five years old; this numbness does not prevent Mitch from leading a normally active life, but it does cause his death, for he does not feel his foot dragging against a wheel as he is hitching rides, and the wheel catches his foot and drags him under the train.[3] Robert Morison in William Maxwell's *They Came Like Swallows* vigorously plays football and baseball and rides a bicycle in spite of having an artificial leg; if anything, his handicap impels him to be more active in sports than he would have been without the handicap. In a later novel by Maxwell, *The Folded Leaf*, thin and undersized Lymie Peters accompanies his athletic friend Spud Latham to the gymnasium for daily workouts. Lymie's weakness and persistence together have an odd effect on Spud. When Spud realizes that Lymie may be his rival in love, he takes comfort in imagining that he can train Lymie to be a good boxer and then beat him up; but as soon as he sees his little friend in a gym suit, he realizes the hopelessness of this dream. "No matter how long Lymie trained, he would never be big enough for anybody to haul off and hit." (P. 194.) In Madeleine L'Engle's *The Small Rain*, Katherine Forrester is slightly lame from a hip injury suffered when she was two. Usually she gets around so well that both she and others forget her injury; but occasionally, if she attempts to run, she is forcibly reminded that she is different from other people.

One novel which does fully portray the emotional and psychological disturbance that is likely to result from physical crippling is Elsie Oakes Barber's *The Trembling Years* (1949). Kathy Storm is a beautiful and lively college freshman when infantile paralysis strikes suddenly and severely, leaving her right arm and her left leg useless. Her next four and a half years are a constant and often bitter struggle as she learns to stand on her own feet, literally and figuratively, and to regard her usefulness to others as more important than their opinion of her.

Blindness is the handicap of adolescents in three novels of 1956. Earlier chapters of this study have mentioned Daphne Athas' *The Fourth World,* set in a boarding school for blind girls and boys (see above, pp. 54–55 and 104). At Canopus Institute, ironically known as "See Eye," the students have learned to do almost everything that seeing people can do, but still feel frightened at the inevitable prospect of facing the world outside the campus. The two adolescents whom the story most concerns, sixteen-year-old Rhea Thomas and seventeen-year-old Gobi Morgan, find security by retreating occasionally into a world which they have created, and where they are absolute masters.

> "Our world is the Fourth World. It is composed of our minds and what our minds see of the real world and also what our minds don't know."
> "Three things, making the fourth?" (P. 32.)

In contrast to the somber naturalism and tragic ending of *The Fourth World,* Margaret Boylen's *The Marble Orchard* presents a satirical and rather symbolic picture of a red-headed Iowa girl who refuses to be martyred by blindness, and finds at last that she does not have to be. Lovey Claypoole is blinded at thirteen by her father's experiment with a gasoline lamp, but refuses to study Braille and to accept either her grandmother's advice of Christian resignation or the local magnate's offer of charity. To avoid both responsibilities and pity, she makes a private playground of the town cemetery, the "marble orchard," and in a bizarre way she finds there love, tolerance, and returning physical sight by the time she is sixteen. Nelson Algren's *A Walk on the Wild Side* tells of the blinding of Dove Linkhorn in late adolescence during a fight with a legless man; but the loss of physical sight seems to give Dove a clear understanding of himself and the world he must live in.

In a number of novels, the physical handicap of the adolescent protagonists is a peculiarity of appearance which sets them off (in their own minds, at least) from other people. In Thomas Wolfe's *Look Homeward, Angel,* Eugene Gant is constantly ridiculed because of his great height and his awkward gait; and in the same author's *The Web and the Rock,* "Monk" Webber receives his nickname because of his fancied resemblance to an ape. In Ruth Suckow's *The Bonney Family,* Warren Bonney is unhappy for many years because of his tall, thin, awkward figure and his conspicuous red hair, and his sister Sarah is just as unhappy for an even longer period because her large size prevents boys from dating her. In Barry Benefield's *April Was When It Began,* the dark, thin Lula Horgos is tormented as a witch by the children of her New York City neighborhood. Robert Marquales in Calder Willingham's *End as a Man* is the victim of some taunting because one of his eyes is brown and the other is blue; but he is a reasonably well-adjusted college student at the time the action of the novel takes place, and is not greatly disturbed by such comments. Much more unfortunate is Robert's roommate, Sow-belly Simmons, whose mule-like appearance and wretched dormitory experiences are described in an earlier chapter of this study (see p. 127 above). One of the many problems troubling Holden Caulfield in Salinger's *The Catcher in the Rye* is his unusual physical appearance; he is excessively tall and thin, and even in adolescence his hair is turning gray.

MENTAL HANDICAPS

Mental handicaps are understandably less common than physical ones in the leading characters of novels, especially the handicap of an inherently low mentality. The story of the deterioration of a fine mind may be grandly tragic, as in *King Lear;* but the inadequate struggles of a feeble mentality can hardly be more than dully pathetic. William Faulkner is perhaps the only modern American novelist who has been able to arouse much reader sympathy for feeble-minded adolescents, and his most successful effort was his first. In *The Sound and the Fury,* the idiot Benjy Compson actually does arouse the reader's sympathy by his incoherent expressions of despair when anything disturbs the pattern of life to which he has become accustomed, and especially when Benjy's earnest grief is contrasted with the callousness of his brother Jason's contemptuous dismissal of any human rights for Benjy. In Faulkner's *As I Lay Dying,* the preadolescent Vardaman Bundren is apparently a low-grade moron who confuses his mother's death with the death of a fish he has caught and with the visit of the doctor who has come to help her; Vardaman's confusions do not seem especially important to himself or to anyone else, although they are at least partly responsible for his older brother Darl's being confined in a mental hospital as a pyromaniac. Ike

245

Snopes in Faulkner's *The Hamlet* is an imbecile who is less interesting as an individual than as a bit of grotesque atmosphere for Faulkner's gothic humor—especially in the account of Ike's love affair with a cow.

Aberration of the adolescent mind is found much more often in novels of the forties and fifties than in those of the twenties and thirties, but even early novels occasionally show traces of it. Fitzgerald's *This Side of Paradise* shows Amory Blaine suffering hallucinations in which he sees the devil with the face of a college friend recently killed in an automobile accident; later in the novel the fey eighteen-year-old Eleanor Savage impulsively decides to gallop her horse over the edge of a cliff, but throws herself to the ground just before the horse goes over.[4] Early novels by William Faulkner show many examples of mental disturbance, but they do not always make it clear which characters are mentally ill, or which characters are adolescents. In *The Sound and the Fury*, Quentin Compson is shown as a freshman at Harvard, greatly disturbed at the circumstances of his own family and eventually committing suicide; but his thinking remains clear and logical until his death. In *As I Lay Dying*, the most intelligent and sensitive member of the Bundren family, Darl, who is definitely beyond the age of adolescence, seems to merit being sent to the mental hospital at Jackson; but, as his older brother Cash comments:

> Sometimes I ain't so sho who's got ere a right to say when a man is crazy and when he ain't. Sometimes I think it ain't none of us pure crazy and ain't none of us pure sane until the balance of us talks him that-a-way. It's like it ain't so much what a fellow does, but it's the way the majority of folks is looking at him when he does it. (Modern Library edition, p. 510.)

Werther's Younger Brother, a strange little book written by Michael Fraenkl and published anonymously in 1931, presents the stream of consciousness of a young intellectual, in love with his brother's wife, who imagines himself to be both Werther and Hamlet. At one time he imagines he has seduced his sister-in-law; at another he fancies he has murdered her. Like Hamlet, he seems torn between madness and suicide, but apparently chooses the former. Vardis Fisher's *In Tragic Life* frequently describes the thoughts of Vridar Hunter in terms of insanity; but they seem rather to be profound and poetic thoughts in a land where there is no time for profound and poetic thinking. Rose Franken's *Strange Victory* (1939) tells of thirteen-year-old Erica Herron's erroneous conviction that her guardian is responsible for the motor-car death of her mother.

The publication of Henry Bellaman's *Kings Row* in 1940 apparently began a more pronounced trend toward the discussion of mental disorders in novels. The assortment of mentally abnormal adolescents in this novel includes the feeble-minded Benny Singer, the homosexual Jamie Wakefield, the incestuous nymphomaniac Cassie Tower, the increasingly neurotic Louise Gordon, the overconscientious Vera Lichinsky, to say nothing of all the adult characters who are abnormal in one way or another. Robert Nathan's *Long After Summer* (1948) is a fascinating though rather unbelievable story of a fourteen-year-old Cape Cod girl who, after seeing her lover drown, fancies that she is moving backward through the summer's experiences with him, and that she will die when she gets as far as April, the month when they met (see page 37 above). Willard Motley's *Knock on Any Door* shows the deterioration of the mind and morals of its protagonist, Nick Romano, from the time he serves as a Catholic altar boy at twelve to the time he is electrocuted, at twenty-one, for the murder of a policeman. Motley shows how various phases of Nick's environment have combined to make him a psychopathic criminal, but intimates that Nick at any stage of the descent, given sufficient will power, could have saved himself. Both psychological motives and physical environment contribute to the making of a criminal mind.

Much fiction of the fifties shows clearly the novelists' interest in abnormal psychology. Charlotte Armstrong's *Mischief* (1950) presents a teen-age girl, Nell Munro, as baby-sitter for a nine-year-old girl whose parents do not realize that Nell is a homicidal maniac. The author's purpose is obviously to give her readers a thrill of horror rather than to add to the understanding of a warped mind, but the actions and the thought processes are a little more convincing than in most thrillers. Another thriller is Howard Pease's *The Dark Adventure* (1950), which tells of sixteen-year-old Johnny Stevens hitch-hiking from Illinois to California, becoming involved in an automobile accident which causes a temporary loss of memory, and making friends with high-school marijuana peddlers and other teen-age trouble-makers before he remembers who he is and what he originally planned to do.

Two of the best fictional studies of psychological abnormality in adolescence are Shirley Jackson's *Hangsaman* and J. D. Salinger's *The Catcher in the Rye*, both published in 1951. An earlier chapter discussed Miss

Jackson's novel (see p. 128 above), telling how the protagonist, Natalie Waite, retreats from life into a world of her own imagination and devotes most of her free time at college to a strange companion who is either completely a figment of her imagination or an actual girl who encourages Natalie to withdraw more and more from reality. Salinger's Holden Caulfield is very introspective and very much afraid of any appearance of "phoniness." He is eager to help other people, and eager to be loved by others, but he does not understand how to communicate with the people around him. When his favorite brother dies, he can express his grief only by breaking windows. He appreciates what his parents try to do for him, but finds it impossible to talk with them. The one adult with whom he feels at ease, his former English teacher Mr. Antolini, frightens him by gently caressing his head as he sleeps; Holden is so afraid of phoniness that he immediately interprets the man's gesture of sympathy as a homosexual approach. Although Holden supposedly relates his adventures from a sanitarium for mental patients, the reader has the impression that he is more confused and frightened than mentally ill and that he will eventually adjust himself to normal life.

A third novel of 1951, William Styron's *Lie Down in Darkness*, depicts the tragedy of a girl whose father fixation drives her to alcoholism and eventually to suicide, although the main emphasis in the novel is on the characters and problems of her parents. Peyton Loftis is a beautiful girl who is spoiled by her devoted father, while her physically and mentally defective older sister Maude is the favorite of their mother. In adolescence, Peyton arouses the jealous hatred of her mother, and is unable to find a man who measures up to the ideal that her father has created in her mind. Her brief married life is miserable for both herself and her husband, and she finally leaps from the window of her New York apartment.

Pamela Oldenburg in Julian Halevy's *The Young Lovers* (1955) is a sensitive art student in New York who hovers on the brink of insanity throughout the novel. When she is first found by the novel's protagonist, Eddie Slocum, she cannot remember anything about herself except her name. Eddie helps her to regain her memory, and the two find happiness for a few months as lovers; but when Pam, knowing she is pregnant, thinks Eddie does not love her, she temporarily loses her mind. Though the novel ends on an optimistic note, the realistic reader wonders whether a person as unstable as Pam could be depended on as a wife and mother.

An adolescent girl who cannot adjust herself to real life appears in Laura Beheler's *The Paper Dolls* (1956). From her childhood on, Ida Erickson has found little love or companionship from her parents, and derives her greatest pleasure from the elaborate lives she invents for the paper dolls that she has cut from magazines and mail-order catalogues. The older she grows the harder it is for her to adjust to reality; and by the time she is an adult, disappointment in a love affair sends her to her bottle as lack of love from her parents formerly sent her to her paper dolls. In Pamela Moore's *Chocolates for Breakfast*, two teen-age girls, Courtney Farrell and Janet Parker, try to make up by means of sex and alcohol for what they have lost in affection from their parents. Janet's suicide at eighteen sobers Courtney into facing life more realistically. A different kind of psychological abnormality appears in two novels based on the Leopold-Loeb murder of Bobby Franks in 1924: Meyer Levin's *Compulsion* and James Yaffe's *Nothing But the Night*, which were discussed in an earlier chapter (see p. 93 above).

Three novels of 1958 deal with adolescents who are mentally handicapped. An adolescent girl in a mental institution is the subject of *The Unbelonging* by Alice M. Robinson, who is a psychiatric nurse and the author of a textbook for psychiatric aides. At the age of twelve, Laurie Hammond is committed to a mental hospital by parents who are unwilling to make sufficient effort to understand her. After six years in various institutions, one of which she tries to burn down, Laura at last meets trained and understanding people who help her return to normal life. In Anne Chamberlain's *The Darkest Bough*, fourteen-year-old Morgan Cavenner is a mentally retarded boy whose male nurse proves to be a menace both to Morgan and to his older sister Bitha. Constance Loveland's *Veronica* tells of a sixteen-year-old New York girl who, in spite of psychiatric help, is unable to find the answers to her problems until her foolish actions lead to a serious accident.

Two later novels feature boys who suffer mental breakdowns in school. Robert Gutwillig's *The Fugitives* (1959) describes Stevie Freeman, after an attempt at suicide, interrupting his college career to go to a sanitarium, where he finds that he is able to help look after others who are in worse condition than he. Less fortunate is Willard McGann in William Wood's *The Fit* (1960); Willard is ill adjusted when he first goes to Warrington Prep in New England, and the lack of sympathy from schoolmates and faculty only makes his condition worse.

The fictional treatment of physical and mental handicaps shows increasing complexity and increasing understanding from 1920 to 1960. The earlier novels tended to suggest admiration for a stoic acceptance of physical limitations, as Gene Stratton-Porter's Freckles in earlier fiction had accepted the loss of his hand. Although the effect of an unusual physical appearance on a developing person's mind and emotions was recognized by early novelists, it was not until the forties that fiction-writers began to illustrate the psychosomatic relationships in all their complexity. As Erik H. Erikson pointed out in 1950:

> . . . we learn that a neurotic person, no matter where and how and why he feels sick, is crippled at the core, no matter what you call that ordered or ordering core. He may not become exposed to the final loneliness of death, but he experiences that numbing loneliness, that isolation and disorganization of experience, which we call neurotic anxiety. (*Childhood and Society*, p. 20.)

By the 1950's novelists were exploring all kinds of psychological difficulties, with or without accompanying physical problems, sometimes seeking for true understanding and sometimes merely exploiting the morbid curiosity which people are likely to feel about the functioning of a distorted mind.

Related to the problem of mental illness, and sometimes contributing to it, is the problem of addiction to drugs or alcohol. In some novels the adolescent himself may be an addict, or may appear to be well on the way to becoming one; in others, his problem is the addiction of a member of his family or someone else who is close to him. In the novels of the twenties and thirties, alcoholism was a not uncommon problem, especially in novels of college life; drug addiction, however, was seldom mentioned. In the flood of juvenile delinquency novels that followed World War II, dope peddling became common and was usually accompanied by at least some use of narcotics on the part of adolescents. In the "beat" literature of the later fifties, the smoking of marijuana was treated almost as casually as the smoking of tobacco, but the use of more powerful drugs was considered a really dangerous practice.

Even in the novels of the early twenties, copious drinking among college students appears to be an accepted part of the tradition of "flaming youth." Philip Sellaby in Benét's *The Beginning of Wisdom* and Neale Crittenden in Mrs. Fisher's *Rough-Hewn* engage in some drinking bouts and enjoy getting "high," but there is no indication that their drinking is compulsive. On the other hand, Amory Blaine in Fitzgerald's *This Side of Paradise* seems to be well on his way toward alcoholism; this chapter earlier mentioned his hallucination of the devil perceived during delirium tremens (p. 246 above), and the portion of the novel which follows Amory's leaving Princeton shows him in alcoholic stupors which last for weeks at a time. An early college novel which clearly traces a student's progression from total abstinence to near alcoholism is Percy Marks's *The Plastic Age*. During his first week at college, Hugh Carver refuses to drink with his roommate, stating as an excuse that he wants to keep in condition for athletics; but before the end of the year he is drinking with the boys occasionally. In his sophomore year Hugh is a member of a fraternity, and at his first fraternity dance he is offended that any drinking is going on, and horrified that some of the girls are drinking. While visiting a friend on Long Island the following summer, Hugh falls in love with Cynthia Day, who is frankly fond of drinking; and when he takes her to the Junior Prom at college, they both get very drunk and go to a dormitory bedroom, where they are discovered by a friend of both of them (see above, page 46). With an effort, Hugh and Cynthia decide it will be best for both of them not to see each other for a while. In remorse, Hugh gives up drinking and busies himself with athletics, music, and academic work to take his mind off Cynthia, while Cynthia busies herself with dates and drinking to take her mind off Hugh. A year later, when Hugh is about to graduate, he asks Cynthia to marry him, but is rather relieved when she refuses. Cynthia remains likable and even admirable, but it is apparent that she may have recurrent lapses into heavy drinking, whereas Hugh will not.

As early as 1928 the problem of heavy drinking among high-school students appeared in Robert S. Carr's *The Rampant Age*. Carr did not suggest that drinking was a universal problem among high-school students, but he did indicate its existence. Paul Benton, the central character of the novel, is introduced to gin when he transfers from a small-town centralized high school to a city school; in order to be accepted in his high-school crowd, he experiments with both liquor and sex, but by the time he is ready for college he seems to be eager to settle down to serious work. Salinger's *The Catcher in the Rye* (1951), J. W. Ellison's *I'm Owen Harrison Harding* (1955), and Pamela Moore's *Chocolates for Breakfast* (1956) are among the comparatively few novels which present drinking among high-school students as a serious problem; but most of the college novels show it as one of the major temptations to the student who is living away from home. John V. Craven's *The Leaf Is Green* (1931), Calder Willingham's *End as a Man* (1947), William Styron's *Lie Down in Darkness* (1951), Glenn Scott's *A Sound of Voices Dying* (1955), Charles Thompson's *Halfway Down the Stairs* (1957), Richard Frede's *Entry E* (1958) and Robert Gutwillig's *After Long Silence* (1958) all give particularly vivid descriptions of drinking scenes at college and the threat of alcoholism to college students.

The problem of the drunkard's child has been treated in fiction almost as long as there has been any fiction. It was a popular device for arousing the sentimental pity that many nineteenth-century authors sought in their readers, and it appears in the first American naturalistic novel, Stephen Crane's *Maggie, A Girl of the Streets* (1893). Many of the young people discussed in this study have drinking fathers: Anderson's Tar Moorehead, Wolfe's Eugene Gant, Farrell's Danny O'Neill, Langston Hughes's Sandy Rogers, Flannery Lewis' Abel Dayton, Betty Smith's Francie Nolan, Richard Erno's Joe Burns, Grace Metalious' Selena Cross, and Peter Feibleman's Cille Morris, to mention only a few. Children of drinking mothers are not nearly so common: Amory Blaine's mother suffers a "nervous breakdown that bore a suspicious resemblance to delirium tremens" (*This Side of Paradise,* p. 8); Katherine Forrester in Madeleine L'Engle's *The Small Rain* is fourteen when her mother dies of a severe cold aggravated by years of excessive drinking; Pamela Oldenburg in Julian Halevy's *The Young Lovers* is shocked into amnesia when she receives a suicide note from her alcoholic mother on the other side of the United States; Miles and Helen in Wingate Froscher's *The Comforts of the Damned* (1960) try to cover up their brilliant mother's alcoholism— but these are just about the only examples of drinking mothers in the novels since 1920.

Addiction to Drugs

Though alcoholic parents contribute to the problems of a number of fictional adolescents, drug-addict parents almost never appear in the novels of the last forty years. The one exception that comes to mind is the physician father of Oliver Alden in Santayana's *The Last Puritan*. Oliver is about fifteen, on a cruise with his father and the devoted Englishman Jim Darnley, when he learns that his father habitually retreats into drugged slumber, leaving Jim to handle his affairs. Seeing Oliver's shocked reaction to this news, Jim takes the boy into his father's cabin, hoping to set his mind at rest.

> His father lay propped high, very lean and bronzed by habitual exposure to the sun and the sea-air; his bald head and thin hands looked dark and swarthy against the white pillow and the white nightgown on which his long fingers were spread out symmetrically. His eyes, rather than in sleep, seemed closed by a voluntary drooping of the eyelids, as if in order that a deeper life might flow undisturbed; and there was a faint ambiguous smile on his lips, not unlike that of the two Buddhas whose golden shrines decorated the Poop. Oliver had expected trouble, and he found an image of peace. He had been nerving himself to tolerate, or if possible to repair, the ravages of vice, and he seemed to be rebuked somehow by a strange spirit of holiness, as if life could ultimately escape from perpetual dying and become supreme recollection. . . . So our budding transcendalist was made inwardly aware, by his father's slumber, of the new possible dimension of moral life. *Dope*, Oliver said to himself, was the worst thing possible. *Dope* was the very denial of courage, of determination to face the facts, a betrayal of responsibility. *Dope* was a cowardly means of escape, of hiding one's head like the ostrich, and choosing not to know or to act or to think. And yet, in close association with that miserable *dope*, appeared this strange serenity, this cool challenge to the world, this smiling and beautiful death in life, or life in accepted death. Here was an ancient, an immortal conviction, which the modern world chose foolishly to ignore: the inscrutable, invincible preference of the mind for the infinite. Could it be that life as the world understands it, was the veritable *dope*, the hideous, beastly, vicious intoxication? Was obedience to convention and custom and public opinion perhaps only an epidemic slavery, a cruel superstition; while to sit with closed eyes in a floating hermitage, as in a Noah's Ark in the Deluge, might be enlightenment and salvation? (Pp. 170–71.)

253

Most novelists are not as philosophical about the morality of drug addiction as Santayana is; since 1947 the use of drugs has been a regular characteristic of the juvenile-delinquency novel, in which the habit is generally one form of rebellion against the standards of parents, teachers, and society as a whole. In Irving Shulman's *The Amboy Dukes*, Frank Goldfarb experiments with marijuana as he does with liquor, sex, and zip-guns—to conform to the accepted standards of his Brooklyn neighborhood gang, whose approbation means more to him than that of his parents, his high-school teachers, or the social workers at the Jewish Center. The protagonist of Hal Ellson's *Duke* (1949) is the fifteen-year-old leader of a Negro gang in New York, whose chief source of income is dope-peddling. He smokes marijuana, assuring himself that it is not habit-forming like heroin or morphine or cocaine; but when he is out of it, he will do almost anything to get more "weed." Johnny Stevens in Howard Pease's *The Dark Adventure* becomes involved in a California dope ring while he is suffering from amnesia, but the story has a happy ending. Hal Ellson's *The Golden Spike* (1952) tells of a sixteen-year-old Puerto Rican boy in New York who is a hopeless drug addict, and George Mandel's *Flee the Angry Strangers* (1952) portrays an eighteen-year-old Greenwich Village girl, a marijuana addict who became a heroin addict and resorted to prostitution and thievery as means of securing her needed supply.

Drug addiction is likely to appear also in novels about jazz musicians, and it may serve as a connecting link between the world of jazz and the underworld of crime. The desire for "kicks" sends young Alfie Lambert (in Douglass Wallop's *Night Light*, 1953) first to playing in a night-club jazz band and later to pointless murder and suicide. In Evan Hunter's *Second Ending* (1956) the young jazz trumpeter Andy Silvera develops from a promising musician at fifteen to a hopeless addict at twenty, who is soon to die from complications brought on by the use of drugs. These are not well written novels, but they illustrate a trend in the popular fiction of the fifties toward exploitation of sensational topics, here related to drug addiction and to jazz. A much better novel is Vance Bourjaily's *Confessions of a Spent Youth*, in which the narrator-protagonist uses marijuana only a few times, noting with concern the great hold which the drug has on his friend the jazz trombonist Hal Folger, in spite of Hal's frequent assurances that hemp is non-habit-forming.

The most famous novel about an adolescent addicted to drugs is Jack

Kerouac's *On the Road* (1957). In New York, San Francisco, and Denver, between their wild automobile rides up and down the country, the adolescent Dean Moriarty and his older friend Sal Paradise find self-expression through dope, jazz, and sex. Marijuana they use freely and casually, believing it to be non-habit-forming; stronger drugs they use only occasionally, when they feel the need of a bigger kick than marijuana can provide.

The problem of drug addiction as it affects fictional adolescents appears mostly in novels published during the fifties, and mostly in novels set in large cities—particularly New York. The problems of alcoholism, on the other hand, may appear in novels published at any time and with settings in any part of the country. Novels of the twenties, if they dealt with the problem of drinking, usually had Eastern college settings; later novels are likely to deal with the drinking problem in any kind of setting, in any part of the country. However, as adolescents are not likely to overindulge in drink while they are under close adult supervision, the problem comes up most often in novels which depict the young people away from home —at college, at boarding school, in military service, or on a trip—and in those which show homes with little parental control—broken homes, or homes where both parents have full-time jobs or time-consuming social activities.

The desperation of the fictional adolescents of the fifties who can find enjoyment only in drugs or liquor, in jazz, sex, and fast cars, and who feel that the death of a person or an animal is a necessary part of their initiation into life, illustrates the climax in a trend that has been noted in discussions of authors' attitudes toward other problem areas of teen-agers as presented in American novels from 1920 through 1960. Novels of the twenties, while completely frank, were more sentimental than those of later decades—also more general and more superficial. Novels of the thirties went into much more detail and tended to arouse sympathy for the adolescent protagonists as victims of an unjust social system; these books offered the hope that the world could be made better if it heeded the novelists' admonitions. Novels of the forties gave still more detail about briefer periods in the adolescents' lives, considering not only the actions, words, and thoughts of the characters but even their subconscious minds, using symbolism both as a literary device and as a clew to lead the reader through a labyrinth of Freudian motives. Novels of the fifties made further use of symbolism and depth psychology to indicate that problems which had once been considered peculiar to perverts could be found, thinly disguised, in the most commonplace lives. And as the complexity of man's problems became more apparent and his faith in traditional values diminished, the hopeful didacticism of the earlier novelists gave way to a desperate ruthlessness which implied, "The world is much worse off than people want to admit, and the best thing anyone can do about his problems is to learn to live with them."

Chapter VIII

PERSPECTIVES AND PROSPECTS

In analyzing the treatment of problems of adolescents in nearly six hundred American novels, published over a period of four decades, this study has grouped the novels according to the kinds of problems they present. In order to make clear some trends found in novels of adolescence in general, and the contributions of particular novelists, the present chapter will group the novels according to the attitudes of the authors toward the problems presented and will trace modifications of these attitudes both chronologically and regionally.

PERSISTENCE OF THE GENTEEL TRADITION

The sentimental attitude of the genteel tradition did not, of course, disappear at once. It is particularly apparent in two novels, both written by Eastern novelists whose reputations were well established during the first two decades of the century: *An Old Chester Secret* (1920) by Margaret Deland and *Blowing Clear* (1930) by Joseph C. Lincoln. Both novels present very similar problems: in each of them a boy of mysterious origin is brought up in a small town whose inhabitants circulate wild rumors as to scandals concerning the boy's birth. Mrs. Deland blames the prejudices of the Pennsylvania village and the misguided pride of the boy's socially prominent mother for Johnny Smith's having to grow up without knowing his own family; Lincoln gives most of his sympathy to the middle-aged Cape Cod fisherman and cabinetmaker who spoils the ungrateful Raymond Heath under the mistaken impression that the boy is his own son by a secret and unhappy marriage. The artificial situations, evoking emotions based on conventional prejudices, seem extremely old-fashioned today and do not generally appear in the better novels of the twenties, especially those dealing with less tradition-bound parts of the country than the northeastern region.

Far more common in the twenties and again in the early forties was

257

the humorous treatment of a mischievous young adolescent or a love-sick older adolescent, in the manner made popular by Booth Tarkington. Tarkington himself extended his Penrod chronicle with *Penrod Jashber* in 1929, and in 1941 he humorously described the seventeen-year-old girl Goody Little and her fourteen-year-old brother Filmer in *The Fighting Littles* as they encounter love problems, family squabbles, and difficulties in adjusting to their environment. Similar condescending humor in the treatment of the problems of adolescence appears in Leona Dalrymple's *Fool's Hill,* Fanny Kilbourne's *A Corner in William,* and John Peter Toohey's *Growing Pains*—all published during the twenties. During the thirties two husband-and-wife teams presented humorous novels about adolescent girls: Florence Ryerson and her husband Colin Clements told of Jane Jones, her love problems, and her literary and dramatic ambitions in *This Awful Age* and its sequel *Mild Oats;* and Graeme and Sarah Lorimer produced four books which laughingly followed the amorous and social adventures of the Philadelphian Maudie Mason between the ages of sixteen and nineteen. The forties saw an outpouring of humorous novels about lovable and memorable adolescent girls: Josephine Bentham's *Janie,* Lillian Day's *The Youngest Profession,* Sally Benson's *Junior Miss,* Dorothy Aldis' *Poor Susan,* F. Hugh Herbert's *Meet Corliss Archer,* Peggy Goodin's *Clementine,* Margaret Millar's *It's All in the Family,* and Sylvia Dee's *And Never Been Kissed.* By 1950 the fad for laughable, lovable subdebs had worn itself out, and the few condescendingly humorous novels about adolescents published during the fifties were about boys: John Faulkner's *Chooky,* Max Shulman's *The Many Loves of Dobie Gillis* and *I Was a Teen-Age Dwarf,* and Harry Ennis Dubin's *Hail, Alma Pater.*

There is a certain amount of realism in these novels, and this is what makes them appealing. Of course the problems of the young people are never taken seriously; although the reader recognizes that the same situations in real life might cause great distress to everybody involved, he joins the author in laughing at the discomfort of the fictional characters, knowing that they are fictional and that a happy ending is inevitable for a novel of this sort. For the most part, the protagonists of these novels have little individuality; their problems are partly contrived and partly the result of the naïveté and enthusiasm that most adolescents are likely to share. The most individualized of these comic adolescents are Miss Benson's Judy Graves, Herbert's Corliss Archer, and Miss Goodin's

Clementine Kelley; each of these young ladies faces some problems which develop inevitably from peculiarities of her own character.

Though the specific locale for each of these novels is not always identified, it is apparent that, with one exception, they are all in the East or the Middle West. Perhaps as a reaction to his brother's creation of grotesque Southerners, John Faulkner demonstrates in *Chooky* that a fictional adolescent of the Penrod tradition can be as much at home in Mississippi as in Indiana.

Just a step removed from the humorously condescending attitude established by Tarkington in *Penrod* and *Seventeen* is the more sympathetic but almost equally romantic attitude of adventure, sentiment, and humor derived from Mark Twain's novels. Edgar Lee Masters' *Mitch Miller* is obviously inspired by *Tom Sawyer;* indeed, Mitch deliberately patterns his life after Tom's. To a less obvious extent, Masters' *Kit O'Brien,* his story of an adolescent ne'er-do-well, is influenced by *Huckleberry Finn.* Ted Robinson's *Enter Jerry* owes something to Mark Twain and something to the schoolboy novel, as it had been popularized by Owen Johnson in his stories of Lawrenceville Prep. Johnson himself added *Skippy Bedelle* to his Lawrenceville chronicle in 1922.

After the middle 1920's the sexless Tom Sawyers virtually disappeared from novels for adult readers, though they continued in juvenile fiction. Older adolescents, who might have been at home in literature of the genteel tradition, occasionally appeared in rather conventional love stories: *Warning Hill* (1930), a fairly early novel by John P. Marquand, gives a rather traditional account of a boy of shabby-genteel family background in love with a girl from a newly rich family; and Mary Austin's *Starry Adventure* (1931) tells of a boy chivalrously offering marriage to a girl who has been caught in an unfortunate love affair. Rose Wilder Lane, in *Old Home Town* (1935), portrays the rather conventional Ernestine Blake in the early years of the twentieth century, growing into long skirts and beginning to take an interest in boys and the usual assortment of small-town eccentrics. Ethel Cook Eliot's *Angel's Mirth* (1936) shows a girl of "enlightened" upbringing being converted to Catholic traditions as she faces problems of adolescence. Percy Marks, who had startled readers with his candid picture of college life in *The Plastic Age,* created in *A Tree Grown Straight* (1936) a youth who readily solves the problems of adolescence because of sane guidance by parents and other older counselors. Robert Nathan in *Winter in April*

(1938) and Barry Benefield in *April Was When It Began* (1939) both presented sentimental pictures of naïve adolescent girls in love with older men. During the early forties Hermann Fetzer, using the pen name "Jake Falstaff," produced three books about young Lemuel Hayden enjoying comfortable and romantic visits to his grandfather's farm in Ohio during the early twentieth century; the author seems to recall his rural Ohio experiences with much the same sort of nostalgia that Mark Twain showed in recalling his Missouri boyhood. Some of Saroyan's books of the forties—notably *My Name Is Aram* and *The Human Comedy*—present affectionate and rather sentimentalized pictures of adolescent boys in California; and R. L. Duffus' *That Was Alderbury* (1941) and *The Waterbury Record* (1959) take a similar attitude toward teen-age boys in small towns in Vermont just about the turn of the century.

Novels about boys and their pets are likely to be rather sentimental, although most of the animal stories published during the period here considered contain a good deal of realism even when they are sentimental. For example, John Steinbeck in "The Red Pony" and Marjorie Kinnan Rawlings in *The Yearling* use stark realism to evoke powerful compassion for their adolescent protagonists. On the other hand, sentiment tends to obscure the realism in Walter D. Edmonds' *The Boyds of Black River* (1953), James Street's *Goodbye, My Lady* (1954), and Clancy Carlile's *As I Was Young and Easy* (1958). Richard B. Erno's *My Old Man* (1955) is almost devoid of sentiment; the ugly cur Orchard responds first with vicious savagery and later with aloof tolerance to seventeen-year-old Joe Burns's patient and long-continued efforts to make the stray dog into a devoted companion.

Obviously a novel which sympathetically portrays an adolescent rising above the corrupting influence of a harsh environment does not have to be considered sentimental or "genteel," although it might be so regarded by many of the naturalistic writers who dominated the fiction of this period. In the second decade of this century Willa Cather had given realistic pictures of adolescent girls triumphing over hostile environments in *The Song of the Lark* (1915) and *My Ántonia* (1918); Dorothy Canfield Fisher in *The Bent Twig* (1915) had written convincingly and without sentiment (though with some didacticism and gentility) of Sylvia Marshall finally rejecting the materialism that had long been her greatest temptation. Such an attitude of clear-eyed faith in the potentiality of human goodness to prevail in the midst of wickedness and

indifference is more common than smiling condescension or blind sentimentality among the novelists of adolescence who wrote between 1920
and 1960, but not nearly as common as the harsh pessimism of the
naturalists. A complete list of the realistic novels which still show faith
in the triumph of human goodness would be too long to include here;
some of the more outstanding ones are Mrs. Fisher's *Rough-Hewn* (1922),
Elizabeth Madox Roberts' *The Time of Man* (1926), William Wister
Haines's *Slim* (1934), H. L. Davis' *Honey in the Horn* (1935) and *Winds
of Morning* (1952), Alvin Johnson's *Spring Storm* (1936), Flannery
Lewis' *Abel Dayton* (1939), Maureen Daly's *Seventeenth Summer*
(1942), Christopher Morley's *Kitty Foyle* (1939) and *Thorofare* (1942),
Walter Van Tilburg Clark's *The City of Trembling Leaves* (1945), Louis
Bromfield's *The Wild Country* (1948), Julian Halevy's *The Young Lovers*
(1955), and Wesley Ford Davis' *The Time of the Panther* (1958). In this
list, all regions of the country and all decades which this study covers
are well represented. Even more striking is the fact that the list includes
many women novelists—certainly more than would be expected from the
great preponderance of male authors in the complete list of novels
studied. These proportions indicate that faith in the ultimate triumph of
right has remained alive in all parts of the country throughout the period
of naturalism's greatest popularity, and that this faith is particularly
characteristic of female writers. Man's persistence in hoping for a bright
future is indicated in the Nobel Prize acceptance speech of the strikingly
naturalistic writer William Faulkner: "I believe that man will not merely
endure: he will prevail. He is immortal, not because he alone among
creatures has an inexhaustible voice, but because he has a soul, a spirit
capable of compassion and sacrifice and endurance. The poet's, the
writer's, duty is to write about these things."

NATURALISTIC NOVELS OF ADOLESCENCE

Certainly the majority of novelists between 1920 and 1960 assumed a
naturalistic attitude toward their subject matter, but it is possible to
trace different emphases within the framework of naturalism, varying
from decade to decade and from region to region. During the twenties
naturalistic writers took a rather broad view of their characters' lives,

covering a number of years superficially instead of analyzing a few days thoroughly, showing that *in the long run* man is likely to be defeated by nature, by society, or by individual human enemies, and that his defeat or triumph is governed by chance and by physical strength rather than by virtue or by divine assistance. Homer Croy's *West of the Water Tower* (1923) covers about twelve years in the lives of Guy Plummer and Bee Chew; Edgar Lee Masters' *Skeeters Kirby* (1923) covers fifteen or twenty years in the life of the narrator-protagonist; John Dos Passos' *Manhattan Transfer* (1925) gives intermittent glimpses, during twenty years or so, at the lives of a number of New Yorkers (notably Jimmy Herf and Ellen Thatcher during the adolescent years); Ernest Hemingway's *In Our Time* (1925) reveals important days in the life of Nick Adams during about ten years; Theodore Dreiser's *An American Tragedy* (1925) follows Clyde Griffiths from the age of twelve to his death at the age of twenty-three. By the end of the 1920's a few naturalistic authors were beginning to concentrate their narratives on shorter periods of time—Robert S. Carr's *The Rampant Age* (1928) describes less than two years of Paul Benton's high-school experiences, and William Faulkner's *The Sound and the Fury* (1929) emphasizes three or four widely scattered days in the lives of the Compsons—but the broader view was still prevalent. During the 1930's some authors, notably Vardis Fisher and James T. Farrell, increased the detail in naturalistic fiction by increasing the number of pages used rather than cutting down on the narrated segment of the characters' lives. Fisher used four volumes to take Vridar Hunter from birth to early middle-age; Farrell used four to take Danny O'Neill from the age of six or seven to twenty-three, and three volumes to follow Studs Lonigan from fifteen to about thirty. During the forties and fifties the majority of novels, naturalistic and otherwise, were likely to concentrate on the events of a short period, from a day or two up to several months in length; but the long chronicle, in one or more volumes, was by no means a thing of the past. Jean Stafford's *Boston Adventure* (1944) follows eight or nine years in the life of Sonia Marburg; John Steinbeck's *East of Eden* (1952) traces the Trask family through two generations, from 1862 to 1918; and William Faulkner reported on the activities of two generations of Snopeses in three volumes: *The Hamlet* (1940), *The Town* (1957), and *The Mansion* (1959).

Some recent novels of the life-history variety are not included in this study because a smaller proportion of their contents is devoted to the adolescent years than in many other novels of the same period, although it is no smaller than the proportion in some novels of the twenties which have been included. For example, Fitzgerald's *This Side of Paradise* (1920) and Stephen Vincent Benét's *The Beginning of Wisdom* (1921) devote only a slightly larger proportion to the adolescent years than does John O'Hara's *From the Terrace* (1958), but the earlier books gave a heavier emphasis on adolescence than was common in their time, especially among serious novels, whereas a great many novels since that time have given their whole attention to the adolescent years, so that *From the Terrace* seems by comparison to give this age rather little emphasis.

PSYCHOLOGY AND SYMBOLISM

One explanation for the tendency to discuss shorter periods in greater detail is the increasing complexity of psychological insight which novelists—especially naturalistic ones—reveal during the years covered by this study. Although such an early writer as Floyd Dell in his autobiographical *Homecoming* (p. 293) admits a great debt to Freud, and Sherwood Anderson has been called by Frederick J. Hoffman in *Freudianism and the Literary Mind* (p. 230) "the one American writer who knew his psychology and, furthermore, possessed a rich fund of knowledge and experience to which it could best be applied," the psychology in novels of the twenties appears fairly obvious and straightforward. Dell's *Moon-Calf* (1920) and Anderson's *Poor White* (1920) are able to present long periods in the lives of their protagonists because the psychological development in each book, while it adds greatly to the appeal, shows a cause-and-effect relationship which can be clearly understood without thorough analysis. In *Tar* (1926), Anderson shows a far more complex psychological development for his protagonist than he showed for Hugh McVey in *Poor White*, and Tar's early adolescence is described at great length while Hugh's is hardly touched. Theodore Dreiser devotes about one-sixth of *An American Tragedy* to Clyde's years in Kansas City between the ages of twelve and seventeen, but the longer and more interesting portion of the novel is that which is closely related to the few months of his tragic love affair with Roberta Alden and the complex psychological pattern woven about it.

It was during the 1940's, however, that American novelists in general began to show a strong interest in the complexities of depth psychology and especially in the interpretation of symbols for hidden desires that had for centuries been considered abnormal and degenerate. This shift in psychological interest is well illustrated by two novels by William Maxwell. *They Came Like Swallows* (1937) shows how a woman's last actions and death during the influenza epidemic of 1918 are seen and emotionally received by her eight-year-old son, her thirteen-year-old son, and her husband. It is a very clever handling of the stream-of-consciousness technique, in which physical events are described entirely through the conscious minds of the people involved—the sort of thing which had already been successfully done by the English novelist Virginia Woolf. *The Folded Leaf* (1945) is concerned with the subconscious mind as well as the conscious, and with many aspects of the peculiar and complex relationship between Spud Latham and Lymie Peters. There is clearly a homosexual element in this relationship, although there is never any genital contact between them, and only once is there a kiss on the lips. Yet they find comfort in assuming positions which are typical of lovers—walking with Lymie's small hand inside Spud's strong one, and sleeping with Spud's body curled protectingly around Lymie's back—and they seem completely unaware that they are behaving like lovers. Maxwell does not explicitly tell, but implies largely through symbols, the causes of the relationship. Lymie is sensitive, unattractive, motherless, neglected by his father, and he finds in Spud not only a friend but a substitute for father, mother, and lover. Spud finds Lymie's helplessness appealing at a time when Spud is friendless in a new community and welcomes the sense of importance which Lymie's dependency gives him. It is the sort of feeling that a strong young man has in the presence of a frail-appearing girl, but Spud is an athlete and has no interest in girls until he is in college. Then Spud and Lymie both fall in love with the same girl, and Spud finds that his athletic ability wins him the acclaim of a fraternity bid. He feels guilty at turning his attention away from the still-dependent Lymie, but is able to sublimate his guilt into jealous hatred when he fancies that Lymie is trying to take his girl away from him. In slashing his own throat and wrists, Lymie is symbolically slashing the ties that bind him to Spud and to Sally. He is also symbolically performing a primitive puberty rite, of the kind that Maxwell specifically referred to earlier in the novel when he described Spud's and Lymie's initiation into a high-school fraternity. Among the many symbols which Maxwell uses in this novel, the homosexual love and the heterosexual love and the self-sacrifice are all treated as aspects which normally appear, though in different guises, in the process of growing up—the unfolding of the folded leaf.

Among the many novels of the forties and fifties which investigate depth psychology of adolescents through symbolism, some of the more important ones are Carson McCullers' *The Heart Is a Lonely Hunter* (1940) and *The Member of the Wedding* (1946); William Faulkner's "The Bear" (1942); Jean Stafford's *Boston Adventure* (1944), *The Mountain Lion* (1947), and *The Catherine Wheel* (1952); Daphne Athas' *The Weather of the Heart* (1947); Peter Taylor's *A Woman of Means* (1950); David Westheimer's *The Magic Fallacy* (1950); Truman Capote's *Other Voices, Other Rooms* (1948) and *The Grass Harp* (1951); Shirley Jackson's *Hangsaman* (1951); James Agee's *The Morning Watch* (1951); William Styron's *Lie Down in Darkness* (1951); Ralph Ellison's *Invisible Man* (1952) Robie Macauley's *The Disguises of Love* (1952); Meyer Levin's *Compulsion* (1956); Peter S. Feibleman's *A Place Without Twilight* (1958); Herbert Gutterson's *The Last Autumn* (1958); and William Humphrey's *Home from the Hill* (1958). Two important psychological novels of 1960 are John Knowles's *A Separate Peace* and Flannery O'Connor's *The Violent Bear It Away.* Most of these can also be listed as naturalistic novels in the sense that they show human lives to be subject to the laws of nature. Even Agee's *The Morning Watch,* which is the most religious of the works just listed, and Capote's *The Grass Harp,* which is the most concerned with the escape from materialism, indicate considerably more weakness of the flesh than was admitted in novels of the genteel tradition. But as the novelists' concern with natural law in human life has shifted from the graphic presentation of observable phenomena to clever guesses about the concealed influences of the unconscious mind, the vaunted objectivity of early naturalism has almost disappeared. The naturalistic novels of the twenties and thirties suggested a hope that the lot of man might be improved through scientific control of his physical and social environment; those of the forties and fifties either painted a dark picture in which human happiness

265

was largely a matter of chance (Nelson Algren's *Never Come Morning,* 1942; Willard Motley's *Knock on Any Door,* 1947; Theodora Keogh's *Meg,* 1950; Jack Karney's *Work of Darkness,* 1956) or sought for hope in specifically human values. Of this latter group, some found hope in religion (Agee's *The Morning Watch;* James Baldwin's *Go Tell It on the Mountain,* 1953; Herman Wouk's *Marjorie Morningstar,* 1955), some in human responsibility (William Faulkner's *Intruder in the Dust,* 1958, and *The Town,* 1957; Richard Frede's *Entry E,* 1958), some in existentialism (John Phillips' *The Second Happiest Day,* 1953; and, on the "beat" fringe of existentialism, Nelson Algren's *A Walk on the Wild Side,* 1956, and Jack Kerouac's *On the Road,* 1957). While many of the elements that are usually called naturalistic are abundant in the hope-seeking novels listed here (in contrast to those listed on page 261 above), the presence of distinctly human values in these same novels has led many critics to insist that truly naturalistic fiction has been on a rapid decline since the late 1940's. Indeed, there is far more fantasy than naturalism in such recent novels as Jack Kerouac's *Doctor Sax* (1959), James Purdy's *Malcolm* (1959), and Conrad Richter's *The Waters of Kronos* (1960).

Charles Child Walcutt in *American Literary Naturalism: A Divided Stream* (1956) attributes the decline in writers' enthusiasm for naturalism partially to "the moral relativism which seems to derive from the century's preoccupation with depth psychology"—the emphasis on a comfortable "adjustment" to life.

> Today the romantic faith in nature is being replaced by existentialism (for the sophisticated) and the return to orthodox Christianity (for those who are less desperate or perhaps less adventuresome). (Pp. 295–96.)

Naturalism predominates, however, throughout the four decades studied, in novels set in all geographical regions and in all sorts of community environment. It is somewhat more noticeable in novels with rural (especially Southern rural) and lower-class large-city environments than in those with small-town and upper-class large-city environments. Far more striking is the fact that practically all the important naturalistic novelists and most of the unimportant ones are masculine. Women writers tend to be humorous or sentimental or uplifting even when they are most realistic. One could count almost on the fingers of one hand the number of feminine novelists who have been clearly naturalistic in writing about adolescence.

Richard Chase, in *The American Novel and Its Tradition,* has pointed out that American naturalistic novelists, from Stephen Crane and Frank Norris through William Faulkner, have used many elements of melodrama, following the gothic tradition that began in this country with Charles Brockden Brown. Such melodramatic or gothic elements appear in many novels about adolescence (especially, but by no means exclusively, those with settings in rural Southern areas and in the slums of New York and Chicago), so that it is sometimes difficult to decide whether the author's attitude should be classified as naturalistic or gothic. The Southern novels of William Faulkner and Erskine Caldwell and the city novels of Nelson Algren, Hal Ellson, and Irving Shulman probably should be considered naturalistic; other novels—such as Allan Seager's *Equinox* (1943), Tommy Wadelton's *Silver Buckles on His Knee* (1945), Blythe Morley's *The Intemperate Season* (1948), Charlotte Armstrong's *Mischief* (1950), John Steinbeck's *East of Eden* (1952), Anne Chamberlain's *The Tall Dark Man* (1955) and *The Darkest Bough* (1958), Virginia Oakey's *Thirteen Summer* (1955), and Alex Karmel's *Mary Ann* (1958)—emphasize the gothic elements, often at the expense of naturalism. It may be noted that gothicism is more evident in novels of the forties and fifties than in those of the twenties and thirties, and that feminine novelists are far more common among the gothicists than among the naturalists. This feminine interest in horror is nothing new: when the gothic novel first made its appearance in England during the eighteenth century, one of the foremost practitioners in the genre was Ann Radcliffe; and the individual horror novel which holds the record for long-continued popularity is *Frankenstein* by Mary Shelley. Some of the most successful writers of modern detective stories are women. Apparently the feminine mind, which is reluctant to record the sordid details of naturalism, is perfectly at ease in inventing cruel torments in stories which are obviously not true.

REGIONAL TRENDS IN NOVELS OF ADOLESCENCE

It is not so easy to pick out characteristics of novels belonging to certain regions as it is to note the characteristics of different decades. Books, authors, ideas, and literary influences travel freely about the country. The literature of the South comes the closest to being distinctive, just as many Southern customs and attitudes are jealously guarded against the intrusion of influence from the North. Adolescents in Southern novels must adapt themselves to certain codes of love and chivalry, to ideas of propriety, to family traditions which may seem strange, or at least not very binding, to readers in other parts of the country. Faulkner is particularly conscious of the effect of Southern traditions on his characters: Quentin Compson in *The Sound and the Fury*, conditioned to the Southern ideals of family honor and the sanctity of women, cannot tolerate the thought that his sister is pregnant by one man and is going to marry another, who was expelled from Harvard for cheating in an examination; Joe Christmas in *Light in August* is miserable throughout his adolescent years and afterward because he believes (but does not know) that he has some Negro blood; the sexually precocious Eula Varner in *The Hamlet* is plagued for years by erotic-minded men and by her brother Jody's frantic attempts to preserve her "honor," and she marries the contemptible Flem Snopes when her family learns that she is pregnant; Ike McCaslin in "The Bear" spends his early adolescence in mastering the hunting tradition of his family, and in his later adolescence he decides to spend his life in poverty in expiation for the sins of his grandfather; Chick Mallison in *Intruder in the Dust* braves the wrath of a whole community and its environs to prove that a Negro to whom he is indebted did not commit the murder of which he has been accused. Other Southern novelists also show adolescent characters embroiled in conflicts resulting, at least in part, from the Southern code of honor and propriety. In Erskine Caldwell's *Trouble in July*, the Negro boy Sonny Clark and the white girl Katy Barlow are caught up in a tragic turmoil resulting from the white crowd's belief in Negroes' constant desire to rape white girls; in Jesse Stuart's *Hie to the Hunters*, fourteen-year-old Did Hargis learns the hillbilly custom of wearing a gun to dances and takes part in the feud between the hunters and the farmers in a mountain community; in John Bell Clayton's *Wait, Son, October Is Near*, young Tucker English learns of adult problems through the conflict between his father's Southern passion and his mother's concept of family honor; in William Humphrey's *Home from the Hill*, Theron Hunnicutt feels compelled to kill the slayer of his father, even though it is the father of the girl he loves. Besides the common bond of the traditions of their region, many Southern novelists are linked by the kind of grotesque comedy to be found in novels by Faulkner, Caldwell, Stuart, Carson McCullers, Truman Capote, and others.

Next to Southerners, Western writers show the most regional characteristics. Novels set in California—especially in the urban areas of San Francisco and Los Angeles—are likely to be much like those set in the Middle West or the East; but the comparatively few novels about the wide open West—Vardis Fisher's tales of Idaho and Utah, H. L. Davis' books about Oregon, Ralph Moody's memoirs of rural Colorado, Oliver LaFarge's and Charles McNichols' accounts of the Indian territories of Arizona, Nevada, and New Mexico—show a rough individualism and a stoic indifference to suffering that are not quite so common in novels set in other parts of the country. Young people growing up in the Far West learn early to look upon nature as an enemy who will grant favors only to those who relentlessly extort them, and they also learn that neighbors are too far away and too busy with their own problems to be counted on for assistance.

The genteel tradition is more apparent in novels of the Midwest and the East than in novels of the South and the West. Sometimes the novelist sympathizes with the genteel tradition, as in most of the sentimental and humorous novels mentioned early in this chapter and in many of the realistic novels that offer hope for man's triumph through traditional virtues; sometimes the author sees the genteel tradition as the enemy of true progress for mankind, as in Glenway Wescott's *The Apple of the Eye*, Dreiser's *An American Tragedy*, most of Ruth Suckow's, Victoria Lincoln's, and Floyd Dell's novels, Santayana's *The Last Puritan*, Christopher Morley's *Kitty Foyle*, Henry Bellamann's *Kings Row*, Grace Metalious' *Peyton Place*, and the serious satires of John P. Marquand and his son John Phillips. In many novels of the East and the Midwest, however, the genteel tradition plays no significant part; each of these regions has produced more novels about adolescents than either the South or the West, and these novels cover the full range of authors' attitudes.

Indeed, it would be a mistake to assume that any part of the country has a monopoly on any of the literary attitudes here mentioned. It may even be misleading to point out the slight regional differences that do exist, because there are far more differences between individual authors of the same region than there are between regions as a whole.

Questions naturally come to mind as to who are the most important American novelists of adolescence and whether they are the same as the novelists who are most admired for general ability. Certainly Theodore Dreiser and Thomas Wolfe are great novelists who have contributed much to the understanding of adolescents, and Ernest Hemingway and William Faulkner are even greater novelists who have made almost as penetrating studies of adolescence as Dreiser and Wolfe; but it is unlikely that any of these (perhaps excepting Wolfe) will ever be known primarily as a novelist of adolescence. Of the well-established American novelists, probably James T. Farrell has made the greatest contributions to the literature of adolescence. Scott Fitzgerald, Floyd Dell, and Sherwood Anderson certainly deserve much credit for sincere and penetrating early studies in the field. Vardis Fisher, although he is not nearly as competent a writer as the others mentioned in this paragraph, introduced a thoroughness and frankness which earlier writers on adolescence had not shown. Among the younger novelists Jessamyn West, Jean Stafford, Carson McCullers, Nelson Algren, and Truman Capote have each contributed more than one outstanding novel of adolescence, and each author is noted for general fictional ability. J. D. Salinger's single novel *The Catcher in the Rye* is already recognized as one of the great classics of the literature about adolescents, and many of his short stories show equally keen understanding of young people of that age. Other top-ranking American novelists have produced at least one outstanding novel of adolescence each, and in some cases this is their best novel: Richard Wright's *Native Son*, Shirley Jackson's *Hangsaman*, William Styron's *Lie Down in Darkness*, Ralph Ellison's *Invisible Man*, James Agee's *The Morning Watch*, and Saul Bellow's *The Adventures of Augie March*. Two novelettes of adolescence by leading novelists—John Steinbeck's "The Red Pony" and William Faulkner's "The Bear"—have become classics, and Katherine Anne Porter's "Old Mortality" is just as memorable, although not as popular.

From the nature of the typical novel of adolescence and the way it is usually produced, it is not surprising that few novelists become known

270

primarily as writers on adolescence. In the beginning of this study (pages 17–18 above) it was pointed out that most novels of adolescence are first novels: a would-be writer who has just completed—or not quite completed—his own adolescence produces a novel about the period of life that he knows best. He may never write another novel; if he does, he generally wants to prove his versatility by writing on another phase of life. The surprising thing is that some novelists—such as Floyd Dell, James T. Farrell, and Jean Stafford—have returned to the theme of adolescence for a number of their novels.

A few of the novelists represented here turned to fiction when they were well advanced in years. George Santayana was a noted philosopher and essayist of seventy-three years when *The Last Puritan* was published; Alvin Johnson was a celebrated economist of sixty-two when his first novel *Spring Storm* appeared; and Madeline Babcock Smith was a housewife and grandmother aged sixty-five when she wrote *The Lemon Jelly Cake.*

The children, and sometimes the brothers, sisters, or spouses, of successful writers are quite likely to try writing novels themselves. Among such works included in this study are *Against the Wall* by Kathleen Millay, the younger sister of Edna St. Vincent Millay; *Joan and Michael* by Barbara Van Doren Klaw ("Martin Gale"), the daughter of Carl Van Doren; *The Intemperate Season* by Blythe Morley, the daughter of Christopher Morley; *Go Home and Tell Your Mother* by Max Wylie, the brother of Philip Wylie; *Morning Song* by Dorshka Raphaelson, the wife of the playwright Samson Raphaelson; *Scotland's Burning* by Nathaniel Burt, the son of Struthers Burt; *The Second Happiest Day* by John Phillips Marquand, Jr. ("John Phillips"); and *The Wheel of Earth* by Helga Sandburg, the daughter of Carl Sandburg. John Faulkner, the younger brother of William Faulkner, had already established himself as a novelist before he wrote *Chooky.* None of these novels by relatives of writers are among the superior works on my list; but all of them are worth reading, and a few (*Scotland's Burning, The Second Happiest Day,* and *The Wheel of Earth*) are definitely above the average.

271

The closing pages of the first chapter of this study (pages 19 to 27 above) noted some opinions expressed by various critics during recent years regarding novels of adolescence, and raised the question whether this study would support all of the observations which these critics had made. It was pointed out that all of these critics had suggested, independently of each other, that the adolescent in modern American fiction is symbolic of mankind in general, or at least of the American in general, going through a period of doubt and confusion as he approaches a new age of greatly increased responsibility. This is a very tempting generalization, especially since the great increase in emphasis on adolescents in fiction came at about the same time that the United States was becoming aware of its imminent need to accept a major responsibility of leadership among the nations of the world. It is probably true that, consciously or unconsciously, many novelists have tended to identify the problems of adolescents with the problems of a society coming of age. However, a preoccupation with the symbolic significance of these problems may lead a critic into the twin errors of finding meanings that do not exist and overlooking meanings that are both obvious and important. Certainly intelligent people today are confused and disturbed about man's responsibility in the modern world; but to explain the increased emphasis on the problems of adolescents in American fiction of the mid-twentieth century by saying that Americans are more confused than other peoples, or that they are more confused today than at any previous time, is to form a hasty conclusion on insufficient evidence. Intelligent people of all eras and all nations have noted the chaos and error of their own times: recall Matthew Arnold's "confused alarms of struggle and flight/Where ignorant armies clash by night"; Shakespeare's "The time is out of joint"; Cicero's "O tempora! O mores!"; Hosea's "They have sown the wind, and they shall reap the whirlwind." If there have ever been times and places which have appeared secure and certain, they have been those which were dominated by strong political leaders or by unquestioned religious hierarchies; American intellectual leaders, in rejecting both political dictatorship and religious domination, face some of the problems which young men face as they revolt from family domination, but these are problems of maturity and responsibility, and their presence in our literature may indicate new strength in our society rather than new weakness. American preoccupation with such problems should not be considered a sign of either strength or weakness until other factors have been carefully studied.

It is obvious, and also important, that American novelists of the twentieth century have been interested in adolescents as adolescents, not merely as symbols for an immature society. Leslie Fiedler called the non-adult in modern literature "a cultural invention," [1] and James William Johnson called the adolescent protagonist as we know him "a distinctly Twentieth-Century manifestation, virtually without precedent in British or American fiction." [2] Fiedler is more accurate than Johnson in tracing the emergence of this sort of protagonist back to Jean Jacques Rousseau, whose *Émile* (1762) is a classic on the education of children and adolescents; but Rousseau's work was preceded by two important English novels of the eighteenth century—Samuel Richardson's *Pamela* (1740) and Henry Fielding's *Tom Jones* (1749)—which emphasize some problems of adolescents. Two novels by Goethe were even more influential in establishing adolescent characters in literature: *The Sorrows of Young Werther* (1774) made popular a sentimental treatment of adolescent *weltschmerz,* and *Wilhelm Meister's Apprenticeship* (1796) set an excellent example of the serious and sympathetic presentation of a young man working out an adjustment to life. Probably the influence of Goethe was greater than that of Richardson, Fielding, or Rousseau on such important nineteenth century English novels of adolescence as Thackeray's *Pendennis,* Dickens' *David Copperfield* and *Great Expectations,* George Meredith's *The Ordeal of Richard Feverel,* and George Eliot's *The Mill on the Floss.* These are all perceptive and realistic studies—not contrived manipulations of an invented symbol of innocence —and they are logical antecedents for modern American novels like *Look Homeward, Angel, Young Lonigan,* and *In Tragic Life.* It is harder to find precedents for the novels which deal intensively with a short period—from a day or two to a year or two—in the life of an adolescent. The nineteenth-century American novels which come closest are Mark Twain's *Huckleberry Finn* and Stephen Crane's *The Red Badge of Courage;* these present psychological struggles during brief periods of adolescence, but they do not probe as deeply into the mind as do novels of the mid-twentieth century. Although literary antecedents and symbolic significance probably play some part in the creating of modern American fictional adolescents, a far more important influence is direct observation (often introspective) aided by modern psychological and sociological concepts.

The difference of opinion among critics as to the date when American novels of adolescence originated (see above, p. 26) is probably due to a difference of opinion about the meaning of the term "novel of adolescence." Certainly adolescents had appeared prominently in some American novels of the nineteenth century and the early twentieth century, but it was not until about 1920 that there began a general trend among American novelists to consider seriously and sympathetically the wide range of problems that may be considered primarily pertinent to adolescents. This was somewhat later than the appearance of similar trends in French and English fiction. Justin O'Brien, in his excellent study *The Novel of Adolescence in France,* gives 1890 as the date for the emergence of this sort of novel, although he mentions a few earlier novels that treated problems of adolescence as distinct from those of children (p. 8).[3] Professor O'Brien suggests several nonliterary reasons for a new interest in adolescents among the French people at that time: (1) the rapidly declining birth rate led French parents to place greater value on their children, and to become aware of the troubles of adolescents; (2) the new emphasis on sports brought adolescent athletes into the limelight; (3) the perfecting of the bicycle about 1890 gave adolescents a convenient way of evading parental surveillance, with corresponding worry on the parents' part (pp. 50–52). Physiologists, educators, sociologists, and psychologists also began to emphasize adolescence during the 1890's; novelists exploited this emphasis increasingly each decade until many critics felt that, during the 1920's, the theme was overexploited (*ibid.,* p. 30). It is not certain to what extent the French novelists of adolescence (the most important of whom was André Gide) directly influenced American writers; undoubtedly the French influenced the English authors, and the English influenced the American.

English novels of adolescence published during the first two decades of the twentieth century include Samuel Butler's *The Way of All Flesh* (1903), D. H. Lawrence's *Sons and Lovers* (1913), Somerset Maugham's *Of Human Bondage* (1915), and James Joyce's *Portrait of the Artist as a Young Man* (1916). Lawrence and Joyce were particularly influential on some of the important American writers about adolescence—specifically, Sherwood Anderson, Thomas Wolfe, and William Faulkner.

Obviously the modern American novel of adolescence did not appear spontaneously about 1920. Besides the earlier French and English traditions, both stemming from eighteenth-century works by Richardson, Fielding, Rousseau, and Goethe, this study has noted serious and perceptive novels of adolescence published before 1920 by Mark Twain, Stephen Crane, Theodore Dreiser, and Willa Cather. Undoubtedly the novels of this sort published in 1920 and later were partly a protestation against the popular but rather false pictures of adolescence presented by such followers of the genteel tradition as Harold Bell Wright, Gene Stratton-Porter, Booth Tarkington, and Owen Johnson.

A chronological listing of the American novels about adolescents published from 1920 through 1960 (see Appendix, pp. 301–32 below) shows a sudden increase in the number of such novels in 1929 and then an almost steady increase each year through 1959, and only a slight decrease in 1960. Probably the spate in 1929 was due partly to the somewhat delayed realization by a number of new writers that their own adolescent experiences might provide very suitable material for novels, but the expected rash of inferior novels was accompanied by some surprisingly good ones. Faulkner's *The Sound and the Fury* and Wolfe's *Look Homeward, Angel* are two first-rate novels published that year, and Myron Brinig's *Singermann*, Dubose Heyward's *Mamba's Daughters*, Anne Parrish's *The Methodist Faun*, O. E. Rölvaag's *Peder Victorious*, and Philip Stevenson's *The Edge of the Nest* are all at least second-rate. In the same year, Booth Tarkington and John Peter Toohey attempted to revive the popularity of the condescending treatment of adolescents in *Penrod Jashber* and *Growing Pains*, respectively; and Charles Samuels satirized the frank confession of erotic experiences in *The Frantic Young Man*.

Practically all of the critics of modern American fiction of adolescence have noted that the novels of the forties and fifties tend to stress symbolism and depth psychology in contrast to the naturalistic novels of the twenties and thirties, which usually imply a need for social reform. The change is a gradual one, but the year 1940 is indicative of this change. Carson McCullers' *The Heart Is a Lonely Hunter* is more representative of the new trend than any other important novel published that year. Three novels by leading naturalists—James T. Farrell's *Father and Son*,

William Faulkner's *The Hamlet,* and Richard Wright's *Native Son*—all reveal deep psychological penetration with a certain amount of symbolism. Some less important novels of 1940 which show great interest in psychology are Henry Bellamann's *Kings Row,* Harlow Estes' *Hildreth,* Christine Whiting Parmenter's *As the Seed Is Sown,* Judy Van de Veer's *November Grass,* Peter Viertel's *The Canyon,* and Dan Wickenden's *Walk Like a Mortal.* Erskine Caldwell's *Trouble in July* and William Saroyan's *My Name Is Aram* show a keener psychological insight than their respective authors are wont to display.

The novels of 1947 also show a shift in novelists' attitudes toward the problems of adolescence. This was the first year of the postwar boom in novels about juvenile delinquents: Willard Motley's *Knock on Any Door* and Irving Shulman's *The Amboy Dukes* tell of delinquent boys in large cities; Daphne Athas' *The Weather of the Heart* and Virgil Scott's *The Dead Tree Gives No Shelter* present delinquent boys in smaller communities, and William E. Henning's *The Heller* and I. S. Young's *Jadie Greenway* describe girls who are well on the way to delinquency. Calder Willingham's *End as a Man* portrays the very depraved life of certain students in a military college which purports to build character.

Novels of adolescence published during the fifties display such a variety of attitudes that it is hard to say which ones are dominant. Novels of depth psychology and symbolism are very much in evidence, and so are novels of juvenile delinquency. Naturalistic novels have not completely disappeared, and there are a few works of fiction that are romantically sentimental and a few that are condescendingly humorous. Many novels of the fifties dwell on morbid traits of abnormal personalities, but this was also true of many novels of the forties and some of the thirties. Two attitudes expressed in much of the fiction of the fifties are not likely to be found in earlier works: existentialism (in John Phillips' *The Second Happiest Day,* C. G. Lumbard's *Senior Spring,* Richard B. Erno's *My Old Man,* and James Whitfield Ellison's *The Freest Man on Earth*) and a "beat" attitude (in Nolan Miller's *Why I Am So Beat,* Nelson Algren's *A Walk on the Wild Side,* Jack Kerouac's *On the Road,* and Charles Thompson's *Halfway Down the Stairs*). There is considerable overlapping of these last two attitudes, and they are both so broadly interpreted that admirers of these trends may claim to find them even in novels that were written long before the attitudes came into vogue. Fantasy and realism are combined, with fascinating

276

originality, in three recent novels: Jack Kerouac's *Doctor Sax*, James Purdy's *Malcolm*, and Conrad Richter's *The Waters of Kronos*.

PROBABLE TRENDS IN THE FUTURE

It seems logical to conclude a survey of a particular kind of novel over the past four decades by venturing an opinion about the future development of this literary type. In 1947 the present writer made a prediction about American literature in general: naturalism, or "unpleasant realism," had about run its course, he said, and would be replaced by a new attitude of faith—not the "rosy, fairy-tale type of faith which prevailed in nineteenth-century romantic literature," but a "realistic faith" based on man's realization that he faces destruction unless he believes in the possibility of a better world and the urgent need to fight to bring it about.[4] This prediction has only partially come true. The dominance of naturalism in our literature has apparently ended, but in place of the literature based on faith, which was prophesied, we have had a literature based on existentialism. Instead of the bleak picture of man as the helpless plaything of nature, which prevailed in naturalistic writing, existentialism offers—in fact, insists on—man's privilege and responsibility of choosing his own way; and there is no promise of a better world for the man who chooses wisely and fights for his choice—only the assurance that man has a free choice and bears the responsibility for his decisions.

This is the status of American literature now, but what about its future? And where does the novel of adolescence fit into the picture? There is still a need for a more positive faith than existentialism offers, but there are no obvious signs of its present emergence, as there appeared to be in some works published about the end of World War II. There will probably be no great decline in the number of novels of adolescence for at least a decade, although there were not quite so many in 1960 as there were in 1959. The novelist and critic Herbert Gold, in the *Atlantic Monthly* for September, 1960, set forth his concepts of the turns which American literature might take during the sixties. Although he spoke slightingly of attempts by Capote and Salinger "to raise elegant eccentricity and child psychology to the level of literature" (p. 54), he recognized the "coming-of-age novel" as one of the main types of modern fiction that will be very hard to replace (p. 56). The young authors who, during the sixties, will publish first novels based on their own adolescent problems are probably now in college or even in high school, and Gold points out some of the differences between the problems their world contains and those presented in earlier apprenticeship novels. They will know only through hearsay of the threats associated with Hitler, Stalin, the Depression, and World War; they are more likely to get through college on a scholarship than on a dishwashing job, and

> when they rebel against their parents, suggests one psychiatrist, the mania for popular psychology will oblige them to rebel against being understood rather than being misunderstood. They will be richer, healthier, groupier, more suburban, rarely driven into the early isolation of economic crisis, second-generation conflict, and rapid changes of class. . . . But these new writers will have grown up among the specters of passivity, isolation, and doubt which haunt American political and family life. (P. 55.)

Gold sees little place in the fiction of the sixties for the meticulous recording of detail that characterized the naturalistic novel; he sees the new novel as "stripped down to poetry and story and the inauguration of passionate conviction" regarding the responsibility of the individual in a society that has become too passive, and the responsibility of Americans in a world where the United States can be neither an isolated paradise nor the universally admired idol of the other nations (pp. 56–57).

Gold does not mention certain other characteristics of the present generation of adolescents. The great population bulge which has long made public schools overcrowded is now beginning to tax college facilities, and will soon flood the labor market with young people competing for the limited number of available jobs—a number which is being constantly reduced by the increasing use of automation in industry and even in professional fields like teaching; the current fashion of "going steady" in early adolescence often leads to getting married and starting a family years before the completion of an increasingly necessary education; increased social tension results from the forced publicity (often forced by adolescents themselves) given certain long-accepted racial inequities in public transportation, public recreation facilities, and private housing.

Certainly all of these things will affect the tone and content of novels which the adolescents and parents of today will write in the near future.

Although some critics during the 1920's decried the large number of semi-autobiographical novels of adolescent experiences, the number has steadily increased, and it appears that this type of fiction is now permanently established. The better novelists in the future will relate these experiences conscientiously and truthfully, occasionally revealing new insights which may help others to attain physical, psychological, social, moral, and economic adjustment. And, as in the past, readers of these future novels may gain both wisdom and catharsis through the vicarious sharing of the harsh blows which pound young people into adults at the forge of life.

NOTES

PREFACE

1. Sigmund Freud, *Delusion and Dream* (New York, 1922), p. 113.

CHAPTER I

1. George Santayana, "The Genteel Tradition in American Philosophy," printed in *Winds of Doctrine* (New York, 1913), pp. 187–88.
2. *Ibid.,* p. 189.
3. O'Connor's list includes (1) G. E. DeMille, *Literary Criticism in America* (New York, 1937); (2) Malcolm Cowley, ed., *After the Genteel Tradition* (New York, 1937); (3) Ludwig Lewisohn, *The Story of American Literature* (New York, 1939); (4) Frederic I. Carpenter, "The Genteel Tradition; A Reinterpretation," *New England Quarterly,* XV (September, 1942), pp. 427–43; (5) Willard Thorp, "Defenders of Ideality," *Literary History of the United States,* ed. Robert Spiller and others (New York, 1948), pp. 809–26; (6) Howard Mumford Jones, *The Theory of American Literature* (Ithaca, N. Y., 1948); (7) Arthur Hobson Quinn, "The Foundations of American Criticism," *The Literature of the American People* (New York, 1951).
4. John F. Carter, Jr., "These Wild Young People," *Atlantic Monthly,* CXXVI (September, 1920), p. 303.
5. Leslie Fiedler, "Good Good Girl and Good Bad Boy," *New Leader,* XLI (April 14, 1958), pp. 22–25. These ideas are adapted in Fiedler's later collection of essays *Love and Death in the American Novel* (New York, 1960), pp. 266–72.
6. Fiedler, "The Invention of the Child," *New Leader,* XLI (March 31, 1958) p. 22.
7. Fiedler, "The Profanation of the Child," *New Leader,* XLI (June 23, 1958), p. 29.

CHAPTER II

1. The general public has been reluctant to accept Freud's insistence that there is considerable sexual activity among children and even among infants. Alfred C. Kinsey and his associates suggest that some of the activity cited by Freud should not be considered truly sexual (thumb-sucking, bed-wetting, scratching and exploration of genitalia), but they offer well-established statistics on pre-adolescent orgasms in 604 boys (*Sexual Behavior in the Human Male* [Philadelphia, 1948], p. 181) and in 659 girls (*Sexual Behavior in the Human Female* [Philadelphia, 1953], p. 106). Impressive though these figures are, they represent considerably less than ten per cent of the persons interviewed.
2. Kinsey and associates report, in *Sexual Behavior in the Human Female,* p. 270,

that 88 per cent of the women interviewed had experienced petting by the age of twenty, that 75 per cent had responded erotically to petting, and that 23 per cent had responded to the point of orgasm.

3. Kinsey *et al.*, *The Human Male*, pp. 534–35, show 87 per cent of males interviewed had petting experience by age twenty, and 23 per cent had responded orgasmically. For figures on masturbation, see note 4 below.

4. Kinsey and associates, in *The Human Female*, p. 173, state that 92 per cent of the men interviewed and 33 per cent of the women had masturbated by the age of twenty. The practice becomes less widespread among men after the teens; among women it becomes more widespread until well into middle age.

5. Kinsey *et al.* found that 70 per cent of the men interviewed (*The Human Male*, p. 550) and 20 per cent of the women (*The Human Female*, p. 286) had experienced premarital coitus by the age of twenty.

6. The following percentages of people interviewed had experienced premarital intercourse by age twenty: boys with no high school, 83 per cent; boys with some high school, 75 per cent; boys with some college, 44 per cent (*The Human Male*, p. 550); girls with no high school, 25 per cent; girls with some high school, 26 per cent; girls with some college, 20 per cent; girls with some graduate school, 15 per cent (*The Human Female*, p. 333). Early marriages probably account for the relatively low proportion of premarital intercourse among girls with no high school education.

7. For statistics and possible explanations of the increase in premarital intercourse during and immediately after World War I, see Kinsey *et al.*, *The Human Female*, pp. 289–301, 339.

CHAPTER III

1. On the other hand, girls are somewhat more likely than boys to be quietly critical of their parents. See Luella Cole, *Psychology and Adolescence* (New York, 1948), p. 297.

2. Wife of the playwright Samson Raphaelson.

3. Cole, *op. cit.*, p. 300.

4. Nelson Algren, reviewing *The Pecking Order* in the *Saturday Review*, XXXVI (June 6, 1953), p. 16.

5. For critical comments on the significance of the road in contemporary American fiction, see Kingsley Widmer, "The Amerian Road," *University of Kansas City Review*, XXVI (Summer, 1960), pp. 309–17.

CHAPTER IV

1. Although Dell mentions twice on p. 102 that the incident occurred in twelfth grade, Felix's age (thirteen) and the mention of his beginning high school in a later chapter make it apparent that Dell momentarily forgot that there are only eight grades before high school.

2. The use of fists to attain recognition is of course not limited to rural schools. James T. Farrell's Studs Lonigan and Danny O'Neill both win approval among their Chicago parochial-school companions by fighting boys bigger than themselves. However, both Studs and Danny find some schoolmates who do not

approve of fighting, whereas approval of Vridar's fighting is practically unanimous.
3. Cole, *op. cit.*, pp. 144–45.
4. Norman Kiell, *The Adolescent Through Fiction* (New York, 1959), p. 222.
5. Perhaps it is significant that the authors of both these novels are sons of novelists of an earlier generation: John P. Marquand and Struthers Burt, respectively.
6. Coffin's book is often classified as autobiography rather than fiction. Fisher's book is also autobiographical, but not to the same extent as Coffin's.
7. Two novels in this survey describe coeducational boarding schools: Mabel Robinson's *Bright Island* (1937) describes a fashionable finishing school in Maine, and Daphne Athas' *The Fourth World* (1956) describes a school for the blind in Pennsylvania.
8. John E. Horrocks, *The Psychology of Adolescence* (Boston, 1951), p. 225.
9. Cole, *op. cit.*, p. 606.
10. Ernest Haveman and Patricia Salter West, *They Went to College* (New York, 1952), p. 16.

CHAPTER V

1. Brother of the better-known novelist Philip Wylie.
2. Leslie Fiedler in *Love and Death in the American Novel* (New York, 1960) discusses this novel at some length (pp. 249–253), suggesting that Airman (born Saul Ehrman), "denying his Jewish birthright . . . by denying his Jewish name," represents the rootless, dissenting Jewish intellectual, while Marjorie, whose change of name and abandonment of religion are temporary and unsuccessful, represents the fundamentally chaste, pious bourgeoise of any religion.
3. G. Stanley Hall, *Adolescence* (New York, 1904), Vol. I, pp. 524–32.
4. Edmund S. Conklin, *Principles of Adolescent Psychology* (New York, 1935), pp. 332, 336.

CHAPTER VI

1. Harper Lee's *To Kill a Mockingbird* (1960) contains a similar incident of a white girl falsely accusing a Negro of raping her. Miss Lee's novel is not included in this study because the only adolescent in it is the accuser, a distinctly minor character.
2. H. L. Mencken, *New York Herald-Tribune Books* (August 25, 1935), p. 1.
3. Basil Davenport, *Saturday Review of Literature*, XII (August 24, 1935), p. 7.
4. See Ima Hanaker Herron, *The Small Town in American Literature* (Durham, N.C., 1939), pp. 365–428, for attitudes expressed in many novels published during the twenties and thirties.
5. Like many novels of adolescents, this was the author's first published work of fiction; unlike most, it was published when the author was sixty-five years old. See *New York Times Book Review* (August 3, 1952), p. 4.
6. *Manhattan Transfer* is important in the development of the American novel, but not very important in the fictional presentation of problems of adolescence. As Blanche Housman Gelfant points out in *The American City Novel* (Norman,

Oklahoma, 1954), p. 134, Dos Passos in this novel focuses "upon the city rather than upon its people."

7. Purdy does not identify the cities which serve as settings for "63" and *Malcolm*. Dame Edith Sitwell, in her introduction to the 1961 editon of Purdy's *Color of Darkness* (p. 11), suggests that "63" is set in Chicago; the city of *Malcolm* is close to an ocean, and might be New York.

8. Space does not permit a discussion here of a number of other novels presenting adolescent Negroes in relation to white people: Florence Means's *Shuttered Windows* (1938), Erskine Caldwell's *Trouble in July* (1940) and *Place Called Estherville* (1949), John R. Tunis' *All-American* (1942), Phyllis Whitney's *Willow Hill* (1947), Hal Ellson's *Duke* (1949), John Faulkner's *Chooky* (1950), Alger Adams' ("Philip B. Kaye") *Taffy* (1950), John Craig Stewart's *Through the First Gate* (1950), Hart Stillwell's *Campus Town* (1950), William Demby's *Beetlecreek* (1950), Thomas Hal Phillips' *The Golden Lie* (1951), Mark Kennedy's *The Pecking Order* (1953), Ruth Seid's ("Jo Sinclair") *The Changelings* (1955), Peter S. Feibleman's *A Place Without Twilight* (1958), Richard Wright's *The Long Dream* (1958), Warren Miller's *The Cool World* (1959), Evan Hunter's *A Matter of Conviction* (1959), Paule Marshall's *Brown Girl, Brownstones* (1959), Beatrice Wright's ("Martin Kramer") *Sons of the Father* (1959), and Charles Beaumont's *The Intruder* (1959). However, most of these books are discussed in other parts of this study (see Index).

CHAPTER VII

1. Leslie Fiedler, "From Redemption to Initiation," *New Leader*, LVI (May 26, 1958), p. 22.
2. The symbolic interpretation of this story has been pointed out in a number of critical works on Faulkner, notably Harry Modean Campbell and Ruel E. Foster, *William Faulkner: A Critical Appraisal* (Norman, Oklahoma, 1951), pp. 146–58, and William Van O'Connor, *The Tangled Fire of William Faulkner* (Minneapolis, 1954), pp. 126–34.
3. This is the account given in *Mitch Miller*, p. 249; but in *Kit O'Brien*, pp. 130–31, Masters suggests that Mitch was killed because a brakeman knocked him off the train.
4. Fitzgerald's fullest and most successful presentation of adolescent mental illness is his study of Nicole Warren (later Nicole Diver) in *Tender Is the Night* (1934), a novel which falls outside the limits of this study because its setting is in Europe.

CHAPTER VIII

1. Leslie Fiedler, "The Invention of the Child," *New Leader*, XLI (March 31, 1958), p. 22.
2. James William Johnson, "The Adolescent Hero: A Trend in Modern Fiction," *Twentieth Century Literature*, V (April, 1959), p. 3.
3. O'Brien lists as French novels of adolescence before 1890 the following: Honoré de Balzac's *Louis Lambert* (1832), Gustave Flaubert's *Novembre* (1842), and Hippolyte Taine's *Etienne Mayran* (1861–62).
4. W. Tasker Witham, *Panorama of American Literature* (1947), p. 362.

BIBLIOGRAPHY

A. American Novels Stressing Problems of Adolescents, 1920–1960

For an explanation of the limits which have been set for this list, and of the inclusion of some works which might be considered short stories or autobiographies, see the Preface (pp. 2–3) and the first page of the Appendix (p. 301).

Abaunza, Virgina. *Sundays from Two to Six.* Indianapolis: Bobbs-Merrill, 1957.

Abel, Hilde. *The Guests of Summer.* Indianapolis: Bobbs-Merrill, 1951.

Abelson, Ann. *The Little Conquerors.* New York: Random House, 1960.

[Adams, Alger] "Philip B. Kaye." *Taffy.* New York: Crown, 1950.

Ader, Paul. *The Leaf Against the Sky.* New York: Crown, 1948.

Agee, James. *The Morning Watch.* Boston: Houghton, Mifflin, 1951.

Albee, George Sumner. *By the Sea, by the Sea.* New York: Simon and Schuster, 1960.

Aldis, Dorothy. *All the Year Round.* Boston: Houghton, Mifflin, 1938.

————. *Poor Susan.* New York: G. P. Putnam's, 1942.

Algren, Nelson. *Never Come Morning.* New York: Harper, 1942.

————. *Somebody in Boots.* New York: Vanguard, 1935.

————. *A Walk on the Wild Side.* New York: Farrar, Straus and Cudahy, 1956.

Amrine, Michael. *All Sons Must Say Goodbye.* New York: Harper, 1942.

Anderson, Sherwood. *Kit Brandon.* New York: Charles Scribner's, 1936.

————. *Tar.* New York: Boni and Liveright, 1926.

Angoff, Charles. *Between Day and Dark.* New York: Thomas Yoseloff, 1959.

————. *In the Morning Light.* New York: Beechhurst Press, 1953.

————. *The Sun at Noon.* New York: Beechhurst Press, 1955.

Armstrong, Charlotte. *Mischief.* New York: Coward-McCann, 1950.

Athas, Daphne. *The Fourth World.* New York: G. P. Putnam's, 1956.

————. *The Weather of the Heart.* New York: Appleton-Century, 1947.

Austin, Mary. *Starry Adventure.* Boston: Houghton, Mifflin, 1931.

Aydelotte, Dora, *Long Furrows.* New York: Appleton-Century, 1935.

Babcock, Havilah. *The Education of Pretty Boy.* New York: Holt, Rinehart, and Winston, 1960.

Baker, Laura Nelson. *The Special Year.* New York: A. A. Knopf, 1959.

Baldwin, James. *Go Tell It on the Mountain.* New York: A. A. Knopf, 1953.

Ballard, James. *The Long Way Through.* Boston: Houghton, Mifflin, 1959.

Barber, Elsie Oakes. *The Trembling Years.* New York: Macmillan, 1949.

Barton, Betsey. *Shadow of the Bridge.* New York: Duell, Sloan and Pearce, 1950.

Baumer, Marie. *The Seeker and the Sought.* New York: Charles Scribner's, 1949.

Beaumont, Charles. *The Intrducer.* New York: G. P. Putnam's, 1959.

Beer, Thomas. *Sandoval: A Romance of Bad Manners.* New York: A. A. Knopf, 1924.

Begner, Edith P. *Just off Fifth.* New York: Rinehart, 1959.

Beheler, Laura. *The Paper Dolls.* Boston: Houghton, Mifflin, 1956.

Bell, Robert E. *The Butterfly Tree.* Philadelphia: Lippincott, 1959.

Bellamann, Henry. *Kings Row.* New York: Simon and Schuster, 1940.

Bellow, Saul. *The Adventures of Augie March.* New York: Viking Press, 1953.

Benefield, Barry. *April Was When It Began.* New York: Reynal and Hitchcock, 1939.

Benét, Stephen Vincent. *The Beginning of Wisdom.* New York: Henry Holt, 1921.

Bennett, Eve. *April Wedding.* New York: Julian Messner, 1960.

Benson, Sally. *Junior Miss*. New York: Harper, 1941.
Bentham, Josephine. *Janie*. New York: Dial Press, 1940.
Bishop, John Peale. *Act of Darkness*. New York: Charles Scribner's, 1935.
Boles, Paul Darcy. *Parton's Island*. New York: Macmillan, 1958.
Bourjaily, Vance. *Confessions of a Spent Youth*. New York: Dial Press, 1960.
Boylen, Margaret. *The Marble Orchard*. New York: Random House, 1956.
Brace, Gerald Warner. *Winter Solstice*. New York: W. W. Norton, 1960.
Bradbury, Ray. *Dandelion Wine*. Garden City, N.Y.: Doubleday, 1957.
Brecht, Harold W. *Downfall*. New York: Harper, 1929.
Brinig, Myron. *Singermann*. New York: Farrar and Rinehart, 1929.
Bro, Margueritte Harmon. *Sarah*. New York: Doubleday, 1949.
————. *Stub: A College Romance*. New York: Doubleday, 1953.
Bromfield, Louis. *The Wild Country*. New York: Harper, 1948.
Bronson, F[rancis] W[oolsey]. *Spring Running*. New York: George H. Doran, 1926.
Broun, Heywood. *The Boy Grew Older*. New York: G. P. Putnam's, 1922.
Brown, Rollo Walter. *The Firemakers*. New York: Coward-McCann, 1931.
————. *Toward Romance*. New York: Coward-McCann, 1932.
Burress, John. *Apple on a Pear Tree*. New York: Vanguard Press, 1953.
Burt, Katharine Newlin. *Escape from Paradise*. New York: Charles Scribner's, 1952.
Burt, Nathaniel. *Scotland's Burning*. Boston: Little, Brown, 1953.
Byron, Gilbert. *The Lord's Oysters*. Boston: Little, Brown, 1957.
Caldwell, Erskine. *Georgia Boy*. New York: Duell, Sloan and Pearce, 1943.
————. *God's Little Acre*. New York: Viking Press, 1933.
————. *Place Called Estherville*. New York: Duell, Sloan and Pearce, 1949.
————. *Tobacco Road*. New York: Charles Scribner's, 1932.
————. *Trouble in July*. New York: Duell, Sloan and Pearce, 1940.
Calitri, Charles. *Rickey*. New York: Charles Scribner's, 1952.
————. *Strike Heaven in the Face*. New York: Crown Press, 1958.
Capote, Truman. *The Grass Harp*. New York: Random House, 1951.
————. *Other Voices, Other Rooms*. New York: Random House, 1948.
Carlile, Clancy. *As I Was Young and Easy*. New York: A. A. Knopf, 1958.
Carlisle, Helen Grace. *The Merry, Merry Maidens*. New York: Harcourt, Brace, 1937.
Carr, Robert S. *The Rampant Age*. Garden City, N.Y.: Doubleday, Doran, 1928.
Carson, Josephine. *Drives My Green Age*. New York: Harper, 1957.
Carson, Katherine. *Mrs. Pennington*. New York: G. P. Putnam's, 1939.
Cather, Willa. *A Lost Lady*. New York: A. A. Knopf, 1923.
Chamberlain, Anne. *The Tall Dark Man*. Indianapolis: Bobbs-Merrill, 1955.
————. *The Darkest Bough*. Indianapolis: Bobbs-Merrill, 1958.
Chamberlain, George Agnew. *The Phantom Filly*. Indianapolis: Bobbs-Merrill, 1942.
Childs, Marquis W. *The Cabin*. New York: Harper, 1944.
Clark, Walter Van Tilburg. *The City of Trembling Leaves*. New York: Random House, 1945.
Clayton, John Bell. *Six Angels at My Back*. New York: Macmillan, 1952.
————. *Wait, Son, October Is Near*. New York: Macmillan, 1953.
Coffin, Robert P. Tristram. *Lost Paradise*. New York: Macmillan, 1934.
————. *Red Sky in the Morning*. New York: Macmillan, 1935.
Cooke, Charles. *The Big Show*. New York: Harper, 1938.
Coursen, Dorothy. *Beauty? I Wonder*. New York: Elliot Holt, 1929.
————. *Fire of Spring*. New York: Henry Holt, 1928.
Craven, John V. *The Leaf Is Green*. New York: A. A Knopf, 1931.

Crawford, Nelson Antrim. *Unhappy Wind.* New York: Coward-McCann, 1930.
[Croy, Homer.] *West of the Water Tower.* New York: Harper, 1923.
Dalrymple, Leona. *Fool's Hill.* New York: Robert McBride, 1922.
Daly, Edwin. *Some Must Watch.* New York: Charles Scribner's, 1957.
———. *A Legacy of Love.* New York: Charles Scribner's, 1958.
Daly, Maureen. *Seventeenth Summer.* New York: Dodd, Mead, 1942.
Davis, Christopher. *Lost Summer.* New York: Harcourt, Brace, 1958.
Davis, Clyde Brion. *The Newcomer.* Philadelphia: J. B. Lippincott, 1954.
Davis, H[arold] L[enoir]. *Honey in the Horn.* New York: Harper, 1935.
———. *Winds of Morning.* New York: William Morrow, 1952.
Davis, Kenneth S. *Morning in Kansas.* Garden City, N.Y.: Doubleday, 1952.
Davis, Reuben. *Shim.* Indianapolis: Bobbs-Merrill, 1953.
Davis, Wesley Ford. *The Time of the Panther.* New York: Harper, 1958.
Day, Lillian. *The Youngest Profession.* New York: Doubleday, Doran, 1940.
Deal, Borden. *The Insolent Breed.* New York: Charles Scribner's, 1959.
DeJong, David Cornel. *Two Sofas in the Parlor.* New York: Doubleday, 1952.
Deland, Margaret. *An Old Chester Secret.* New York: Harper, 1920.
Dell, Floyd. *Janet March.* New York: A. A. Knopf, 1923.
———. *Moon-Calf.* New York: A. A. Knopf, 1920.
———. *Souvenir.* Garden City, N.Y.: Doubleday, Doran, 1929.
Demby, William. *Beetlecreek.* New York: Rinehart, 1950.
DeMott, Benjamin. *The Body's Cage.* Boston: Atlantic-Little, Brown, 1959.
Dempsey, David K. *All That Was Mortal.* New York: E. P. Dutton, 1958.
Derleth, August. *Evening in Spring.* New York: Charles Scribner's, 1941.
DiDonato, Pietro. *Three Circles of Light.* New York: Julian Messner, 1960.
Doan, Daniel. *The Crystal Years.* New York: Abelard Press, 1952.
Dos Passos, John. *The Big Money.* New York: Harcourt, Brace, 1936.
———. *The Forty-Second Parallel.* New York: Harper, 1930.
———. *Manhattan Transfer.* New York: Harper, 1925.
———. *1919.* New York: Harcourt, Brace, 1932.
Dougherty, Richard. *A Summer World.* New York: Doubleday, 1960.
Downes, Anne Miller. *Until the Shearing.* New York: Frederick A. Stokes, 1940.
Dreiser, Theodore. *An American Tragedy.* New York: Boni and Liveright, 1925.
Dubin, Harry Ennis. *Hail, Alma Pater.* New York: Hermitage House, 1954.
DuBois, William. *A Season to Beware.* New York: G. P. Putnam's, 1956.
Duffus, R[obert] L[uther]. *That Was Alderbury.* New York: Macmillan, 1944.
———. *The Waterbury Record.* New York: W. W. Norton, 1959.
Dutton, Louise. *Going Together.* Indianapolis: Bobbs-Merrill, 1923.
Eddy, Roger W. *The Bulls and the Bees.* New York: Crowell, 1956.
———. *The Rimless Wheel.* New York: Macmillan, 1947.
Edmonds, Walter D. *The Boyds of Black River.* New York: Dodd, Mead, 1953.
Edwards, E[dward] J. *The Chosen.* New York: Longmans, Green, 1949.
Ehle, John. *Kingstree Island.* New York: Morrow, 1959.
Eliot, Ethel Cook. *Angels' Mirth.* New York: Sheed and Ward, 1936.
Elliott, George P. *Parktilden Village.* Boston: Beacon Press, 1958.
Ellison, James Whitfield. *The Freest Man on Earth.* New York: Doubleday, 1958.
———. *I'm Owen Harrison Harding.* New York: Doubleday, 1955.
Ellison, Ralph. *Invisible Man.* New York: Random House, 1952.
Ellson, Hal. *Duke.* New York: Charles Scribner's, 1949.
———. *The Golden Spike.* New York: Ballantine Books, 1952.

————. *Rock.* New York: Ballantine Books, 1955.
————. *Summer Street.* New York: Ballantine Books, 1953.
————. *Tomboy.* New York: Charles Scribner's, 1950.
Emery, Anne. *Sorority Girl.* Philadelphia: Westminster Press, 1952.
Erno, Richard B. *The Hunt.* New York: Crown, 1959.
————. *My Old Man.* New York: Crown, 1955.
Estes, Harlow. *Hildreth.* New York: Dodd, Mead, 1940.
Faralla, Dana. *Black Renegade.* Philadelphia: J. B. Lippincott, 1954.
————. *The Madstone.* Philadelphia: J. B. Lippincott, 1958.
————. *The Magnificent Barb.* Philadelphia: J. B. Lippincott, 1947.
Farnham, Mateel Howe. *Rebellion.* New York: Dodd, Mead, 1927.
Farrell, James T. *Ellen Rogers.* New York: Vanguard Press, 1941.
————. *Father and Son.* New York: Vanguard Press, 1940.
————. *My Days of Anger.* New York: Vanguard Press, 1943.
————. *No Star Is Lost.* New York: Vanguard Press, 1938.
————. *Young Lonigan.* New York: Vanguard Press, 1932.
————. *The Young Manhood of Studs Lonigan.* New York: Vanguard Press, 1934.
Farris, John. *Harrison High.* New York: Rinehart, 1959.
Faulkner, John. *Chooky.* New York: W. W. Norton, 1950.
Faulkner, William. *Absalom, Absalom!* New York: Random House, 1936.
————. *As I Lay Dying.* New York: Jonathan Cape and Harrison Smith, 1930.
————. "The Bear" in *Go Down, Moses.* New York: Random House, 1942.
————. *The Hamlet.* New York: Random House, 1940.
————. *Intruder in the Dust.* New York: Random House, 1948.
————. *Light in August.* New York: Harrison Smith and Robert Haas, 1932.
————. *Sanctuary.* New York: Jonathan Cape and Harrison Smith, 1931.
————. *The Sound and the Fury.* New York: Jonathan Cape and Harrison Smith, 1929.
————. *The Town.* New York: Random House, 1957.
Feibleman, Peter S. *A Place Without Twilight.* Cleveland: World, 1958.
Fenwick, Elizabeth. *Days of Plenty.* New York: Harcourt, Brace, 1956.
[Fetzer, Hermann] "Jake Falstaff." *The Big Snow: Christmas at Jacoby's Corners.* Boston: Houghton, Mifflin, 1941.
————. *Come Back to Wayne County.* Boston: Houghton, Mifflin, 1942.
————. *Jacoby's Corners.* Boston: Houghton, Mifflin, 1940.
Field, Hope. *Stormy Present.* New York: E. P. Dutton, 1942.
Fillmore, Parker. *Yesterday Morning.* New York: Century, 1931.
Fineman, Irving. *This Pure Young Man.* New York: Longmans, Green, 1930.
[Fisher,] Dorothy Canfield. *The Deepening Stream.* New York: Harcourt, Brace, 1930.
————. *Rough-Hewn.* New York: Harcourt, Brace, 1922.
Fisher, Steve. *Giveaway.* New York: Random House, 1954.
Fisher, Vardis. *In Tragic Life.* Caldwell, Idaho: Caxton Printers, 1932.
————*Passions Spin the Plot.* Caldwell, Idaho: Caxton Printers, 1934.
Fitzgerald, F. Scott. *This Side of Paradise.* New York: Charles Scribner's, 1920.
"Flagg, Kenneth." *Andrew.* New York: G. P. Putnam's, 1958.
Foff, Arthur. *Glorious in Another Day.* Philadelphia: J. B. Lippincott, 1947.
[Fraenkel, Michael.] *Werther's Younger Brother: The Story of an Attitude.* New York: Carrefour Editions, 1931.
[Franken, Rose D., and William B. Meloney] "Franken Meloney." *Strange Victory.* New York: Farrar and Rinehart, 1939.

Frede, Richard. *Entry E.* New York: Random House, 1958.
Friesen, Gordon. *Flamethrowers.* Caldwell, Idaho: Caxton Printers, 1936.
Froscher, Wingate. *The Comforts of the Damned.* New York: Appleton-Century-Crofts, 1960.
Frost, Frances. *Innocent Summer.* New York: Farrar and Rinehart, 1936.
——. *Yoke of Stars.* New York: Farrar and Rinehart, 1939.
Gardner, Mac. *Mom Counted Six.* New York: Harper, 1944.
Garrett, Zena. *The House in the Mulberry Tree.* New York: Random House, 1959.
Gilman, Mildred Evans. *Fig Leaves.* New York: Siebel, 1925.
Gipson, Fred. *The Home Place.* New York: Harper, 1950.
——. *Old Yeller.* New York: Harper, 1956.
——. *Hound-Dog Man.* New York: Harper, 1949.
Glasgow, Ellen. *The Sheltered Life.* Garden City, N.Y.: Doubleday, Doran, 1932.
Gold, Herbert. *The Optimist.* Boston: Atlantic-Little, Brown, 1959.
——. *Therefore Be Bold.* New York: Dial Press, 1960.
Gollomb, Joseph. *Unquiet.* New York: Dodd, Mead, 1935.
Goodin, Peggy. *Clementine.* New York: E. P. Dutton, 1946.
——. *Take Care of My Little Girl.* New York: E. P. Dutton, 1950.
Goodman, Aubrey. *The Golden Youth of Lee Prince.* New York: Simon and Schuster, 1959.
Gorham, Charles. *The Future Mr. Dolan.* New York: Dial Press, 1948.
——. *Trial by Darkness.* New York: Dial Press, 1952.
Grace, Carol. *The Secret in the Daisy.* New York: Random House, 1955.
Granberry, Edwin. *The Erl King.* New York: Macaulay, 1930.
Grant, Dorothy Fremont. *Devil's Food.* New York: Longmans, Green, 1949.
Guerard, Albert J. *The Past Must Alter.* New York: Henry Holt, 1938.
Gutterson, Herbert. *The Last Autumn.* New York: William Morrow, 1958.
Gutwillig, Robert. *After Long Silence.* Boston: Little, Brown, 1958.
——. *The Fugitives.* Boston: Little, Brown, 1959.
Haines, William Wister. *Slim.* Boston: Little, Brown, 1934.
Halevy, Julian. *The Young Lovers.* New York: Simon and Schuster, 1955.
Halper, Albert. *The Chute.* New York: Viking Press, 1937.
——. *The Golden Watch.* New York: Henry Holt, 1953.
Ham, Roswell, G., Jr. *Fish Flying Through the Air.* New York: G. P. Putnam's, 1957.
Harnden, Ruth. *I, a Stranger.* New York: Whittlesey House, 1950.
Harriman, John. *Winter Term.* New York: Howell, Soskin, 1940.
Harris, Mark. *Something About a Soldier.* New York: Macmillan, 1957.
Harris, Sara. *The Wayward Ones.* New York: Crown, 1952.
Head, Ann. *Fair with Rain.* New York: McGraw-Hill, 1957.
Hemingway, Ernest. *In Our Time.* New York: Boni and Liveright, 1925.
Henning, William E. *The Heller.* New York: Charles Scribner's, 1947.
Herbert, F. Hugh. *Meet Corliss Archer.* New York: Random House, 1944.
Herlihy, James Leo. *All Fall Down.* New York: E. P. Dutton, 1960.
Heyward, DuBose. *Mamba's Daughters.* New York: Doubleday, Doran, 1929.
Hill, Fowler. *Plundered Host.* New York: E. P. Dutton, 1929.
Hill, Margaret. *Really, Miss Hillsbro!* Boston: Atlantic-Little, Brown, 1960.
Hitchens, Dolores. *Fool's Gold.* New York: Doubleday, 1958.
Horgan, Paul. *A Lamp on the Plains.* New York: Harper, 1937.
Hormel, Olive Deane. *Co-Ed.* New York: Charles Scribner's, 1926.
Hubler, Richard G. *True Love, True Love.* New York: Duell, Sloan and Pearce, 1959.

Hughes, Langston. *Not Without Laughter*. New York: A. A. Knopf, 1930.
Hull, Helen. *Candle Indoors*. New York: Coward-McCann, 1936.
Humphrey, William. *Home from the Hill*. New York: A. A. Knopf, 1958.
Hunter, Evan. *Blackboard Jungle*. New York: Simon and Schuster, 1954.
———. *A Matter of Conviction*. New York: Simon and Schuster, 1959.
———. *Second Ending*. New York: Simon and Schuster, 1956.
Jackson, Charles. *The Sunnier Side*. New York: Farrar, Straus, 1950.
Jackson, Shirley. *Hangsaman*. New York: Farrar, Straus and Young, 1951.
Jennison, Peter S. *The Mimosa Smokers*. New York: Crowell, 1959.
Johnson, Alvin. *Spring Storm*. New York: A. A. Knopf, 1936.
Johnson, Curtis. *Hobbledehoy's Hero*. Chicago: Pennignton Press, 1959.
Johnson, Josephine W. *Wildwood*. New York: Harper, 1946.
Johnson, Nora. *The World of Henry Orient*. Boston: Atlantic-Little, Brown, 1958.
Johnson, Owen. *Skippy Bedelle*. Boston: Little, Brown, 1922.
Jones, Dorothy Holder. *The Wonderful World Outside*. New York: Dodd, Mead, 1959.
Jordan, Elizabeth. *Daddy and I*. New York: Appleton-Century, 1935.
Joseph, Donald. *October's Child*. New York: Frederick A. Stokes, 1929.
Kapelner, Alan. *All the Naked Heroes*. New York: George Braziller, 1960.
Karig, Walter. *Lower than Angels*. New York: Farrar and Rinehart, 1945.
Karmel, Alex. *Mary Ann*. New York: Viking Press, 1958.
Karney, Jack. *Work of Darkness*. New York: G. P. Putnam, 1956.
Kehoe, William. *A Sweep of Dusk*. New York: E. P. Dutton, 1945.
Kelley, Ethel M. *Beauty and Mary Blair*. Boston: Houghton, Mifflin, 1921.
Kelley, William. *Gemini*. New York: Doubleday, 1959.
Kennedy, Mark. *The Pecking Order*. New York: Appleton-Century-Crofts, 1953.
Keogh, Theodora. *Meg*. New York: Creative Age Press, 1950.
———. *The Tattooed Heart*. New York: Farrar, Straus and Young, 1953.
Kerouac, Jack. *Doctor Sax*. New York: Grove Press, 1959.
———. *Maggie Cassidy*. New York: Avon, 1959.
———. *On the Road*. New York: Viking Press, 1957.
Kilbourne, Fanny. *A Corner in William*. New York: Dodd, Mead, 1922.
King, Mary. *Quincie Bolliver*. Boston: Houghton, Mifflin, 1941.
Kirkwood, Jim. *There Must Be a Pony!* Boston: Little, Brown, 1960.
Kirsch, Robert R. *In the Wrong Rain*. Boston: Little, Brown, 1959.
Kirstein, Lincoln. *Flesh Is Heir*. New York: Brewer, Warren, and Putnam, 1932.
[Klaw, Barbara Van Doren] "Martin Gale." *Joan and Michael*. New York: Viking Press, 1941.
Knowles, John. *A Separate Peace*. New York: Macmillan, 1960.
Kohner, Frederick. *Cher Papa*. New York: G. P. Putnam, 1959.
———. *Gidget*. New York: G. P. Putnam, 1957.
Kozol, Jonathan. *The Fume of Poppies*. Boston: Houghton, Mifflin, 1958.
Kroll, Harry Harrison. *Waters Over the Dam*. Indianapolis: Bobbs-Merrill, 1944.
LaFarge, Oliver. *The Enemy Gods*. Boston: Houghton, Mifflin, 1937.
Laing, Alexander. *End of Roaming*. New York: Farrar and Rinehart, 1930.
Lampell, Millard. *The Hero*. New York: Julian Messner, 1949.
Lamson, Peggy. *The Charmed Circle*. Philadelphia: J. B. Lippincott, 1950.
Lane, Rose Wilder. *Old Home Town*. New York: Longmans, Green, 1935.
Larrimore, Lida. *No Lovelier Spring*. Philadelphia: Macrae-Smith, 1935.
Latimer, Margery. *This Is My Body*. New York: Jonathan Cape and Harrison Smith, 1930.

Leahy, Jack Thomas. *Shadow on the Waters.* New York: A. A. Knopf, 1960.
Lee, Harry. *Fox in the Cloak.* New York: Macmillan, 1938.
L'Engle, Madeleine. *Camilla Dickinson.* New York: Simon and Schuster, 1951.
——. *The Small Rain.* New York: Vanguard Press, 1945.
Leslie, Ann George. *Dancing Saints.* New York: Doubleday, Doran, 1943.
Leslie, Warren. *Love or Whatever It Is.* New York: McGraw-Hill, 1960.
Levin, Meyer. *Compulsion.* New York: Simon and Schuster, 1956.
——. *The Old Bunch.* New York: Simon and Schuster, 1937.
Levy, Melvin P. *Lafayette Carter.* Philadelphia: J. B. Lippincott, 1956.
Lewis, Flannery. *Abel Dayton.* New York: Macmillan, 1939.
Lewis, Sinclair. *Bethel Merriday.* New York: Doubleday, Doran, 1940.
Lewiton, Mina. *The Divided Heart.* Philadelphia: David McKay, 1947.
Lincoln, Joseph C. *Blowing Clear.* New York: D. Appleton, 1930.
Lincoln, Victoria. *Celia Amberley.* New York: Rinehart, 1949.
——. *February Hill.* New York: Farrar and Rinehart, 1934.
——. *Out from Eden.* New York: Rinehart, 1951.
Linkletter, Monte. *Cricket Smith.* New York: Harper, 1959.
Lorimer, Graeme and Sarah. *Acquittal.* Boston: Little, Brown, 1938.
——. *First Love, Farewell.* Boston: Little, Brown, 1940.
——. *Heart Specialist.* Boston: Little, Brown, 1935.
——. *Men Are Like Street Cars.* Boston: Little, Brown, 1933.
——. *Stag Line.* Boston: Little, Brown, 1934.
Loveland, Constance. *Veronica.* New York: Vanguard, 1958.
Lumbard, C[harles] G[ilbert]. *Senior Spring.* New York: Simon and Schuster, 1954.
Lundberg, Daniel. *River Rat.* New York: Reynal and Hitchcock, 1941.
Macauley, Robie. *The Disguises of Love.* New York: Random House, 1952.
McCarthy, Catherine Ridgeway. *Definition of Love.* Boston: Houghton, Mifflin, 1949.
McCormick, Jay. *November Storm.* New York: Doubleday, Doran, 1943.
McCoy, John Pleasant. *Swing the Big-Eyed Rabbit.* New York: E. P. Dutton, 1944.
McCullers, Carson. *The Heart Is a Lonely Hunter.* Boston: Houghton, Mifflin, 1940.
——. *The Member of the Wedding.* Boston: Houghton, Mifflin, 1946.
MacDonald, John D. *The End of the Night.* New York: Simon and Schuster, 1960.
McFarland, Philip. *A House Full of Women.* New York: Simon and Schuster, 1960.
McGivern, William Peter. *Savage Streets.* New York: Dodd, Mead, 1959.
[McLean, Kathryn] "Kathryn Forbes." *Transfer Point.* New York: Harcourt, Brace, 1947.
MacLeod, Norman. *The Bitter Roots.* New York: Smith and Durrell, 1941.
MacMullan, Hugh. *Louder than Words.* New York: Loring and Mussey, 1935.
McNichols, Charles L. *Crazy Weather.* New York: Macmillan, 1944.
Mandel, George. *Flee the Angry Strangers.* Indianapolis: Bobbs-Merrill, 1952.
Manfred, Frederick. *Conquering Horse.* New York: McDowell, Obolenksy, 1959.
Manoff, Arnold. *Telegram from Heaven.* New York: Dial Press, 1942.
Marks, Percy. *The Plastic Age.* New York: Century, 1924.
——. *A Tree Grown Straight.* New York: Frederick A. Stokes, 1936.
——. *What's a Heaven For?* New York: Frederick A. Stokes, 1938.
Marquand, John P. *B.F.'s Daughter.* Boston: Little, Brown, 1946.
——. *Point of No Return.* Boston: Little, Brown, 1949.
——. *Warning Hill.* Boston: Little, Brown, 1930.
[Marquand,] John Phillips [Jr.]. *The Second Happiest Day.* New York: Harper, 1953.
Marquis, Don. *Sons of the Puritans.* New York: Doubleday, Doran, 1939.

Marshall, Lenore. *The Hill Is Level.* New York: Random House, 1959.
Marshall, Paule. *Brown Girl, Brownstones.* New York: Random House, 1959.
Martin, Helen R. *Emmy Untamed.* New York: Appleton-Century, 1937.
Martin, Peter. *The Building.* Boston: Little, Brown, 1960.
Masters, Edgar Lee. *Kit O'Brien.* New York: Boni and Liveright, 1927.
———. *Mitch Miller.* New York: Macmillan, 1920.
———. *Skeeters Kirby.* New York: Macmillan, 1923.
[Masters, Kelly R.] "Zachary Ball." *Piney.* Boston: Little, Brown, 1950.
Maxwell, William. *The Folded Leaf.* New York: Harper, 1945.
———. *They Came Like Swallows.* New York: Harper, 1937.
[Mayer, Jane, and Clara Spiegel] "Clare Jaynes." *Early Frost.* New York: Random House, 1952.
Mayhall, Jane. *Cousin to Human.* New York: Harcourt, Brace and World, 1960.
Means, Florence. *Shuttered Windows.* Boston: Houghton, Mifflin, 1938.
Mende, Robert. *Spit and the Stars.* New York: Rinehart, 1949.
Metalious, Grace. *Peyton Place.* New York: Julian Messner, 1956.
Michaelson, John Nairne. *Morning, Winter, and Night.* New York: Sloane, 1952.
Millar, Margaret. *It's All in the Family.* New York: Random House, 1948.
Millay, Kathleen. *Against the Wall.* New York: Macaulay, 1929.
Miller, Nolan. *Why I Am So Beat.* New York: G. P. Putnam's, 1954.
Miller, Warren. *The Cool World.* Boston: Little, Brown, 1959.
[Miller, Warren] "Amanda Vail." *The Bright Young Things.* Boston: Little, Brown, 1958.
———. *Love Me Little.* New York: McGraw-Hill, 1957.
Mitchner, Stuart. *Let Me Be Awake.* New York: Crowell, 1959.
Moody, Ralph. *The Fields of Home.* New York: W. W. Norton, 1953.
———. *Little Britches.* New York: W. W. Norton, 1950.
———. *Man of the Family.* New York: W. W. Norton, 1951.
Moore, Pamela. *Chocolates for Breakfast.* New York: Rinehart, 1956.
Moore Ruth. *Candlemas Bay.* New York: William Morrow, 1951.
———. *The Fire Balloon.* New York: William Morrow, 1948.
———. *Walk Down Main Street.* New York: William Morrow, 1960.
Morley, Blythe. *The Intemperate Season.* New York: Farrar, Straus, 1948.
Morley, Christopher. *Kitty Foyle.* Philadelphia: J. B. Lippincott, 1939.
———. *Thorofare.* New York: Harcourt, Brace, 1942.
——— and Don Marquis. *Pandora Lifts the Lid.* New York: Doran, 1924.
Morrison, Ray. *Angels Camp.* New York: W. W. Norton, 1949.
Motley, Willard. *Knock on Any Door.* New York: Appleton-Century, 1947.
Nabokov, Vladimir. *Lolita.* New York: G. P. Putnam's, 1958.
Nathan, Robert. *Long After Summer.* New York: A. A. Knopf, 1948.
———. *Winter in April.* New York: A. A. Knopf, 1938.
Nemerov, Howard. *The Homecoming Game.* New York: Simon and Schuster, 1957.
Newman, Robert H. *Fling Out the Banner.* Philadelphia: J. B. Lippincott, 1941.
Norman, Charles. *The Well of the Past.* Garden City, N.Y.: Doubleday, 1949.
Nusser, J. L. *Scorpion Field.* New York: Appleton-Century-Crofts, 1957.
Oakey, Virginia. *Thirteenth Summer.* New York: A. A. Wyn, 1955.
O'Connor, Flannery. *The Violent Bear It Away.* New York: Farrar, Straus and Cudahy, 1960.
O'Donnell, Eugene. *Berdoo.* New York: Rinehart, 1959.
Offit, Sidney. *He Had It Made.* New York: Crown, 1959.
O'Hara, John. *Butterfield 8.* New York: Harcourt, Brace, 1935.

O'Higgins, Harvey. *Julie Cane.* New York: Harper, 1924.

Osborn, Mary Elizabeth. *Days Beyond Recall.* New York: Coward-McCann, 1942.

Ostenso, Martha. *Wild Geese.* New York: Dodd, Mead, 1925.

Parmenter, Christine Whiting. *As the Seed Is Sown.* New York: Crowell, 1940.

Parrish, Anne. *The Methodist Faun.* New York: Harper, 1929.

Patterson, Vernon. *All Giants Wear Yellow Breeches.* New York: William R. Scott, 1935.

Pease, Howard. *The Dark Adventure.* New York: Doubleday, 1950.

Petrakis, Harry Mark. *Lion at My Heart.* Boston: Atlantic-Little, Brown, 1959.

Phillips, Thomas Hal. *The Golden Lie.* New York: Rinehart, 1951.

———. *The Loved and the Unloved.* New York: Harper's, 1955.

Plagemann, Bentz. *Into the Labyrinth.* New York: Farrar, Straus, 1948.

———. *This Is Goggle.* New York: McGraw-Hill, 1955.

Porter, Katherine Anne. "Old Mortality" in *Pale Horse, Pale Rider.* New York: Harcourt, Brace, 1939.

Porter, Monica E. *Mercy of the Court.* New York: W. W. Norton, 1955.

Pratt, Theodore. *Valley Boy.* New York: Duell, Sloan and Pearce, 1946.

Price, Emerson. *Inn of That Journey.* Caldwell, Idaho: Caxton Printers, 1939.

[Proffitt, Josephine] "Sylvia Dee." *And Never Been Kissed.* New York: Macmillan, 1949.

Prokosch, Frederic. *Night of the Poor.* New York: Harper, 1939.

Purdy, James. *Malcolm.* New York: Farrar, Straus and Cudahy, 1959.

———. "63: Dream Palace" in *Color of Darkness.* New York: New Directions, 1957.

Raphaelson, Dorshka. *Morning Song.* New York: Random House, 1948.

Rawlings, Marjorie Kinnan. *The Yearling.* New York: Charles Scribner's, 1938.

Raymond, Margaret Thomsen. *A Bend in the Road.* New York: Longmans, Green, 1934.

———. *Linnet on the Threshold.* New York: Longmans, Green, 1930.

———. *Sylvia, Inc.* New York: Dodd, Mead, 1938.

Rehder, Jessie C. *Remembrance Way.* New York: G. P. Putnam's, 1956.

Rendina, Laura Cooper. *Roommates.* Boston: Little, Brown, 1948.

Richter, Conrad. *The Waters of Kronos.* New York: A. A. Knopf, 1960.

Ricks, Peirson. *The Hunter's Horn.* New York: Charles Scribner's, 1947.

Ritner, Ann. *The Green Bough.* Philadelphia: J. B. Lippincott, 1950.

Roark, Garland. *The Cruel Cocks.* New York: Doubleday, 1957.

Roberts, Dorothy James. *A Durable Fire.* New York: Macmillan, 1945.

———. *With Night We Banish Sorrow.* Boston: Little, Brown, 1960.

Roberts, Elizabeth Madox. *The Time of Man.* New York: Viking Press, 1926.

Robinson, Alice M. *The Unbelonging.* New York: Macmillan, 1958.

Robinson, [Edwin Meade] "Ted." *Enter Jerry.* New York: Macmillan, 1921.

Robinson, Mabel Louise. *Bright Island.* New York: Random House, 1937.

Robinson, Oliver. *Triumvirate.* Boston: Bruce Humphries, 1943.

Rollins, William, Jr. *The Obelisk.* New York: Brewer and Warren, 1930.

Rölvaag, O[le] E[dvart]. *Peder Victorious.* New York: Harper, 1929.

Rooney, Frank. *The Heel of Spring.* New York: Vanguard Press, 1956.

Rosaire, Forrest. *East of Midnight.* New York: A. A. Knopf, 1945.

Rosenfeld, Isaac. *Passage from Home.* New York: Dial Press, 1946.

Ryerson, Florence, and Colin Clements. *Mild Oats.* New York: D. Appleton, 1933.

———. *This Awful Age.* New York: D. Appleton, 1930.

Salamanca, J. R. *The Lost Country.* New York: Simon and Schuster, 1958.

Salinger, J[erome] D[avid]. *The Catcher in the Rye.* Boston: Little, Brown, 1951.

Samuels, Charles. *The Frantic Young Man*. New York: Coward-McCann, 1929.
Sandburg, Helga. *The Wheel of Earth*. New York: McDowell, Obolensky, 1958.
Santayana, George. *The Last Puritan*. New York: Scribner's, 1936.
Saroyan, William. *The Human Comedy*. New York: Harcourt, Brace, 1943.
———. *My Name Is Aram*. New York: Harcourt, Brace, 1940.
Scott, Glenn. *A Sound of Voices Dying*. New York: E. P. Dutton, 1954.
Scott, Jessie. *Charity Ball*. New York: Macmillan, 1946.
Scott, Virgil. *The Dead Tree Gives No Shelter*. New York: William Morrow, 1947.
Seager, Allan. *Equinox*. New York: Simon and Schuster, 1943.
[Seid, Ruth] "Jo Sinclair." *The Changelings*. New York: McGraw-Hill, 1955.
Seley, Stephen. *The Cradle Will Fall*. New York: Harcourt, Brace, 1945.
Shaw, Irwin. *Lucy Crown*. New York: Random House, 1956.
———. *The Young Lions*. New York: Random House, 1948.
Sheean, Vincent. *Bird of the Wilderness*. New York: Random House, 1941.
Shenton, Edward. *The Gray Beginning*. Philadelphia: Penn, 1924.
Shippey, Lee. *The Great American Family*. Boston: Houghton, Mifflin, 1938.
Shulman, Irving. *The Amboy Dukes*. New York: Doubleday, 1947.
———. *Children of the Dark*. New York: Henry Holt, 1956.
———. *Good Deeds Must Be Punished*. New York: Henry Holt, 1956.
———. *The Square Trap*. Boston: Little, Brown, 1953.
Shulman, Max. *I Was a Teen-Age Dwarf*. New York: Bernard Geis, 1959.
———. *The Many Loves of Dobie Gillis*. New York: Doubleday, 1951.
Simmons, Helen. *Lark*. New York: Smith and Durrell, 1942.
Simmons, Herbert. *Corner Boy*. Boston: Houghton, Mifflin, 1957.
Sklar, George. *The Two Worlds of Johnny Truro*. Boston: Little, Brown, 1947.
Smith, Betty. *Maggie-Now*. New York: Harper, 1958.
———. *A Tree Grows in Brooklyn*. New York: Harper, 1943.
Smith, Madeline Babcock. *The Lemon Jelly Cake*. Boston: Little, Brown, 1952.
Solomon, Barbara Probst. *The Beat of Life*. Philadelphia: Lippincott, 1960.
Soman, Florence Jane. *A Break in the Weather*. New York: G. P. Putnam, 1959.
Sourian, Peter. *Miri*. New York: Pantheon Books, 1957.
Stafford, Jean. *Boston Adventure*. New York: Harcourt, Brace, 1944.
———. *The Catherine Wheel*. New York: Harcourt, Brace, 1952.
———. *The Mountain Lion*. New York: Harcourt, Brace, 1947.
Steinbeck, John. *East of Eden*. New York: Viking Press, 1952.
———. "The Red Pony" in *The Long Valley*. New York: Viking Press, 1938.
Sterling, Dorothy. *Mary Jane*. New York: Doubleday, 1959.
Stern, Daniel. *Miss America*. New York: Random House, 1959.
Steuer, Arthur. *The Terrible Swift Sword*. New York: Coward-McCann, 1956.
Stevenson, Philip. *The Edge of the Nest*. New York: Coward-McCann, 1929.
———. *The Gospel According to St. Luke's*. New York: Longmans, Green, 1931.
Stewart, John Craig. *Through the First Gate*. New York: Dodd, Mead, 1950.
Stillwell, Hart. *Campus Town*. New York: Doubleday, 1950.
Stolz, Mary. *Pray Love, Remember*. New York: Harper, 1954.
———. *Ready or Not*. New York: Harper, 1953.
Stone, Grace Zaring. *The Almond Tree*. Indianapolis: Bobbs-Merrill, 1931.
Stong, Phil. *The Long Lane*. New York: Farrar and Rinehart, 1939.
———. *The Rebellion of Lennie Barlow*. New York: Farrar and Rinehart, 1937.
———. *State Fair*. New York: Century, 1932.
Street, James. *Good-bye, My Lady*. Philadelphia: J. B. Lippincott, 1954.

———. *In My Father's House.* New York: Dial Press, 1941.

——— and Don Tracy. *Pride of Possession.* Philadelphia: Lippincott, 1960.

Stuart, Jesse. *Hie to the Hunters.* New York: Whittlesey House, 1950.

———. *Taps for Private Tussie.* New York: E. P. Dutton, 1943.

[Sture-Vasa, Mary] "Mary O'Hara." *My Friend Flicka.* Philadelphia: J. B. Lippincott, 1941.

———. *The Green Grass of Wyoming.* Philadelphia: J. B. Lippincott, 1946.

———. *Thunderhead.* Philadelphia: J. B. Lippincott, 1943.

Styron, William. *Lie Down in Darkness.* Indianapolis: Bobbs-Merrill, 1951.

Suckow, Ruth. *The Bonney Family.* New York: A. A. Knopf, 1928.

———. *The Folks.* New York: Farrar and Rinehart, 1934.

———. *The John Wood Case.* New York: Viking Press, 1959.

———. *The Odyssey of a Nice Girl.* New York: A. A. Knopf, 1925.

Summers, Hollis. *City Limit.* Boston: Houghton, Mifflin, 1948.

Sumner, Cid Rickett. *Tammy Out of Time.* Indianapolis: Bobbs-Merrill, 1948.

———. *Tammy Tell Me True.* Indianapolis: Bobbs-Merrill, 1959.

Swados, Harvey. *Out Went the Candle.* New York: Viking Press, 1955.

Swarthout, Glendon. *Where the Boys Are.* New York: Random House, 1960.

Sykes, Hope Williams. *Second Hoeing.* New York: G. P. Putnam's, 1935.

Tamkus, Daniel. *The Much-Honored Man.* New York: Doubleday, 1959.

[Tanner, Edward Everett] "Patrick Dennis." *Auntie Mame.* New York: Vanguard Press, 1955.

Tarkington, Booth. *Alice Adams.* New York: Doubleday, Page, 1921.

———. *The Fighting Littles.* Garden City, N.Y.: Doubleday, Doran, 1941.

———. *Penrod Jashber.* Garden City, N.Y.: Doubleday, Doran, 1929.

Taylor, Peter. *A Woman of Means.* New York: Harcourt, Brace, 1950.

Taylor, Ross McLaury. *Brazos.* Indianapolis: Bobbs-Merrill, 1938.

"Tembler, Paul." *The Spring Dance.* New York: Viking Press, 1959.

Thacher, Russell. *The Tender Age.* New York: Macmillan, 1952.

Thompson, Charles. *Halfway Down the Stairs.* New York: Harper, 1957.

Thompson, Mary Wolfe. *Highway Past Her Door.* New York: Longmans, Green, 1938.

Tigue, Ethel Erkkilla. *Betrayal.* New York: Dodd, Mead, 1959.

Toohey, John Peter. *Growing Pains.* New York: Dial Press, 1929.

Treynor, Blair. *She Ate Her Cake.* New York: William Morrow, 1946.

Tunis, John R. *All-American.* New York: Harcourt, Brace, 1942.

———. *Go, Team, Go!* New York: William Morrow, 1954.

———. *Iron Duke.* New York: Harcourt, Brace, 1938.

———. *Son of the Valley.* New York: William Morrow, 1949.

Van der Veer, Judy. *November Grass.* New York: Longmans, Green, 1940.

Van Etten, Winifred. *I Am the Fox.* Boston: Little, Brown, 1936.

Vidal, Gore. *The City and the Pillar.* New York: E. P. Dutton, 1948.

———. *The Season of Comfort.* New York: E. P. Dutton, 1949.

Viertel, Peter. *The Canyon.* New York: Harcourt, Brace, 1940.

Villarreal, José Antonio. *Pocho.* New York: Doubleday, 1959.

Wadelton, Tommy. *Silver Buckles on His Knee.* New York: Coward-McCann, 1945.

Wagoner, David. *Rock.* New York: Viking Press, 1958.

Walker, Mildred. *The Body of a Young Man.* New York: Harcourt, Brace, 1960.

———. *Winter Wheat.* New York: Harcourt, Brace, 1944.

Wallop, Douglass. *Night Light.* New York: W. W. Norton, 1953.

Ware, Edmund. *Rider in the Sun.* Boston: Lothrop, Lee and Shepard, 1935.

Warrick, LaMar. *Yesterday's Children*. New York: Crowell, 1943.
Weaver, John V. A. *Her Knight Comes Riding*. New York: A. A. Knopf, 1928.
Webster, Henry Kitchell. *The Innocents*. Indianapolis: Bobbs-Merrill, 1924.
Weeks, Joseph. *All Our Yesterdays*. New York: Rinehart, 1955.
Weidman, Jerome. *The Enemy Camp*. New York: Random House, 1958.
———. *The Lights Around the Shore*. New York: Simon and Schuster, 1943.
Weldon, John Lee. *The Naked Heart*. New York: Farrar and Straus, 1953.
Weller, George Anthony. *Not to Eat, Not for Love*. New York: Harrison Smith and Robert Haas, 1933.
Wescott, Glenway. *The Apple of the Eye*. New York: Dial Press, 1924.
West, Jessamyn. *Cress Delahanty*. New York: Harcourt, Brace, 1954.
———. *The Witch Diggers*. New York: Harcourt, Brace, 1951.
Westheimer, David. *The Magic Fallacy*. New York: Macmillan, 1950.
Wetzel, Donald. *The Rain and the Fire and the Will of God*. New York: Random House, 1957.
Whitney, Phyllis A. *Willow Hill*. New York: Reynal and Hitchcock, 1947.
Wickenden, Dan. *The Running of the Deer*. New York: William Morrow, 1937.
———. *Walk Like a Mortal*. New York: William Morrow, 1940.
———. *The Wayfarers*. New York: William Morrow, 1945.
Widdemer, Margaret. *The Boardwalk*. New York: Harcourt, Brace and Howe, 1920.
Willingham, Calder. *End as a Man*. New York: Vanguard Press, 1947.
———. *Geraldine Bradshaw*. New York: Vanguard Press, 1950.
Wilson, Sloan. *A Summer Place*. New York: Simon and Schuster, 1958.
Windham, Donald. *The Dog Star*. New York: Doubleday, 1950.
Winnek, Marian. *Juniper Hill*. Indianapolis: Bobbs-Merrill, 1932.
Winslow, Anne Goodwin. *The Springs*. New York: A. A. Knopf, 1949.
Winsor, Kathleen. *America, with Love*. New York: G. P. Putnam's, 1957.
Winther, Sophus Keith. *Mortgage Your Heart*. New York: Macmillan, 1937.
Witherspoon, Mary-Elizabeth. *Somebody Speak for Katy*. New York: Dodd, Mead, 1950.
Wolf, Robert L. *Springboard*. New York: Albert and Charles Boni, 1927.
Wolfe, Thomas. *Look Homeward, Angel*. New York: Scribner's, 1929.
———. *The Web and the Rock*. New York: Harper, 1939.
Wood, Playsted. *The Presence of Everett Marsh*. Indianapolis: Bobbs-Merrill, 1937.
Wood, William. *The Fit*. New York: Macmillan, 1960.
Woodbury, Helen. *The Misty Flats*. Boston: Little, Brown, 1925.
Wouk, Herman. *The City Boy*. New York: Simon and Schuster, 1948.
———. *Marjorie Morningstar*. New York: Doubleday, 1955.
[Wright, Beatrice Ann] "Martin Kramer." *Sons of the Fathers*. New York: Macmillan, 1959.
Wright, Richard. *The Long Dream*. New York: Doubleday, 1958.
———. *Native Son*. New York: Harper, 1940.
Wylie, Max. *Go Home and Tell Your Mother*. New York: Rinehart, 1950.
Yaffe, James. *Nothing but the Night*. Boston: Little, Brown, 1957.
Yoseloff, Martin. *The Family Members*. New York: E. P. Dutton, 1948.
———. *The Girl in the Spike-Heeled Shoes*. New York: E. P. Dutton, 1949.
Young, I[sador] S. *Jadie Greenway*. New York: Crown, 1947.
Zietlow, E[dward] R[obert]. *These Same Hills*. New York: A. A. Knopf, 1960.
Zugsmith, Leane. *The Reckoning*. New York: Harrison Smith and Robert Haas, 1934.

B. *Secondary Sources of Information on Problems of Adolescents in Modern American Fiction*

A complete listing of the 3,000 or more book reviews which were read in preparing this book would only serve to confuse the reader; if he is interested, he may find these reviews readily by consulting the *Book Review Digest.* Listed here are those reviews which are cited in footnotes; for the rest, it seems enough to say that for every novel mentioned in this study, from three to ten reviews were read, usually including those in the *New York Herald-Tribune Book Review,* the *New York Times Book Review,* and the *Saturday Review.* Other frequent sources for reviews were the *Boston Transcript,* the *Chicago Sunday Tribune,* the *Christian Science Monitor, Commonweal,* the *Library Journal,* the *Nation,* the *New Republic,* the *New Yorker, Time,* the *Times* (London) *Literary Supplement,* and the *Virginia Kirkus Bookshop Service Bulletin;* less frequent sources were the *Atlantic Monthly,* the *Bookman,* the *Chicago Sun Book Week,* the *Christian Century,* the *Independent,* the *Literary Digest,* the *Literary Review,* the *Manchester Guardian,* the *San Francisco Chronicle,* the *Springfield* (Massachusetts) *Republican,* and the *Yale Review.*

Aldridge, John W. *After the Lost Generation.* New York: McGraw-Hill, 1951.
————. *In Search of Heresy.* New York: McGraw-Hill, 1956.
Algren, Nelson. "Jungle of Tenements." *Saturday Review,* XXXVI (June 6, 1953), 16.
Allen, Frederick Lewis. "Best-Sellers: 1900-1935." *Saturday Review of Literature,* XIII (December 7, 1935), 3 ff.
Barr, Donald. "Freud and Fiction." *Saturday Review,* XXXIX (May 5, 1936), 36.
Beach, Joseph Warren. *American Fiction, 1920-1940.* New York: Macmillan, 1941.
————. *The Twentieth Century Novel.* New York: Century, 1932.
Berdie, Ralph F. "Why Don't They Go to College?" *Personnel and Guidance Journal,* XXXI (March, 1953), 352-356.
Bone, Robert A. *The Negro Novel in America.* New Haven: Yale University Press, 1958.
Brooks, Van Wyck. *The Writer in America.* New York: E. P. Dutton, 1953.
Campbell, Harry Modean, and Ruel E. Foster. *William Faulkner: A Critical Appraisal.* Norman: University of Oklahoma Press, 1951.
Carpenter, Frederic I. "The Adolescent in American Fiction." *English Journal,* XLVI (September, 1957), 313-319.
————. *American Literature and the Dream.* New York: Philosophical Library, 1955.
————. "The Genteel Tradition: A Reinterpretation." *New England Quarterly,* XV (September, 1942), 440-441.
Carter, John F., Jr. "The Wild Young People." *Atlantic Monthly,* CXXVI (September, 1920), 301-304.
Chase, Richard. *The American Novel and Its Tradition.* New York: Doubleday Anchor, 1957.
————. *The Democratic Vista.* New York: Doubleday Anchor, 1958.
Childers, Helen White. "American Novels about Adolescence, 1917-1953." Nashville, Tenn.: unpubl. diss., George Peabody Teachers College, 1958.
Cole, Luella. *Psychology and Adolescence,* 3rd ed. New York: Rinehart, 1948.
Conklin, Edmund S. *Principles of Adolescent Psychology.* New York: Henry Holt, 1935.
Cowley, Malcolm. *After the Genteel Tradition.* New York: W. W. Norton, 1937.
————. *The Literary Situation.* New York: Viking Press, 1954.

————. "Psychoanalysts and Writers." *Harper's*, CCLX (September, 1954), 87-93.
Davenport, Basil. "Huck Finn in New Guise." *Saturday Review of Literature*, XII (August 24, 1935), 7.
Dell, Floyd. *Homecoming.* New York: Farrar and Rinehart,. 1933.
Erikson, Erik H. *Childhood and Society.* New York: W. W. Norton, 1950.
Fiedler, Leslie A. "Boys Will Be Boys!" *New Leader*, XLI (April 28, 1958), 23-26.
————. *An End to Innocence.* Boston: Beacon Press, 1955.
————. "From Redemption to Initiation." *New Leader*, XLI (May 26, 1958), 20-23.
————. "Good Good Girl and Good Bad Boy." *New Leader*, XLI (April 14, 1958), 22-25.
————. "The Invention of the Child." *New Leader*, XLI (March 31, 1958), 22-24.
————. *Love and Death in the American Novel.* New York: Criterion Books, 1960.
————. "The Profanation of the Child." *New Leader*, XLI (June 23, 1958), 26-29.
Frank, Mary H. and Lawrence K. *Your Adolescent at Home and in School.* New York: Viking Press, 1955.
Freud, Sigmund. *Delusion and Dream,* trans. Helen M. Dowley. New York: Moffat, Yard, 1917.
————. *An Outline of Psychoanalysis,* trans. James Strachey. New York: W. W. Norton, 1949.
Friedenberg, Edgard Z. *The Vanishing Adolescent.* Boston: Beacon Press, 1959.
Frohock, W[ilbur] M[errill]. *The Novel of Violence in America,* 2nd ed. Dallas: Southern Methodist University Press, 1957.
Gauss, Christian. *Life in College.* New York: Scribner's, 1932.
Geismar, Maxwell. *American Moderns: From Rebellion to Conformity.* New York: Hill and Wang, 1958.
————. *The Last of the Provincials: The American Novel, 1915-1925.* Boston: Houghton, Mifflin, 1947.
————. "Naturalism Yesterday and Today." *College English*, XV (January, 1954), 195-200.
————. *Writers in Crisis: The American Novel, 1925-1940.* Boston: Houghton, Mifflin, 1942.
Gelfant, Blanche Housman. *The American City Novel.* Norman: University of Oklahoma Press, 1954.
Gesell, Arnold, *et al. Youth: The Years from Ten to Sixteen.* New York: Harper's, 1956.
Gloster, Hugh M. *Negro Voices in American Fiction.* Chapel Hill: University of North Carolina Press, 1948.
Gold, Herbert. "Fiction of the Sixties." *Atlantic Monthly*, CCVI (September, 1960), 53-57.
————. "The Sexual Stalemate." *Nation*, CLXXXVII (November, 1958), 309-311.
Gordon, Caroline. *How to Read a Novel.* New York: Viking Press, 1957.
Grene, Marjorie. *Dreadful Freedom: A Critique of Existentialism.* Chicago: University of Chicago Press, 1948.
Gurko, Leo. *The Angry Decade.* New York: Dodd, Mead, 1947.
Guyot, Charly. *Les Romanciers américains d'aujourd'hui.* Paris: Éditions Labergerie, 1948.
Hall, G. Stanley. *Adolescence,* 2 vols. New York: D. Appleton, 1904.
Hartwick, Harry. *The Foreground of American Fiction.* New York: American Book, 1934.
Hassan, Ihab H. "The Idea of Adolescence in American Fiction." *American Quarterly,*

X (Fall, 1958), 312-324.

Hatcher, Harlan. *Creating the Modern American Novel.* New York: Farrar and Rinehart, 1935.

Havemann, Ernest, and Patricia Salter West. *They Went to College.* New York: Harcourt, Brace, 1952.

Herr, Paul. "The Small, Sad World of James Purdy." *Chicago Review,* XIV (Spring, 1960), 19-25.

Herron, Ima Honeker. *The Small Town in American Literature.* Durham, N.C.: Duke University Press, 1939. (Reissued, apparently without change, New York: Pageant Books, 1959).

Hicks, Granville. *The Great Tradition.* New York: Macmillan, 1933.

Hoffman, Frederick J. *Freudianism and the Literary Mind.* Baton Rouge: Louisiana State University Press, 1945.

———. *The Modern Novel in America, 1900-1950.* Chicago: Regnery, 1951.

Holmes, John Clellon. "Existentialism and the Novel: Notes and Questions." *Chicago Review,* XIII (Summer, 1959), 144-151.

Horrocks, John E. *The Psychology of Adolescence.* Boston: Houghton, Mifflin, 1951.

Hyman, Stanley Edgar. "Some Trends in the Novel." *College English,* XX (October, 1958), 1-9.

James, William. *The Varieties of Religious Experience.* New York: Longmans, Green, 1902.

Johnson, James William. "The Adolescent Hero: A Trend in Modern Fiction." *Twentieth Century Literature,* V (April, 1959), 3-11.

Kazin, Alfred. *On Native Grounds.* New York: Reynal and Hitchcock, 1942.

Kiell, Norman. *The Adolescent through Fiction: A Psychological Approach.* New York: International Universities Press, 1959.

Kinsey, Alfred C., *et. al. Sexual Behavior in the Human Female.* Philadelphia: W. B. Saunders, 1953.

———. *Sexual Behavior in the Human Male.* Philadelphia: W. B. Saunders, 1948.

Lesser, Simon O. *Fiction and the Unconscious.* Boston: Beacon Press, 1957.

Lisca, Peter. *The Wide World of John Steinbeck.* New Brunswick, N.J.: Rutgers University Press, 1958.

Mahoney, Stephen. "The Prevalence of Zen." *Nation,* CLXXXVII (November 1, 1958), 311-315.

Maillard, Denyse. *L'Enfant américain au XXe siècle d'après les Romanciers du Middle-West.* Paris: Librairie Mizet et Bastard, 1935.

May, Henry F. *The End of American Innocence.* New York: A. A. Knopf, 1959.

Mencken, H[enry] L[ouis]. "History and Fable and Very Good Stuff." *New York Herald Tribune Books* (August 25, 1935), p. 1.

Mohrt, Michel. *Le Nouveau Roman américain,* 4e édition. Paris: Gallimard, 1955.

Nye, Ivan. "Adolescent-Parent Adjustment—Rurality as a Variable." *Rural Sociology,* XV (December, 1950), 334-339.

O'Brien, Justin. *The Novel of Adolescence in France.* New York: Columbia University Press, 1937.

O'Connor, William Van. *An Age of Criticism: 1900-1950.* Chicago: Regnery, 1952.

———. "The Grotesque in Modern Fiction." *College English,* XX (April, 1959), 342-346.

———. *The Tangled Fire of William Faulkner.* Minneapolis: University of Minnesota Press, 1954.

———, ed. *Forms of Modern Fiction: Essays Collected in Honor of Joseph Warren*

Beach. Minneapolis: University of Minnesota Press, 1948.

Podhoretz, Norman. "The New Nihilism and the Novel." *Partisan Review,* XXV (Fall, 1958), 576-590.

Reichler, George Reinhart. "A Reading Ladder of Novels Dealing with Problems of Adolescence." Cincinnati: unpubl. thesis, University of Cincinnati, 1951.

Rexroth, Kenneth. "San Francisco's Mature Bohemians." *Nation,* CLXXXIV (February 23, 1957), 159-162.

Salisbury, Harrison E. *The Shook-Up Generation.* New York: Harper, 1958.

Santayana, George. *The Genteel Tradition at Bay.* New York: Scribner's, 1931.

————. *Winds of Doctrine.* New York: Scribner's, 1913.

Scott, James F. "Beat Literature and the American Teen Cult." *American Quarterly,* XIV (Summer, 1962), pp. 150-60.

Simon, Jean. *Le Roman américain au XXe siècle.* Paris: Boivin, 1950.

Spiller, Robert E., *et al. Literary History of the United States,* 3 vols. New York: Macmillan, 1948.

Splaver, Sarah. "The Career Novel." *Personnel and Guidance Journal,* XXI (March, 1953), 371-372.

Stevenson, David L. "Fiction's Unfamiliar Face." *Nation,* CLXXXVII (November 1, 1958), 307-309.

Thorp, Willard. *American Writing in the Twentieth Century.* Cambridge, Mass.: Harvard University Press, 1960.

Wagenknecht, Edward. *Cavalcade of the American Novel.* New York: Henry Holt, 1952.

Walcutt, Charles Child. *American Literary Naturalism: A Divided Stream.* Minneapolis: University of Minnesota Press, 1956.

Wattenberg, William W. *The Adolescent Years.* New York: Harcourt, Brace, 1955.

Wedge, Bryant M., ed. *Psychosocial Problems of College Men.* New Haven: Yale University Press, 1958.

Wellek, René, and Austin Warren. *Theory of Literature.* New York: Harcourt, Brace, 1949.

White, George L., Jr. *Scandinavian Themes in American Fiction.* Philadelphia: publ. diss., University of Pennsylvania, 1937.

Widmer, Kingsley. "The American Road: The Contemporary Novel." *University of Kansas City Review,* XXVI (Summer, 1960), 309-317.

Witham, W. Tasker. *Panorama of American Literature.* New York: Stephen Daye Press, 1947.

Wolfe, Bernard. "Angry at What?" *Nation,* CLXXXVII (November 1, 1958), 316-322.

Appendix

CHRONOLOGICAL LIST OF AMERICAN NOVELS
DEALING WITH PROBLEMS OF ADOLESCENTS

This list of nearly 600 works covers all the major American novels of adolescence published between 1920 and 1960 and most of the minor ones. It deliberately excludes (1) novels about adolescents living outside the United States, (2) historical novels with settings before 1870, and (3) most novels specifically intended for juvenile readers. As explained in the Preface, the list includes a few books that are on the borderline between autobiographical fiction and fictionalized autobiography, or between episodic novels and closely related short stories; these are indicated in the list by a superior *a* or *s*, respectively, preceding the title.

To save space in the columns, periods are omitted after all abbreviations except authors' initials. Abbreviations in the column headed *Locale* refer mainly to states; a few refer to major cities (NYC, Chi, LA, SF, NO, Phil) and a few to regions (NE, Midw). "DC" refers to the city of Washington; "Wash" to the state. "Road" indicates that important events occur while traveling.

In column headed *Sex and Age:* before colon, f = female, m = male; after colon, b = birth, c = childhood, m = maturity, gs = grade school age, hs = high school age, col = college age.

In column headed *Author's Treatment*, D = didactic, G = gothic, H = humorous, J = juvenile, N = naturalistic, P = psychological, R = realistic, Sa = satirical, Se = sentimental, Sy = symbolic.

In column headed *Problems*, numbers correspond to chapter numbers; see Contents as key. Number underscored indicates that the novel is specifically discussed in the chapter indicated.

Author and Title	Locale	Sex & Age(s)	Author's Treatment	Problem(s)
1920				
Deland, Margaret AN OLD CHESTER SECRET	Pa	m:b–m	Se	III
Dell, Floyd MOONCALF	Ill, Iowa	m:b–20	R, P	II, III, IV, V
Fitzgerald, F. Scott THIS SIDE OF PARADISE	Minn, NE, NJ	m:b–m	R	II, III, IV, V, VII

Author and Title	Locale	Sex & Age(s)	Author's Treatment	Problem(s)
1920				
Masters, Edgar Lee MITCH MILLER	Ill	m:12	Se,H	II,<u>V</u>,V<u>II</u>
ˢWiddemer, Margaret THE BOARDWALK	NJ(?)	m:hs f:hs	P	II
1921				
Benét, Stephen Vincent THE BEGINNING OF WISDOM	Cal, Conn	m:b-m	R,Sy	II,<u>IV</u>,<u>V</u>,V<u>II</u>
Kelley, Ethel M. BEAUTY AND MARY BLAIR	NYC	f:18	Sa,N	II,III,<u>VI</u>
Robinson, [Edwin Meade] "Ted" ENTER JERRY	Ind	m:c-16	H,Se	II,IV
Tarkington, Booth ALICE ADAMS	Ind	f:23 m:19	Se,R	<u>III</u>,VI
1922				
Broun, Heywood THE BOY GREW OLDER	NYC	m:b-17	Se	III,<u>V</u>
Dalrymple, Leona FOOL'S HILL	?	m:17	H	II,III
[Fisher,] Dorothy Canfield ROUGH-HEWN	NJ, NY	m:b-m	R	<u>II</u>,<u>IV</u>,<u>V</u>
Johnson, Owen SKIPPY BEDELLE	NJ	m:hs	H	IV
Kilbourne, Fanny A CORNER IN WILLIAM	NY(?)	f:15	H	II
1923				
Cather, Willa A LOST LADY	Neb	m:12-m	R	<u>II</u>
[Croy, Homer,] WEST OF THE WATER TOWER	Mo	m:19-m f:17-m	N,P	<u>II</u>,III,<u>V</u>
Dell, Floyd JANET MARCH	Minn, NYC	f:c-21	R,P,D	II,III,IV, <u>V</u>II
Dutton, Louise GOING TOGETHER	?	f:15	Se	II
Masters, Edgar Lee SKEETERS KIRBY	Ill	m:12-m	N	<u>V</u>,VII
1924				
Beer, Thomas. SANDOVAL: A ROMANCE OF BAD MANNERS	NY	m:17	Se	III,V

Author and Title	Locale	Sex & Age(s)	Author's Treatment	Problem(s)
1924				
Marks, Percy THE PLASTIC AGE	NE	m:17-21	R,P	II,IV,VII
Morley, Christopher,and Don Marquis. PANDORA LIFTS THE LID	NY	f:18	Sa	III,IV
O'Higgins, Harvey JULIE CANE	NJ	f:c-m	P,R	IV,VI
Shenton, Edward THE GRAY BEGINNING	Pa	m:c-m	P	V
Webster, Henry Kitchell THE INNOCENTS	Midw	m:18	P	III,IV
Wescott, Glenway THE APPLE OF THE EYE	Wis	m:15	P,Sy	II,V,VI,VII
1925				
Dos Passos, John MANHATTAN TRANSFER	NYC	m:c-m f:b-m	N	II,III,V,VI
Dreiser, Theodore AN AMERICAN TRAGEDY	Mo,NY	m:14-22	N	II,III,VI,VII
Gilman, Mildred Evans FIG LEAVES	Mich	f:c-m	P,Se	II,IV
[s]Hemingway, Ernest IN OUR TIME	Mich, Ill	m:12-m	N,Sy	II,VII
Ostenso, Martha WILD GEESE	Minn(?)	f:17-18	N	II,III,VI
Suckow, Ruth. THE ODYSSEY OF A NICE GIRL	Iowa, Mass	f:11-m	R,P	III,V
Woodbury, Helen THE MISTY FLATS	Conn, NYC	f:c-m	P	III,V
1926				
[a]Anderson, Sherwood TAR	Ohio	m:b-14	R,P	II,III,IV, V,VII
Bronson, F. W. SPRING RUNNING	NJ,NY, Conn	m:c-m f:c-m	N	II,IV,V
Hormel, Olive Dean CO-ED	Ill	f:17-21	Se	IV
Roberts, Elizabeth Madox THE TIME OF MAN	Ky	f:11-m	R,P	III,VI
1927				
Farnham, Mateel Howe REBELLION	Kan	f:c-m	P	III

303

Author and Title	Locale	Sex & Age(s)	Author's Treatment	Problem(s)
1927				
Masters, Edgar Lee KIT O'BRIEN	III	m:15	Se,D	VI
Wolf, Robert L SPRINGBOARD	III,O, Mass	m:b–20	Sa	II,IV
1928				
Carr, Robert S. THE RAMPANT AGE	?	m:16–18	N	II,IV,VII
Coursen, Dorothy FIRE OF SPRING	Ind	f:11 f:13	P	II,V
Suckow, Ruth THE BONNEY FAMILY	Iowa	f:12–m m:14–m	R,P	III,IV,V, VI,VII
Weaver, John V. A. HER KNIGHT COMES RIDING	NY	f:c–m	P	II
1929				
Brecht, Harold W. DOWNFALL	Pa	m:14–16	P,R	III,IV
Brinig, Myron SINGERMANN	Mont	m:b–17 m:c–m f:c–m	R	II,III,V, VI
Coursen, Dorothy BEAUTY? I WONDER	?	f:c–m	Sy,P	II,III
Dell, Floyd SOUVENIR	NYC	m:19	R,P,D	II,III,V
Faulkner, William THE SOUND AND THE FURY	Miss, Mass	m:20	N,Sy	III,IV,VI, VII
Heyward, Du Bose MAMBA'S DAUGHTERS	SC,NYC	m:14–m f:b–17	R	V,VI
Hill, Fowler PLUNDERED HOST	?,NYC	m:c–m	R	II,III,V
Joseph, Donald OCTOBER'S CHILD	Ga	m:c–18	P	III,IV,VI
Millay, Kathleen AGAINST THE WALL	Me,NY	f:18–19	N	IV,VI
Parrish, Anne THE METHODIST FAUN	Ind, NYC	m:20–25	P	II,III,V
Rolvaag, O[le] E[dvart] PEDER VICTORIOUS	SD	m:c–m	N	II,III,IV, VI,VII
Samuels, Charles THE FRANTIC YOUNG MAN	NYC?	m:18	Sa	II,VI
Stevenson, Philip THE EDGE OF THE NEST	NYC	m:14 f:17	P	II,III,IV

304

Author and Title	Locale	Sex & Age(s)	Author's Treatment	Problem(s)
1929				
Tarkington, Booth PENROD JASHBER	Ind	m:12	H	III
Toohey, John Peter GROWING PAINS	?	m:18	H	II, III
Wolfe, Thomas LOOK HOMEWARD, ANGEL	NC	m:b-18	N, Sy	II, III, IV, V, VI, VII
1930				
Crawford, Nelson Antrim UNHAPPY WIND	Midw	m:c-m	P	II, V
Dos Passos, John THE 42ND PARALLEL	Chi, SF, DC, Md, Minn, ND, road	m:c-m f:c-m	N	II, III, V, VI, VII
Faulkner, William AS I LAY DYING	Miss	f:17	N, Sy	II, III, VI, VII
Fineman, Irving THIS PURE YOUNG MAN	Pa	m:17-m	R	II, IV, V
[Fisher,] Dorothy Canfield THE DEEPENING STREAM	Midw, NY	f:4-m	R	II, III, V
Granberry, Edwin THE ERL KING	Fla	m:c-18	Sy	II, III
Hughes, Langston NOT WITHOUT LAUGHTER	Kan	m:c-16 f:16-m	N	II, III, IV VI, VII
Laing, Alexander AN END OF ROAMING	NE	m:b-m	R	II, IV, V
Latimer, Margery THIS IS MY BODY	NYC	f:16-m	P, Sy	II, IV, V
Lincoln, Joseph C. BLOWING CLEAR	Mass	m:11-m	Se	III, VI
Marquand, John P. WARNING HILL	NJ	m:c-m	R, Se	V, VI
Raymond, Margaret Thomsen LINNET ON THE THRESHOLD	?	f:14-15	R, J	III, V
Rollins, William, Jr. THE OBELISK	Boston	m:c-m	P, Sy	V
[S] Ryerson, Florence and Colin Clements. THIS AWFUL AGE	Midw?	f:12-15	H	II, III, IV, V
1931				
Austin, Mary STARRY ADVENTURE	NMex	m:c-m	R, Sy	II, V

Author and Title	Locale	Sex & Age(s)	Author's Treatment	Problem(s)
1931				
Brown, Rollo Walter THE FIREMAKERS	Ohio	m:14-m	N,D	V,VI
Craven, John V. THE LEAF IS GREEN	NJ,NY	m:19	N	II,IV
Faulkner, William SANCTUARY	Miss	f:18	N,Sy	II,III,VII
Fillmore, Parker YESTERDAY MORNING	NY?	m:c-m	Se	III,VI
[Fraenkel, Michael] WERTHER'S YOUNGER BROTHER	?	m:17?	P,Sy	II,V,VII
Stevenson, Phillip. THE GOSPEL ACCORDING TO ST. LUKE'S	NE?	m:15-18	R	IV
Stone, Grave Zaring THE ALMOND TREE	DC	m:16	P	II,III
1932				
Brown, Rollo Walter TOWARD ROMANCE	Ohio	m:c-19	Sy,Se	II,III,V, VI
Caldwell, Erskine TOBACCO ROAD	Ga	f:18 f:13 m:16	N	II,III,VI, VII
Dos Passos, John 1919	Chi, NYC, Mass, NJ,Road	f:c-m m:c-m	N	II,III,IV, V,VI,VII
Farrell, James T YOUNG LONIGAN	Chi	m:15-17	N	II,III,IV, VI,VII
Faulkner, William LIGHT IN AUGUST	Miss	f:18-19 m:b-m	N,Sy	II,III,VI
Fisher, Vardis IN TRAGIC LIFE	Idaho	m:b-18	P,N	II,III,IV, V,VI,VII
Glasgow, Ellen THE SHELTERED LIFE	Va	f:c-17	P	II,V,VII
S Kirstein, Lincoln FLESH IS HEIR	NY? Eur	m:15-m	P,Sy	IV,V
S Lorimer, Graeme and Sarah MEN ARE LIKE STREET CARS	Phil	f:16	H	II

Author and Title	Locale	Sex & age(s)	Author's treatment	Problem(s)
1932				
Stong, Phil STATE FAIR	Iowa	m:18 f:19	H,Se	II,VI
Winnek, Marian JUNIPER HILL	Mass	f:14–16	N,P	II,III
1933				
Caldwell, Erskine GOD'S LITTLE ACRE	Ga	f:15–16	N	II,VI
[s] Ryerson, Florence, and Colin Clements. MILD OATS	Midw	f:15–17	H	II,V
Weller, George Anthony NOT TO EAT, NOT FOR LOVE	Mass	m:col	P,Sa,Sy	IV
1934				
[a] Coffin, Robert P. Tristram LOST PARADISE	Maine	m:11	Se,R	IV,V,VI
Farrell, James T. THE YOUNG MANHOOD OF STUDS LONIGAN	Chi	m:17–m	N	II,III,V, VI,VII
Fisher, Vardis PASSIONS SPIN THE PLOT	Idaho, Utah	m:18–m	P,N	II,IV,V, VI
Haines, William Wister SLIM	Ky(?), road	m:18	R,D	II,V,VI
Lincoln, Victoria FEBRUARY HILL	Mass, RI	f:17–m	R,H	II,III,V
[s] Lorimer, Graeme and Sarah STAG LINE	Phil	f:16–17	H	II
Raymond, Margaret Thomsen A BEND IN THE ROAD	?	f:16–20	R,J	II,V
Suckow, Ruth THE FOLKS	Iowa	m:c–m f:c–m	R	II,III,IV, VI
Zugsmith, Leane THE RECKONING	NYC	m:15	N	III,IV,VI
1935				
Algren, Nelson SOMEBODY IN BOOTS	Texas, road, Chi	m:15–m	N	II,III,VI, VII
Aydelotte, Dora LONG FURROWS	Ill	f:c–m	Se,H	II,VI
Bishop, John Peale ACT OF DARKNESS	WVa	m:16	Sy,N	VII
Coffin, Robert P. Tristram RED SKY IN THE MORNING	Maine	m:15–m	Sy	III,VI,VII

Author and Title	Locale	Sex & Age(s)	Author's Treatment	Problem(s)
1935				
Davis, H[arold] L[enoir] HONEY IN THE HORN	Ore	m:16-18 f:16-18	R,H	II,III,<u>VI</u>
Gollomb, Joseph UNQUIET	NYC	m:c-m	R,D	II,III,IV, V,VI
Jordan, Elizabeth DADDY AND I	NE	f:15	Se,H	III,<u>VI</u>
S Lane, Rose Wilder OLD HOME TOWN	Midw	f:c-m	Se	<u>VI</u>
Larrimore, Lida NO LOVELIER SPRING	NYC	f:17	Se,H	II
S Lorimer, Graeme and Sarah HEART SPECIALIST	Phila	f:18	H	<u>II</u>
MacMullan, Hugh LOUDER THAN WORDS	Mass	m:c-hs	D,R	II,III,IV
O'Hara, John BUTTERFIELD 8	NYC	f:c-22	N,Sa	II,<u>VI</u>
S Patterson, Vernon. ALL GIANTS WEAR YELLOW BREECHES	Mo	m:c-16	R	II,III,IV
Sykes, Hope Williams SECOND HOEING	Colo	f:16	N,D	II,III,<u>VI</u>
Ware, Edmund RIDER IN THE SUN	West	m:15-m	R,P	III,<u>VI</u>
1936				
Anderson, Sherwood KIT BRANDON	Tenn, Va	f:c-m	N	II,III,V, VI
Dos Passos, John THE BIG MONEY	Col, Chi,NY	f:c-m	N	II,III,V, VI,VII
Eliot, Ethel Cook ANGEL'S MIRTH	Conn	f:16	P,D	III,<u>V</u>,VII
Faulkner, William ABSALOM, ABSALOM!	Miss, Mass	m:20	N,Sy	<u>IV</u>,VI
Friesen, Gordon FLAMETHROWERS	Kans, Okla	m:c-m	P,N,Sy	III,IV,<u>V</u>, <u>VI</u>,VII
S Frost, Frances INNOCENT SUMMER	Vt	m:10-15 f:5-14	P,N	II,III,VI
Hull, Helen CANDLE INDOORS	NY	f:c-m m:c-m	Se,P,D	III,II,V
Johnson, Alvin SPRING STORM	Neb	n:15-17	R	<u>II</u>,VI
Marks, Percy. A TREE GROWN STRAIGHT	?	m:c-m	Se,D	II,III,IV

Author and Title	Locale	Sex & Age(s)	Author's Treatment	Problem(s)
1936				
Santayana, George THE LAST PURITAN	Conn, Mass	m:c-m	P,Sa,Sy	III,IV,V, VII
Van Etten, Winifred I AM THE FOX	Iowa NY,Pa	f:c-m	P,Sy	II,V,VII
1937				
Carlisle, Helen Grace THE MERRY, MERRY MAIDENS	NYC	f:hs-m	Se	II,V,VI
Halper, Albert THE CHUTE	Chi	m:17	N,D	V,VI
Horgan, Paul A LAMP ON THE PLAINS	NMex	m:hs	R	II,III,IV, V,VII
LaFarge, Oliver THE ENEMY GODS	NMex	m:c-m	R,D	II,III,IV, V,VI
Levin, Meyer THE OLD BUNCH	Chi	m:hs-m f:hs-m	N	II,III,IV, V,VI
Martin, Helen R. EMMY UNTAMED	Pa	f:c-m	Se	III,VI
Maxwell, William THEY CAME LIKE SWALLOWS	Ill	m:13	R,Se	III,VII
Robinson, Mabel Louise BRIGHT ISLAND	Me	f:hs	Se,J	II,IV,VI
Stong, Phil. THE REBELLION OF LENNIE BARLOW	Iowa	m:13-14	Se,H	IV,VI
Wickenden, Dan. THE RUNNING OF THE DEER	NY	m:15	R,Sy	III,IV,V, VI
Winther, Sophus Keith MORTGAGE YOUR HEART	Neb	m:12-19	N	II,III,VI
Wood, Playsted. THE PRESENCE OF EVERETT MARSH	Wis	m:hs	Se,Sa	IV
1938				
Aldis, Dorothy ALL THE YEAR ROUND	?	m:20 f:18 f:13	D,Se,H	III
Cooke, Charles THE BIG SHOW	NY, NYC	m:18-19?	Se,R	II,V,VII
Farrell, James T. NO STAR IS LOST	Chi	m:c-15	N	III,IV,V, VI,VII
Guerard, Albert J. THE PAST MUST ALTER	Ia, Cal,Eur	m:c-m	P	III

Author and Title	Locale	Sex & Age(s)	Author's Treatment	Problem(s)
1938				
Lee, Harry FOX IN THE CLOAK	Ga	m:16-m	R	V
Lorimer, Graeme and Sarah ACQUITTAL	Midw	m:17	P	III
Marks, Percy. WHAT'S A HEAVEN FOR?	Cal	m:hs-m	D	IV,V
Means, Florence SHUTTERED WINDOWS	Minn, SC	f:hs	J	III,IV,VI
Nathan, Robert WINTER IN APRIL	NYC	f:15	Se	II
Rawlings, Marjorie Kinnan THE YEARLING	Fla	m:12-13	R,Se	III,VII
Raymond, Margaret Thomsen SYLVIA, INC.	Pa?	f:col	J,R	V
Shippey, Lee. THE GREAT AMERICAN FAMILY	Cal	m:c-m	Se,H	III
Steinbeck, John. "The Red Pony" in THE LONG VALLEY	Cal	m:10-12	N,Sy	III,VII
Taylor, Ross McLaury BRAZOS	Tex, Kan	m:16-m	R,Se	II,V,VI
Thompson, Mary Wolfe HIGHWAY PAST HER DOOR	NJ	f:17	J	V
Tunis, John R THE IRON DUKE	Iowa	m:col	J	IV
1939				
Benefield, Barry APRIL WAS WHEN IT BEGAN	NYC	f:13-16	Se,H	II,VII
Carson, Katherine MRS. PENNINGTON	Kan	m:14,20 f:16,18	Se	III,VI
[Franken, Rose D., and William B. Meloney] "Franken Meloney" STRANGE VICTORY	NY	f:13	P	III,VII
Frost, Frances YOKE OF STARS	Vt	f:c-m	P	III,V
Lewis, Flannery ABEL DAYTON	Cal	m:13-18	R,P	II,III,V, VI,VII
Marquis, Don. SONS OF THE PURITANS	Ill	m:c-m	H,Se	II,III,V
Morley, Christopher KITTY FOYLE	Phil, Ill, NYC	f:c-m	R,Sa,Se	II,III,V

Author and Title	Locale	Sex & Age(s)	Author's Treatment	Problem(s)
1939				
Porter, Katherine Anne "Old Mortality" in PALE HORSE, PALE RIDER	La, Tex	f:c-18	P	III,<u>V</u>
Price, Emerson. INN OF THAT JOURNEY	Ohio	m:12-14	R,P	II,III,IV, <u>VI</u>
Prokosch, Frederic NIGHT OF THE POOR	Wis, road, Tex	m:17	R,Sy	<u>III</u>,VII
Stong, Phil THE LONG LANE	Iowa	m:12	Se,H	III,V
Wolfe, Thomas THE WEB AND THE ROCK	NC	m:b-m	N,Sy	II,III,IV, <u>V</u>,VI
1940				
Bellamann, Henry KINGS ROW	Mo?	m:c-m	P,N	II,III,<u>V</u>, <u>VI,VII</u>
^s Bentham, Josephine JANIE	Cal	f:16	H	II
Caldwell, Erskine TROUBLE IN JULY	Ga	m:18	N,Sy,D	<u>VI</u>
Day, Lillian THE YOUNGEST PROFESSION	Cal	f:15-16	H	II,<u>V</u>
Downes, Anne Miller UNTIL THE SHEARING	NY	m:c-m	Se,Sy,D	II,III,IV, <u>V</u>
Estes, Harlow HILDRETH	Me	f:19	P,R	<u>II,III</u>
Farrell, James T. FATHER AND SON	Chi	m:14-19	N	II,III,IV, <u>V,VI</u>
Faulkner, William THE HAMLET	Miss	f:11-16	N,Sy,P	II,<u>III</u>,VII
[Fetzer, Hermann] "Jake Falstaff" JACOBY'S CORNERS	Ohio	m:13	Se	VI
Harriman, John WINTER TERM	Mass?	m:14	R	<u>IV</u>
Lewis, Sinclair BETHEL MERRIDAY	Conn, NYC,road	f:c-22	R,Se,Sa	<u>V</u>
^s Lorimer, Graeme and Sarah FIRST LOVE, FAREWELL	Phila	f:19	H	<u>II</u>

Author and Title	Locale	Sex & Age(s)	Author's Treatment	Problem(s)
1940				
McCullers, Carson THE HEART IS A LONELY HUNTER	Ga	f:12-16	P,N	II,III,V
Parmenter, Christine Whiting AS THE SEED IS SOWN	Mass	m:c-m f:c-m	P,D	II,III
s Saroyan, William MY NAME IS ARAM	Calif	m:c-18	H,Se	III,IV,V
Van der Veer, Judy NOVEMBER GRASS	Calif	f:c-m	P,Sy	III,VI
Viertel, Peter THE CANYON	Calif	m:c-m	R,P	II,III,VI
Wickenden, Dan WALK LIKE A MORTAL	NY	m:17	R,P	III,IV
Wright, Richard NATIVE SON	Chi	m:20	N,P,D	II,III,VI, VII
1941				
s Benson, Sally JUNIOR MISS	NYC	f:12 f:15	H,Se	III
Derleth, August EVENING IN SPRING	Wis	m:hs f:hs	Se,H	II,III,V
Duffus, R[obert] L[uther] THAT WAS ALDERBURY	Vt	m:13	Se,R	VI
Farrell, James T. ELLEN ROGERS	Chi	f:19	N	II
[Fetzer, Hermann] "Jake Falstaff" THE BIG SNOW	Ohio	m:13	Se	IV,VI
King, Mary QUINCIE BOLLIVER	Tex	f:12-18	N,P	II,III,VI
[Klaw, Barbara Van Doren] "Martin Gale" JOAN AND MICHAEL	Conn	f:16-17 m:17-18	P,J	III
Lundberg, Daniel RIVER RAT	Mass	m:17	H	II,III,IV, VI
MacLeod, Norman THE BITTER ROOTS	Mont	m:12-16	N,P	II,IV
Newman, Robert H. FLING OUT THE BANNER	Mass	m:17	N	IV,V
Sheean, Vincent BIRD OF THE WILDERNESS	Ill	m:16-17	R,P	II,III,IV, VI

Author and Title	Locale	Sex & Age(s)	Author's Treatment	Problem(s)
1941				
Street, James IN MY FATHER'S HOUSE	Miss	m:14 f:16	R,Se	II,III,VI, VII
[Sture-Vasa, Mary] "Mary O'Hara" MY FRIEND FLICKA	Wyo	m:10	Se,J	VII
Tarkington, Booth THE FIGHTING LITTLES	Ind, Me	f:17 m:14	H	II,III,VI
1942				
Aldis, Dorothy POOR SUSAN	?	f:14	H,R	III
Algren, Nelson NEVER COME MORNING	Chi	m:17-18	N,P	II,III,VI
Amrine, Michael. ALL SONS MUST SAY GOODBYE	Kan	m:18	R,P	II,III,IV
Chamberlain, George Agnew THE PHANTOM FILLY	Ohio	m:15-19	Se	VII
Daly, Maureen SEVENTEENTH SUMMER	Wis	f:17	R,P	II,III
Faulkner, William. "The Bear" in GO DOWN, MOSES	Miss	m:10-m	N,P,Sy	VII
S[Fetzer, Hermann] "Jake Falstaff" COME BACK TO WAYNE COUNTY	Ohio	m:14	Se,H	VI
Field, Hope STORMY PRESENT	WVa, Ohio	f:16-17	Se	II,III
Manoff, Arnold TELEGRAM FROM HEAVEN	NYC	f:17?	R,Se	II,III,V, VII
Morley, Christopher THOROFARE	Eng, Md	m:c-m	R,H,Se	IV,VI
Osborn, Mary Elizabeth DAYS BEYOND RECALL	NY	f:c-16	Se	II,VI,VII
Simmons, Helen LARK	Cal	f:c-18	Se,Sy	II,III
Tunis, John R. ALL-AMERICAN	?	m:hs	R,D,J	IV,VI
1943				
S Caldwell, Erskine GEORGIA BOY	Ga	m:12	H,N	III,VI
Farrell, James T. MY DAYS OF ANGER	Chi	m:21-23	N	II,III,IV, V,VI
Leslie, Ann George DANCING SAINTS	?	m:c-m	R,D	II,III,V

Author and Title	Locale	Sex & Age(s)	Author's Treatment	Problem(s)
1943				
McCormick, Jay NOVEMBER STORM	Gr. Lakes ship	m:18–19?	R	III,V,VI
Robinson, Oliver TRIUMVIRATE	Ind	f:c–m m:c–m m:c–m	R	II,III,VI
Saroyan, William THE HUMAN COMEDY	Cal	m:14–15	Se	III,VI,VII
Seager, Allan EQUINOX	NY	f:17	P,G	II,III
Smith, Betty. A TREE GROWS IN BROOKLYN	NYC	f:11–16	Se	II,III,V, VI,VII
Stuart, Jesse. TAPS FOR PRIVATE TUSSIE	Ky	m:13?	H	III,VI,VII
[Sture-Vasa, Mary] "Mary O'Hara" THUNDERHEAD	Wyo	m:13–14	Se,J	VII
Warrick, LaMar YESTERDAY'S CHILDREN	Midw	m:17–18	H,Se	III,IV, VII
Weidman, Jerome. THE LIGHTS AROUND THE SHORE	NYC, Eur	m:15	P	III
1944				
Childs, Marquis W THE CABIN	Iowa	m:13	P	III,V,VI
Gardner, Mac MOM COUNTED SIX	Wash	f:c–18	H,N	II,III,VI
ᔆ Herbert, F. Hugh MEET CORLISS ARCHER	?	f:15	H,Se	II,III
Kroll, Harry Harrison WATERS OVER THE DAM	Ala	m:18	N	II,VI
McCoy, John Pleasant SWING THE BIG-EYED RABBIT	Va	m:16	H	III,IV,VI
McNichols, Charles L. CRAZY WEATHER	Ariz	m:14	N,P	III,V,VI
Stafford, Jean BOSTON ADVENTURE	Mass	f:10–20	N,P,Sy	II,III,IV, V,VI,VII
Walker, Mildred WINTER WHEAT	Mont, Minn	f:19–21	R	II,III,IV, V,VI

314

Author and Title	Locale	Sex & Age(s)	Author's Treatment	Problem(s)
1945				
Clark, Walter Van Tilburg THE CITY OF TREMBLING LEAVES	Nev, Cal	m:b-m	R,P	II,IV,<u>V</u>
Karig, Walter LOWER THAN ANGELS	NYC, NJ	m:b-m	N	II,III,IV, V,<u>VII</u>
Kehoe, William A SWEEP OF DUSK	Midw	m:hs-col	P,R	III,IV
L'Engle, Madeleine THE SMALL RAIN	NYC, NE,Eur	f:10-20	P	II,<u>V,VII</u>
Maxwell, William THE FOLDED LEAF	Chi Ind?	m:15-19	P,R,Sy	II,III,<u>IV,</u> <u>VII</u>
Roberts, Dorothy James A DURABLE FIRE	Ohio	f:c-m	P,N	II,III,VI
Rosaire, Forrest EAST OF MIDNIGHT	Chi,Cal, Fla	f:c-m	P	II,<u>V</u>,VII
Seley, Stephen THE CRADLE WILL FALL	NJ	m:11	P,N	III
Wadelton, Tommy. SILVER BUCKLES ON HIS KNEE	Ind	m:c-m	G,Se	VII
Wickenden, Dan THE WAYFARERS	Mich	f:19-20	R,P,Sy	II,III
1946				
Goodin, Peggy CLEMENTINE	Ind	f:10-16	H,R	<u>II</u>,IV,<u>V</u>
Johnson, Josephine WILDWOOD	NE	f:13-22	P	III,<u>V</u>
McCullers, Carson THE MEMBER OF THE WEDDING	Ga	f:12	P,Sy	III,V
Marquand, John P. B.F.'S DAUGHTER	Conn	f:c-m	P,Sa	II,III,VI
Pratt, Theodore VALLEY BOY	Cal	m:11	Se	<u>VII</u>
Rosenfeld, Isaac PASSAGE FROM HOME	Chi	m:14	N	<u>III</u>
Scott, Jessie CHARITY BALL	Midw	f:17 f:18	G,Se	III
[Sture-Vasa, Mary] "Mary O'Hara" THE GREEN GRASS OF WYOMING	Wyo	m:16-18	Se,R	II,<u>VII</u>
Treynor, Blair SHE ATE HER CAKE	Iowa, Cal	f:15-19 m:15-19	G,Se	II,III,<u>V,</u> VII

Author and Title	Locale	Sex & Age(s)	Author's Treatment	Problem(s)
1947				
Athas, Daphne THE WEATHER OF THE HEART	Me	f:c-m m:c-m	N,P	II,III,VI
Eddy, Roger W. THE RIMLESS WHEEL	NE	m:c-19	P,R,Sy	II,II,V, VI,VII
Faralla, Dana THE MAGNIFICENT BARB	Ga	m:12 f:17?	Se	II,VII
Foff, Arthur. GLORIOUS IN ANOTHER DAY	SF	m:18?	N	II,III
Henning, William E. THE HELLER	Midw	f:17-18	R	II,III,IV
Lewiton, Mina THE DIVIDED HEART	?	f:15	P,J	III,IV
[McLean, Kathryn] "Kathryn Forbes" TRANSFER POINT	SF	f:10-12	Se,H,R	III,VI
Motley, Willard KNOCK ON ANY DOOR	Col, Chi	m:12-21	N	III,VI,VII
Ricks, Peirson THE HUNTER'S HORN	NC	m:15?	P,Sy	II,III,VII
Scott, Virgil. THE DEAD TREE GIVES NO SHELTER	Ohio	m:17-21	N	III,IV
Shulman, Irving THE AMBOY DUKES	NYC	m:16	N,P	II,III,V, VII
Sklar, George. THE TWO WORLDS OF JOHNNY TRURO	Conn	m:17	P,N	II,V,VII
Stafford, Jean THE MOUNTAIN LION	Cal, Col	m:10-16 f:8-14	P,Sy	III,VI, VII
Whitney, Phyllis A. WILLOW HILL	Midw?	f:17	R,D,J	IV,V,VI
Willingham, Calder END AS A MAN	Tenn?	m:18	N,Sa	II,IV,VII
Young, I[sador] S. JADIE GREENWAY	NYC	f:16	N,P	II,III,IV, VI
1948				
Ader, Paul. THE LEAF AGAINST THE SKY	NC	m:14-18	N,P	II,III,IV, V
Bromfield, Louis THE WILD COUNTRY	Mo	m:13-14	R,P	II,III,VI
Capote, Truman. OTHER VOICES, OTHER ROOMS	Miss	m:13	P,Sy	II,III,VII

Author and Title	Locale	Sex & Age(s)	Author's Treatment	Problem(s)
1948				
Faulkner, William INTRUDER IN THE DUST	Miss	m:16	N,Sy	<u>III</u>,<u>VI</u>
Gorham, Charles THE FUTURE MR. DOLAN	NYC	m:19	N	II,III,VII
Millar, Margaret IT'S ALL IN THE FAMILY	?	f:11	H,Se	III
Moore, Ruth THE FIRE BALLOON	Me	f:16	Se,Sy	II,IV,<u>VI</u>
Morley, Blythe THE INTEMPERATE SEASON	Conn	m:17	P,G	<u>II</u>,VII
Nathan, Robert LONG AFTER SUMMER	Mass	f:14	Se,Sy	<u>II,III,VII</u>
Plagemann, Bentz INTO THE LABYRINTH	Ohio	m:18	P,Sy	II,V
Raphaelson, Dorshka MORNING SONG	NYC	f:c–16	H,Se	II,<u>III</u>,V
Rendina, Laura Cooper ROOMMATES	?	f:16	P,J	II,III,IV
Shaw, Irwin THE YOUNG LIONS	Cal, NYC, Eur	m:19–m	N,P	II,III,VI, <u>VII</u>
Summers, Hollis CITY LIMIT	Ky, Ind	f:16 m:17	R,P	<u>II,IV</u>
Sumner, Cid Ricketts TAMMY OUT OF TIME	Miss	f:17	H,Sa,Se	II,VI
Vidal, Gore THE CITY AND THE PILLAR	Va, road	m:16–m	N	<u>II</u>
Wouk, Herman THE CITY BOY	NY	m:11	H,Se	II,IV,<u>VI</u>
Yoseloff, Martin THE FAMILY MEMBERS	Iowa	f:17	R,Se	<u>II</u>,III,VI
1949				
Barber, Elsie Oakes THE TREMBLING YEARS	Mass	f:17–21	P,R,D	II,IV,<u>VII</u>
Baumer, Marie. THE SEEKER AND THE SOUGHT	NYC	m:15	N,P,D	<u>III</u>
Bro, Margueritte Harmon SARAH	Midw	f:11–m	D,J,R	II,III,IV, V
Caldwell, Erskine. PLACE CALLED ESTHERVILLE	Ga	m:16 f:17	N,G	II,III,VI

Author and Title	Locale	Sex & Age(s)	Author's Treatment	Problem(s)
1949				
Edwards, E[dward] J. THE CHOSEN	NYC, Midw	m:col	D	IV, V
Ellson, Hal DUKE	NYC	m:15	N	III, VI, <u>VII</u>
Gipson, Fred HOUND-DOG MAN	Tex	m:12	H, Se, R	III, <u>VII</u>
Grant, Dorothy Fremont DEVIL'S FOOD	NYC, SF	f:18	D	II, III, IV, V
Lampell, Millard THE HERO	NJ, Va	m:18-19	Sa	IV
Lincoln, Victoria CELIA AMBERLEY	RI, Phil, Mass	f:c-m	P	II, IV, VI
McCarthy, Catherine Ridgway DEFINITION OF LOVE	Bost	f:20-21	Se, P	II, IV
Marquand, John P. POINT OF NO RETURN	Mass	m:12-m	R, P, Sa	II, III, <u>V</u>, VI
Mende, Robert SPIT AND THE STARS	NYC	m:c-m	R, Se, D, H	II, V, VI
Morrison, Ray ANGELS CAMP	Cal	m:16	P, D	III
Norman, Charles THE WELL OF THE PAST	NYC, S Am, Eur	m:hs-m	R, Sy, Sa	III, IV, V
[Proffitt, Josephine] "Sylvia Dee" AND NEVER BEEN KISSED	Midw?	f:15-16	H	II
Tunis, John R. SON OF THE VALLEY	Tenn	m:15-m	R, D, J	<u>V</u>, VI
Vidal, Gore THE SEASON OF COMFORT	DC, NY, Eur	m:c-m	P	III, IV, <u>V</u> VII
Winslow, Anne Goodwin THE SPRINGS	Tenn	f:17	H, Se	II, III, VI
Yoseloff, Martin. THE GIRL IN THE SPIKE-HEELED SHOES	Midw	f:14-m	N	II, III, V
1950				
[Adams, Alger] "Philip B. Kaye". TAFFY	NYC	m:17-18	N	III, VI
Armstrong, Charlotte MISCHIEF	NYC	f:19	G, P	III, <u>VII</u>
Barton, Betsey SHADOW OF THE BRIDGE	NE	f:18 f:17	P	iI, III, <u>IV</u> V
Demby, William BEETLECREEK	WVa?	m:14	P, R, Sy	<u>II, VI</u>, VII

Author and Title	Locale	Sex & Age(s)	Author's Treatment	Problem(s)
1950				
Ellson, Hal TOMBOY	NYC	f:15	N	III
s Faulkner, John CHOOKY	Miss	m:11	H	III,VI
Gipson, Fred THE HOME PLACE	Tex	m:10-11	R,Se,H	III,VI
Goodin, Peggy. TAKE CARE OF MY LITTLE GIRL	Midw	f:18	Sa,H	IV
Harnden, Ruth I, A STRANGER	Bost	f:10-12	P,Sy	III,IV
s Jackson, Charles THE SUNNIER SIDE	NY	m:10-15	P	II,III,VI
Keogh, Theodora MEG	NYC	f:12	N,P	III,IV,<u>VI</u>
Lamson, Peggy THE CHARMED CIRCLE	?	m:col f:col	P,D	II,IV
[Masters, Kelly R.] "Zachary Ball." PINEY	Miss, La	m:14-15	R,G,Se	III,VI,VII
a Moody, Ralph LITTLE BRITCHES	Col	m:8-11	R,Se	<u>V</u>,VI,VII
Pease, Howard THE DARK ADVENTURE	Ill, road, Cal	m:16	G,P,J	III,<u>VII</u>
Ritner, Ann THE GREEN BOUGH	Pa	f:18	Se	II,III,V, VI
Stewart, John Craig THROUGH THE FIRST GATE	South	m:17?	R,D,Sy	II,IV,VI
Stillwell, Hart CAMPUS TOWN	Tex?	m:18-19	N,D	II,III,IV, VI
Stuart, Jesse HIE TO THE HUNTERS	Ky	m:14 m:16	H,Se	<u>III,VI</u>,VII
Taylor, Peter A WOMAN OF MEANS	Mo	m:11-14	P,Sy	III
Westheimer, David THE MAGIC FALLACY	Tex	m:16 m:14	P,Sy	II,III
Willingham, Calder GERALDINE BRADSHAW	Chi	f:18?	N	II
Windham, Donald THE DOG STAR	Ga	m:15	N,P,Sy	II,<u>III</u>,VI
Witherspoon, Mary-Elizabeth SOMEBODY SPEAK FOR KATY	Fla, NYC	f:17-20	Se,D	II,IV,V, VI

319

Author and Title	Locale	Sex & Age(s)	Author's Treatment	Problem(s)
1950				
Wylie, Max. GO HOME AND TELL YOUR MOTHER	Ohio	m:12-13	R, Se	II, III, IV, <u>V</u>
1951				
Abel, Hilde THE GUESTS OF SUMMER	NY	f:17	P, Sy	II, III, <u>V</u>, VI
Agee, James THE MORNING WATCH	Tenn	m:12	P, Sy	<u>IV</u>, <u>V</u>
Capote, Truman THE GRASS HARP	La?	m:16	Sy, Se	III, <u>V</u>, VII
Jackson, Shirley HANGSAMAN	Vt?	f:17	P, Sy	III, <u>IV</u>, V, <u>VII</u>
L'Engle, Madeleine CAMILLA DICKINSON	NYC	f:15	P	II, III
Lincoln, Victoria OUT FROM EDEN	Conn	f:18 m:16	P, H, Se	II, III, IV, <u>VI</u>
[a]Moody, Ralph MAN OF THE FAMILY	Col	m:11-13	R, Se	III, <u>V</u>, <u>VI</u>
Moore, Ruth CANDLEMAS BAY	Me	m:16	R, P	III, IV, V, <u>VI</u>
Phillips, Thomas Hal THE GOLDEN LIE	Miss	m:16	R, P, D	III, <u>V</u>, VI
Salinger, J[erome] D[avid]. THE CATCHER IN THE RYE	Pa, NYC	m:16	P, R, Sy	II, III, IV, V, <u>VII</u>
[s]Shulman, Max. THE MANY LOVES OF DOBIE GILLIS	Minn	m:18	H	II, IV
Styron, William LIE DOWN IN DARKNESS	Va, NYC	f:c-m	P, N, Sy	II, III, IV, <u>VII</u>
West, Jessamyn THE WITCH DIGGERS	Ind	f:18 f:13	Sy, P, G	II, III, <u>V</u>, VI
1952				
Burt, Katherine Newlin ESCAPE FROM PARADISE	NY	f:c-18? f:c-m m:c-m	P, Se, G	II, III
Calitri, Charles RICKEY	NY	m:15	P, D	II, III
Clayton, John Bell SIX ANGELS AT MY BACK	Fla	m:19	N, P	<u>III</u>
Davis, H[arold] L[enoir] WINDS OF MORNING	Ore	f:15 m:20	R	II, III, VI

320

Author and Title	Locale	Sex & Age(s)	Author's Treatment	Problem(s)
1952				
Davis, Kenneth S. MORNING IN KANSAS	Kan	m:17	P,G	III
[a]De Jong, David Cornel TWO SOFAS IN THE PARLOR	Mich	m:13	H,Se	III,VI
Doan, Daniel THE CRYSTAL YEARS	Bost, NH	m:11-15	Se,H,P	III,VI
Ellison, Ralph INVISIBLE MAN	South, NYC	m:17-m	N,P,Sy	II,IV,V, VI
Ellson, Hal THE GOLDEN SPIKE	NYC	m:16	N,P	II,III,VI, VII
Emery, Ann SORORITY GIRL	?	f:15	P,J	II,IV
Gorham, Charles TRIAL BY DARKNESS	Conn, NY	m:c-20	P,Sy,D	II,III,IV
Harris, Sara THE WAYWARD ONES	?	f:16-17	N,P,D	II,III,IV
Macauley, Robie THE DISGUISES OF LOVE	Midw	m:16	P	III
Mandel, George FLEE THE ANGRY STRANGERS	NYC	f:18	P,N	II,III,VI, VII
[Mayer, Jayne, and Clara Spiegel] "Clare Jaynes." EARLY FROST	Cal	f:17-18	P	II,III,IV
Michaelson, John Nairne MORNING, WINTER AND NIGHT	Ohio	m:12-13	P	II,III,IV, VI
Smith, Madeline Babcock THE LEMON JELLY CAKE	Ill	f:11	H,Se	III,VI
Stafford, Jean THE CATHERINE WHEEL	Maine	m:12	P,Sy	III
Steinbeck, John EAST OF EDEN	Cal	f:c-m m:b-18	P,Sy,G	II,III,V, VI
Thacher, Russell THE TENDER AGE	NJ	m:17	N,P	II,III
1953				
[a]Angoff, Charles IN THE MORNING LIGHT	Bos	m:12-17	R	III,IV,V, VI
Baldwin, James. GO TELL IT ON THE MOUNTAIN	NYC	m:14	P,Sy	III,V,VI
Bellow, Saul. THE ADVENTURES OF AUGIE MARCH	Chi	m:c-m	N,P	II,III,IV, V,VI

Author and Title	Locale	Sex & Age(s)	Author's Treatment	Problem(s)
1953				
Bro, Margueritte Harmon STUB: A COLLEGE ROMANCE	?	m:18	Se,J	II,IV
Burress, John APPLE ON A PEAR TREE	Tenn	m:11-12	R,Se	III,VI
Burt, Nathaniel SCOTLAND'S BURNING	Pa? Md	m:14	P,Sy,R	II,<u>IV</u>
Clayton, John Bell WAIT, SON, OCTOBER IS NEAR	Va	m:10-11	N,P,H	III,<u>VII</u>
ˢDavis, Reuben SHIM	Miss	m:14	R,Se	VI,VII
ˢEdmonds, Walter D. THE BOYDS OF BLACK RIVER	NY	m:12-15	R,Se	<u>VI</u>,VII
Ellson, Hal SUMMER STREET	NYC	m:16	N	II
Halper, Albert THE GOLDEN WATCH	Chi	m:c-16	R,Se	III,VI
Kennedy, Mark THE PECKING ORDER	Chi	m:11 m:15	N	<u>III</u>,VI
Keogh, Theodora THE TATTOOED HEART	NY	f:15 m:11	P,N,Sy	II,III
[Marquand,] John Phillips, [Jr.] THE SECOND HAPPIEST DAY	Mass, NYC	m:13-m	P,R,Sy	II,III,<u>IV, V</u>,<u>VII</u>
ᵃMoody, Ralph THE FIELDS OF HOME	Mass, Maine	m:14-15	R,Se,H	III,<u>V</u>,<u>VI</u>
Shulman, Irving THE SQUARE TRAP	LA	m:18-20	N,P,D	III,V,<u>VI</u>
Stolz, Mary READY OR NOT	NYC	f:16	R,P,J	II,III,IV
Wallop, Douglass NIGHT LIGHT	NY	m:16	N,P	III,V,VI, <u>VII</u>
ˢWeldon, John Lee THE NAKED HEART	Ala	m:c-20	P,G,Sy	II,III,VI
1954				
Davis, Clyde Brion THE NEWCOMER	Midw?	m:13	P,H	II,<u>IV</u>,VI
Dubin, Harry Ennis HAIL, ALMA PATER	NY	m:13-17	H	III,IV
Faralla, Dana BLACK RENEGADE	Ga	m:13-14	Se,D,J	VII
Fisher, Steve GIVEAWAY	Ind,LA	m:17	Sa,R	II,III,<u>V</u>

Author and Title	Locale	Sex & Age(s)	Author's Treatment	Problem(s)
1954				
Hunter, Evan BLACKBOARD JUNGLE	NYC	m:16	N,P	III,IV,VI
Lumbard, C[harles] G[ilbert] SENIOR SPRING	Cal	m:21	R,P	II,IV,V
Miller, Nolan WHY I AM SO BEAT	Ohio	m:18	H	II,IV
Scott, Glenn A SOUND OF VOICES DYING	Va	m:18-19	R,P	II,IV
Stolz, Mary PRAY LOVE, REMEMBER	NY	f:18	R,P,J	II,III,IV, V
Street, James GOODBYE, MY LADY	Miss	m:14	R,Se	II,VI,VII
Tunis, John R. GO, TEAM, GO!	Ind	m:16?	R,D,J	II,III,IV
ˢWest, Jessamyn CRESS DELAHANTY	Cal	f:12-16	R,P,H	II,III,IV, V
1955				
ᵃAngoff, Charles THE SUN AT NOON	Bos	m:17-21	R	II,III,IV, V,VI
Chamberlain, Anne THE TALL DARK MAN	Midw?	f:13	G,P	III,IV,V, VII
Ellison, James Whitfield I'M OWEN HARRISON HARDING	Mich	m:15-16	N,P,H	II,III,IV
Ellson, Hal ROCK	NYC	m:15	N	II,III,VI
Erno, Richard B. MY OLD MAN	Mich	m:17	N,P	III,V,VI, VII
Grace, Carol THE SECRET IN THE DAISY	?	f:c-16	P,Se	II,III
Halevy, Julian THE YOUNG LOVERS	NYC	m:18 f:18	P,R	II,III,IV, VII
Oakey, Virginia THIRTEENTH SUMMER	Miss	f:13	P,G	III
Phillips, Thomas Hal THE LOVED AND THE UNLOVED	Miss	m:14-m	G,Sa	II,VI,VII
ᵃPlagemann, Bentz THIS IS GOGGLE	NY	m:10-18	H,R	II,III,IV
Porter, Monica E. MERCY OF THE COURT	Mich	m:17	R,P	III,VI
[Seid, Ruth] "Jo Sinclair" THE CHANGELINGS	Ohio	f:13	P,Sy,R	III,VI

323

Author and Title	Locale	Sex & Age(s)	Author's Treatment	Problem(s)
1955				
Swados, Harvey OUT WENT THE CANDLE	NJ, Cal	f:18-m	N,P	II,III,IV
s[Tanner, Edward Everett] "Patrick Dennis." AUNTIE MAME	NYC	m:10-m	H,Sa	II,III,IV
Weeks, Joseph ALL OUR YESTERDAYS	Mich	m:18	N	II,III,V
Wouk, Herman MARJORIE MORNINGSTAR	NY	f:17-m	R,P	II,III,V, VI
1956				
Abaunza, Virginia SUNDAYS FROM TWO TO SIX	?	f:16	P,Se	II,III,V
Algren, Nelson A WALK ON THE WILD SIDE	Tex, road, NO	m:15-19	N,Sy,H	II, III, V VI,VII
Athas, Daphne THE FOURTH WORLD	Pa	m:16-17 f:15-16	N,P	II,IV,VII
Beheler, Laura THE PAPER DOLLS	Tex, NYC	f:c-m	P	II,III,V, VII
Boylen, Margaret THE MARBLE ORCHARD	Iowa	f:13-16	P,Sa,Sy	II,III,VI VII
DuBois, William A SEASON TO BEWARE	Fla, NYC	m:18-m	P	II,IV,V
aEddy, Roger W. THE BULLS AND THE BEES	Conn	m:c-m	H	II,III,IV, V,VI
Fenwick, Elizabeth DAYS OF PLENTY	Mich	f:14	P,Se	III
Gipson, Fred OLD YELLER	Tex	m:14	R,Se	VI,VII
Hunter, Evan SECOND ENDING	NYC	m:20	P,N	II,IV,V, VII
Karney, Jack WORK OF DARKNESS	NYC	m:16?	N,P	II,III,VII
Levin, Meyer COMPULSION	Chi	m:18 m:19	N,P	II,III,VI, VII
Levy, Melvin LAFAYETTE CARTER	Cal	m:16	P,D	III
Metalious, Grace PEYTON PLACE	NH	f:15-20	N,P,Sy	II,III,V, VI,VII
Moore, Pamela CHOCOLATES FOR BREAKFAST	NYC, LA	f:15-16	P,N	II,III,VI, VII

324

Author and Title	Locale	Sex & Age(s)	Author's Treatment	Problem(s)
1956				
Rehder, Jessie C. REMEMBRANCE WAY	NC	f:16	P	II
Rooney, Frank THE HEEL OF SPRING	NY,Cal,Midw	m:12-22	P	III
Shaw, Irwin LUCY CROWN	Vt, NYC	m:13-m	P, R,	III, IV
Shulman, Irving CHILDREN OF THE DARK	Midw	m:hs	N, D	III
Shulman, Irving. GOOD DEEDS MUST BE PUNISHED	NYC, WVa	m:col	D	II, _IV_, _VI_
Steuer, Arthur THE TERRIBLE SWIFT SWORD	Ga	m:col	N, P	IV
1957				
[s]Bradbury, Ray DANDELION WINE	Ill	m:12	Sy, Se	III, V, _VI_
[a]Byron, Gilbert THE LORD'S OYSTERS	Md	m:c-12	H, Se	III
Carson, Josephine DRIVES MY GREEN AGE	Kan	f:12-13	P, R	_III_, VI
Daly, Edwin SOME MUST WATCH	O, Ill, Mich	m:18	P, D	II, III, IV, VII
Faulkner, William THE TOWN	Miss	f:14-16	P, N, Sy	_II_, III, IV, VI
Ham, Roswell G., Jr. FISH FLYING THROUGH THE AIR	Conn	m:16-m	H	IV, VII
Harris, Mark SOMETHING ABOUT A SOLDIER	Ga	m:17	P	II, VI, _VII_
Head, Ann FAIR WITH RAIN	SC, NJ	m:20 f:16	H, Se	II, IV
Kerouac, Jack ON THE ROAD	NYC, Cal, road	m:19-m	N, Sy, P	II, _III_, _V_, _VII_
Kohner, Frederick GIDGET	Cal	f:15	H, D, R	II, III
[Miller, Warren] "Amanda Vail" LOVE ME LITTLE	NY	f:15 f:15	Sa, H	II
Nemerov, Howard THE HOMECOMING GAME	?	m:col	H, Sa	II, IV

Author and Title	Locale	Sex & Age(s)	Author's Treatment	Problem(s)
1957				
Nusser, J[ames] L. SCORPION FIELD	Midw	f:14 m:15	P,N	II,III,VII
Purdy, James "63:Dream Palace" in COLOR OF DARKNESS	Chi?	m:19	P,Sy,G	VI,VII
Roark, Garland THE CRUEL COCKS	La	m:13	R,D	VI,VII
Simmons, Herbert CORNER BOY	StL	m:18-19	N	III,VI
Sourian, Peter MIRI	NYC, Mass	f:18 m:18 m:18	P,R	II,IV,VI
Thompson, Charles HALFWAY DOWN THE STAIRS	Mass, NY	m:col	N	II,IV,VI
Wetzel, Donald. THE RAIN AND THE FIRE AND THE WILL OF GOD	Ala	m:14	P,R,Sy	II,VI
Winsor, Kathleen AMERICA WITH LOVE	?	f:12	N	II
Yaffe, James NOTHING BUT THE NIGHT	Chi	m:17 m:17	P,G	III,VII
1958				
Boles, Paul Darcy PARTON'S ISLAND	Ala	m:14-15 m:16-17	R,Se,H	VI,VII
Calitri, Charles STRIKE HEAVEN ON THE FACE	NH	m:17-18 f:17-18	R,P	II,III,IV, V
Carlile, Clancy AS I WAS YOUNG AND EASY	Okla	m:12	Se,H	II,VI,VII
Chamberlain, Anne THE DARKEST BOUGH	?	m:14 f:18?	P,G	II,III,VII
Daly, Edwin A LEGACY OF LOVE	Mich	f:20	P,R,D	II
Davis, Christopher LOST SUMMER	Pa	f:18	P,N	II,III,VI, VII
Davis, Wesley Ford THE TIME OF THE PANTHER	Fla	m:14	R,H,Sy	II,III,VI, VII
Dempsey, David K. ALL THAT WAS MORTAL	Ill	f:16-m	R	II,III,V

Author and Title	Locale	Sex & Age(s)	Author's Treatment	Problem(s)
1958				
Elliott, George P. PARKTILDEN VILLAGE	Cal	f:19	P,Sy,R	II,III,IV
Ellison, James Whitfield THE FREEST MAN ON EARTH	NYC	m:18	P,R	III,VII
Faralla, Dana THE MADSTONE	Minn	f:12 f:13 m:10	P	III
Feibleman, Peter S. A PLACE WITHOUT TWILIGHT	NO	f:10–23	P,R,Sy, H	II,III,IV, VI,VII
"Flagg, Kenneth" ANDREW	Col, NYC	m:20	P,D	II,III,IV
Frede, Richard ENTRY E	Conn	m:20	P,Sy	II,IV,V
Gutterson, Herbert THE LAST AUTUMN	Mass?	m:14	P	II,III,IV
Gutwillig, Robert AFTER LONG SILENCE	Conn?	m:18–m	P	II,IV,VII
Hitchens, Dolores FOOL'S GOLD	Cal	m:17 f:16	P,G	II,III
Humphrey, William HOME FROM THE HILL	Tex	m:17–19	P,Sy,G	II,III,VI,VII
Johnson, Nora THE WORLD OF HENRY ORIENT	NYC	f:13	P,Sy	II,III,IV
Karmel, Alex MARY ANN	NYC	f:18?	P,G	II,III
Kozol, Jonathan THE FUME OF POPPIES	Mass Me, NYC Eur	f:19–20 m:19–20	R	II,IV
Loveland, Constance VERONICA	NYC Ohio	f:16 f:18	R,P	II,III,IV, V,VII
[Miller, Warren] "Amanda Vail" THE BRIGHT YOUNG THINGS	NE, NYC	f:18	Sa,H	II,III,IV
Nabokov, Vladimir LOLITA	road	f:12–17	Sa,P	II,III,VII
Robinson, Alice M. THE UNBELONGING	NY	f:12–18	P,D	II,III,VII
Salamanca, J. R. THE LOST COUNTRY	Va	m:b–17	P	II,III,IV, V
Sandburg, Helga THE WHEEL OF EARTH	Ky, Ill	f:16–m	N,P	II,III,VI

327

Author and Title	Locale	Sex & Age(s)	Author's Treatment	Problem(s)
1958				
Smith, Betty MAGGIE-NOW	NYC	f:c-m	R,P,Se	II,III,<u>VI</u>
Wagner, David ROCK	Ill	m:18?	N,P	II,III,VI
Weidman, Jerome THE ENEMY CAMP	NYC, Conn	m:c-m	P,R	II,III,<u>VI</u>
Wilson, Sloan A SUMMER PLACE	Me,NY Fla	f:18-m m:18-m	P,Se	II,III
Wright, Richard THE LONG DREAM	Miss	m:c-m	P,N	II,III,VI
1959				
[a]Angoff, Charles BETWEEN DAY AND DARK	Bos, NYC	m:21-23	R	II,V,VI
Baker, Laura Nelson THE SPECIAL YEAR	Midw	m:17	J,P	II,IV,V, VII
Ballard, James THE LONG WAY THROUGH	WVa, Cal	m:17-21	N,P	II,VI,VII
Beaumont, Charles THE INTRUDER	Tenn?	f:15	R,P,D	II,III,<u>IV</u>, VI
Begner, Edith P. JUST OFF FIFTH	NYC	m:13	P	VI
Bell, Robert E. THE BUTTERFLY TREE	Ala	m:20	Sy	II,V,VI
Bental, Pearl Bucklen FRESHMAN AT LARGE	?	f:col	J,D	II,IV,V
Deal, Borden THE INSOLENT BREED	Tenn	m:c-m f:c-m	R,Sy	II,V,VI
DeMott, Benjamin THE BODY'S CAGE	NE	m:19	G,P	III,V,VII
[a]Duffus, R[obert] L[uther] THE WATERBURY RECORD	Vt	m:18-19	R	V,VI
Ehle, John KINGSTREE ISLAND	NC	f:19 m:24	R,P	II,III,VI
Erno, Richard B. THE HUNT	Mich	m:15?	G,P	<u>VII</u>
Farris, John HARRISON HIGH	Midw	m:17-18 f:17-18	N,Se,D	II,III,IV, <u>V</u>,VI,VII
Garrett, Zena. THE HOUSE IN THE MULBERRY TREE	Tex	f:11	G,Sy,P	III,V

Author and Title	Locale	Sex & Age(s)	Author's Treatment	Problem(s)
1959				
Gold, Herbert THE OPTIMIST	Mich	m:17-m	P,R	II,IV,V
Goodman, Aubrey. THE GOLDEN YOUTH OF LEE PRINCE	Conn, NYC	m:18-23	P,Sa,D	II,IV,V
Gutwillig, Robert THE FUGITIVES	NE?	m:col	P	II,V,<u>VII</u>
Hubler, Richard G. TRUE LOVE, TRUE LOVE	Pa	m:10	Se,H	II,IV
Hunter, Evan A MATTER OF CONVICTION	NYC	m:hs	N,P	<u>III</u>,VI,VII
Jenison, Peter S. THE MIMOSA SMOKERS	NY, Eur	f:c-m m:c-m	P,G	II,III,VII
Johnson, Curtis L. HOBBLEDEHOY'S HERO	Iowa	m:16	H,P	II,III,IV, VII
Jones, Dorothy Holder THE WONDERFUL WORLD OUTSIDE	?	f:16	J,Se,D	II,III
Kelley, William GEMINI	NYC	m:18-21?	P,R,Sy, Sa	II,<u>V</u>,VI
Kerouac, Jack DOCTOR SAX	Mass	m:c-14	Sy,G	<u>II</u>,<u>V</u>,VI
Kerouac, Jack MAGGIE CASSIDY	Mass, NYC	m:16-20 f:17-21	R,Sy,P	<u>II</u>,IV,V, <u>VI</u>
Kirsch, Robert R. IN THE WRONG RAIN	LA	f:17	R,P	II,V
Kohner, Frederick CHER PAPA	Idaho	f:17	H,Sa	II,III
Linkletter, Monte CRICKET SMITH	Iowa	m:15-17	H,R	II,III,IV <u>V</u>
McGivern, William Peter SAVAGE STREETS	NY	m:19 f:16?	N,D	II,<u>III</u>,VI
Manfred, Frederick CONQUERING HORSE	ND,SD Neb, road	m:17	R,Se	II,V
Marshall, Lenore THE HILL IS LEVEL	NH	f:b-m	Se,D	II,III,V
Marshall, Paule BROWN GIRL, BROWNSTONES	NYC	f:10-m	N,P	II,III,V, VI,<u>VII</u>
Miller, Warren THE COOL WORLD	NYC	m:14	N,D	II,<u>III</u>,V, VI,<u>VII</u>

Author and Title	Locale	Sex & Age(s)	Author's Treatment	Problem(s)
1959				
Mitchner, Stuart LET ME BE AWAKE	Ind, NYC, Pa	m:18-19	P,R	II,IV,V
O'Donnell, Eugene BERDOO	NH	m:19?	N,G,H, P	II,VI,VII
Offit, Sidney HE HAD IT MADE	NY	m:17	R	II,V
Petrakis, Harry Mark LION AT MY HEART	Chi	m:20	R	II,III,VI
Purdy, James MALCOLM	NYC?	m:14-15	Sa,Sy	II,III,V, VI,VII
ˢShulman, Max I WAS A TEEN-AGE DWARF	Midw	m:13-m	H	II,III,IV
Soman, Florence Jane A BREAK IN THE WEATHER	NY	f:19 f:11	P,R	II,III,VI
Sterling, Dorothy MARY JANE	South	f:12	J,D	IV,VI,VII
Stern, Daniel MISS AMERICA	NJ, NYC, LA	f:18-m	P,R	II,III,V
Suckow, Ruth THE JOHN WOOD CASE	Iowa	m:17	R,P	III,VI
Sumner, Cid Ricketts TAMMY TELL ME TRUE	Miss?	f:18	Se,H	II,IV,VI
Tamkus, Daniel THE MUCH-HONORED MAN	?	f:c-m	P,G	II,III
"Tembler, Paul" THE SPRING DANCE	NE	m:15	R,P,H	II,IV
Tigue, Ethel Erkkilla BETRAYAL	Idaho	m:hs f:hs	D	IV
Villarreal, José Antonio POCHO	Cal	m:c-m	R,P	II,III,VI
[Wright, Beatrice Ann] "Martin Kramer" SONS OF THE FATHERS	Cal	m:col-m	N,P	II,III,IV, V,VI
1960				
Abelson, Ann THE LITTLE CONQUERORS	NE	m:c-m f:c-m	R	II,III,V, VI
Albee, George Sumner BY THE SEA, BY THE SEA	NE?	m:20?	Sa,H	II,VI
Babcock, Havilah THE EDUCATION OF PRETTY BOY	Va	m:14?	J,Se	III,VII

Author and Title	Locale	Sex & Age(s)	Author's Treatment	Problem(s)
1960				
Bennett, Eve APRIL WEDDING	?	f:hs m:hs	J,R,D	II,V
Bourjaily, Vance CONFESSIONS OF A SPENT YOUTH	Va,NY NE,Fla, abroad	m:17-24	N,P	II,III,IV, V,VII
Brace, Gerald Warner WINTER SOLSTICE	Mass	m:col	N,P	II,III,VI, VII
DiDonato, Pietro THREE CIRCLES OF LIGHT	NJ	m:c-14	N,Sy,Se	II,III,VI, VII
Dougherty, Richard A SUMMER WORLD	NY	m:17-18	P,R,Se	II,VI
Froscher, Wingate THE COMFORTS OF THE DAMNED	NYC	m:20? f:22?	G,P	II,III,V, VII
Gold, Herbert THEREFORE BE BOLD	Ohio	m:16-17	P,Sa	II,III,IV, V,VI
Herlihy, James Leo ALL FALL DOWN	Ohio, Fla	m:14-16	P,Sy,G	II,III,V
Hill, Margaret REALLY, MISS HILLSBRO!	West	f:21-22	J	II,V,VI
Kapelner, Alan ALL THE NAKED HEROES	NYC, road	m:22? m:24?	N,P	II,III,V, VII
Kirkwood, Jim THERE MUST BE A PONY!	LA	m:16	G	VII
Knowles, John A SEPARATE PEACE	NH	m:16-17	R,P,Sy	IV,VII
Leahy, Jack Thomas SHADOW ON THE WATERS	Wash	m:16	R,Se	VI
Leslie, Warren LOVE OR WHATEVER IT IS	NE	f:col	G,P	II,III
MacDonald, John D. THE END OF THE NIGHT	South	m:col	G,P	II,III
McFarland, Philip A HOUSE FULL OF WOMEN	South	m:12-13	G,P	II,III,VII
Martin, Peter THE BUILDING	NY	m:b-m	R	II,III,IV, V,VI
Mayhall, Jane COUSIN TO HUMAN	Ky	f:15-16	P	III,V
Moore, Ruth WALK DOWN MAIN STREET	Me	m:hs	R,H	IV,VI
O'Connor, Flannery THE VIOLENT BEAR IT AWAY	Tenn.	m:14	G,P	III,V,VI, VII

Author and Title	Locale	Sex & Age(s)	Author's Treatment	Problem(s)
1960				
Richter, Conrad THE WATERS OF KRONOS	Pa	m:14?	Sy	III
Roberts, Dorothy James WITH NIGHT WE BANISH SORROW	Va, NYC	f:c–m	R	II, III, VI
Solomon, Barbara Probst THE BEAT OF LIFE	NYC	f:col m:col	N, P	II, III, VII
Street, James Howell, and Don Tracy PRIDE OF POSSESSION	Tenn?	m:12	R, Se	III, VII
Swarthout, Glendon WHERE THE BOYS ARE	Fla	f:18	R, Sa	II, IV
Walker, Mildred THE BODY OF A YOUNG MAN	Ill	m:hs	R, P	IV
Wood, William THE FIT	NE, NYC	m:hs	P	IV, VII
Zietlow, E[dward] R[obert] THESE SAME HILLS	SD	m:18	R, Sy, D	IV, V, VI, VII

INDEX

This Index includes, under both title and author, every novel mentioned in the main part of the text. Other novels of adolescence may be found in the Bibliography and the Appendix. The Index also includes some outstanding fictional characters (cross-referenced under the names of their respective authors), a number of background books and articles, and a few general topics other than those which can readily be found by consulting the Contents.

Index

336

337

Index

resulting in revolt of an adolescent from the family are sometimes obvious and sometimes obscure—usually more subtle and complex in the novels of the forties and fifties than in those of the twenties and thirties. In the next group of novels the causes of revolt are more readily apparent, and for that reason they may perhaps be discussed more briefly.

Rebellion Against Family Status

It is not surprising that inadequate finances in the home frequently cause an adolescent to seek his happiness elsewhere. Not only is the poverty itself distressing, but it usually causes friction and bitterness among members of the household, so that the home is psychologically as well as physically an unpleasant place in which to be. In *Moon-Calf*, the Fays struggle for years to keep together, but when Felix is sixteen, the family dissolves. Felix goes to live with a married brother in Port Royal, but his brother's house is never home to him. In Booth Tarkington's *Alice Adams* (1921), Alice's adolescent brother Walter spends as little time at home as he can, turns to undesirable companions and pastimes, and finally embezzles funds from his employer; Alice herself, though she is twenty-two years old, has an adolescent's dread that her friends will realize her family is not as affluent as it once was. In Sherwood Anderson's *Tar* (1926), young Tar Moorehead resents his home because of the constant poverty there. During his childhood, Tar often imagines himself belonging in the family of a nearby grocer who has many daughters; as the only son in the family, Tar would be treated like a prince, and would have all he wanted to eat. When he is old enough to sell papers at the railroad station, he likes to imagine that he is not really a Moorehead, but the son of a wealthy man who left him in Mrs. Moorehead's care while he traveled abroad. Tar frequently dreams that a well-dressed man getting off the train will say to him, "My son, my son. I am your father. I have been in foreign parts and have accumulated a huge fortune. Now I have come to make you rich." (P. 287.) Sometimes Tar eats at the home of his friend Hal Brown, where he enjoys the rich variety of food and the jovial friendliness of the family; but he never dares ask his friends to eat at his house, where corn meal mush or cabbage soup is often the only dish served at a meal.

Mention has been made (p. 68 above) of the aversion that Farrell's Danny O'Neill feels for the impoverished home of his parents. Mick Kelly in Carson McCullers' *The Heart Is a Lonely Hunter* (1940) dreams of escaping from the family poverty and going to some far-off place where she will become a famous painter or writer or musician; but the poverty traps her into taking a job at Woolworth's before she has a respectable education, and she knows that her dreams of escape will never be realized. Francie Nolan in Betty Smith's *A Tree Grows in Brooklyn* (1943) is more fortunate—or perhaps more determined—than Mick. Although Francie also has to leave school to get a full-time job, as soon as she is put on a night shift she bluffs her way into college. Francie's childhood and early adolescence, in a home with a likable but improvident father, have been very hard; and her later adolescence, after her father's death, has been even harder. Yet she and her brother, as they discuss their mother's forthcoming marriage with a second and rather well-to-do husband, can feel sorry for their baby sister who, if she will never know the hard times they have known, will never know the fun their father brought into the home.

The family background of Mary Millar in *Morning Song* (1948) by Dorshka Raphaelson[2] is remarkably similar to that of Sonie Marburg in *Boston Adventure*, mentioned earlier in this chapter. Sonie is the daughter of a scholarly, improvident German father and grasping Russian mother; they live in a small fishing village near Boston. Mary is the daughter of a scholarly, improvident Austrian father and grasping Russian mother; they live in a part of New York City (near Broadway and 175th Street) which was almost a suburb about the time of World War I, when their story takes place. Sonie's father deserts his family when Sonie is twelve; her mother becomes mentally unbalanced after giving birth to a son, and Sonie devotes her adolescent years to supporting her mother and brother until the child dies and the mother is placed in a mental institution. Mary's parents are divorced when she is eight, and her father dies when the girl is fourteen; Mary soon has to leave school and work full time to support her mother and younger brother. But at this point the resemblance ends. *Boston Adventure* is somber, symbolic, full of hatred and evil: *Morning Song* is humorous and sentimental. In spite of her difficult home life and the greedy amorality of the theater world where she earns her living, Mary remains excitedly happy and naïvely idealistic, overcoming dangers and difficulties as inevitably as Sonie is overcome by

Index

Index

Index

Weather of the Heart, The, 60, 89, 196-97, 265, 276
Weaver, John V. A., 39, 168
Web and the Rock, The, 168, 173, 178, 244
Webster, Henry Kitchell, 71
Webster, Jean, 38-39
Weeks, Joseph, 179-80
Weidman, Jerome, 202, 206
Weldon, John Lee, 202
Well of the Past, The, 142
Weller, George Anthony, 124
Werther's Younger Brother, 168-69, 246
Wescott, Glenway, 172, 186, 235, 242, 269
West, Jessamyn, 2, 19, 32, 33, 43, 61, 75, 103, 112, 142, 176, 192, 198, 199, 270
West of the Water Tower, 52-53, 71, 84, 153, 262
Westheimer, David, 265
Wetzel, Donald, 36-37, 189, 217
What's a Heaven For?, 165, 174
Wheel of Earth, The, 55, 58, 187, 224, 271
Where the Boys Are, 132
"White Heron, The," 227
Whitney, Phillis, 142
Why I Am So Beat, 130-31, 276
Wickenden, Dan, 84, 276
Wild Country, The, 187, 261
Wild Geese, 60, 71, 74, 186
Wildwood, 83, 175
Wilhelm Meister's Apprenticeship, 273
Willinghham, Calder, 58, 61, 127, 245, 252, 276
Willow Hill, 142
Windham, Donald, 92, 202
Winds of Morning, 190, 191, 261
Windy McPherson's Son, 12
Winesburg, Ohio, 12, 21
Winning of Barbara Worth, The, 9
Winter in April, 42, 44, 259-60
Winter Term, 116
Winter Wheat, 163-64, 165, 186

Winther, Sophus Keith, 83, 96
Witch Diggers, The, 61, 176
Witham, W. Tasker, 284
Witherspoon, Mary-Elizabeth, 166
Wolf, Robert, 122-23
Wolfe, Thomas, 16, 25, 60, 61, 66-67, 104, 113, 123, 139-40, 143, 146, 150, 168, 173, 178, 197, 230, 236-37, 244, 252, 270, 275. See also Gant, Eugene
Woman of Means, A, 265
Wood, Playsted, 105-06
Wood, William, 249
Woodbury, Helen, 67, 140
Work of Darkness, 266
World of Henry Orient, The, 113
World War I, 15, 24, 101, 178, 206-07, 229-30, 232, 233, 239, 278, 282
World War II, 16, 24, 230-33, 278
Wouk, Herman, 33, 84, 155, 181, 203-04, 266
Wright, Beatrice Ann, 149-50
Wright, Harold Bell, 9, 13, 275
Wright, Richard, 16, 81, 92, 97, 98, 201, 211, 212-13, 270, 276
Wylie, Max, 180, 271

Yaffe, James, 93, 242, 249
Yearling, The, 189, 221-22, 225, 260
Yesterday's Children, 133, 233
Yoke of Stars, 145, 146
Yoseloff, Martin, 54, 202
Young, I. S., 89, 276
Young Lions, The, 83, 232
Young Lonigan, 35-36, 47-48, 87, 108, 112, 273
Young Lovers, The, 62, 129-30, 233, 248, 252, 261
Young Manhood of Studs Lonigan, The, 58, 87
Youngest Profession, The, 154, 258

Zietlow, E. R., 186-87, 228
Zugsmith, Leane, 87-88, 104, 200-01

345